HISTORY OF THE
Bodleian Library

1845-1945

By SIR EDMUND CRASTER

BODLEY'S LIBRARIAN, 1931-45

OXFORD
AT THE CLARENDON PRESS
1952

Oxford University Press, Amen House, London E.C. 4
GLASGOW NEW YORK TORONTO MELBOURNE WELLINGTON
BOMBAY CALCUTTA MADRAS CAPE TOWN
Geoffrey Cumberlege, Publisher to the University

PRINTED IN GREAT BRITAIN

Preface

In the first year of my service in the Bodleian Library, Mr. Falconer Madan, who was then Librarian, brought into the little study in which I worked, a big, benevolent-looking and extremely old clergyman whom he introduced to me as Mr. W. D. Macray. So I was able to have a few minutes chat with a man who joined the Bodleian staff in 1840 and who had compiled the *Annals of the Bodleian Library*. The first edition of that work was published in 1868. It was greatly expanded and brought down to the year 1881 in a second edition, nearly half as long again as its precursor, which came out in 1890. Both editions were published by the Delegates of the Clarendon Press.

Madan was greatly interested in the history of the library, and on more than one occasion he suggested to me that I should revise and continue 'Macray'. The course that I have adopted since retirement from office is a different one. A revision of an account already given of an earlier period seemed less clamant than the recording of later events before they were forgotten. And I have adopted a different method, attempting to write a history where Macray had confined himself to annalistic arrangement. Annals have their convenience if the writer aims at ease of reference (though even there, as any one who has constantly used Macray must have found, there are catches despite an excellent index), but they do not produce a picture or allow the presentation of conclusions.

The following pages cover the history of a century—the hundred years that preceded the conclusion of the Second World War. All the developments of modern librarianship may be said to fall within this period, and, by tracing them back to their not-too-remote past, one may observe the growth of institutions and customs that are now taken for granted, their origin and the very reason for their existence perhaps forgotten. That, after all, is one of the main aims of history, the fuller realization of the present through the study of the past which lives on in the present.

This is not merely a history of one of the world's great libraries during an important phase of its existence. It is the history of a university department which has impinged at many points upon the life of the university. To some little extent it is even a history of learning, for, as Macray says in the preface to his *Annals*, 'a history of the University library can afford in some sort an outline of the progress of learning and of the development of studies'.

v

PREFACE

In deciding to start with 1845 I have intentionally overlapped Macray. As a subordinate member of the staff he was not concerned with library policy and had no access to current Curatorial papers. In particular, annals which he added to his second edition form but a scanty record of those years, and are almost wholly limited to the recording of accessions. Therefore I have raised the curtain upon 1845, and have then recounted the history of three successive periods of which each extended over a generation. Each section traverses the same ground, covering subjects in much the same order: each surveys the same scene as it appeared at a different epoch. The method adopted involves some repetition and breaking off of narratives that are resumed in later chapters, but it is better suited for giving a picture of a period. If I have succeeded in making some of my predecessors live again in these pages I shall have achieved one of my main purposes.

I have to tender my thanks to the Delegates of the University Press for undertaking publication, and to the Curators of the Bodleian Library for sanctioning it as well as for the unrestricted use they have allowed me to make of their library records. I desire also to thank Bodley's Librarian and the various members of his staff, more especially Dr. Richard Hunt, for the assistance they have never failed to give me. Their criticisms and suggestions have been most helpful. But I should add that this is in no sense an official history, and that I accept sole responsibility for any opinions and judgements that are expressed in it.

H. H. E. C.

Table of Contents

Part I. *The Bodleian in* 1845

Part II. *Bandinel and Coxe,* 1845–81

TABLE OF CONTENTS

TABLE OF CONTENTS

Part IV. *Three Librarians*, 1912–45

TABLE OF CONTENTS

List of Illustrations

PART I

The Bodleian in 1845

Chapter I

Library Buildings

1. SURROUNDING BUILDINGS

EXTERNALLY the Bodleian Library did not appear to be very different in 1845 from what it is now; only it had an air of greater antiquity. The stonework of its upper story was black with age and scaling off in tatters. The Tower of the Five Orders over the great gates of the Schools, with the statue of King James I on its west face looking out over the quadrangle, was patched with cement, its mouldering surface imparting to it a soft mellow tone.[1] Ivy grew in great masses up the buttresses which Sir Christopher Wren had constructed in Exeter garden against the south face of the library and festooned its mullion windows.[2] A hundred years ago the building looked at least a century older than it does today.

Before entering the Schools quadrangle let us take a quick glance round at the neighbouring buildings. On the east side, in Catte Street, Magdalen Hall occupied the site of the future Hertford College, and there was a *porte cochère* and flanking stone screen[3] where the College lodge and hall now stand. To the south, in the centre of the Radcliffe Square, the Radcliffe Library, hereafter to be called the Camera, was an independent library under the governance of the Radcliffe Trustees, the grilled openings of its lower story still un-

---

[1] A good idea of the uniform tone of the building before the Tower of the Five Orders and the upper story of the quadrangle were refaced may be obtained from Mackenzie's sepia drawings (Bodl. Arch. F. e. 13, foll. 30–4) made in 1835 and engraved in Ingram's *Memorials of Oxford*, vol. ii. A large and excellent photographic print of the west front of the tower, taken by Henry Taunt before its restoration, is to be found in Bodl. G. A. Oxon. a. 8.

[2] The rampant growth of ivy can be traced by comparing the views of the Bodleian Library from Exeter garden in Nash's aquatint of 1813 (Ackermann's *History of Oxford*) and in Delamotte's drawing of 1835 (Bodl. Arch. F. e. 13, fol. 18, reproduced as a woodcut in Ingram's *Memorials*) with the photograph in Aymer Vallance's *Old Colleges of Oxford*, 1912, p. 10. But ivy-clad walls have fallen out of fashion, and the library was stripped of its creepers in 1921.

[3] Shown in Mackenzie's drawing of Magdalen Hall engraved in Ingram, vol. ii.

glazed. Its entrance was on the ground level, opposite to St. Mary's Church,[1] for the flight of steps and entry on the north side had not yet been made; and a heavy red cast-iron railing, punctuated by gas-lamps, enclosed the surrounding grass-plot. To the north of the quadrangle, and facing Broad Street, the Clarendon Building, which the University Press had evacuated fourteen years earlier, held the Delegates' Room, in which the Hebdomadal Board, soon to be transformed into the Hebdomadal Council, met (as they still do) on Mondays in term-time for the transaction of university business. Here also the Vice-Chancellor and the Registrar had their offices. On the first floor what is now the Board Room was the lecture-room of the Reader in Experimental Philosophy, for whom the Clarendon Laboratory was to be one day built. The room adjoining it to the north was a general lecture-room shared by university professors. The present offices of the Registry and the rooms over them held Dr. Buckland's geological and mineralogical collections, then recently extruded from the Ashmolean Museum. This last-named institution occupied what is now termed the Old Ashmolean, its crowded and multifarious contents reduced, after long neglect, to some order by the two Duncan brothers who had been its successive keepers. Stuffed quadrupeds and heads, and anthropological exhibits, filled its great pillared ground-floor room.[2] In its upper rooms natural history collections and antiquities found common lodgement with a coin-cabinet and the Ashmolean Library in which early scientific works predominated and which contained the manuscripts and printed books left to the university by Elias Ashmole, by Dr. Lister, and by Anthony Wood. The basement of the building formed an unenviable residence for the Professor of Chemistry and provided him also with lecture-room and laboratory. Between the Clarendon Building and the Ashmolean Museum, Wren's massive Sheldonian Theatre served, as it still does, as scene for the ceremonies of the Encaenia, for occasional concerts, and for the holding of Convocations when urgent whips brought up country clergy to vote in numbers that the Convocation House could not accommodate. The entry to the Convocation House was then, as now, in the angle south of the Ashmolean

[1] The south entrance is clearly shown in the *Oxford Almanack* for 1790, and in Mackenzie's aquatint in Ackermann. The railings were erected in 1826 and are said to have cost more than £1,500. Hebdomadal Register 1823–33, p. 57; Radcliffe Trustees' minutes, 8 June 1827.
[2] Shown in a woodcut in Ingram's *Memorials*, vol. iii. A full account of the contents of the museum at this time is given in the 1838 edition of the *Stranger's Guide through the University and City of Oxford*, pp. 52–56, from which the reader may derive much instruction and some amusement.

Museum, through the Apodyterium in which the Vice-Chancellor held his court.

2. SCHOOLS QUADRANGLE: GROUND-FLOOR ROOMS

And now it is time to explore the quadrangle itself. The Schools quadrangle might still be regarded at this date as the heart of the university, and as late as 1858 proctorial regulations forbade undergraduates to pass through it unless they wore cap and gown. There is a staircase turret in each of its four corners. On its west side the stone-panelled frontage of the Proscholium, which faces the spectator as he stands under the tower archway, screens the Divinity School. That splendidly lighted, splendidly roofed hall still at this time retained a tenuous connexion with sacred studies, for here the candidates for degrees in divinity continued to perform their exercises. Enriched oak doors open into ground-floor schools on the other three sides. At the time of which we write these schools were given up to public examinations, professorial lectures, and the storage of departmental libraries and of classical statuary. Let us visit them in turn, beginning with the southern range.

As one enters the quadrangle under an arch out of the Radcliffe Square, and turns to the left, before reaching the door that led up to the Bodleian Library, one comes to the School of Natural Philosophy. This room had recently served as a lecture-hall for university professors, but now the professors had migrated to the Clarendon Building, and the School was virtually out of use. On the other side of the archway, forming the eastern portion of the south range, lies the Music School, in which still hung the lovely portraits of early musicians, now quite recently transferred to a new Music School in Holywell after being long immured in a room in the New Examination Schools.[1] Here the Professor of Music lectured and exercises were performed for musical degrees, and here was kept a music library which the Bodleian subsequently absorbed. The door to the corner tower in the south-east angle originally gave on to a staircase, but the stairs had been taken out in 1835, and it now opened into the Clerk of the Schools' Office, over which a mezzanine floor had been constructed; and in the newly formed upper chamber the library of the Savilian Professors of Geometry and Astronomy huddled in its seventeenth-century book cupboards. The neighbouring doorway, south of the Tower of the Five Orders, gives access to the Logic School. Up to the year in which our narrative begins, the Logic

---

[1] The collection, said to be unique of its kind in England, has been described by Mrs. Poole, *Catalogue of Oxford Portraits* (Oxf. Hist. Soc., 1912), vol. i, pp. xii, 151–65.

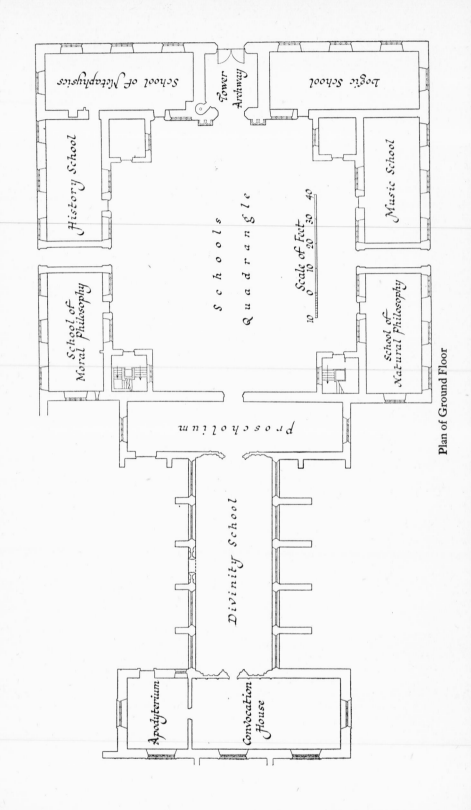

School of Metaphysics

Tower Archway

Logic School

History School

Music School

Schools Quadrangle

School of Moral Philosophy

School of Natural Philosophy

Scale of Feet
10 0 10 20 30 40

Proscholium

Divinity School

Apodyterium

Convocation House

Plan of Ground Floor

School, which at that time included the present Curators' Room, had sheltered a collection of Romano-Greek statuary presented to the university ninety years before by the Countess of Pomfret.[1] The Pomfret Marbles, as they are called, represent the greater part of the statues gathered together at Arundel House in James I's time by Thomas Howard, Earl of Arundel. They had just been moved to the newly completed University Galleries in Beaumont Street and lodged in the basement whence they were exhumed in 1894 to fill the ground-floor gallery, their present resting-place. So the Logic School was left empty, and on 5 June 1845 Convocation accepted a decree annexing it to the library.

The next two schools—one on the north side of the gateway tower and the other forming the eastern half of the north range—termed respectively the School of Metaphysics and the History School, were given up to examinations. When the university reformed its examination system in 1800 the new statute provided that the final examination for the B.A. degree, as well as the B.C.L. examination, should be held in the Schola Metaphysicae. Hence the School acquired the name of Writing School which has since been transferred to the great rooms in the new Examination Schools in the High Street. And the adjoining History School had been brought into use for viva voce examinations, and came to be known as the Old School or, from the rising seats at one end of the room, as the Cockpit.[2]

The one remaining ground-floor school not yet noticed is the former School of Moral Philosophy in the western half of the north range, adjoining the present back staircase to the library. In it, and in part built into its walls, were the inscribed stones and monuments from the Arundel collection which Lord Arundel's grandson, Lord Henry Howard, had presented to the university at the instigation of John Evelyn. Here likewise were the Selden Marbles, the gift of the learned John Selden. From its contents it was styled the Arundel Marble Room or Marble School.

3. THE OLD READING-ROOM

Turning back to the south-west corner of the quadrangle, and climbing the long ascent of shallow stairs that leads to the Bodleian

[1] Ackermann contains a good aquatint, by Westall, of the 'Statue Gallery'. A list of the statues as they stood in the gallery is given in the contemporary Oxford guides, e.g. the *Oxford University and City Guide*, 1822 ed., pp. 79–80.
[2] The room is depicted in R. W. Buss's aquatint, 'Examination of candidates for the degree of Bachelor of Arts', published in 1842. A proposal by Council for 'the removal of the rising seats in the present viva-voce school and its conversion into a writing school' was approved by Convocation on 12 Dec. 1862.

Library, up which the Prince Regent had toiled, groaning audibly, when the Allied Sovereigns came to Oxford,[1] one came to a swing door,[2] then covered with green baize reminiscent of a butler's pantry, and pushing it open, entered Arts End, to be confronted by the Founder himself, limned by a Venetian artist.[3] Here one is in the heart of Bodley, the first of three great apartments which, linked together in the shape of the capital letter H, together form what is now called the Old Reading-Room. Arts End is built over the Proscholium, and has received its name from the arts folios which fill the shelves lining its walls below the level of a gallery.[4] From the outset, and down to about 1840, all printed folios—other than those that came in great collections kept intact in memory of their former owners—were referenced into one of the four faculties of Theology, Law, Medicine, and Arts. A similar classification of quartos and octavos had been pretty well abandoned before 1824. The octavos and quartos of arts, as well as those of theology and medicine, retain their place on the shelves of the Arts End Gallery; but portraits of former librarians, which then depended from the gallery rail, have been recently rehung in the Curators' Room. On the floor of Arts End, near the entrance, a flimsy exhibition-case displayed a few of the library's treasures; and in the middle, in front of the great east window and facing the cross-piece of the H, was a large table; on it a black inkstand with wafers and pounce, and behind it a capacious high-backed Gothic chair in which sat the librarian.[5]

The central portion of the Old Reading-Room, down which the librarian gazed as he sat at his work, had not yet come by its name of Duke Humphrey's Library. Built over the Divinity School, it had been the fifteenth-century university library, and, when Sir Thomas Bodley restored it, he retained its original hammer-beam roof, affixing to it panels painted with the university arms. At the point of junc-

---

[1] G. V. Cox, *Recollections of Oxford*, 2nd ed. (1870), p. 82.

[2] The door was ordered by the Curators at their Visitation in 1813.

[3] Bodley's portrait hung previously over the entrance to the Picture Gallery; *Oxford University and City Guide*, 1822 ed., p. 73. It had been moved into Arts End by 1847; Parker's *Handbook for Visitors to Oxford*, p. 83.

[4] The wooden staircases to the gallery are modern restorations, on the ancient model, made in 1919.

[5] The library bills for 1832 record payment for 'a large Wainscote oak table with glass-case top to contain manuscripts for the library'. The librarian's chair was made out of oak removed in the preceding year from the roof of the Picture Gallery; Macray's *Annals*, p. 18. A water-colour by R. W. Buss, hanging near the north door of Arts End, shows the room as it was about 1843. It has been reproduced in aquatint. The reminiscences of H. J. Shuffrey, who was appointed a member of the library staff in 1863, are useful for reconstructing the general appearance of Arts End and Duke Humphrey's Room at a yet earlier period. They are among the library records.

ARTS END IN 1843
from a water-colour by R. W. Bass

tion with Arts End, where a gate now stands, a shallow step took one down on to an oaken floor at a slightly lower level, so that a *revenant* of 1845 would find himself walking ankle-deep in the present floor, as Archbishop Laud's ghost is fabled to do in his library at St. John's College. Just beyond the gate there stands, on either side of the room, a massive oak case holding drawers in which were then kept a slip-catalogue of accessions, and, then as now, the busts of Sir Thomas Bodley and of King Charles I looked down on them from above. Over the right-hand case there hung a framed Holbein drawing—a design for a cup—since removed to the Ashmolean. Just beyond each of the cases is the open-work door of a little closet. The closet on the right was the librarian's lower study; the one on the left was occupied by one of the sub-librarians; on its shelves the long row of Thomas Hearne's publications which a former librarian, Dr. Humphrey Owen, had collected in pious memory of that industrious but impossible member of the Bodleian staff. And, immediately beyond these studies but facing the visitor, are the two grilled cupboards called the Archives. Between them, low lattice gates gave access to the main reading-room.

Down its length runs a corridor, its floor at this date covered with rush matting. It was broader then than it is today, for the bookcases that front it are a late addition, and, in their place, copies of the *Oxford Almanack* for years between 1812 and 1833 less usefully filled the frames which Sir Thomas Bodley had contrived for the 'tables' or catalogues of the books in his oak book-presses. The presses jut out between the library windows and divide each side of the room into eight readers' alcoves, once raised slightly above the level of the central gangway. Half that number, namely, the first two and the last two alcoves on either side, were screened off, each by a pair of latticed doors backed by green curtains.[1] They served as enclosed studies for privileged readers, such as Dr. Pusey and his friend Charles Marriott, who occupied the farthest two on the south side. Oak benches originally ran down the centre of each alcove, but had been replaced since 1766 by more comfortable Windsor chairs. Theology folios fill the three shelves over the readers' desks in each southern alcove, and continue on the north side in which are also the folios of the two faculties of Law and Medicine. Over the alcoves dark galleries then extended. That on the south contained the quartos and octavos named 'Linc.' and 'Marshall' after their donors—Dr. Thomas Barlow, Bishop of Lincoln, and Dr. Thomas Marshall. The northern

---

[1] Macray's annotated copy of his *Annals*.

gallery was called 'Jur.', since it held the quartos and octavos of the faculty of Law. The room has ever been a haunt of ancient learning, well adapted for study and quiet contemplation in summertime, when honey-questing bees droned lazily in through ivy-framed windows opening on to Exeter College garden, but in winter it could be bitterly cold, and became dark as day and year wore on, for all artificial light was strictly forbidden under Sir Thomas Bodley's statute. *Dominus illuminatio mea* said the text on each panel of its painted ceiling.

Two closets similar to those at Arts End, one on each side, terminate the room, that on the left forming a study for a sub-librarian. And just beyond them one then stepped up into the western wing over the Convocation House and Apodyterium. A reader's table stood in the centre, a high bookcase of reference books on either side, but the floor was probably at this time free of other furniture.[1] The wing receives its name of Selden End from the library of the lawyer, parliament man, scholar, and orientalist, John Selden, whose folios are ranged on the shelves of its eastern wall. But there was much more besides crowded into this room. To the right of the west window which fronts the east window of Arts End the Sutherland collection of historical prints and drawings, received in 1837, had been placed on the deep shelves of a blocked window recess. And the well-filled galleries held thousands of quartos and octavos, not merely those that had come by Selden's gift, but a far greater number of miscellaneous accessions referenced B.S. (for Bibliotheca Seldeniana), for the most part no longer classified into faculties. The system of subject-classification with fixed shelf-marks had in fact begun to break down early in the eighteenth century under pressure of library growth; and though books continued until long afterwards to be referenced into faculties, their shelf-mark ceased to correspond with their subject-matter. As books of smaller size than the ordinary folio poured into the library, additional space had been found for them by removing panelling from above the wall-cases in the Selden galleries, and so increasing the number of shelves in each tier from eight to ten; by similar additions to the gallery shelves at Arts End; and by the insertion of two shelves under the readers' desks at both ends as well as in the main reading-room, for large quartos and folios of the smaller size. The walls of Selden End and Arts End alike were now lined with books from floor to ceiling; further contrivances were impossible, and, at the date at which we are taking our survey, it could have been said

---

[1] A sepia drawing by Mackenzie (Bodl. Arch. F. e. 13, fol. 35) engraved in Ingram's *Memorials of Oxford*, shows Selden End as it appeared in 1835.

8

that, for a year past, there was no room left in this portion of the building for any further accessions.[1]

4. THE PICTURE GALLERY

Nevertheless space had to be found somewhere for new books which were coming in at the rate of three or four thousand volumes a year. Sir Thomas Bodley had long ago foreseen that 'stowage for books', as he termed book-storage, would form a perennial problem for future librarians; and, with that end in view, he left funds for the construction of an upper story to the University Schools. The gallery, which runs round the three sides of the Schools quadrangle and forms its second floor, is reached by continuing up the main staircase, past the entry into Arts End. Since the Restoration it had developed into a picture gallery. It ranks as the oldest public gallery in England and formed the sole university art collection down to the year of which we are writing, when the Randolph Gallery was opened in Beaumont Street and some seventy pictures were transferred to it from Bodley. Those which were left, and which for the most part still remain upon its walls, were almost all of them portraits of the English school of painting. Though heavily weighted with Knellers, the collection contained such fine examples of portraiture as Gheeraerts's full-length of Sir Henry Savile, and the interesting picture by an unknown artist of Lord Burleigh riding on a white jennet. Immediately to the left of the gallery door came, in chronological order, Sonmans's series of founders of colleges,[2] since rehung on the walls over the readers' alcoves in Duke Humphrey. A serried row of chancellors of the university confronted the pious founders. Ensconced in window embrasures were a number of busts, some of them of merit: such were Edward Pierce's bust of Christopher Wren since transferred to the Ashmolean; Bacon's bust of Lord North, and the Chantrey busts of the Duke of Wellington and of Dean Ireland, now in the Examination Schools. In a window near the entrance Guy Fawkes's lantern attracted the attention of curious visitors who will also not have failed to notice, near to it, Drake's chair, made out of the timbers of the *Golden Hind*.[3] And under glass cases on stands in the centre of the

[1] For further details see G. W. Wheeler's two papers on 'Bodleian Press-marks in relation to Classification' in the *Bodleian Quarterly Record*, vol. i, pp. 280–92, 311–20.

[2] *Oxford University and City Guide*, 1822 ed., p. 74. From the 1859 edition of this guide, p. 73, it appears that the founders had been extruded by that date from the gallery and were hanging on the staircase.

[3] Accounts of the contents of the Picture Gallery are to be found in all the early Oxford guides, the fullest being that in the *Oxford University and City Guide*, 1859 ed., pp. 66–73. *A Catalogue of the Pictures, Models, Busts, &c, in the Bodleian Gallery*

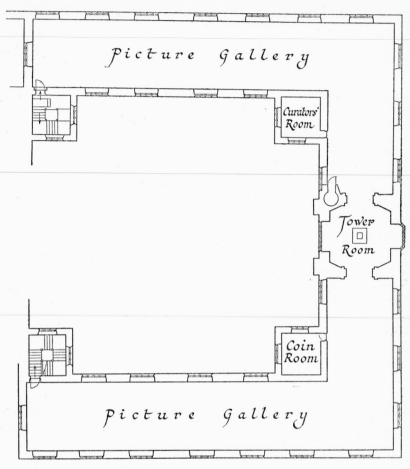

Plan of Second Floor

room were plaster casts of the Parthenon and other Greek and Roman buildings, the work of Fouquet of Paris,[1] which had been bought in 1823 for about £400 out of a subscription fund raised by the Ashmolean keepers, the brothers Duncan.

But it was not for this that Sir Thomas had planned his gallery, and it is therefore surprising to find that, although manuscript collections had begun to be placed in it at least as early as 1747, and two minor collections of printed books (Crynes and Godwyn) were put up in its southern wing in the third quarter of the eighteenth century, it was not brought into general use for book-storage until 1824. From that year, under the pressure of growing congestion in the Old Reading-Room, all new octavos other than serials were referenced into a fresh category called Year-Books. In this the breakdown of the faculty classification was frankly recognized by the abandonment of any attempt at subject arrangement. The octavo accessions of each year were simply placed in alphabetical order of authors' names, and were given a pressmark consisting of the last two numerals of the year date and a running number. Thus the first volume in the year-book series has for its pressmark the symbol 24, 1.[2] Year-Books filled wall-cases in the northern range of the Picture Gallery, blocking up its north windows,[3] and extended into the east range. There was already no room for more, and the acquisition of the Logic School in this year (1845) had come just in time to provide space for future Year-Books.

The southern wing of the Picture Gallery was not as yet so full as the northern. Its north windows, like those of the north range, had been blocked since 1831 by wall-cases. These shelved the Crynes and Godwyn books and long runs of pamphlets, and, in addition, an unclassified section named Δ, which had been formed for quarto accessions at the same time that the Year-Books series had been instituted for octavos.[4] From 1840 room had also had to be found for folio accessions, for folio space in the reading-room had at length given

and Library was produced by the library janitor, John Norris, in 1847. All earlier lists have been superseded by Mrs. Poole's Catalogue of Oxford Portraits, vol. i, pp. 1–130.
[1] A list of the Fouquet models is given in The Strangers' Guide through the University and City of Oxford, 1838, pp. 33–37; also by Macray, Annals, p. 312. All references to Macray's work are to the 2nd edition (1890).
[2] Wheeler in Bodleian Quarterly Record, vol. i, p. 291.
[3] Le Blon's copies of Raphael's seven cartoons, presented to the University by the Duke of Marlborough in 1807, are recorded as hung on the north side of the gallery (Oxford University and City Guide, 1819 ed., p. 43). They can only have done so till 1831 when the Picture Gallery was reconstructed and its north windows blocked. In 1845 they were transferred to the Randolph Gallery.
[4] Foreign quartos were referenced into 1 Δ and subsequently into 3 Δ; English quartos into 2 Δ.

out; and so a new section was made for them and named Fol. Δ.[1] And now in 1844–5, when space could no longer be found in the Selden galleries for any additions to the older octavos which had continued to be put there, these were given a home in the east range of the Picture Gallery in a category called Θ.

Two doors open off this eastern range. Each of them leads into a chamber over one of the corner staircases of the Schools. The south chamber, into which no one was allowed to enter unless accompanied by the librarian, was the Medal Room or Coin Room. It housed the Bodleian collection of coins and medals, started by Archbishop Laud and enriched by numerous subsequent donations of which the most recent and one of the finest was that received in 1834 from Francis Douce. The northern chamber is now the librarian's study, but was at this time called the Curators' Room, having been fitted up for Curators' meetings in 1814.[2]

The middle portion of the east range forms the second floor of the Tower of the Five Orders. It has arched openings to the north and south, and in one of the archways, facing Vandyke's portrait of Sir Kenelm Digby, there formerly hung Sir Joshua Reynolds's portrait of the architect James Paine and his son, now one of the ornaments of the Ashmolean Museum. Its oriel windows are filled with carrels of stained glass:[3] the embrasures once held a few casts of classical busts and Rysbrack's bust of the great Duke of Marlborough now in the Ashmolean. In the centre of the room stood till recently Le Sueur's fine bronze statue of William Herbert, Earl of Pembroke, in suit of armour. The rich stucco ceiling, work of an Oxford plasterer named Thomas Roberts, was put up in 1753. Above it are the two top stories of the tower. The lower of the two has held the university archives ever since they were placed there in 1640. The upper one, now known as the Upper Archives Room, was not assigned to the Keeper of the Archives until 1854, and, at the time of which we are writing, was, nominally at least, in the occupation of the Reader in Experimental Philosophy.[4]

Floor and ceiling of the Picture Gallery had been renewed in

[1] Reserved for modern folios from 1845 when the class Fol. Θ was formed for older folios. Wheeler, op. cit., p. 292.

[2] Curators' minutes, 24 Mar. 1814. It had previously been known as the Bodley Chest Room.

[3] An inscription, which disappeared when the stonework of the eastern window was renewed about 1880, recorded the gift of the glass in it by the Oxford antiquary, Alderman William Fletcher, in 1797.

[4] Proposals have been made on more than one occasion to transfer the archives to the Clarendon Building (Council committee minute-book, 1857–73, p. 11; Curators' minutes, 31 Oct. 1885, 8 Nov. 1887).

1831.[1] In the same year the west end of its north wing was partitioned off to make an unpacking room. Here the library binder later sat and worked. The door leading out of the gallery at this point gives on to the top of the backstairs, over which there had been constructed in 1795 an upper study for the librarian.[2] At the bottom of the first flight of stairs a door leads one back into the northern half of Arts End.

5. FIRST-FLOOR ROOMS

The schools on the first floor were originally reached by the staircases already mentioned as being in the corners of the quadrangle. Of these the south-east staircase was transformed into three small rooms in 1835; the north-east stair may have been blocked about the same date; the other two remain as the front and back stairs of the library. Half-way up the front stairs a door leads into the old Anatomy School, over the School of Natural Philosophy. Dissections had long been banished from the room, which came, in Charles II's time, to be a museum of curiosities. And now the antiquated rarities that once were in it had given place in their turn to manuscripts, bibles, and early editions of the classics, for it had been fitted up as a library room in 1787–9 to plans of the architect, James Wyatt. As the first addition to be made to the seventeenth-century library building, it was styled 'Auctarium', and the title *Bibliothecae Bodleianae Auctarium* remains painted on a label over its door. Tall wire-fronted bookcases, lettered A to Z, lined its walls and blocked its north and west windows, and, below them, pierced panels enclosed cupboards added in 1812. Here were kept the Barocci collection of Greek manuscripts; biblical, patristic, and classical manuscripts which still bear the pressmarks Auct. D, Auct. E, and Auct. F; portions of the Canonici collection of manuscripts bought in Venice in 1817; early editions of the Bible; *editiones principes* and fifteenth-century editions of the classics; Aldines, and texts of Greek and Latin authors annotated with scholia and marginalia by classical scholars. The floor was free except for a table at which 'persons employed in any considerable collation'[3] had the felicitous privilege of sitting and working.

[1] An engraving from a drawing by Whessell in 1829 shows the gallery as it appeared before the old ceiling was removed.
[2] 'The fitting up of the staircase from the Bodleian Library to the Law School', i.e. the present back staircase, was ordered by the Curators, 26 Mar. 1795; Curators' minutes.
[3] Curators' minutes, 21 Jan. 1789. Among the persons so privileged was Gustav Haenel, who found himself 'involved in a cloud of dust, poured with profusion over my blowing face by the venerable Fathers of the manuscripts in the Auctarium,

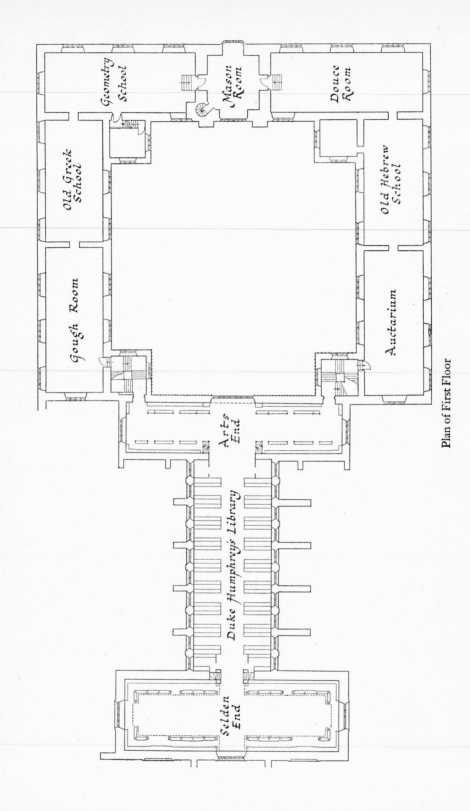

Geometry School

Mason Room

Douce Room

Old Greek School

Old Hebrew School

Gough Room

Auctarium

Arts End

Duke Humphrey's Library

Selden End

Plan of First Floor

A door leads through from the Auctarium to the old Hebrew School, sometime called the School of Rhetoric, over the Music School. It had degenerated into a drying-room for the University Press[1] before it was taken over for the library to which it was formally annexed in 1821.[2] Partitions were erected dividing the room into three. The first was planned as an Oriental manuscript-room; but, about 1825, the need for finding further space for folios in the reading-room upstairs brought hither the incunabula and early sixteenth-century printed books which up to then had found their place on the ordinary library shelves. They supplemented the classical incunabula already shelved in the tier of the Auctarium marked Q; and thus it was that they were given the pressmark Auct. 1Q–7Q, and that the room in which they stood came to be called the Q Room.

The middle room was devoted to Western manuscripts. The chief of its contents was the series formed in or about 1760 out of minor collections and single accessions. This series, into which isolated manuscript accessions were still being referenced, was termed MSS. Bodley, and from it the room took its name of the Bodley Room. Beyond it came a third room, called Laud; but, besides the miscellaneous manuscripts of Archbishop Laud's great donations, it contained a portion of the still vaster and more multifarious collection of manuscripts bequeathed to the library in 1755 by Dr. Richard Rawlinson; a collection so extensive that it swamped the meagre staff, and that, for a century to come, large parts of it lay unsorted in cupboards and obscure hiding-holes. A short flight of steps led out of the Laud Room up into a small lumber-room below the Medal Room. This had been constructed in 1835 in the south-east corner stair-turret, and for a time it held the University Armoury of ancient muskets and halberds.[3]

The Auctarium and the adjoining school together occupied the first floor of the southern range. Beyond them, and turning left, one comes to the old Astronomy School, which lies over the Logic School. It had been annexed to the library in 1828, and in 1834 a bequest of 17,000 volumes by Francis Douce made it necessary to

which Dr. Bliss and Dr. Nicoll have given free access to me to'. Letter to Sir Thomas Phillipps, 25 Feb. 1827, *penes* W. H. Robinson Ltd., Pall Mall.

[1] Ingram's *Memorials*, vol. ii (The Schools), p. 14.

[2] But nine years earlier, on 9 Nov. 1812, the Curators had ordered an estimate to be made of the cost of fitting it up; and in 1817 the oriental collections of Laud, Pococke, Huntington, Marsh, and Clarke were already installed in it. (W. M. Wade, *Walks in Oxford*, vol. ii, p. 301.) A letter from Dr. Philip Bliss to Sir Egerton Brydges shows that they were moved into the new room in 1813. Bodl. MS. Eng. letters, d. 74, fol. 287.

[3] Shuffrey's reminiscences.

shelve it forthwith.[1] As had been done in both the schools of the south range, its window looking into the quadrangle was blocked. So also was the door which had originally led into it from the staircase.[2] Its walls were lined with cases which were carried across the room near its south end, cutting off the southern portion to form a separate room—subsequently named the Spanish Room—for Douce manuscripts.

None of the great collections which make up the treasures of Bodley is so strongly marked with the individuality of the man who formed it as that of Francis Douce. It was gathered together in the Dibdin age of unrestricted enthusiasm for fine print. It was rich in incunabula (of which it contained 311), in block-books, and in books printed on vellum. Here were fragments of works by the first English printers and much early French literature. Many of its books were in the finest bindings; some in embroidered and ivory covers. It was very strong in bibles, Horae, Primers, and other liturgical works. History and biography formed a dominant feature; and the whole was stamped with a romantic antiquarianism worthy of a correspondent of Walter Scott. Here was abundance of books on antiquities; of works dealing with manners and customs, sports and pastimes; of literature on the fine arts. Its 400 manuscripts included superb specimens of illumination by artists of the Middle Ages. An individual note which runs throughout the collection is Douce's love of the singular, the recondite, and the grotesque. Here were black-letter ballads; large collections of chap-books and children's books of the eighteenth and early nineteenth centuries; even playing-cards. Albums, boxes, and portfolios were filled with scraps—much that was precious (like Caxton's advertisement of his works), much that was purely ephemeral. A small but choice collection of charters contained many seals of the first quality. Of Douce's coin-cabinet we have already spoken. Besides coins it held fine series of fifteenth-century Italian medals and of English tradesmen's tokens. Douce's collection of prints and drawings (which Thomas Dodd, a London print-dealer, had been employed to catalogue) was especially rich in the products of the German Renaissance,[3] and would alone have sufficed to make his name famous.

The spacious room was worthy of its contents. Its light oak wall-cases, and the harmonious colouring of the gilt-lettered bindings

[1] A woodcut in Ingram's *Memorials*, vol. ii, shows it as it was in 1835.

[2] The door has now been removed to ground-floor level and gives admittance to the new Curators' Room.

[3] Douce's collections form the subject of a series of articles in the *Bodleian Quarterly Record*, vol. vii, pp. 360–80.

behind the metal grills, charmed young Mary Arnold, when, an impressionable girl of seventeen, she was permitted by the fatherly indulgence of the librarian to work in the adjoining room. Many years afterwards she recorded what she felt.[1] The treasures of the Douce collection 'shone', she said, 'like jewels in the golden light of the room. That light was to me something tangible and friendly. It seemed to be the mingled product of all the delicate browns and yellows and golds in the bindings of the books, of the brass lattice-work that covered them, and of reflections from the beautiful stone-work of the Schools quadrangle outside. In these noble surroundings there sank deep into me the sense of history, and of that vast ocean of the recorded past, from which generations rise and into which they fall back.'

A few steps lead up out of the Douce Room into a square oriel-lighted room over the tower archway. From the first it had been the Savile Study, occupied by the professors of Sir Henry Savile's twin chairs. It had been annexed to the library and fitted up to capacity with new shelving in 1835. A handsome bequest of £40,000 made to library funds in 1841 by Dr. Robert Mason was commemorated by giving to this chamber the name of the Mason Room. And now it was filled up to the curved vault of its ceiling with editions de luxe, books with plates, and other expensive publications, all fitted into its shelves with the exactitude of tesserae in a mosaic.

A door similar to that by which one enters leads down on the north side to what was the Geometry School before it was attached to the library in 1828. It lies over the Schola Metaphysicae. Here were the great Oriental collections, and the northern portion of the room was partitioned off to house the 5,000 Hebrew books and manuscripts collected by Rabbi Oppenheimer and bought in Hamburg in 1829. Thence—passing on the left a flight of stairs up to a room below the Curators' Room in the north-east corner-turret, containing Edmund Malone's much-prized library of Shakespeariana and English drama-tic literature, which Lord Sunderlin had presented in 1821—one comes, in the north range of the quadrangle, on the old Greek School or Schola Linguarum, over the History School. This had been ab-sorbed in 1821 and had been converted into three rooms for the English and foreign periodicals now coming into the library in rapidly increasing numbers. Beyond it one is over the Arundel Marble Room and in the old Law School, the first of the Schools after the Auctarium to be taken over by the library. It was annexed in 1805 and was at once fitted up with ornamental wall-cases. It was

[1] Mrs. Humphry Ward, *A Writer's Recollections*, 1918, p. 112.

probably intended from the first to receive the library of works on British topography which Richard Gough had formed and promised to bequeath, and which came in upon his death in 1809. A few years later, further shelving was added,[1] and a number of eighteenth-century manuscript collections were brought in.[2] The west end of the room, just beyond the point where an entrance door gives on to the backstairs, was cut off from the rest, and came to be known from its contents (MSS. Rawlinson A–C) as the Rawlinson Room.

Thus between the years 1797 and 1835 the whole of the first floor of the Schools had been taken over for library purposes. The library, although already overtaken in the race by the British Museum, was increasing rapidly, and in 1837 it had been calculated that upwards of 80,000 volumes (in addition to tracts and dissertations) had been added to it since 1813.[3] In 1849, four years after the date of our survey, it was computed to hold 220,000 printed volumes and 21,000 manuscripts.[4]

[1] Curators' minutes, 19 Dec. 1816.
[2] Namely, Dodsworth, Carte, Tanner, Willis, and Ballard. W. M. Wade, *Walks in Oxford* (1817), vol. ii, p. 302. A very careful pencil drawing by Joseph Fisher, in Bodl. MS. Top. Oxon. a. 36, fol. 79, shows the room as it was in 1819. (The date is supplied by MS. Eng. Misc. d. 293, fol. 37.)
[3] Letter from the librarian, entered in Curators' minutes.
[4] Macray, *Annals*, p. 352. The British Museum had some 227,000 printed books by 1837; Esdaile, *The British Museum Library* (1946), p. 102.

Chapter II

Organization and Personnel

1. COPYRIGHT ACCESSIONS AND PURCHASES

IN surveying the library buildings mention has been made (pp. 16–18) of the greater donations (Gough, Malone, and Douce) of the first half of the nineteenth century. A more constant stream of accessions flowed in under successive copyright acts under which the Bodleian Library claimed from the publishers a copy of every book published in the United Kingdom. This privilege[1] originated in an agreement made by Sir Thomas Bodley with the Stationers' Company as far back as 1611. It had been confirmed by a series of Acts of Parliament, of which the most recent was that of 1842 (5 and 6 Vic., c. 45). It was shared with other libraries, but the number so privileged had been reduced in 1836 from eleven to five, namely, the British Museum, the universities of Oxford and Cambridge, the Advocates' Library at Edinburgh, and Trinity College, Dublin. The recognition of the Bodleian as a library of national deposit was greatly valued, and Oxford had rejected out of hand an offer made in 1836 to substitute for the copyright privilege an annual State grant of £500. But from the outset, and particularly during the eighteenth century, administration of the agreement with the Stationers' Company, and of the subsequent licensing acts and copyright acts, had been woefully ineffective owing chiefly to failure on the part of publishers to enter their books at Stationers' Hall. So it was not until the Copyright Act of 1814 (54 Geo. III, c. 156), following upon a judgement in the Court of Kings Bench, recognized the right of the privileged libraries to every publication, whether entered at Stationers' Hall or not, that the Bodleian began to reap the full benefit of that to which it was legally entitled. Books and periodicals were now claimed from the publishers and sent off to Bodley in monthly parcels by the clerk of the Stationers' Company, who received from that library for his pains 50 guineas a year out of which he was required to meet the cost of collection. The Stationers' Hall lists for 1845 show that about 2,500 different works were received in that year, over and above parts and periodicals, sheet music, and maps.

The copyright privilege relieved the library from the necessity of

---

[1] The history of the copyright privilege has been fully recounted in Robert Partridge's *Legal Deposit of Books*, 1938.

buying new English publications, and left its funds free for the purchase of foreign literature as well as of manuscripts and rare books and for the making up of its extensive arrears. Down to 1780 the library revenue available for book purchase had been almost nil; but in that year, upon the initiative of Sir William Scott, afterwards Lord Stowell, a statute had been passed which produced a substantial and growing income earmarked for this special purpose. It imposed, for the benefit of the library, an annual fee of 4s. upon all members of colleges and halls who had resided four years in the university or who had been admitted to the library as readers. It also doubled undergraduates' matriculation fees and assigned the additional amount to the library.[1] The sum brought in by the two new taxes amounted in the first full year to no more than £451: but both were doubled in 1813; and by 1845, with the growth of numbers in the university, the library was drawing from these two sources a revenue amounting to the respectable sum of £2,277.[2]

The fund was well laid out on substantial purchases made during the first half of the nineteenth century.[3] The manuscripts of the Dutch scholar, J. P. D'Orville, consisting of Greek and Latin classics, collations, and correspondence of classical scholars, were bought in 1805 for £1,025. In 1809 £1,000 was paid for the manuscripts, partly Greek and partly Oriental, of the English traveller, E. D. Clarke. The great Canonici collection was purchased in 1817 for £5,444.[4] In 1820 the library acquired for £500 fifty Greek codices from the Saibante collection. Four years later large purchases, to the amount of £925, were made at the sale at The Hague, of another Dutch library, that of Meerman, comprising a number of very early classical manuscripts besides much foreign history and law. The Oppenheimer

[1] *Corpus Statutorum Univ. Oxon.*, addenda, pp. 104–5.

[2] The clearest account of these sources of library revenue is that given in a printed paper headed 'Information collected by a Committee of the Hebdomadal Council' and dated 16 May 1855. Matriculation fees varied with the social status of the person matriculating, or rather with that of his father. Thus, down to 1855, an esquire's son paid £2. 19s.; a gentleman's son got off with £2. 1s. and the proportion of their fees payable to the library was 33s. and 21s. respectively. The average amount received by the Bodleian on each matriculation was reckoned in 1855 at £1. 7s. 9d.

[3] Catalogues of books purchased for the library were published annually from 1780 to 1861. The accounts annexed to these lists are amplified in some measure by a volume of library accounts among the library records. Booksellers' bills remain for a few years scattered over the first half of the nineteenth century: an unbroken series begins in 1851.

[4] Canonici's printed books were not included in the sale, nor all his manuscripts. Of these the Bodleian secured 2,047. Some 915 others were purchased in 1835 by the Rev. Walter Sneyd. The manuscripts now referenced Add. MSS. 10629–10919 were resold by him in 1836 to the British Museum, the remainder were dispersed in 1903 and subsequent sales.

Hebrew collection was bought *en bloc* in 1829 for £2,080. More recently some smaller but valuable collections of Oriental manuscripts had been added to the library. These included the Wilson collection of Sanskrit manuscripts purchased in 1842 for £500; the Bruce collection of Arabic and Ethiopic manuscripts, bought in the following year for £1,000; and the 750 Oriental manuscripts, chiefly Persian, acquired in 1844 for £2,000 from the representatives of Sir William Ouseley.

Occasionally large prices were paid for single manuscripts. Bodley had been outbid in its attempt to acquire the Towneley Homer in 1814,[1] but a fifteenth-century manuscript of Suidas was bought in 1817 for £220, and the lovely Codex Ebnerianus of the New Testament in 1820 for £150. Of a different order were the purchases made in 1812, for £150, of Richard Gough's materials for a third edition of his *British Topography*, and in 1835, for £240, of the original manuscript of Bishop Burnet's *History of his Own Time*.

As for printed books, the library authorities at first directed their energies in the main to the purchase of early bibles and *editiones principes* of the classics. A provident outlay of £70 had secured for Bodley in 1819 a magnificent copy of Fust and Schoeffer's 1459 Mainz Psalter, printed on vellum. Money was not always so well expended, and comparatively high prices were paid for the large folios of foreign travel and of natural history with coloured plates, which were so much the fashion in public as in private libraries at the close of the eighteenth and beginning of the nineteenth century. The Bodleian set of Aldines was gradually brought to practical completion, largely through purchases made at M. Renouard's and Bishop Samuel Butler's sales in 1828 and 1840. And its defects in other directions were gradually recognized and remedied. Astonishing though it may seem, the *Acta Sanctorum* were acquired for the first time in 1815, and such standard works as Baronius's *Annales Ecclesiastici* and the *Bibliotheca Maxima Veterum Patrum* as late as 1830. It was not until 1813 that the library acquired a set of the *Gentleman's Magazine*, or until 1816 that it secured the *Annual Register*, or until 1829 that it got its first copy of Hansard. But foreign literature was by no means neglected; French official and academical publications were secured despite the interruptions of the Revolutionary and Napoleonic wars, though the need for subscribing to German learned periodicals was hardly recognized until 1826. Growing attention was paid to sales upon the Continent, such as those of the libraries of

---

[1] It fell at £620 to Dr. Burney, from whose family it was purchased four years later, with the rest of the Burney library, for the British Museum.

Professor Te Water at Leyden in 1823, of Meerman at The Hague in 1824, of M. Langlès at Paris in 1825 (which yielded some rare products of Far Eastern presses), and of Dr. Kloss of Frankfurt in 1835. From 1824 special attention began to be devoted to the acquisition of early Spanish books. A collection of Lutheran tracts, filling eighty-four volumes, had been bought in 1818. And the year 1827 was marked by the purchase at Altona, for £333, of no fewer than 43,000 academic dissertations.

Purchases in the home market were hardly less frequent or extensive. One may instance the eleven or twelve thousand seventeenth- and eighteenth-century plays, and the large collection of booksellers' catalogues and sale-catalogues of books and coins, all prior to 1814, bought in 1834; and an enormous collection of English pamphlets, 19,380 in number, and covering the years 1660–1820, bought in 1837 from the bookseller Thomas Rodd. Advantage was taken of knock-down prices to make large purchases in 1834–5 at the sales of Richard Heber's vast library; and from then onwards, under the stimulus of the Malone and Douce gifts, early English printing and Shake-speariana make more frequent appearance in the annual purchase lists. Money was still plentiful. The librarian was watchful, and, though sometimes beaten in the race by Dr. Routh, the ancient President of Magdalen,[1] he could rightly claim to be generally in advance of competing libraries. Thomas Rodd usually bid for Bodley at English auctions; local agents were generally employed at continental sales. Current foreign books and periodicals were acquired in the main through the firm of Treuttell and Wurz in Soho, and subsequently through that of Bossange, Barthes, and Lowell in Great Marlborough Street, or direct from Asher of Berlin. Payne and Foss were the principal source for rare books and manuscripts. During the ten years preceding 1845 the average sum (apart from extraordinary purchases) expended on manuscripts and printed books works out at £1,685 a year.

2. LIBRARY CATALOGUES

Annual lists were printed of purchases and donations,[2] though these gave no shelf-marks. The general library catalogue, superseding one that was then more than a hundred years old—the Bodleian catalogue

---

[1] Tuckwell, *Reminiscences of Oxford*, 1901 ed., p. 167.

[2] They were distributed, under orders given by the Curators, 28 Nov. 1788 and 27 Oct. 1789, to heads of houses, college librarians, senior common rooms, curators, and resident professors.

of 1738—had been published only two years back, that is, in 1843, in three folio volumes, which lay open in the great east window, behind the librarian's chair. It had made slow progress, for it had been under way for thirty years. It had cost about £2,150 to compile, and more than as much again—namely, about £2,300—to print.[1] It was eight years out of date at the time of its appearance, and staff were already at work on a supplementary volume which should contain accessions from 1835. Gough, Douce, and Oppenheimer collections were also excluded, for each had its own separate catalogue, the first a very imperfect one seeing that a very large portion of Gough pamphlets and tracts received no notice.[2] Academic dissertations were likewise to be looked for in a separate printed list. Music remained as yet uncatalogued, unarranged, and piled up in cupboards. Prints were in better case, thanks to the elaborate three-volume catalogue of the Sutherland collection, the compilation and gift of the munificent donor.

A reader in 1845 who desired to see any recent accession would consult the cataloguers' written slips. These were arranged in an alphabetical series filling the drawers of the heavy cases on either side of the entry to Duke Humphrey's Library. There were no order-forms in those days; and it was usual for a reader to summon a library attendant and point out to him, in the printed catalogue or in the slip-drawer, the catalogue-entry of the book he wanted.[3] If he were in quest of a manuscript, he would refer in the first place to the interleaved copy of the *Catalogus Manuscriptorum Angliae et Hiberniae* published in 1697/8, or, if he were an Orientalist, to the two catalogues of Oriental manuscripts edited respectively by Uri and Nicoll. For Gough and Douce manuscripts he would use the separate catalogues of those collections. The D'Orville and the E. D. Clarke collections each had its own catalogue, as had a small collection of Icelandic codices purchased in 1828 from Finn Magnusen for £350. But for a very large number of the library's manuscripts there was no published catalogue at all, and it was necessary to refer for descriptions to written handlists. However, the sub-librarian, H. O. Coxe, had been actively engaged since 1840 in cataloguing the Douce manuscripts and Canonici collection, and was now hard at work preparing a catalogue of all the library's Greek manuscripts.

[1] *Bodleian Quarterly Record*, vol. ii, p. 87; Macray, *Annals*, pp. 345-7.
[2] Their omission was not noticed until 1878 (letter from the librarian to the Vice-Chancellor, 26 Oct. 1878).
[3] The practice continued until the Curators, on 22 Nov. 1859, ordered a notice to be put up requesting readers to search the catalogues for themselves, and directed the librarian to provide printed order-slips.

3. LIBRARY READERS

Who, it may be asked, were the readers at this time, and what use was being made of Bodley? Under the Founder's Statute the privilege of using the library was given to all graduate members of the university. But for this privilege, whether exercised or no, they had to pay down, upon graduating, a fee fixed in 1804 at 11s. of which the librarian pocketed 10 and handed 1 on to the humble janitor.[1] Other persons who desired to read were originally required to obtain a grace in Congregation; and, although this was apparently no longer enforced, admission of strangers continued to be a matter of some trouble and difficulty. There still remained upon the statute-book—though it had become a dead letter—a provision that a non-graduate reader might not read manuscripts unless he brought with him a Master of Arts or a Bachelor of Civil Law to sit by his side as invigilator and surety.[2] Undergraduates made no use of Bodley but had to be content with their college libraries. There were no women readers. Every reader, on graduation or (if not a graduate) on admission, had in old times to take a solemn oath on a Testament that he would not mutilate or embezzle books, but would observe library regulations; and the oath continued to be required down to 1838 when a statute was passed substituting for it a new form of simple declaration.[3] Fines of the amount of 3s. 4d. were exacted for improper treatment of books, as for leaning on an open book or resting notebook or writing-paper upon it. B.A.'s of less than two years' standing were required to come in cap and gown,[4] and the custom of wearing academic dress in the library, although not compulsory for senior members, seems to have been general.

Attendance of readers, though mounting, was extremely thin judged by later standards. One day in August 1822 the sub-librarian, Philip Bliss, had noted that not a single member of the university came into the library. But that was in the dead of the long vacation, and, even so, may be regarded as exceptional. A fairer idea can be derived from the entry books in which readers' orders of books and manuscripts were recorded.[5] They reveal that the number of separate

---

[1] Hebdomadal Register, 1802–23, p. 62. The janitor's share of admission fees was subsequently fixed at £20 per annum; Curators' minutes, 23 Apr. 1842.

[2] *Laudian Code*, ed. Griffiths (1888), p. 227.

[3] *Corpus Statutorum*, addenda, pp. 320–1.

[4] *Statuta Antiqua Univ. Oxon.*, ed. Gibson (1931), p. 514.

[5] In a return made to Parliament in Jan. 1849 the librarian stated, 'No register is kept of persons consulting the Library; accordingly, the number of students who have frequented it during the last ten years cannot be ascertained.' (Macray, *Annals*, p. 352.) He did less than justice to his own records.

persons making use of Bodley in 1845 was 215. The highest number
ordering books or manuscripts on one day in May of that year (when
the library was probably at its busiest) was eleven; the average number
throughout the month was between four and five. Since books might
be reserved, one should probably double that number to obtain an
approximate estimate of the total of daily readers. A few came almost
daily. In fact a constant use was made of the place by a very limited
number.

Amongst the most regular readers at this date were Dr. Greenhill,
the learned physician to the Infirmary; Charles Marriott, working
away in his private study on the Library of the Fathers; Mr. (subsequently Bishop) Jacobson, who walked in every day from a curacy
at Begbroke to produce his *Patres Apostolici*; Mark Pattison, still
under the spell of Tractarianism; and Count Mortara, who might be
found cataloguing the Italian manuscripts of the Canonici collection
and treating the staff with elaborate foreign courtesy. Here also one
might frequently meet Dr. Travers Twiss, who was later to become
a Regius Professor of Civil Law; Mr. Westwood, relaxing himself
upon early illumination; Mr. Haddan, future partner of Mr. Stubbs
in the edition of ecclesiastical documents; and Charles Eden, vicar
of the University Church, engaged in editing the works of Jeremy
Taylor.

Not all who came to read stayed to read. Times of opening were
not convenient for all would-be readers. It is true that the library was
open on all days but thirty-eight throughout the year, Sundays excepted. From Lady Day to Michaelmas its doors were opened at nine
o'clock; during the winter at ten. Only on days when university sermons were preached at St. Mary's, which all senior members of the
university might be expected to attend, the library was not opened
until the sermon was over, that is, till about eleven.[1] And it stayed open
until the warning tinkle of a little handbell, suggestive of muffins to
older ears, and the hands of Dr. Rawlinson's eighteenth-century clock
pointing to four in summer or to three o'clock in winter announced
the closing time so welcome to the library staff and discomposing
to its readers.[2] But though these times might well enough suit the
leisured student, the absence of evening opening made the university
library practically useless in term-time to that growing class, the
hard-worked college tutors.

And two terms out of the three it was impossible to read in the
library with comfort unless endowed with physical hardihood or

[1] The practice continued down to 1889 when the statute was altered.
[2] *Corpus Statutorum*, addenda, p. 206.

25

clad in suitable apparel. Foreigners in particular found its cold intolerable, 'unless arriving', it is said, 'from a very northerly latitude'.[1] In 1818 the Vice-Chancellor had received a memorial containing proposals for rendering the contents of the library more accessible. Stirred up by it, he had consulted Mr. Rennie, of Waterloo Bridge fame, as to the best means of warming the university buildings; and, after a three-years' interval, a small furnace or hypocaust had actually been installed on Exeter College ground, whence hot air rose up through two gratings into Selden End. W. D. Macray, the Bodleian annalist, has described how he used to see old Professor Reay, the Oriental sub-librarian, standing over one of those gratings for half an hour at a time, in vain efforts to thaw himself.[2] Despite hot air, the cold of Bodley remained a standing jest, though not with those who used the place. The library remained, it was said, 'either close or cold, and for a great part of the year both'.[3] In a cold spell in January of 1841 its temperature had fallen below freezing-point. Professor Reay's colleague, H. O. Coxe, might work imperturbably on his catalogues of Greek and Latin manuscripts, 'very gay in my new spencer and very comfortable'. But even he must have shuddered one day in March of this year, 1845, when he let himself into the library at seven o'clock in the morning to carry on private work before breakfast and found the thermometer registering 17 degrees Fahrenheit.[4] 'When I became a B.A.', the Vice-Principal of St. Alban Hall told the first University Commission, 'I was romantic enough to think of working in the Bodleian. Although I protected myself even to encumbrance with clothing against the cold, I could not work there more than two hours at a time.'[5] And young Max Müller recorded his early impressions:[6]

Bodley's Library seemed a perfect paradise for a student. I must confess that I slightly altered my opinion when I had to sit there every day during a severe winter without any fire, shivering and shaking and almost unable to hold my pen, till kind Mr. Coxe, the sub-librarian, took compassion on me and brought me a splendid fur that had been sent him as a present by a Russian scholar, who had witnessed the misery of the librarian in this Siberian library.

[1] *Oxford in 1888*, p. 45. This *jeu d'esprit* was written in 1838 by Richard Walker, a Fellow of Magdalen. [2] *Annals*, p. 310, n. 2.
[3] G. V. Cox, *Recollections of Oxford*, 2nd ed., p. 223.
[4] Coxe's diaries form an important source for the history of the library during the time when he was a member of the staff. The originals remain in the possession of his family, but very full extracts have been made by his son, the Rev. Hilgrove Coxe, and these are among the library records.
[5] *Oxford University Commission Report*, 1852, Evidence, p. 150.
[6] *My Autobiography, a Fragment* (1901), p. 249.

Despite hot-air inlets, the cold of that early spring of 1845 was too great to be endured. The librarian took the simple course of absenting himself in the cold spell and, when summer came, his Curators resolved to try out the steam heating which had lately been introduced at the University Press. At a cost of £150 a steam boiler was installed,[1] and pipes were run along either side of Duke Humphrey's Library below the windows. Henceforward readers doubtless expected to study in comparative comfort.

They sat in their alcoves, reading and copying; dipping quill-pens into large pewter inkpots. Only the most privileged scholar might hope to have assigned for his sole and separate use one of the eight enclosed studies. Others sat at oak benches in front of the wall-cases of Arts and Selden Ends. Silence was enjoined, but there was a frequent disturbing amount of conversation,[2] not least from the librarian.

4. THE LIBRARIAN

For in this as in every other matter the great Dr. Bulkeley Bandinel was a law unto himself. Son of the Public Orator and first Bampton Lecturer, Dr. James Bandinel of Jesus College, he came of a family that had been settled in Jersey since the beginning of the seventeenth century; and when his obituary came to be written in the *Gentleman's Magazine*,[3] he was described in it as 'descended from one of the oldest and noblest families of Italy'. On this he may have prided himself; yet it was dangerous to address him as Dr. Bandinelli, for, as he remarked to that eminent German philologist, Max Müller,[4] 'I have never been one of those dirty foreigners'. It was easy to make him angry. At his christening his father's colleague at Jesus College, old John Price, then Bodley's Librarian, had renounced on his behalf the pomps and vanities of this wicked world, little thinking then that, when he himself died at the age of seventy-nine, his little godson would succeed to his own exalted station.

Young Bulkeley was sent to Winchester, and became in turn a

---

[1] Steam-heating was eventually found inadequate and was replaced in 1863 upon the advice of Mr. (afterwards Sir William) Siemens by a hot-water system. But, as fires were drawn every evening and the boilers relit every morning, the library is likely to have remained a chilly place in winter weather.

[2] Mr. Walker of Magdalen pictures a reader trying to study in one of the alcoves in 1838. 'Perchance the adjoining study might contain two students, studying aloud with all their might; and the only resource left to him was to read as loud as they, and to drown their duetto, thus relieving himself but contributing to increase the hubbub.' *Oxford in 1888*, p. 46.

[3] 1861, pt. 1, p. 465.

[4] *My Autobiography*, p. 251.

scholar and a Fellow of New College. He commenced his clerical career by serving as naval chaplain on board the famous *Victory*, then, in 1808, in the Baltic under the command of another Channel Islander, Admiral Sir James Saumarez. Two years later his godfather brought him on to the Bodleian staff, appointing him sub-librarian; and, when Mr. Price died in the long vacation of 1813, after holding office for forty-five years, he was promptly nominated by the Curators to succeed, and no one opposed his election in Convocation. So at the age of thirty-two he became Bodley's Librarian.

He was then still a bachelor, as was required by the Founder; but a new statute, passed three months after his election, released the librarian and sub-librarians from the obligation of perpetual celibacy,[1] and he married two years later. The same statute permitted these officers to hold benefices—it had been previously forbidden. Consequently in 1823, in which year he took the degree of D.D., Bishop Barrington of Durham, a former Bodleian Curator, was able to present him to the distant rectory of Haughton-le-Skerne with Sadberge. He occasionally visited his parish on his summer holidays. Wytham, where he was curate, was near at hand and saw more of him.

The 1813 Statute raised the librarian's salary from £300 to £400 and it had since been further increased in 1842 to £550.[2] In addition, he had the 10s. fee which all members of the university paid upon graduation, and his income in fees was computed in 1837 to amount to about £120 a year.[3] He had also his New College Fellowship and his Durham Rectory.

Although an instance of spiritual nepotism, Dr. Bandinel was very far from being a negligible librarian. He was accurate and industrious. So at least Thomas Dibdin thought him.[4] An American traveller who came to Oxford in 1838 describes him as possessing 'more bibliographical knowledge than anybody I have met with in England except Hallam'.[5] He was really knowledgeable in the book-lore of the period, that is in incunabula and *editiones principes*, and compiled an alphabetical list of those in Bodley which never got beyond proof-stage.[6] The account that has already been given of the accessions to the library during his period of office gives proof of the activity and remarkable success with which he followed up the opportunities of

[1] *Corpus Statutorum*, addenda, p. 202.
[2] Convocation Register, 1837–46, p. 349.
[3] Curators' minutes, 30 Nov. 1837.
[4] *Bibliographical Decameron*, 1817, vol. i, p. xcv.
[5] *Life of George Ticknor*, 1876, vol. ii, p. 169.
[6] *Catalogus editionum principum vel Saec. XV in Bibliotheca Bodleiana*, printed in 1827.

the book market. It was said of him when he died, that to the very last he knew the size, appearance, and position of every volume in the library;[1] and there must have been some little warrant for that rash assertion.

There was no denying his learning. In his younger days he had been co-editor with Ellis and Cayley in their great but pretentious edition of Dugdale's *Monasticon*. He had also edited, in 1826, for the University Press Clarendon's *History of the Rebellion*. He was bosom friend of his contemporary, Philip Bliss—antiquary, bibliophile, Registrar, and Keeper of the Archives—who had been on the staff when Bandinel first came to Bodley. The two old cronies chatted away together in the library, regardless of the rule for silence, and in their lighter moments exchanged poetic epistles on their respective attacks of gout.[2] When Isaac D'Israeli brought Francis Douce to visit the library, Bandinel received them both with the greatest charm and courtesy. The Douce collection is the lasting memorial of that memorable encounter.

Yet not all visitors could reckon on being so well received. He was said to have a quick eye for a charlatan; and visitors and readers alike had to prove their worth before they could obtain the attention which all expected or at least desired. He had his favourites, and one could only win his favour by establishing a claim to it. Seated one day at his table, he perceived a young reader daring to take down a volume from its shelf. Instantly he pounced upon him; but, on discovering that the young man was godson to his brother James in the Foreign Office, all became smiles, and nothing could exceed the dread Librarian's good humour. It was said 'there was no trouble that he would not take for the most obscure scholar if he was persuaded of his integrity and good faith'.[3]

His staff could not expect such good treatment. Coxe stood up to him, and bore with characteristic patience the old man's rambling reminiscences, while pining to get back to his beloved manuscripts. But the Senior Sub-Librarian, mild ineffective old Professor Reay, had much to suffer from him, and the language in which he was ordered about, says Max Müller, 'was such as would not now be

[1] *Gentleman's Magazine*, 1861, pt. 1, p. 465. George Ticknor gives similar testimony; loc. cit.

[2] MS. Phillips 18132.

[3] *Gentleman's Magazine*, loc. cit. Ill-natured Sir Frederic Madden, to whom Bandinel had shown considerable attention, even letting him have a Bodleian manuscript to collate at his lodgings, describes him with some insight as 'a very weak and vain man, with a dash of the bully; but *au fond* a great deal of good nature, which must however be brought forth to the satisfaction of his own self-esteem or not at all'. Bodl. MS. Eng. hist. c. 149, fol. 149.

addressed to any menial'.[1] And Macray, then a young assistant in the library, testifies that 'all the staff trembled at Jupiter's nod'.[2] Bandinel could lash with his tongue, and had learned vigour of expression on the quarter-deck of the *Victory*.

Even the Curators were cowed by their alarming Librarian—that ponderous eighteenth-century figure in doctor's gown and capacious white bands—when he told them that such and such had been the invariable custom of the library for years and could not be altered. Max Müller says[3] that there were only two men of whom Dr. Bandinel was afraid: one was Dr. Pusey; the other was Benjamin Jowett, afterwards Master of Balliol.

Other librarians since his day have been as autocratic, but none so terrifying. The library's treasures were his treasures, jealously guarded as his private property. He dispensed himself from the regulations which he enforced so strictly upon others, and had no scruple in carrying home its books and manuscripts to exhibit to his friends, or even in borrowing coins out of the cabinet, being himself a numismatist. He had been a great figure. Now in 1845 he was sixty-four; well past his prime.

5. SUBORDINATE STAFF

The two sub-librarians were nominated by him. Both were clergymen. The senior of the two, Stephen Reay, whom his chief treated with such contumely, was nearly as old as Bandinel but more infirm. He had been at one time Vice-Principal of St. Edmund Hall, and since 1840 he held the Laudian Chair of Arabic. 'I remember once', says Max Müller in his account of Bandinel,[4] 'when Professor Reay had been looking for ever so long to find his spectacles without which he could not read the Arabic manuscripts, and had asked everybody whether they had seen them, a voice came at last thundering through the Library—"You left your spectacles on my chair, you old idiot, and I sat on them".' Yet others than Bandinel could not but feel deep respect for the tall, spare, handsome, bowed old man; for his old-fashioned churchmanship and for his kindliness, his gentleness, his simplicity. 'If a character could be drawn by a single word,' says his obituary notice in the *Gentleman's Magazine*,[5] 'guilelessness would express that of Mr. Reay. He was never heard to utter an unkind word of anybody. He never could be got to assent to an ill-natured observation. The present writer'—one may be sure that it is H. O.

[1] *My Autobiography*, p. 251. [2] *Annals*, p. 371, n.
[3] *My Autobiography*, p. 251. [4] Loc. cit.
[5] 1861, pt. 1, pp. 463–5.

BULKELEY BANDINEL
LIBRARIAN 1813–60
from a daguerreotype

Coxe who writes—'would often playfully offer satirical comments on their mutual acquaintance, and give his aged friend the opportunity, if he pleased, of expressing dislike. But he can never remember an instance where Mr. Reay assented. His common resource was to feign himself "rather deafer today than usual", and, on whichever side one might happen to be, one received a hint that he never was "able to hear with *that* ear".'

His colleague, Coxe, had a more winning charm, and was in every respect a more forceful personality than the gentle old Laudian Professor. A country clergyman's eighth son, as his name Henry Octavius testifies, he came of a family that had rented for the past 200 years the small farm of Ardington Mill, near Lockinge, under leases taken from New College. He was a Worcester College man, and had rowed in the College boat. At the time of which we are writing he was thirty-four. He was physically robust and constantly in the saddle, an untiring rider. He had the fresh complexion of a countryman, and looked out on the world with quizzical but kindly steel-blue eyes from below his bushy eyebrows. He was as Victorian as his chief was Georgian. His piety was unaffected, but his humour was irresistible. He was an accomplished mimic: his rendering of an imaginary conversation between tart old Dr. Routh and obsequious Mr. Burgon was a *tour de force*.[1] He had great social gifts. His attitude to his fellows was one of genial *camaraderie*. He had nicknames for all. Bandinel to him was B. B., or sometimes 'Proto', a shortened form of Proto-bibliothecarius. His courtesy was enlivened by his wit. He liked young life, enjoyed female society, and had a knack of making himself *persona grata* in higher circles than his own. He inspired affection in every quarter, by his kindheartedness as much as by the ease of his manner. No one daunted him—except Benjamin Jowett; but that comes later in the story.

He was a skilled palaeographer, and his fame depends on his palaeographical *expertise* more than upon his general librarianship. He had had his training on the staff of the manuscript department in the British Museum before coming to Bodley, and had been employed there to catalogue the Arundel manuscripts. His appointment as a Bodleian sub-librarian at the beginning of 1839 had been made possible by a decree raising the salary of that office from £150 to £250.[2] He was then about to be married, and, after qualifying for election by postponing his wedding, took to wife Miss Charlotte Turner, daughter of an old general, Sir Hilgrove Turner, who had once

---

[1] Tuckwell, *Reminiscences of Oxford*, 1901, p. 168.
[2] Convocation Register, 1837–46, p. 107.

been private secretary to George IV and had brought the Rosetta Stone from Egypt. His father-in-law bought him a house in Oxford, 17 Beaumont Street, in which he lived for close on forty years.

Since £250 a year was not much on which to bring up a family, even in those days, it was necessary to augment it from other quarters. A curacy at Culham brought him in at first £80 and then £100 to add to his salary. Dr. Bliss was specially helpful in obtaining him literary work, and, though all the Doctor's offers were not accepted—he suggested that Coxe should become leader-writer of his paper, the *Oxford Herald*—it was through Bliss that he became an editor for the Roxburghe Club as well as for the English Historical Society. Then there was work to be done—some, but not all of it, paid—in cataloguing the manuscripts of the Oxford colleges. Rising at half past five in the morning he used to walk from his house through the echoing streets of Oxford and knock up some sleepy college porter for admittance, so getting two or three hours' work done in a college library before breakfast. Half an hour sufficed for breakfast; half an hour for lunch; or perhaps after lunch, with college cap on his head, he would try out friends' horses over the fence in Charles Symonds's paddock. His industry was phenomenal. Here is a bare time-table of a day in August in this very year of 1845. 'Transcribing at 5 for Warden of New College. 6.30–9, St. John's. 9.30–10, transcribing. 10–1.30, Bodley. 1.30–2, transcribing. 2–4 Bodley. 4.30–5.30, 7.45–9.45, transcribing.' In other words, five and a half hours' work at the library, two and a half spent on college manuscripts, and perhaps five and a half copying. Even his holidays were frequently given up to some college catalogue.

Yet he was happy in his work. He had refused to leave Oxford and England for the United States, to become head of a college in Georgia. Warden Sneyd had offered him the chaplaincy of All Souls; and, at the beginning of this year (1845), he had been made Chaplain of Corpus and a member of its high table. 'Bodley Coxe' as he was called, to distinguish him from Heyward Cox, the Rector of Carfax, and from old Valentine Cox, the Esquire Bedel, was rapidly becoming a figure in the university.

The statute of 1813 provided that, in addition to the librarian and the two sub-librarians, there should be two assistants or *ministri*. They fulfilled the duties of what are today called 'pages' in American libraries, fetching books for readers and replacing them on the shelves; and they carried out clerical work in the intervals of book-service. Their salaries were left to be regulated by the Curators, and were in practice limited to £50 a year. Under the library statute they had to be B.A.'s or undergraduates.[1] They were nominated by the librarian, and Dr. Bandinel usually found in his own college of New College promising young undergraduates who were content to work in the library until they took their M.A. degree, when they passed on to some country living or curacy. One of the two *ministri* appointed in 1845 was a young Aberdonian, W. D. Macray, academical clerk at Magdalen. At the time of his appointment, Macray had already done more than five years' service in the library of which he was to become the historian; for since the age of fourteen he had attended upon the compilers of the General Catalogue. But there were other assistants besides the statutory *ministri*. Attendance at college lectures, and the need for preparation for public examinations, were already being felt a hindrance to the employment of undergraduates, and in 1840 H. S. Harper had been appointed as the first non-academic *minister*. Though his place was subsequently filled by an undergraduate of the normal type, Harper was kept on at an increased salary (£75) as a member of the permanent staff. It was a sign of change in the times; a realization of the need for recruitment of lower grades by permanent appointment, and perhaps some faint perception that, for the performance of routine duties, practical experience of the working of a library might be a better asset than a university education.

On or off the library staff—it is difficult to say how he was at first regarded, though in time he came to be reckoned as an assistant—was another clergyman, a prominent Anglo-Catholic. He was the Rev. Mr. Hackman, the energetic curate for a year past at the new church of St. Paul's in Walton Street. Mr. Hackman was employed, at £150 a year, on producing the supplementary volume to the General Catalogue. With his broad wide mouth, his kindly eyes, and his shock of tousled curly hair, he might be seen at his work in the end study on the right, perched on a thick folio volume, the one book which he forgot to catalogue.[2]

Finally, there was the janitor, John Norris—porter and cleaner and collector of fees (and tips) from strangers who came to visit the library or Picture Gallery unaccompanied by a member of the university. The fees, fixed by custom at 1s. a head,[3] went to swell his £40 salary. An under-janitor was engaged at £10 a year to stoke the boiler. This staff of nine persons ran the library.

---

[1] *Corpus Statutorum*, addenda, p. 200.
[2] Macray, *Annals*, p. 388, n.; A. T. Bassett, *St. Barnabas, Oxford*, 1919, p. 5.
[3] Macray, p. 186. They were reduced in 1862 to 3d.; op. cit., p. 344.

6. FINANCE

To meet the cost of staff (including cataloguing staff), of purchases, of binding, of repairs, and general maintenance, the library had in 1845 a revenue of £4,647,[1] apart from librarian's and janitor's fees. As has been already stated (p. 20), £2,277 of this sum came from university dues originally earmarked for book purchase. In addition, the university paid over the annual surplus (after certain charges had been met) of a tax of 4s. a head imposed in 1802 on members of Convocation.[2] The 1813 statute sets out this additional revenue as intended to meet the cost of increased staff, of the production of the General Catalogue, and of library repairs hitherto defrayed out of general university funds.[3] As the surplus mounted up beyond expectation, the Curators consented in 1824 to its reduction by the addition of new examiners' fees to the prior charges on the fund, provided that there was always left for Bodleian use not less than £500 a year.[4] They were justified in their action. In 1845 the Convocation tax brought in to the library £920.

Other smaller sums contributed from university revenue were the ancient stipend of £6. 9s. 6d. which had come down from Henry IV's time as the yearly wage of the university librarian; and a supplement to that exiguous salary in the form of £40 paid to the librarian under a statute of 1769.[5] There were also payments out of a trust fund which Lord Crewe, the princely Bishop of Durham, had left to the university in 1721, from which £60 was paid annually towards the librarian's salary and £10 was allocated to the purchase of books.

[1] The £200 granted in 1838 to supplement the sub-librarians' salaries is not included in the library revenue. Owing to a flaw in drafting, it was paid to these officers direct out of university funds.

[2] Convocation tax (as it was called) of 4s. a year from all members of the university (*ab Academicis*), of which a surplus only was paid to Bodley, is not to be confused with the tax of 4s., subsequently raised to 8s., on all resident members of more than four years' standing, which went wholly to Bodley for the purpose of book-purchase. It has a not uninteresting history. Originally voted on 5 July 1798 to meet the expenses of the corps of Oxford University Volunteers raised in the Napoleonic War, when that corps was disbanded at the Peace of Amiens it was converted by Convocation, under a decree passed on 7 May 1802, into a permanent tax, having for its primary charge the payment of public examiners (Convocation Register, 1793–1802, p. 555). After the surplus of the income so raised had been assigned by resolution of the Hebdomadal Board, taken on 25 Jan. 1805, to certain specific library purposes (Hebdomadal Register, 1803–23, pp. 67–68), it was made a permanent addition to library revenue by the statute of 1813. The tax was finally abolished on 4 Dec. 1845 and the loss of income made up by an annual payment out of the funds of the University Press of a sum amounting to the average of the tax during the previous three years (Convocation Register, 1837–46, p. 532).

[3] *Corpus Statutorum*, addenda, p. 203.

[4] Curators' minutes, 5 Feb. 1824.   [5] *Corpus Statutorum*, addenda, p. 99.

Mention may also be made in this connexion, if it be not too insignificant a detail, of the trifling sum of £5, which still today figures as a university payment. This was a rent-charge on Wyck Rissington in Gloucestershire, devised to the library as far back as 1633 and devoted, like Lord Crewe's £10, specifically to book-purchases.[1]

In addition to what it derived from the university, the library had its own estate. Sir Thomas Bodley had endowed it with two properties: certain houses in Distaff Lane in the City of London, and land at Cookham near Maidenhead called Hindhay Farm. These were let on seven-year leases; and, although during the eighteenth century the university had been allowed to pocket the fines paid for renewal, the library had since made good its claim to fine as well as rent. The income derived from these estates, including an average of the fines, had been calculated in 1813 at £178. 5s. The actual net yield in 1845 amounted to £221.

Two other benefactions make up the tale of library assets. In describing the Picture Gallery passing mention has been made (p. 11) of books left to the Bodleian by the Rev. Charles Godwyn, who was also an important contributor to the coin collection. Dying in 1770, Mr. Godwyn devised to the university the residue of his property; and, when the business of the bequest was finally settled, this was invested in £1,050 3 per cent. Consols, and the interest upon it paid annually to the library. A very much larger legacy was that of £40,000, recently left, in 1841, under the will of Dr. Robert Mason, whose name, as we have seen, is commemorated in the Mason Room. This had been invested in £36,000 3 per cent. Consols, and produced, after tax deduction, an annual yield of £1,048. 10s.

Thus the library had at its disposal (apart from officers' fees and sub-librarians' supplementary stipends) income from real estate to the approximate amount of £221; a capital sum of £37,050 held in Consols and yielding, before payment of income tax, a dividend of £1,110; and an assemblage of various contributions from the university amounting in all to some £3,320 per annum. In 1845 its revenue came to £4,647. Its outgoings in that same year were £3,893. During the preceding ten years they had averaged £4,153. Balances were carried over from one year to the next; but the 1813 statute had provided that any surplus in excess of £1,000 should be invested.[2] The last remaining invested balance had just been sold out to allow of the purchase of the Ouseley collection.

The year 1845 happened to be one in which purchases fell con-

---

[1] A note on the rent-charge is given in *Oxford*, vol. ix, no. 1, p. 22.
[2] *Corpus Statutorum*, addenda, p. 203.

siderably below the average,[1] and were but £1,201, or, if commissions and customs duties be added, £1,260. Binding bills came to £407. Salaries, including payments to the cataloguing staff and the copyright agents' fee, amounted to £1,205.[2] Repairs and maintenance formed a not inconsiderable figure, since there was a constant need for new shelving, and came to £364; in addition to which there was an exceptional payment this year of £481 on the new warming apparatus. Other outgoings were small indeed. Fifty pounds sufficed to meet household expenses, and the little warmth that the library had hitherto got was cheap at £11. The printing bill was only £10. Stationery and postage came to £48, and there were miscellaneous charges to the amount of £56.

The Vice-Chancellor acted as treasurer of the library, and was responsible for the collection of its revenues, for paying out to the librarian the sums required by him for current expenses, and for the direct discharge of all other bills. The library accounts were kept for him by the librarian, and were audited, usually by Dean Gaisford, at the annual Visitation.[3] That great event came on 8 November, and Bodley closed its doors to the public on this anniversary of its first opening. At ten or eleven in the morning the Vice-Chancellor arrived in state, preceded by the bedels with their silver pokers. The ceremony lasted till two in the afternoon, the librarian absenting himself until he was specially summoned. The original purposes of the Visitation were that the Bodleian Curators should satisfy themselves, by a count of the library, that no books were missing from its shelves; that they should give any orders that were necessary for the efficient management of the library; that they should pass and sign the year's accounts; and, not least, that they should meet together at an annual dinner. The custom had arisen of exhibiting, upon this festal day, the donations made to the library during the previous twelve months; and the Curators also ran through the list of purchases and ascertained that they had been duly catalogued. At some stage in their proceedings, or perhaps at the close, they adjourned to the School of Natural Philosophy,[4] where a Master of Arts of Christ Church was waiting to deliver what was known as the Bodleian Oration. This was a set

[1] As has been stated above (p. 22) the average amount spent annually in 1835–44 was £1,685 apart from extraordinary purchases.

[2] Or £1,405 if one adds the £200 paid to the sub-librarians which is not shown in the library accounts.

[3] The practice continued till 1863. The date for closing the account was then changed to Michaelmas and subsequently to 15 July. From 1882 the financial became the calendar year, and so continued till 1925 when it was made 1 Aug.–31 July.

[4] John Walters, *The Bodleian Library*, 1780, p. 28, n.; W. M. Wade, *Walks in Oxford* (1817), vol. ii, p. 303.

form, recording in Latin the praises of Sir Thomas Bodley, and laud-
ing the study of Hebrew.[1]

Macray has recorded the method by which the count was conducted when he was a young assistant.[2] He himself attended on the
Vice-Chancellor in his easy and dignified task of counting the folios
in Duke Humphrey's Library. The two University proctors each
took one of the dark galleries over the alcoves. The Regius Professor
of Greek, Dr. Gaisford, counted the contents of his favourite Auctarium. Dr. Pusey betook himself to the Oriental collections. The
remaining Curators dispersed themselves into different parts of the
library. Armed with 'hand-lists' or shelf-lists, they checked the contents of the shelves by these official records. But, as the library grew
in extent, the Curators' check must have become increasingly per-
functory. In practice the real count was carried out by the staff, and
the library was closed for eight days before the Visitation to set them
free for this purpose.

As the real count had preceded the Visitation, so the auditing of
accounts before they were presented to Convocation might be delegated to one or two of the Curators to carry out on a subsequent day.
The afternoon was drawing on, and it was time to dine. The Bodleian
dinner was given by the Vice-Chancellor at his lodgings. He had an
allowance of £2 towards the cost of entertainment, but presumably
trenched also on the £7. 13s. 4d. given to him in payment of his services as chairman of the Board and Library Treasurer. Dinner was
attended by all the other Curators, namely, by the Proctors and the
Regius Professors of Divinity, Law, Medicine, Hebrew, and Greek;
by the two Savilian Professors and the Laudian Professor of Arabic
who were called in to assist at the count; by the Pro-Vice-Chancellors,
the Registrar, and the Bodleian Orator; likewise by the Librarian and
his two Sub-Librarians. In the course of the meal the Yeoman Bedel
in Arts came round the table and presented to diners the rewards
assigned to them by Sir Thomas Bodley in his Foundation Statute,
namely, 10s. to each Curator and attendant Professor, and £2 besides
to each Proctor for the now nominal duty of keeping the keys of
the founder's strong-box in which the library funds had used to be
deposited.[3] Dinner was otherwise a dull affair, and Coxe notes in his
diary upon one occasion that he was glad to escape it.

[1] But the orator also touched on the events of the year, e.g. on the Copyright Bill
in 1818, and on the introduction of heating and the Malone donation in 1821. Bodl.
MS. Eng. misc. d. 293, foll. 30, 60.
[2] *Bodleian Quarterly Record*, vol. i, p. 329.
[3] G. V. Cox, *Recollections*, 2nd ed., p. 226. The Visitation dinner was abolished
a silentio by the Bodleian statute of 1856.

From being the one stated meeting of the year, the Visitation had ceased to be an occasion for the transaction of ordinary library business. Under an order made by the Curators in 1817, they met once a term, on the last Wednesday.[1] Their place of meeting was usually the old Bodley Chest Room, opening off the Picture Gallery: it had been fitted up for the purpose in 1814[2] and was now known as the Curators' Room. They had no agenda before them, nor were any papers circulated. Acta were recorded in a minute-book, but, up to May of this year (1845), no entry had been made in it for three years past.

The constitution of the library was regulated in the main by the statute passed by Convocation in 1813.[3] It prescribed, however, that older statutes should remain in force except in so far as they were hereby repealed; and, in consequence, the establishment of what statutory regulations were still current was a matter of some little research. The general direction of library affairs was entrusted to the eight Curators. Owing to the small size of the Board, there was no need for committees, though from time to time two or more of its number might be delegated to audit accounts, to investigate some question of finance, or to arrange for purchases at one of the more important sales. All were *ex-officio*. Vice-Chancellor and Proctors were only members of the Board during their short terms of office; and, of the five regius professors who were its permanent members, it cannot be said that Dr. Hampden, Dr. Kidd, or Dr. Phillimore took any lively interest in Bodleian affairs. The control of the library, for which the whole body of Curators was nominally responsible, was in fact left in the hands of Dr. Pusey and Dr. Gaisford. The latter in particular, with his enthusiasm for Greek manuscripts and his intimate knowledge of book values, was the real ruler.[4] Fortunately for Coxe, the grim laconic Dean of Christ Church took a fancy to him, and encouraged him in his cataloguing. 'At work on MS. 11', Coxe writes in his diary. 'Just as the Dean came in, found it out to be Psellus. The Dean nudged me and chuckled.'

With Gaisford's quiet chuckle we will take our leave of 1845 and proceed to sketch the history of the library during the subsequent hundred years.

[1] Curators' minutes, 26 Feb. 1817.
[2] Ibid., 24 Mar. 1814.
[3] *Corpus Statutorum*, addenda, pp. 199–207.
[4] His successor in the Deanery describes him as 'an unreasonable man in all things except Philology and bookselling and the management of libraries.' Mallet, *History of the University of Oxford*, vol. iii, p. 219.

PART II
Bandinel and Coxe, 1845–81

Chapter III
Library Administration

I. THE BOARD OF CURATORS

READERS of Mark Pattison's *Memoirs*[1] will remember his vivid account of the enormous effect produced upon the academic world in 1845 by the announcement that John Newman, leader of the Oxford Movement, had been received into the Church of Rome. The years of theological agitation were ended, and, in the quiet which ensued, minds were set free to pursue secular aims. 'From that moment', according to Pattison, 'dates the regeneration of the University. Hence the flood of reform which broke over Oxford in the next few years following 1845, which did not spend itself till it had produced two Government Commissions, until we had ourselves enlarged and remodelled all our institutions.'

Immediate effects were not everywhere apparent. The sudden lull which Pattison describes as falling upon Oxford did but soothe Bodley to a deeper sleep. Only three meetings of its Curators are recorded as having been held in the next eight years. Bandinel sank slowly into lethargy. His health was failing; he was absent throughout the winter of 1846–7; and one night in February 1849 was noted by Coxe as 'a critical one for poor Proto. On the brink of death from 2 to 4.30.'

Nevertheless he rallied, and was to continue in office for more than eleven years to come. No wonder his active-minded sub-librarian chafed. 'I wish sometimes', Coxe wrote in his diary, 'I had the direction of Bodley for ten years.' He prayed for patience,[2] that prime requisite of librarians, and against the thoughts of succeeding his chief which constantly obtruded themselves in his mind. So he schooled himself, rejecting offers of ecclesiastical preferment which would have removed him from Oxford—a colonial bishopric was one —and at the end of 1852 could describe himself as 'certainly better in my B. B. feelings'.

---

[1] *Memoirs*, 1885, pp. 212, 238.
[2] 'Talk with B. B. about former times. He does not grumble! ! ! Pray that I may be patient.' Coxe's diary, 17 Apr. 1850.

There was little chance of library reform being initiated by the ageing Bandinel; pressure had perforce to come from without. The appointment, at the end of August 1850, of a Royal Commission 'for the purpose of inquiring into the state, discipline, studies and revenue of the University of Oxford', naturally led to inquiry into the administration of the university library; and among the points on which the University Commissioners invited evidence was 'the means of rendering Bodley's Library more generally useful than at present'. In their report, published in 1852, they adopted a suggestion made to them by the leading Balliol tutor of his day, Benjamin Jowett (who was to play a prominent part in Bodleian history during the next thirty years), 'that the Bodleian Library should be placed under the management of the Professors'.

The substitution of a Professorial Delegacy for the existing Board of Curators did not commend itself to a committee which the Hebdomadal Board set up to examine the Commission's proposals. 'We think', they said, 'that this body need be neither increased nor changed.' But change could not be so easily averted. Dean Gaisford's death in 1855 terminated an era in Bodleian history in which he had been the leading figure; while the appointment of Jowett to fill his place as Regius Professor of Greek brought on to the Curatorial Board a man who, by his energy, at once succeeded to Gaisford's authoritative position. Jowett was a man full of ideas, not all of them sound, who lost no opportunity for pressing them upon his colleagues and upon the library officers. He found in Coxe a not wholly willing ally. 'Shall get into a scrape by my coalition with Jowett', Coxe wrote in his diary, 'but never mind.'[1]

The old Hebdomadal Board of Vice-Chancellor, Proctors, and Heads of Houses itself was changed, giving place in 1854 to a democratically elected Hebdomadal Council. In the spate of measures that followed came a new Bodleian statute, codifying and amending all earlier statutes, which was passed by Convocation in May, 1856. It added to the existing *ex officio* members of the Board of Curators five additional members, elected by Congregation for a term of ten years.[2] The first Curatorial contest brought on to the Board, at the head of the poll, the learned and cultivated Dr. Wellesley, Principal of New Inn Hall; Professor Max Müller; and a capable financier, 'Bat' Price, Master of Pembroke. The Curators now met in the Delegates' Room in the Clarendon Building. The 1856 statute enacted that their meetings should be held twice a term; but this statutory requirement failed

[1] Diary, 8 Mar. 1858.
[2] *Corpus Statutorum*, addenda, p. 564.

to satisfy their new-found zeal, and they agreed, a year later, to meet at 2 p.m. on alternate Saturdays in term.[1]

For the infusion of new blood into the old Curatorial body led immediately to a general overhaul of the library system in all its branches, and to seven or eight years of radical reform. In those reforms the Curators received no help from their librarian. Bandinel belonged to a past generation and stood, a dread but lonely figure, upon the ancient ways. Ever since the House of Lords passed the Reform Bill he had breasted, but failed to stem, 'the fatal current which is overwhelming both church and state'.[2] He remained active in adding to the treasures of the library. But so far as the initiation of changes went, his demise might have already occurred.

Great changes were to come, all destined to bring the Bodleian closer to the general life of the university. No longer would it be the privileged sanctum of a few scholars, with learned clerics monopolizing its chief offices. The employment of a larger professional staff allowed new enterprises to be undertaken. The revival of classification, and the production of a revised author-catalogue in a form completely different from the printed and interleaved volumes of an earlier period, would come to show that the Bodleian was ready, if not to originate, at least to copy the innovations of other leading libraries. In a very few years the Bodleian was to acquire, in the great rotunda now called the Radcliffe Camera, a substantial increase of accommodation both for books and readers. Prolonged discussions were to follow as to the best form of further extension, even as to whether it would not be best to abandon the old buildings and construct an entirely new library; and though debates led to little action, they were at least a sign of the ferment of the times.

Yet it was possible to regret, as Bandinel must have regretted, the passing of the old unregenerate days when Bodley still had large resources and when it was still making great purchases and receiving great gifts. The attempt, begun under Bandinel, to acquire the vast collection of manuscripts formed by Sir Thomas Phillipps was to end in failure. From now onwards purchases—that keynote of a library's prosperity—began to decline, for Bodley was entering upon a period

---

[1] Curators' minutes, 31 Oct. 1857. Altered by resolution of 29 Oct. 1859 to alternate Tuesdays. On 14 Feb. 1860 it was agreed that meetings should be held monthly. The decision to revert to two stated meetings a term and to hold these at 2 p.m. on the second and last Saturday in Full Term, was taken in 1869 on Jowett's motion and has since been maintained except that the seventh Saturday has been substituted for the eighth.

[2] Bandinel to Bishop Thomas Burgess, 5 Apr. 1832; Bodl. MS. Eng. letters, c. 133, fol. 37.

of financial stringency from which it would not emerge for another eighty years.

2. STAFF CHANGES

Hitherto there had been no provision for retiring or pensioning the librarian. He held his office for life, unless deprived of it for high misdemeanour. Only the statute of 1813 had provided that, if he became unfitted for his duties by serious illness or old age, the Vice-Chancellor and Curators might appoint a deputy to act for him and require the librarian to contribute to his deputy's salary.[1] The 1856 statute partially remedied this defect by fixing pensions for librarians and sub-librarians of thirty years' standing who wished to retire for reasons of age or illness. The amounts fixed were £300 for the librarian and £150 for a sub-librarian[2]—sums increased by a subsequent (1873) statute to £500 and £200 respectively. But there was as yet no retiring age,[3] and resignation continued to be voluntary. Bandinel, though advancing in his seventies, clung to office. He did indeed give up in 1855 the curacy of neighbouring Wytham,[4] and let in Coxe, who was to find in its parsonage a happy country home for the remaining twenty-five years of his life.

But, though increasingly irregular in his attendance at the library, Bandinel could not bring himself to quit it. 'I cannot but think', wrote Coxe in January 1857, 'that B. B. has behaved very wrongly in retaining his Librarianship after having statutably vacated it so long. This past year he has not been in the library more than thirty days within $1\frac{3}{4}$ hours of his time.' Doubtless he was conscious of the course he ought to have taken, and in the following July he tantalized Coxe with a 'touching conversation about his resigning'. Yet nothing came. As the great Panizzi, Principal Librarian of the British Museum, remarked to him with characteristic Italian irony, 'The older you grow, my dear Bandinel, the more you love your work. The older I grow, the less I feel equal to it.'[5]

'Oh, my God, pardon me the impatience I have shown throughout the year; the desire that others should give up that I should inherit their position.' Such was the prayer with which Coxe closed his diary

[1] *Corpus Statutorum*, addenda, p. 200.

[2] Op. cit., pp. 559, 560.

[3] When Bandinel at length resigned, the Vice-Chancellor (Jeune) gave notice that he would propose that no librarian or under-librarian in future retain office after the age of seventy. (Curators' minutes, 9 June 1860.) Perhaps he received no backing, for he did not proceed with his motion.

[4] Bishop Wilberforce, whose standards were presumably high, had found Bandinel 'active and earnest' in his parish. Bodl. MS. Oxf. Dioc. Papers, d. 550, p. 141.

[5] The story is told in the *Standard* for 10 Apr. 1879.

for 1858. The Curators themselves were showing signs of restiveness. That year they had censured Bandinel at their Visitation. They treated Coxe as *de facto* librarian; but he, with perfect loyalty, 'insisted on their seeing Bandinel, to which they demurred, but I carried my point'.[1] At last the end came. Bandinel was brought to resign after striking a bargain over the amount of his pension.

On the last day of May 1860, as Coxe passed his chief's house in Beaumont Street, the old man called him in from his window to say that the Curators had offered him a retiring pension of £500 a year, and that he had accepted. It was indeed, as Coxe described it, a 'very memorable day'. For it was agreed that Bandinel should retire at Michaelmas; that he should have an extraordinary pension of £200 in addition to his statutory £300;[2] and that he should be specially enrolled among the Curators of the library. Michaelmas Day came, and there was a pathetic little scene in the Medal Room where, the Curators all assembled, Bandinel handed the key of the room to the Vice-Chancellor and resigned the headship. 'How strange it seems', wrote Coxe, 'that it is really vacant.'

And the senior sub-librarianship was vacant also, for Professor Reay was retired on a pension at the same time as his chief. He was equally old. He had been very ill in the summer of 1855, when Bandinel talked of filling his place; and two years later another clergyman, Robert Payne Smith, was appointed sub-librarian *extra ordinem*,[3] to serve as Reay's deputy. Reay having retired, Payne Smith was naturally nominated to succeed him.

There was no doubt (unless it were in his own mind) that Coxe would follow Bandinel as Bodley's Librarian. Just as Panizzi directed the affairs of the British Museum long before his genial old chief, Sir Henry Ellis, resigned; so, at Bodley, Coxe had for some years past been the real head of the library. His election took place on 6 November 1860. But there was a difficulty that had to be overcome. A statute had been passed in 1847 repealing the prohibition against electing a married person to library office, but reimposing, at Gaisford's instance, the old ban on holding a benefice with cure of souls.[4] This last was modified under the 1856 statute, which permitted an absolute majority of the Curators to dispense from the obligation if their decision was confirmed by Convocation.[5] Jowett was at first

[1] Coxe's diary, 2 Apr. 1859.
[2] Macray (*Annals*, p. 371) makes a slip in saying that Bandinel retired on a full stipend, for the librarian's salary, which had formerly been £550 plus fees, was fixed by the 1856 statute at £700 per annum. *Corpus Statutorum*, addenda, p. 561.
[3] 3 Feb. 1857.   [4] *Corpus Statutorum*, addenda, p. 342.
[5] Op. cit., p. 560. As originally drafted the clause prohibited absolutely the holding

averse to Coxe retaining his Wytham curacy, but permission was eventually given him to continue in it,[1] on his undertaking to reside in Oxford throughout the year, except during the Long Vacation. In the other vacations and in term-time Coxe used to ride out to his parsonage for week-ends on his rat-tailed chestnut cob Punch, 'a wonder to jump but a slug on the road', who came to be almost as well known as his master.[2]

The conflict of library and clerical duties came to the fore again over the appointment of a second sub-librarian to take Coxe's place. Dr. Liddell, Dean of Christ Church, moved that the post be kept vacant. Alternatively, he and Jowett appear to have favoured the election of Dr. Aufrecht, a German savant who had been employed in Bodley since 1855 on a catalogue of Sanskrit manuscripts. But the existing sub-librarian was also an Orientalist, and Coxe objected. Hackman had a better claim to the post, having been appointed to perform the duties of a sub-librarian in 1857 during four and a half months when Coxe was absent on a Government mission to report on collections of manuscripts in the Levant. Still there was opposition to him. It was argued that it would 'be disadvantageous to set a precedent of promoting a person from a subordinate office in the Library to that of Sub-Librarian'.[3] Also, as Vicar of St. Paul's, he was a beneficed clergyman. That obstacle was removed by legislation. Pusey pressed on the Curators a statute abrogating in its entirety the prohibition of library officers from holding cures of souls.[4] The statute was opposed by Jowett, but passed Convocation after a pamphlet warfare, and allowed Coxe to nominate Hackman. The appointment of this genial and cultured clergyman, innocent cause of the fracas, was approved by Convocation on 18 April 1862.

By that time Bandinel was already dead. He was seventy-nine when he retired from office. His life's occupation gone, he told Macray that he had a foreboding that his life would soon cease also.[5] Only twice or thrice did he again toil breathlessly up the long flight of library stairs. He just outlived his gentle old subordinate, Reay.

of a cure of souls in any parish more than 5 miles distant from Oxford or having a population of over 200.

[1] By decree of Convocation, 28 Feb. 1861.

[2] Years afterwards (26 Nov. 1874) Goldwin Smith wrote to Coxe from Toronto— 'If you were with me now and had your rat-tailed pony with you, you might have a fast thing after a bear which has appeared in the woods near my house. You would find the stake fences stiff enough.'

[3] Printed fly-sheet by 'A Curator of the Bodleian Library', headed 'Is there any ground why the Librarian and Under-Librarians of the Bodleian should not have cure of souls?'

[4] *Corpus Statutorum*, addenda, p. 654.   [5] *Annals*, p. 370.

On the afternoon of Reay's funeral Coxe called on the Bandinels and was told by Mrs. Bandinel that Dr. Symonds could do no more for her husband. Four days later Coxe wrote in his diary: 'Gave Proto the sacrament; scarcely appreciating it fully.' And in another four days the old man died, on 6 February 1861, little more than four months after his long-deferred resignation.

3. STAFF SALARIES

The librarian's salary, fixed in 1856 at £700, was raised in 1873 to £1,000, a figure at which it remained until after the First World War. At the same time he and his sub-librarians were cut off from a possible source of additional income by a statute[1] that reimposed the old prohibition against holding benefices. The sub-librarian's yearly salary had been increased in 1851 to £300.[2] On Coxe's suggestion, a Curatorial committee appointed in 1873 to consider assistants' pay looked into sub-librarians' stipends also, with the result that these were redefined as £300 rising to £400.[3]

Lower grades changed their character. The statutory *ministri*— B.A.'s who earned £50 a year by working in the library until they took their Master of Arts degree—gave place to a new type of assistant, usually non-graduate, who came to stay. Their duties were those rather of a library clerk than of an assistant of the present day, for, in addition to attendance on readers, they were charged with book-replacement and the posting up of library records. Some assistants were mere boys, employed on fetching and carrying. Cataloguing formed no part of their duties. It was left to a special cataloguing staff, and assistants were merely required to incorporate slips, not to write them.

The 1856 library statute fixed assistants' maximum rate of pay at £100, their minimum as low as £20 a year.[4] Subsequently, the amount of their salaries came to be determined by the Curators. The earliest regulations for assistants, made in 1867, recognized three classes, the third advancing from £25 to £40, the second ranging from £50 to £80, and the first from £90 to £130.[5]

Wages on this scale clearly needed supplementing; and, though

---

[1] 14 June 1873. Coxe received dispensation from the statute by a decree which allowed him to claim the augmented salary without resigning his living.
[2] Convocation Register, 1846–54, p. 333. The increase was made statutory in 1856.
[3] By statute of 21 Nov. 1874.
[4] *Corpus Statutorum*, addenda, p. 561.
[5] A subsequent regulation (repealed in May 1906) laid down that assistants should be selected for Class I after an examination in languages. Curators' minutes, 13 Nov. 1880.

some assistants were able to earn a little extra as copyists and pedigree-hunters, one cannot be surprised that in 1873 the whole body petitioned for an advance in salaries, basing their claim on the ground of increase in cost of living and the practice of other institutions. The Curators agreed to certain changes.[1] The maximum wage of first-class assistants was raised from £130 to £200 a year, but the rates of the two lower grades was left very much as before. The assistants were left dissatisfied, and there were critics outside Oxford who voiced the feeling that they were 'shamefully underpaid'.[2] That was not Jowett's view. In giving evidence to the University Commission in 1877 he affirmed his belief that present staff stipends were sufficient. Professor Stubbs, a fellow Curator, who was also called to give evidence, did not conceal his dissent from that opinion. 'I have always thought', he said, 'that it was a matter of very great importance to have a staff of people who are attached, not only by feeling and affection and sentiment, but by a substantial salary, to the interest of the Bodleian.'[3]

The number of lower-grade staff increased considerably. A main cause of increase was an event which occurred in 1862 and which will be described in a later chapter (pp. 123–7)—the acquisition of the Radcliffe Camera as a second reading-room. The new room was kept open for twelve hours every day and required the presence of three to four assistants and a janitor. By 1881 the permanent staff of the library had grown from nine to seventeen. And over and above these there was a special staff engaged on the formation of a new library catalogue as well as three extra assistants employed on special cataloguing projects.

Increases in numbers and in rates of pay account for the steep advance in staff expenditure which occurred between 1845 and 1881. In 1845 it amounted to £1,205 and represented no more than 26 per cent. of receipts: in 1881, if the wages of the catalogue staff be included, it totalled £4,806, and, though library revenue had increased, two-thirds of it was now taken up by the payment of the staff.

4. SOURCES OF INCOME

To meet the cost of its staff and other expenses the Bodleian had a revenue that was derived in part from grants made by the university and in part from the library's own endowment, this last consisting of houses and lands and investments in Government funds. The library

[1] Confirmed by statute, 21 Nov. 1874.
[2] Compton Reade in *Belgravia*, vol. xxv (1875), p. 180.
[3] *University Commission*, minutes of evidence, 1881, pp. 248, 319.

continued to hold the farm of Hindhay at Cookham, and relet it in 1847 on a twenty-one-year lease at an improved rent of £220. Ray Mills in the same parish produced, from 1869, a rental of £528. But the houses in Distaff Lane in the City of London, which formed the remaining portion of Sir Thomas Bodley's original endowment, were sold in 1853, and the proceeds of the sale were invested in £3,543. 10s. 3 per cent. Consols. The library also possessed £37,050 Consols, derived from the Mason and Godwyn benefactions. And that holding was further increased in 1847, when the university allocated £30,000 Consols to the library in composition for its share in the impost of four shillings on all members of the university known as the Convocation Tax.

University contributions to library revenue varied slightly from year to year until they were replaced by fixed annual grants. This was in part effected by the 1856 library statute which instituted a grant of £850 per annum in lieu of the library's share of matriculation fees and certain minor charges (sub-librarians' supplementary salaries, librarian's fees, and the ancient stipends of library officers including the £40 paid to the librarian under the 1769 statute).[1] And in 1861 that allowance and the 8s. university due paid since 1813 by senior members of colleges and halls were consolidated in a fixed annual grant of £2,800.[2]

So, in addition to real estate at Cookham producing £748 a year, the library came to hold £70,600 3 per cent. Consols, and it also received yearly a university grant of £2,800 in addition to such subsidiary sources as the Crewe benefaction. There had been variation in the sources of income but no material increase of the amount, which totalled £4,647 in 1845 and £5,125 in 1861; and, as expenditure in the same period grew from £3,894 to £5,552, balances dwindled. In 1858–9 the library sold out the reserve of £3,000 which it had accumulated in 1848–50, but all the same was faced by a rising deficit which had grown by 1861 to £1,402.

By way of improving their finances the Curators took statutory powers to sell their duplicates.[3] In May 1862 they held a five days' sale at Sotheby's where duplicate books (including prints from the Rawlinson collection) were sold to the net amount of £615. Choice was unfettered by sentiment: the highest price fetched (£110. 5s.)

---

[1] *Corpus Statutorum*, addenda, p. 561.

[2] Op. cit., p. 644. It will be remembered that the tax on members of colleges and halls, and the share in matriculation fees, together constituted a fund originally intended to be applied solely to book-purchase. Since 1813 they had been brought into the library general account.

[3] Op. cit., p. 652.

was obtained for a 1489 specimen of the St. Alban's press, cut out of a manuscript presented to the university by Archbishop Laud.[1] A second sale, in 1865, realized £687 net. It comprised English works of the sixteenth and seventeenth centuries and included copies of Chettle's *Kind-Harts Dreame* (1593) and of Dekker's *Guls Horne-Booke* (1609).[2] A third, but smaller, sale held in 1870 which produced £172, was also unfortunate in its selection, for the library then disposed of twenty-five volumes of tracts of the Popish Plot period (1680–90) which William Smith of Melsonby, the northern antiquary, had presented to it in 1726. It did not benefit much thereby, for they were knocked down for 13s.[3]

Much harm and little profit could come from such sales. And when, in 1861, the library took over and staffed the Radcliffe Camera, it became necessary to ask the university for a specific grant to meet the additional financial burden. The sum of £150 granted by decree in 1862, though increased next year to £200 and in 1865 to £300, failed to cover Camera expenses which soon reached £650 per annum. And another new form of expenditure was now imposed upon the library. This was the production of a new general catalogue. The university made a special grant of £500 a year for that purpose in 1865 and continued it till the work was completed in 1879. But £500 went little way when the wages of the cataloguing staff rose as they did in 1875 to £1,133. Little wonder that the Curators began to be alarmed. For some years the library had been kept going by grants for special purposes and thereby been able to show a small credit balance; but expenditure in 1875 exceeded income by £679, and the library was once more faced with a deficit.

5. DEMAND FOR INCREASED ENDOWMENT

Up to 1873 the financial duties of the Curators had been limited to auditing[4] and passing the annual statement of accounts. The Vice-Chancellor had acted as treasurer of library funds and the librarian as accountant. But a revised statute passed in that year transferred responsibility for library finance from the Vice-Chancellor to the

[1] The *Rhetorica Nova* of Gulielmus de Saona, formerly in MS. Laud misc. 749. For an instance of a book (4to T. 33. Art) gutted at the same time of a number of early English plays, see *Oxford Bibliographical Society Papers and Proceedings*, vol. i, p. 222.

[2] Macray, p. 376. The figures there given are presumably gross proceeds, for the library accounts show the smaller totals given in the text.

[3] Lot 1028 in sale of Aug. 1870.

[4] After 1873 the Curators annually delegated the audit to two of their own number, but the appointment of a university auditor eventually rendered a separate audit necessary.

Curatorial Board. The Curators applied their minds at once to the financial position. It was agreed that library revenue, which in 1875 amounted to £6,423, needed to be increased by at least £2,000 a year. If the university were to add £1,000 a year to the grants it made for the Camera and the catalogue, so as to cover the expenditure they were supposed to satisfy,[1] it would ease the library general fund to the extent of allowing it to extinguish its deficit and leave something over to meet much-needed binding. Over and besides this, the library had been starved in its book-purchases. An additional thousand a year could well be spent in that way, and it was suggested that applications might be made to certain colleges for subventions towards that sum.[2]

The Curators, however, were not unanimous. Jowett thought it right to see first what could be done to effect economies. So when the Curators' application came before Council he proposed that it should be referred back and, at a meeting of the Curators at which Coxe found himself 'bullied by questions from Jowett, Pusey and Price', moved for the appointment of a committee 'for the purpose of conferring with the Librarian on the expenses and management of the Library'.[3] The committee, after holding inquisition into the various branches of expenditure, modified the earlier application to Council. They now asked the university to clear off the existing deficit, to increase the permanent annual grant from £2,800 to £3,350, and, while continuing the grants for the Camera and the catalogue at the existing levels, to make a five-year grant of £250 per annum for binding expenses. In its new form the application was approved.[4] And thus from July 1876 the library came to receive £4,400 a year from the university, of which £3,350 was a permanent annual grant and £1,050 took the form of temporary subventions. The library's total revenue was thereby increased to £7,365.

It was out of the power of the university to make a larger grant than that which it now accorded. Its revenues were insufficient to meet all the demands that were made upon it. This was clearly brought out in the report (published in 1874) of the 1871 University Commission. It was recognized that provision must be made for enabling or requiring the colleges to contribute more largely out of their revenues to university purposes. With that end in view a

---

[1] The Curators reported that the sum expended to date on the catalogue was £9,571, and that the grants received from the University Chest were only £4,625, also that the grants made for the Camera in 1862–74 amounted to £3,475, but that expenses totalled £5,348.
[2] Communications from the Curators to Council, 20 Apr. and 11 Nov. 1875, printed as Council papers.   [3] Curators' minutes, 27 Nov. 1875, and Coxe's diary.
[4] By decrees of 23 May and statute of 13 June 1876.

Statutory Commission was set up in 1877 to frame new statutes for university and colleges alike.

Meeting in the autumn of that year the Commission heard evidence. Among other witnesses who came before them there was C. H. Robarts, a Fellow of All Souls who, as College Librarian, had succeeded in getting the Codrington Library thrown open to law students of the university. A strong plea by him for increased endowment of the university library had appeared in *Macmillan's Magazine* for February 1876. He proposed, in that article, that £5,000 a year should be appropriated to Bodley out of the revenues of his own college. The Bodleian should not rest content, he argued, until it had an independent endowment of £10,000 a year.

These ideas quickly developed into a grandiose scheme which he unfolded in the summer of 1877 to a conference of librarians held in London and repeated in a letter to the Vice-Chancellor. The Bodleian and all other libraries within the university were to be brought under one management like those of Harvard are today. In order to endow and provide for this complex of libraries, he proposed that the bulk of the revenues and nearly all the buildings of his college should be devoted to library purposes; that Bodley's librarian should be *ex officio* Warden of All Souls, chosen by the Curators; that the incorporators of the college should include six sub-librarian Fellows, and that the balance of its revenues, which he estimated at £8,000 a year after payment of Fellowships and maintenance, should be applied for the benefit of what he called the university library system, including therein the upkeep of the All Souls Library.

Robarts failed to convince either his college or the Commissioners. The latter listened with greater attention to Coxe as well as to Jowett and Professor Stubbs whom the Curators had deputed to give evidence. Coxe was moderate in his request and contented himself with asking for an additional £2,000 a year for book-purchases and an extra £200 a year for binding. Jowett thought that another £1,000 a year spent on books would be sufficient. But Stubbs told the Commissioners without reserve that he thought the Bodleian ought to have an income of not less than £15,000 a year. That was not too large a sum: the annual income of the library departments of the British Museum was reckoned at this time to be more than four times that amount.[1]

The Commissioners were sympathetic though cautious. In their report, dated 25 April 1878, they estimated that a fixed annual sum of at least £3,000 ought to be added to the existing library revenue; they

[1] *University Commission*, minutes of evidence, 1881, pp. 244–9, 317–20, 356–66.

pointed out that this amount must necessarily be obtained from the colleges, and advised that it and other contributions to university needs should be fairly apportioned among the colleges best capable of bearing them. Their recommendation was in part implemented by the college statutes which they drew up in 1882, imposing on All Souls an annual contribution to the Bodleian of £1,000, and upon Sir Thomas Bodley's old college of Merton a yearly grant of £300.

The need for a considerable increase in endowment was certainly obvious. Only thirty years before the library was spending well within its resources, was able to meet exceptional charges out of ordinary income, and was still in a position to pile up reserve funds. Those happy days were past. Bodley closed its financial year in 1881 with a credit balance of only £2.

6. THE NEW AUTHOR-CATALOGUE

The main task of Coxe's librarianship, extending over almost the whole of his period of office, was the production of a new general catalogue. For its origin we must go back a little, to the days when Bandinel was still librarian.

It has been told in Chapter II (p. 23) that a three-volume alphabetical library catalogue was published in 1843, and the preparation of a fourth, supplementary volume put immediately in hand. This was published, under Hackman's editorship, in 1851. It had cost about £1,000 to compile, and £814 had been spent on its printing. It comprehended the accessions of the years 1835–47. Gough and Douce books still had to be looked up in separate catalogues, and current acquisitions in the slip-drawers.

Was the Bodleian to go on printing supplements? They were expensive, and, as Coxe pointed out, printed appendixes would soon swell to a size commensurate with the original catalogue. Any work of reference that consists largely of supplements becomes impossible to use, and this is especially true of library catalogues. It was bad enough that the Gough and Douce collections were catalogued separately. The continued existence of special catalogues of particular collections, Coxe rightly observed, was not to be tolerated for a moment.

The British Museum had found a solution of its cataloguing troubles by adopting in 1849 a cataloguing system based on what was known as the movable slip. Under that system catalogue entries were made on separate written slips instead of on the interleaved pages of a printed catalogue; and the slips, instead of being filed in drawers as in Bodley, were laid down in guard-books from which they could be lifted when a particular guard-book needed respacing. A committee of the Curators set up on Jowett's motion in March 1857 instructed Coxe to report on the British Museum method of cataloguing. He advised its adoption. Thereby the three printed volumes of the 1843 catalogue, the printed supplement, the Gough and Douce catalogues, and the recent accessions slips, could all be blended in a single alphabetical series.[1]

The Curators approved Coxe's proposals and the specimen of a catalogue which he submitted, and desired him to proceed at once with the work. He was given Hackman as his principal colleague and the services of three other assistants, but, that proving insufficient, the cataloguing staff was doubled in size in 1862,[2] and henceforward two teams were employed consisting of four persons each. They worked at Selden End, screened by tall bookcases from public gaze, and seated at broad tables which have since furnished, and still furnish, make-shift desks for privileged readers.

There was a hitch at the outset owing to the discovery of about 10,000 unreferenced volumes. A decision had also to be taken as to whether ephemeral literature should be catalogued. At Coxe's suggestion, a discretionary power was given to him to omit from the main catalogue certain classes of elementary and ephemeral literature received under the Copyright Act.[3] This was the practice adopted, and still maintained, in the University Library of Cambridge. But at Bodley the works which Coxe excluded from the catalogue were eventually brought into it by his successor.

A committee of four Curators, of whom Jowett was chief, was appointed to supervise the preparation of the catalogue. At the beginning of 1869 Coxe, pressed by Jowett to report on progress and cost, was able to announce that the catalogue was half-way through: work had been completed on the letters A–E and G–H. Macray, who had succeeded Hackman as catalogue superintendent, went off the cataloguing staff at the end of 1870 on his presentation to the country living of Ducklington, and was succeeded by W. H. Bliss. When Bliss resigned six years later in order to examine the Vatican archives for the Public Record Office, the catalogue was near its end. For some time the slow rate of its progress and its mounting cost had been

---

[1] Report dated 1 Nov. 1858 (Bodl. G. A. Oxon. b. 29).

[2] Coxe had asked for this two years earlier; Curators' minutes, 30 Oct. 1860.

[3] The classes selected for omission included theological tracts printed for parochial distribution; lives of eminent persons abridged from larger biographies; elementary school-books; works of fiction, including anonymous novels and tales, with reprints for railway-station circulation; plays and poetical pieces that were anonymous or appeared to be of trifling importance. Curators' minutes, 11 Dec. 1860.

giving the Curators some uneasiness. On Jowett's motion in 1871 they called a second time for a report on cost, and directed the librarian to present a progress report at each meeting. The commission of inquiry into library expenses and management, set up by the Curators in November 1875, again gave an opportunity for investigating catalogue costs. What, it was asked, was the cost of production of each catalogue slip? They were written out by transcribers, drawing salaries ranging from £50 to £100 a year. Inquiry made at the British Museum showed that its transcribers produced on an average about fifty slips a day. Taking a transcriber's pay at £100 a year, that would work out at about $1\frac{1}{2}d$. per slip for transcription, to which would have to be added a fraction for cost of sorting and arrangement. But, when a return was called for from the Bodleian staff, it gave the daily average as only eighteen slips a day. Coxe was dismayed. 'Flabbergasted', he wrote in his diary, adding 'Dreadfully taken in by the transcribers. Took blame to myself and tendered resignation'.[1] Fortunately the return was found at fault; fresh calculations brought the average up to thirty-one and the cost per slip down to $2\frac{3}{4}d$.[2] Honour was partially satisfied, and Coxe remained librarian.

In June 1878 Coxe was able to inform the Curators that the catalogue was at last completed. It had taken eighteen years to make and had proved far more expensive than the three printed volumes and their supplement which it replaced. They had cost just over £3,000 to compile and as much again to print. But the cost of the new written catalogue worked out at £14,540, and, as only £7,000 had been met by special grants, more than half the expense had fallen upon the ordinary funds of the library. Still it was far more usable than the earlier printed edition. The 724 large folio volumes, shelved in Arts End, provided a catalogue of the whole of the library's contents. It was no longer necessary to consult supplementary catalogues or to rummage in drawers of tightly packed slips. Additional entries could be inserted in their proper places without overcrowding. But the new catalogue had one great defect. Its entries had been taken over from the 1843 catalogue, which in its turn had been based on an earlier printed catalogue of 1738; and so it perpetuated many of the errors and all the faults of arrangement of its predecessors. No sooner was it completed than the need for its revision became apparent, but it was not to revision that the cataloguers turned.

[1] Diary, 14 Dec. 1875.
[2] Report of Bodleian Curators on expenses and management of the library, Mar. 1876.

7. CLASSIFICATION

We have seen in the opening chapter (pp. 6, 11) how the original Bodleian classification of books into faculties had broken down under pressure of space, and how, from 1824, all attempt at subject-classification had been frankly abandoned. The proposal for resumption of classification came up somewhat unexpectedly and suddenly in the form of a clause appended to the 1856 statute. This laid down that, if the library should be enlarged so as to permit resumption of faculty classification, the Curators should consider the arrangement of books (other than collections given on the express condition that they should be kept separate) in a rational order within the faculties.[1] There is reason to think that the proposal originated with Jowett.[2] The Curators were at this time concerning themselves with the production of their new general library catalogue; and Jowett moved that they should commission Coxe to visit the British Museum and the principal foreign libraries in order that he might collect information respecting their catalogues, mode of arrangement, and other details of management.[3] The proposal fell through so far as foreign libraries were concerned; but Coxe was deputed to visit the British Museum and Cambridge University Library, and, on 24 November 1858, addressed a letter to the Vice-Chancellor[4] in which he described the method of arranging books followed in the British Museum.

The British Museum references were, and still remain, pressmarks in the strictest sense. That is to say, their first element is the number of a press or bookcase. The characteristic feature of the system is that, runs of presses being devoted to particular classes of books, the press-number also indicates subject-matter. Intervals in the numerical sequence, Coxe reported, were allowed for expansion. 'Presses 100 and 101 may contain English Bibles, and at present be sufficient for all the Bibles now in the collection; but, as it is probable that editions will greatly increase, the next adjoining press, containing, we will say, commentaries on Scripture, will not be labelled 103 but 110.'[5]

---

[1] 'Consilium ineant Bibliothecae Curatores ut intra singulas etiam facultates, si ita commode fieri possit, libri distincte et ordinate disponantur.' *Corpus Statutorum*, addenda, p. 565.

[2] Coxe wrote in his diary on 26 Jan. 1858: 'Jowett's hobby will be a trial and hard work. Never mind.'

[3] Curators' minutes, 30 Jan. and 27 Feb. 1858.

[4] Printed as a Curatorial paper.

[5] There would be no intervening empty presses. As a subject expanded, the next subject was moved one press farther on, and the vacated press renumbered. All presses being of uniform dimensions, this system of expansion avoided changes of

This method of pressmarking was known as the expansive system. Coxe recommended its adoption by Bodley.

The Curators accepted Coxe's proposals, resolving that the provision of the Bodleian statute relating to arrangement be carried out simultaneously with the execution of the catalogue, keeping in mind the British Museum arrangement.[1] Coxe had pointed out in his report that additional room was essential for applying the new system of classification, and this was now to hand through the acquisition of the Radcliffe Camera. In January 1862, a few days before the Camera was first opened to Bodleian readers, new octavos and small quartos began to be placed in the wall-cases below the reading-room gallery, arranged in nine sections in accordance with Coxe's modification of the British Museum classification scheme.[2] Coxe was not pleased with their appearance. 'Hideous', he comments in his diary. 'A warehouse. Still I can see my way, only patience.'

By January 1865 the basement below the Camera reading-room had been fitted up for additional storage, and a bookshift into it out of the reading-room commenced.[3] And Coxe had produced by then a second and minuter classification, increasing the original nine sections by a process of subdivision to seventy-three.[4] It has been claimed[5] that his scheme is 'one of the earliest, if not the earliest, arranged on the principle of relative location'. By that is meant the system under which books are given reference numbers that are independent of the shelves they occupy, and so may have their position changed (so long as they remain in the same order) without any

pressmarks in the books themselves and in the catalogues. It is described by Richard Garnett in a paper 'On the system of classifying books on the shelves followed at the British Museum'; *Essays in Librarianship and Bibliography*, 1899, pp. 210–24.

[1] Curators' minutes, 11 Dec. 1858.

[2] Namely, theology (100), medicine (150), arts and trades (170), mathematics and physics (180), history (200), miscellaneous literature (250), poetry (280), classics (290), and philology (295). New folios and large quartos were placed in similar but unnumbered classes, with shelf-marks of the type 'Poetry a. 18'. As local classification was already in use for topography (Gough adds.), drama (Malone adds.), parliamentary papers, law reports, and a few other sections, these subjects were omitted from the scheme. Old books were retained in the Bodleian building. For the classification simultaneously adopted for them, and for further details generally, see G. W. Wheeler's article on 'Bodleian Pressmarks in relation to Classification' in *Bodleian Quarterly Record*, vol. i, pp. 311–12, 317–19.

[3] By Apr. 1875 47,578 volumes had come to be shelved in the basement, and there were 14,719 in the reading-room.

[4] A table showing the development of the classification scheme of 1864 out of that of 1861 is given by Mr. Wheeler in *Bodleian Quarterly Record*, vol. i, pp. 318–19.

[5] By H. R. Purnell, a former Bodleian assistant, in a paper on 'Development of notation in classification', printed in the *Library Assistant*, Feb.–Mar. 1911. His assumption, though accepted by Mr. Wheeler, is disproved by the notes 'case full' entered in early handlists, e.g. under 100a, 100b, 100c.

alteration of pressmark or of catalogue-entry. The substitution of 'relative' for 'fixed' location is an important event in the history of library management. But it is impossible to maintain the claim that Coxe's scheme inaugurated a new system. He did but copy from the British Museum.

Relative location, without class numbers, had in fact been in use in the library for quartos and octavos ever since its foundation.[1] Coxe's numerical classification, like that of the British Museum which he followed, was still a form of fixed location, though relative location developed out of it by stages that may no longer be possible to trace. A system under which numbers represented presses and—only secondarily—classes was transformed, almost imperceptibly, into one in which numbers represented classes and nothing else.

New accessions were henceforward arranged upon the shelves according to subject. Coxe originally contemplated bringing the older contents of the library likewise into his classification scheme. Certain collections had to be preserved as separate entities, but even they might be rearranged on the same principle within the collection. These were his views when he reported in 1858 that

> Without an entire rearrangement of the whole Library, we might still considerably improve our present condition to the readers' convenience, by commencing our system of classification with the books which have been added to the Library since the year 1823, leaving the rest to be completed as future opportunities of additional room might chance to occur. It appears to me however that it would be far better to commence *ab ovo* and rearrange the whole Library.

Jowett's influence may be detected in that pronouncement, for Jowett was a determined advocate of reclassification.

Actual experience in classification,[2] coupled with advice he received from Winter Jones, Panizzi's successor at the British Museum, and from Edward Edwards, the Manchester City Librarian, convinced Coxe that he was mistaken. In the report which he made to the Curators in May 1864[3] he said that he would not advocate the breaking up of a large portion of the library as it then stood: it would be a pity to mix up early printing with modern textbooks, and he did not think the result would compensate for the labour and pains bestowed. He suggested that re-referencing should for the present be limited to

[1] This was pointed out by Mr. Wheeler in the *Bodleian Quarterly Record*, vol. i, p. 285.

[2] Coxe notes in his diary that it was begun on 25 Mar. 1859, 'Very hard work, and quite a question whether it succeeds.'

[3] Printed as a Curatorial paper.

the series previously referred to as Year-Books. These were the accessions received since 1824; books which had never been classified but had been arranged alphabetically by authors under the year of publication. The series had been closed in 1860 and its place taken by the class arrangement which Coxe inaugurated in 1861. He now proposed to classify the Year-Books into the class-divisions of his new scheme.

On receiving Coxe's report the Curators ordered classification to be resumed at once. At the same time they approved a curious and ·ingenuous scheme[1] for classifying books without alteration of their position on the shelves. This was to be done by affixing to the back of each volume a label which, by its colour and the letters printed on it, indicated the main subject and the special branch of that subject with which the book was concerned. But, unfortunately for a scheme which depends for its success not merely on the strength of the gum which holds a label but on that of the dye that tints it, colours in the course of years have become indistinguishable, nor is there any longer an explanatory key to give them meaning. There is little served by a faded label lettered CL if that may equally well denote calculus (if green) or colonial history (if pink). Anyway, the experiment was not carried far. It was applied in a most haphazard way, perhaps as books were ordered up by readers. It can at no time have rendered assistance except, to a minor degree, to the staff. Today the labels serve no purpose except to stir up wonder at their origin and meaning.

Coxe meanwhile proceeded with the classification of the accessions of 1851–60, and, when that was done, he quietly abandoned further effort. His thoughts were moving in a new direction, namely, in that of a class catalogue.

8. THE CLASSIFIED CATALOGUE

Although in 1857 Mr. Meyrick, then junior proctor, had suggested the preparation of a 'systematized index' to the existing catalogue,[2] the idea of a classed or subject-catalogue, supplementing the author-catalogue, received its first practical expression in the report which Coxe made in 1864 upon Jowett's scheme for reclassification. He there argued that the advantages to be derived from a rearrangement of books upon the shelves could be gained more effectively 'by a classified catalogue, i.e. the titles of books written out and arranged according to their subject-matter'. As the slips for the author-catalogue were being produced by manifold process in triplicate, and

---

[1] Described by Wheeler in *Bodleian Quarterly Record*, vol. i, pp. 312–13, 320.
[2] Curators' minutes, 12 Dec. 1857.

only two copies of that catalogue were needed, a third slip was left available for other purposes.[1] These extra slips could be arranged under subjects. He therefore proposed that the alphabetical catalogue should be pressed forward to completion, and that the cataloguing staff should then be turned on to classify the extra slips and produce by that supposedly simple method a complete classified catalogue of the whole library.[2]

Jowett in the end accepted Coxe's project for a classified catalogue, but he did not regard it as a sufficient substitute for reclassification of the books upon the shelves. He made his view very clear in the following peremptory order which he issued, on his own responsibility, in December 1873 to Douglas Galton, whom the Curators had called in to advise on library extension. 'You will further take care in your report', he wrote, 'to provide for the classification of the books. I am aware that the other Curators and the Librarian disapprove of classificatory arrangement, but that circumstance is immaterial.'[3] Four years later he returned to the same topic in the evidence he gave before the University Commission.

In February 1877 he persuaded the Curators to set up a committee with powers sufficiently wide to allow shelf-arrangement to be discussed along with many other matters. The committee's report,[4] dated 1 December, attempted to reconcile Jowett's views with those held by Coxe. It recommended reclassification, but only after the production of a subject-catalogue. The terms of the report are as follows:

We think that the time has arrived when the Bodleian, like other large public libraries, should be arranged according to subjects. Such an arrangement . . . has hitherto from want of room extended only to books purchased since 1851. . . . We agree with the Librarian in thinking that the best way of proceeding with the task will be first by classifying the Library on paper, or, in other words, making a classified catalogue, which would be very useful in itself and not very expensive. We recommend that this work should be commenced at once.

So reclassification was postponed until a subject-catalogue should be completed. Jowett still insisted on eventual total rearrangement of the whole library, though a talk with Coxe 'opened his eyes a little on the subject of classification'.[5] 'I do not of course say', Coxe com-

[1] As at the British Museum, where the extra set went to form shelf-lists.
[2] Report to the Curators of the Bodleian Library, May 1864.
[3] Library records, 'Buildings, etc., 1855–81'.
[4] Report of committee of Curators on the general arrangement of the rooms of the library.
[5] Coxe's diary, 13 and 14 Feb. 1878.

mented on the committee's report, 'that such a thing [as reclassification] is impossible, but I do feel that it is most doubtful whether what would be gained by such a plan would at all compensate for the extravagant cost of time and labour.' And, as he more nearly approached the subject, he began to cool in his advocacy even of a classified catalogue. It might be worth while, he told the Curators, 'to consider whether it would not be well to wait until the work in a certain sense be done for us, namely, by the publication of what has long been contemplated by Librarians, a universal class catalogue of all published works of all countries and languages'.[1] The idea of a universal catalogue is completely Utopian; but Coxe was right in his main point, that it is the duty of librarians to concern themselves with catalogues and leave it to others to compile bibliographies. He calculated that a classified catalogue could scarcely be completed in less than five or six years.

The author-catalogue was finished, as we have said, in June 1878; and Coxe, in spite of his misgivings, had hoped to turn at once to the classified catalogue. But the difficulties of the work became apparent at the very outset. The slips out of which it was to be compiled were ready for arrangement; but there was the problem set by large collections of texts, like Migne's *Patrologia Latina* and Pertz's *Monumenta Germaniae Historica*, which were entered in the author-catalogue only under the name of a general editor. And over and besides these, there was the case of authors whose writings appear only in the Proceedings of learned societies at home and abroad. An extensive and almost limitless task lay ahead, of what is called 'breaking up', that is to say, the separate cataloguing of works published in series, as well as of articles in periodicals. Though Coxe may not have realized it, the librarian who attempts to catalogue not merely a printed book but its contents is inevitably lost, for there is no end to his labour.

Expert opinion was discouraging. The sub-librarian Neubauer, commissioned by the Curators to inspect the class catalogues in use in the libraries of Berlin, Leipzig, and Munich, reported unfavourably upon the project. Munich had already given over the attempt, and no work had been done upon its catalogues since 1860. 'I was told', said Neubauer, 'that the class catalogue is very seldom used, and bibliographical handlists supply in most cases the necessary information.' A printed volume was infinitely easier to consult than boxes of loose slips.[2]

---

[1] Observations by the librarians on the report of the committee of Curators, Feb. 1878, printed as a Council paper.
[2] At Berlin, however, the class catalogue was in bound form.

The Curators had themselves grown sceptical as to the advantages of a subject-catalogue; nevertheless, they could not resist Jowett, and on his motion sanctioned the proposals which Coxe had made for what one may term analytical cataloguing, agreeing at the same time that the commencement of the classified catalogue should be postponed for one year.[1] They obtained the consent of Convocation to the renewal, for three years, of the annual grant of £500 previously paid for the author-catalogue, and to the allocation of £270 a year out of that sum to the production of the classified catalogue;[2] and they appointed two of their number—Stubbs and Mark Pattison—to consult with Coxe on the classes or divisions to be adopted. The classification of slips, once begun, proceeded apace, and by June 1882 336,816 had been sorted into thirteen main sections.[3] The ultimate fate of the ill-starred enterprise will be told in a later chapter (pp. 165–7).

[1] Curators' minutes, 8 June 1878. Coxe's letter setting out his proposals is entered on the minutes.
[2] Decree of 11 Mar. 1879.
[3] *The Bodleian Library in 1882–7*, p. 31. Coxe originally proposed nine principal headings or classes, with some ninety subdivisions.

Chapter IV

Printed Books, &c.

It has recently been calculated that, ever since they started, the libraries of American universities have been doubling their size every sixteen years.[1] This alarming conclusion does not hold good of English libraries, for here the period is longer. In a return which he made to Parliament at the beginning of 1849, Bandinel estimated the number of printed volumes in the Bodleian at about 220,000. The first attempt at an exact return was made in 1885, the figure then supplied by the Librarian to the Curators being 406,159. If Bandinel's estimate is near accuracy, it follows that the Bodleian had not quite doubled its size in thirty-six years. Still, that it should have nearly done so in little more than a generation was sufficiently formidable.

On the figures given, the average annual increase over the years 1849–85 works out at just over 5,000 volumes. Very varying estimates were made from time to time within the period in question, and gave the annual intake at figures ranging from 5,000 to 8,000.[2] In analysing returns one has always to be on one's guard against confusing separate pieces with bound volumes, a caution that applies specially to periodical literature. And, in the absence of annual returns, it would be difficult, and perhaps not very profitable, to attempt any precise assessment. It is sufficient for present purposes to point out that the annual rate of increase was continually rising, and that towards the end of the period it probably rose very steeply. A detailed return made by a Curatorial committee in 1880 gives the number of foreign books bought in the previous year as 2,179, and the copyright intake as 6,067 volumes; a total, if foreign books are taken to represent volumes, of 8,246. This is exclusive of periodicals and parts.

1. COPYRIGHT ACCESSIONS

The major portion of the yearly accessions came to the library under the terms of the Copyright Act. We have already seen (p. 19) that the number of different works received from Stationers' Hall in

[1] F. Rider, *The Scholar and the Future of the Research Library*, 1944, chap. 1.
[2] Five thousand was the figure supplied to Douglas Galton in 1874. But in his report of 1855 Gilbert Scott had reckoned it at six to seven thousand. And in a later architect's report, that made by Graham Jackson in 1881, it is given as seven to eight thousand. The figure 3,000, excluding periodicals, given by Macray in the first edition of his *Annals* (1868), is fairly certainly an underestimate.

1845 was about 2,500, without reckoning parts and periodicals, and the supply was on the increase. In the past the Bodleian had admittedly failed to receive many of the books to which it was entitled by Act of Parliament. In 1852 the University Commission recommended in its report[1] that agents should be appointed in provincial towns to collect local literature; and Mr. Strickland, in giving evidence before it, observed that no attempt was made by the Bodleian to secure the colonial publications to which it was doubtfully entitled under the Imperial Copyright Act of 1842.[2] Neither suggestion was followed up. It was more practical to concentrate on the London publishers. Panizzi was just at this time launching his campaign against recalcitrant publishers on behalf of the British Museum. Its effect was magical: between 1851 and 1858 the Museum's annual copyright intake was almost exactly doubled. Stirred up by his example, the Curators deputed Coxe, in March 1858, to visit the British Museum and Cambridge University with the view of ascertaining whether the copyright privilege could be better secured. At the same time they instructed their officers to maintain strictly the rights of the Bodleian Library under the Copyright Act. They were directed to compare the books actually received with the Publishers' Circular and with the books received at the British Museum, and to apply for all books not sent.[3]

The 1842 Act had made the deposit of copies in the British Museum obligatory upon publishers, thereby relieving the Museum of any need for the services of a paid agent. But the other privileged libraries were not in so good a case. They had to demand copies within twelve months of publication. It was clearly to their advantage to design more efficient machinery for collection than that hitherto provided by the Stationers' Company. With that object, the Curators deputed Jowett, Wellesley, and Max Müller to concert measures with Cambridge, Dublin, and Edinburgh. Wellesley threw himself actively into the business, and was able to lay before his colleagues a set of resolutions agreed upon by representatives of the four libraries at a meeting held in London on 31 May 1859.[4] The main obstacle in the past had been lack of energy on the part of Mr. Greenhill, clerk of

---

[1] p. 120.
[2] Evidence, p. 102. The act provided no penalty for non-compliance. Any theoretical privilege which libraries of deposit, other than the British Museum, may have had under the act disappeared with the International Copyright Act of 1886 and was not revived by the Imperial Copyright Act of 1911. Partridge, *Legal Deposit of Books*, pp. 149, 152; Esdaile, *The British Museum Library*, 1946, p. 142.
[3] Curators' minutes, 13 Mar. and 24 Apr. 1858.
[4] Set out in the Curators' minutes.

the Stationers' Company. It was resolved that he should continue as heretofore to invoice and transmit to the four privileged libraries the books delivered to his office, but should be relieved of the duty of claiming books, and that claims should henceforward be made by an agent not connected with the Stationers' Company acting on behalf of the four libraries. The plan was sound, but was opposed by Greenhill, who saw himself threatened with a loss of income, and based his legal rights upon a clause of the Copyright Act which required all books to be received through the Clerk of the Stationers' Company. So he was allowed to continue on his existing salary on trial and was supplied with lists of books which he was required to claim.[1] The result was still unsatisfactory, and the libraries eventually accepted his proposal that they should jointly pay him 250 guineas a year on the understanding that he obtain for them all books of the value of 3d. and upwards, and all periodicals received at the British Museum.[2] Jowett continued to be dissatisfied with Greenhill's returns; and at length, the Curators' patience exhausted, the Bodleian joined with Cambridge and a third library in appointing a new agent, Mr. Eccles of the British Museum, who was installed in place of Greenhill after some trouble and difficulty. At the same time the Curators set up a committee to watch the administration of the Act.[3]

Thenceforward things improved. In 1852 Bodley had received under the Copyright Act 3,447 works in 3,711 volumes, and 4,308 parts and periodicals. In 1864 the number of works received was 4,316, and the number of parts and periodicals was 7,469. The corresponding figures for 1879 were 5,367 works in 6,067 volumes, and 8,550 periodicals and parts.

In 1878 the copyright privilege, long resented by publishers, was seriously threatened by a report of a Copyright Commission recommending that the legal requirement to present copies to libraries other than the British Museum should be repealed. Coxe, in opening the Library Association annual meeting at Oxford, opposed the recommendation for the sound reason that the preservation of a single copy in London was insufficient protection against loss, and argued that there should be other centres than London where any English book could be consulted.[4] A bill to give effect to the Copyright Commission's proposal was actually drafted. The Hebdomadal Council sent up a deputation to London to wait upon its promoter, Lord John Manners; and the bill was eventually dropped after a proposal that

---

[1] Minutes, 1 June 1860.   [2] Minutes, 2 Nov. 1861.
[3] Minutes, 16 May 1863; Coxe's diary, 6 Feb. 1864.
[4] *Proceedings of Library Association Conference*, 1878, p. 122.

the privilege should be commuted for an annual payment of £1,200 had been rejected as inadequate.[1] This was neither the first nor the last occasion on which the library had to fight for the retention of its statutory right.

2. DONATIONS: THE ASHMOLEAN LIBRARY

The days of great donations to Bodley had ended in 1841 with Dr. Mason's bequest of £40,000. The two great Oxford bibliophiles of their day, Dr. Routh, the President of Magdalen, and Dr. Bliss, the Registrar, might have been counted as prospective benefactors, since both collected books that they knew were not in Bodley. But Routh settled his library of printed books on Durham University, and failed to carry out his professed intention of leaving half his manuscripts to the Bodleian and half to his college.[2] Bliss contented himself with bequeathing to Bodley his interleaved copy of Wood's *Athenae* (now MSS. Top. Oxon. c. 8–12), preferring that his library should be put up to auction. And the only substantial gifts of books made by private donors in the forty years following the Mason bequest were two which will be described later (pp. 77, 89)—the first, a collection of British periodicals presented in 1862 by Dr. F. W. Hope; the second, a bequest of autograph letters and extra illustrated and other printed books, made in the following year by Captain Montagu Montagu, a naval officer of literary tastes who had retired to live at Bath.

Nevertheless, the contents of the library were swollen by transfers made to it from three other repositories. The Ashmolean Visitors transferred to Bodley in 1860 the books and manuscripts of their Museum; the Radcliffe Trustees deposited their Oriental manuscripts in 1872; and the Archdeacon of Oxford transferred in 1878 the earlier records from his Registry. An account of the second and third of these collections will be given hereafter.

The Ashmolean Library came to Bodley as an indirect result of long abortive negotiations for the acquisition of Sir Thomas Phillipps's great collection of manuscripts. The story of the Phillipps

---

[1] Partridge, *Legal Deposit of Books*, p. 99. A letter from the Copyright Commissioners inquiring as to the value set upon the university's privilege was laid before the Curators on 1 July 1876. No estimate seems to have been sent in at that time; but in 1879 a calculation was made on the basis of published prices of books and periodicals issued in 1877, and the privilege was valued at £2,108.

[2] Bloxam, *Magdalen College Register*, vol. vii, p. 22. Routh's manuscripts were put up for auction, and the most valuable were bought by Sir Thomas Phillipps.

manuscripts will be told in the next chapter (pp. 83–7): and it is sufficient here to say that the Ashmolean Visitors made their offer in October 1858; that it was accepted; and that their books and manuscripts arrived in 1860. They comprised the collections of four famous antiquaries—Sir William Dugdale (d. 1686); his son-in-law, Elias Ashmole, founder of the Museum (d. 1692); Anthony Wood (d. 1695), and John Aubrey (d. 1697); as well as the medical and scientific library, in 1,260 volumes, of Dr. Martin Lister (d. 1712), physician and zoologist.[1] From Dugdale came forty-eight volumes of manuscript; almost all being transcripts from private archives, public records, chartularies, and chronicles, made by him for the most part by way of material for his *Baronage* and his *Antiquities of Warwickshire*. A separate catalogue of them was published in 1692 by Edmund Gibson, later Bishop of London.[2] Aubrey's printed books are characteristically promiscuous. They have not been kept separate but are mixed up with other accessions to Ashmole's collections.[3] His manuscripts, not more than twenty in number, include the autograph copy of his Brief Lives;[4] his descriptive accounts of north Wiltshire (MSS. 1–3) and Surrey; and his correspondence, 1644–95.[5]

The books formerly belonging to Elias Ashmole and the additions that have been made to them fall into two series. The main collection consists of runs of manuscripts and of printed books, numbered consecutively 1–1,836, of which some 1,100 are printed books. Supplementary to this are 350 printed volumes referenced Ashmole A–H. But the latter, as well as many of the higher numbers in the main series (1549–1836), are accessions to Ashmole's original collection received from John Aubrey; from the Museum's second keeper, Edward Lhuyd (d. 1709), and from other donors; and they include likewise the contents of the university chemical library founded in 1683.[6]

[1] Lister's books are mainly seventeenth-century. Besides medicine and anatomy, natural philosophy, chemistry, and botany, they include a number of voyages and travels. Some have drifted into the section referenced Ashmole A–H.

[2] It has been superseded by the descriptions in the *Summary Catalogue*, nos. 6491–536.

[3] They have been listed by Dr. Gunther in the *Bodleian Quarterly Record*, vol. vi, pp. 230–6.

[4] MSS. Aubrey 6–9, edited by Andrew Clark in 1898.

[5] Letters from Aubrey to Edward Lhuyd are to be found in Ashmole 1814 and 1829, and his letters to Anthony Wood are in MSS. Wood F. 39, 40, &c. His 'Monumenta Britannica', which are invaluable for their early accounts and detailed drawings of Avebury and Stonehenge, were bought for Bodley in 1836, and are now referenced MSS. Top. gen. c. 24–25.

[6] Listed in *Bodleian Quarterly Record*, vol. vi, pp. 201–3, by Dr. Gunther, who has also given a general account of the Ashmole printed books, op. cit., pp. 193–4.

Ashmole's manuscripts, of which there are 706, are well known, thanks to the extremely full catalogue of them which W. H. Black compiled for the Delegates of the Press.[1] Astrology, alchemy, and medicine are widely represented in them, especially by the papers of Dr. Simon Forman (d. 1611); by the medical and astrological practice-books of Dr. Richard Napier (d. 1634); and by the prognostications, nativities, and the like, of John Booker (d. 1667), William Lilly (d. 1681), and Ashmole himself. Here are some manuscripts from Dr. Dee's library, and MSS. 487–8 are his diary (A.D. 1577–1601). The tracts on alchemy are chiefly sixteenth- to seventeenth-century transcripts; but there are various early manuscripts on medicine as well as on astronomy and mathematics; also medieval calendars and computistic works. MS. 1511 is a late twelfth-century illuminated bestiary which once belonged to John Tradescant,[2] and MS. 1431 is an early illuminated herbal. The drawings in MS. 304 have been recently identified[3] as from the hand of Matthew Paris.

Under the headings of heraldry and local history mention may be made of Ashmole's own collections (including many original documents) for his history of the Order of the Garter, for the history of the College of Windsor, and for that of Lichfield. There are various volumes of the heraldic and genealogical collectanea of Robert Glover (d. 1588) and of Ashmole himself; church-notes, genealogical rolls, heraldic visitations, grants of arms, volumes of peers' patents, funeral ceremonies, and numerous papers relating to the College of Heralds. There is a little section (MSS. 33–53) devoted to Middle-English and seventeenth-century poetry; and also various pieces relating to English history, chiefly parliamentary and of the seventeenth century, but including such earlier manuscripts of historical interest as Bishop Beckynton's letter-book, A.D. 1442 (MS. 789); Bishop Redman's Premonstratensian Register, A.D. 1474–1503 (MS. 1519); and a volume of original royal warrants and letters missive from Henry VIII to Charles I (MS. 1729). MS. 1136 contains Ashmole's own Memoirs.[4] Appended to the collection (MSS. 1814–21, 1825, 1829–30) is the correspondence of the Museum Keeper, Dr.

---

[1] Begun in 1831 but not published till 1845, and then without an index. An index was subsequently compiled by Macray and published in 1866. Black's catalogue with the index is now numbered part X of the Bodleian series of quarto catalogues of manuscripts. Dr. R. W. Hunt has given a note on its history in the *Review of English Studies*, vol. xxiii (1947), p. 200.

[2] As pointed out by Mrs. Poole in *Bodleian Quarterly Record*, vol. vi, p. 221.

[3] By Mr. F. Wormald in *Walpole Society*, vol. xxxi (1942–3), pp. 109–12.

[4] Published in 1774 as *Memoirs of the Life of Elias Ashmole*. Richard Rawlinson bought some of Ashmole's miscellaneous papers from his heirs (Macray's *Annals*, p. 241, n. 4). They are now MSS. Rawlinson D. 864–5.

Edward Lhuyd, A.D. 1691–1709, which was given to the Museum in 1769.[1]

The printed books[2] fall into two main categories. One is a very extensive collection of contemporary pamphlets; the other is a library, unique in character, of works on astrology and kindred topics. The former and major portion has in it numerous volumes of Civil War tracts—acts and ordinances, royal and parliamentary declarations, speeches and addresses; and an immense number of pamphlets, dealing in the main with English political and theological controversy; also collections of sermons, poems, newspapers, and (Ashmole 1052–60) book-catalogues; all amassed by Ashmole between 1679 and 1690. The reason for the paucity of pamphlets earlier than the Popish Plot is not far to seek, for on 26 January 1679, as Ashmole tersely tells us in his Memoirs, 'the fire in the Temple burned my library'.[3] Whether from this or from some other cause, the library of printed books now lacks both the heraldry and the alchemy which Ashmole's tastes would have led one to look for in it. In 1667 he had bought his astrological friend John Booker's study of books, and given the large sum of £140 for it.[4] Yet hardly more than a dozen of Booker's books are now traceable. Perhaps the bulk of them also perished in the fire: for the case is very different with Ashmole's later purchase, made in June 1681. This was the library of another fellow-astrologer, William Lilly, self-styled Merlinus Anglicanus, which Ashmole bought from Lilly's widow for £50.[5] At least 146 of Ashmole's volumes contain Lilly's signature on their title-page. Lilly's and Ashmole's books taken together make up a most comprehensive library of astrology and astronomy, with prognostications and works on magic and witchcraft and suchlike products of human credulity. To a long series of ephemerides or astronomical calendars must be added a set of almanacs (Ashmole 62–92, 245–68, 583–618, 868–93) for the years 1571–1690, which in part duplicates, in part supplements, the more extensive collection of almanacs previously acquired by Bodley by gift from Dr. Richard Rawlinson.[6] And among the older Ashmole

[1] Macray's *Annals*, p. 367. Lhuyd's correspondents are listed in the *Summary Catalogue of Western Manuscripts*, vol. v, pp. 83–85. Other valuable material for the history of science in Oxford is to be found in the Journal and Letter-books of the Philosophical Society of Oxford, A.D. 1681–8 (MSS. 1810–13), edited by R. T. Gunther in *Early Science in Oxford*, vols. iv (Journal) and xii (Letter-books).

[2] A detailed list of them, in two folio volumes, compiled in 1839 by W. Kirtland, under Keeper of the Ashmolean, is kept among the library records.

[3] *Memoirs of the Life of Elias Ashmole*, p. 355.

[4] Op. cit., p. 333. [5] Op. cit., p. 360.

[6] The Rawlinson almanacs, for which see Macray's *Annals*, p. 249, cover the years 1607–1752: those in the Anthony Wood collection, mentioned below, are for 1630–95.

books mention may be made of two that are printed on vellum—a fine Sarum missal printed by W. Hopyl at Paris in 1514 (Ashmole 1764), and a curious little set of seaman's charts dating from about 1500 (Ashmole 1352).

Anthony Wood had in his lifetime sold to the Bodleian Library some twenty-five medieval manuscripts, including several monastic chartularies and statute-books.[1] The rest of his library he bequeathed to the Ashmolean Museum. It consisted of 960 printed volumes (containing a far greater number of printed pieces) and about 130 manuscripts. The printed section is strong in books printed at Oxford or written by Oxford men in the seventeenth century, and is chiefly remarkable for an abundance of contemporary pamphlets—particularly Oxford pamphlets—fly-sheets, ballads, chap-books, book-catalogues, and almanacs; the bric-à-brac of literature which the old antiquary was constantly picking up in Oxford bookshops and recording in his carefully kept journals.[2]

Wood's manuscripts comprise his own collections for the history of Oxfordshire and of the city, university, and colleges of Oxford, together with many original documents bearing upon those subjects. They also contain his collections for the famous *Athenae Oxonienses*; his correspondence (MSS. Wood F. 39–45) with Dugdale, Evelyn, Aubrey, and other celebrated scholars of his time; and, in addition, a number of heraldic manuscripts, chiefly from the library of Ralph Sheldon (d. 1684). Taken as a whole they form a mine of material for Oxford history which the work of many later writers has totally failed to exhaust.[3] And besides printed books and manuscripts, there

[1] Wood's *Life and Times*, vol. iii, pp. 342–4; Macray's *Annals*, p. 157. The collection is called 'MSS. Wood empt.', and is described in the *Summary Catalogue*, nos. 8589–613. 'MSS. Wood donat.' is the name given to a small collection comprising nine volumes of Dr. Gerard Langbaine's Adversaria, catalogued by Coxe as Langbainii Adversaria 22–30 in his *Quarto Catalogue*, vol. i, cols. 886–7.

[2] Wood's interleaved almanacs for 1657–95, thirty-nine in number, are referenced 'MSS. Wood's Diaries' and listed in the *Summary Catalogue*, vol. v, p. 351. They form one of the main sources for Andrew Clark's *Wood's Life and Times* (Oxf. Hist. Soc., vols. xix, xxi, xxvi, xxx, xl), a work that cannot be too highly praised as a reconstruction of the life and work of a scholar of an earlier age. Vol. i (Oxf. Hist. Soc., vol. xix) gives a general account of the Wood collection and a helpful list of the almanacs, newspapers, and volumes of pamphlets, catalogues, ballads, &c., to be found therein.

[3] A full list of the Wood manuscripts was compiled by William Huddesford, Keeper of the Museum, and printed in 1761. They have been recently recatalogued as MSS. 8463–588 in the *Summary Catalogue*, vol. ii, pt. 2, pp. 1164–96. The series is arranged in five divisions according to a size classification, viz. B. (duodecimo), nos. 8572–88; C. (octavos) and D. and E. (quartos), nos. 8505–71; and F. (folios), nos. 8463–504. The fifth volume of the *Summary Catalogue* gives at pp. 86–92 descriptions of volumes made up from loose papers, additional to the original bound collection, viz. C. 52–53, D. 32, E. 32–33, F. 39–51. The exhaustive 'Catalogue of the MS. authorities

were bundles of charters and deeds, largely in poor condition, representing Wood's pilferings from the Treasury of Christ Church, and others acquired perhaps with a greater show of legality.[1]

It was altogether a notable accession. It amounted to about 3,700 volumes and these, when they came, were crowded into the little room described in the opening chapter (p. 15) as reached by a steep flight of stairs from the Laud Room, and which, from being the University Armoury, now became the Wood-Ashmole Room.

3. PURCHASES

It has been told (p. 22) how the average annual outlay on books in the years 1835–44, apart from extraordinary purchases, was £1,685. In the years that followed, exceptional purchases became fewer, ceasing altogether after 1859.[2] And although between the years 1845 and 1881 annual receipts rose from £4,647 to £7,355, the amount available for purchases actually fell after 1859. For whereas the average yearly amount spent upon ordinary purchases during the quinquennium 1855–9 was £1,946, the corresponding figure for the quinquennium 1875–9 was no higher than £1,377.[3] Periodicals were growing in importance, and an increasing proportion of what was spent on books went in paying subscriptions, leaving so much the less for buying older books or foreign non-periodical literature.[4] The reason for diminishing resources is not far to seek. With library growth staff salaries and overhead charges ever increase and, in default of special endowment, book purchase is always the residuary legatee of library funds. Only between the years 1780 and 1813 had the library possessed a growing endowment hypothecated to purchases, and even then the Curators had been unable to resist the temptation to draw upon it for the fitting up of new rooms.

Current foreign literature formed the first charge upon the sum

used by Wood in his treatises on Oxford', given in vol. iv of Andrew Clark's *Wood's Life and Times* (Oxf. Hist. Soc., vol. xxx), pp. 87–312, is in effect a *catalogue raisonné* of the Wood manuscripts arranged under sources.

[1] They are all included in W. H. Turner's *Calendar of Charters and Rolls preserved in the Bodleian Library* (1878), which, however, does not distinguish the Wood charters from those acquired by the Bodleian from other sources. For Wood's work in Christ Church Treasury see his *Life and Times*, vol. ii, pp. 112–14.

[2] The principal were: 1848, Michael (Hebrew) MSS., £1,030; 1849, Mill (Sanskrit) MSS., £350; 1850, 'Libri Polonici', £366; 1852, Mortara (Italian printed books), £1,000; 1854, Lathbury collection of prayer books, £300; 1856, Lutheran tracts, £300; 1858, Ouseley (Persian) MSS., £500; 1859, Libri sale (MSS.), £720.

[3] The averages for the quinquennia following 1844 work out as follows: 1845–9, £1,432; 1850–4, £1,913; 1855–9, £1,946; 1860–4, £1,543; 1865–9, £1,743; 1870–4, £1,466; 1875–9, £1,377.

[4] In 1879 the library bought 2,179 foreign books and 3,786 periodicals or parts.

left available for purchases. From the establishment of the Taylor Institution for the study and teaching of Modern Languages in 1845, Bodley considered itself relieved from the necessity of buying European *belles lettres*. Provision for science was similarly left to the Radcliffe Library. And there were other gaps. The sub-librarian, Dr. Neubauer, reported to the Curators in 1878 that Bodley was taking in no foreign works on natural science, general literature, or law.[1] Funds were insufficient. The Curators resolved in 1878 to inform a new University Commission that a considerable sum was needed for the purchase of current foreign literature. Three years earlier they had placed on record the desirability of applying for an additional £1,000 a year for book purchases.[2] Such an increase would have given the library about £2,500 to spend every year upon books; in itself a modest sum since it was but a quarter of the amount which the British Museum was spending annually during the second half of the century. Convocation contented itself with a chary annual grant of £230 made in 1879 for three years.[3]

Book-selection had tended to be left in the hands of the library officers. In giving evidence before the first University Commission in 1852, Jowett advocated that it should be entrusted to the professors.[4] The Bodleian statute of 1856, doubtless prompted by Jowett, followed on these lines: in the selection of books the librarian was empowered to take the advice of curators and other learned men, and in particular of professors in their respective faculties.[5] There is little to show how far the librarian availed himself of the permission accorded to him.

We have seen how in 1845 Bodley was acquiring its foreign books from various booksellers in Oxford, in London, and abroad. Inquiries made at the close of 1858, as to the terms upon which they would continue to trade, resulted in the whole supply being entrusted to Messrs. Parker of Oxford, who thereby obtained a monopoly as Bodleian foreign agents.[6]

In the auction-room Bodley became a less frequent buyer than in the past. From the time that Bandinel went, the library fell steadily behind in the competition for book rarities. It was no longer in a position to pile up reserve funds out of which large purchases might be made as opportunity offered. The great patrons of the sale-room

[1] Report of 2 Feb. 1878 issued as a Curatorial paper.
[2] Curators' minutes, 6 Nov. 1875 and 28 Mar. 1878.
[3] Decree, 11 Mar. 1879.
[4] *Oxford University Commission Report*, 1852, Evidence, p. 39.
[5] *Corpus Statutorum*, addenda, p. 559.
[6] Curators' minutes, 5 Feb. 1859.

at this period were private buyers like Lord Ashburnham and Henry Huth. Only at the Bliss sales of 1858, and at the Libri sale of 1859 (of which more will be said later) did the Bodleian come forward as a purchaser on a large scale.

The Rev. Dr. Philip Bliss had at one time combined the offices of Sub-Librarian, of Keeper of the University Archives, and of Registrar to the University. He was a born bibliophile. He bought at auction sales, from booksellers in Oxford and out of it, and off book-stalls, always entering on its fly-leaf the source of his copy, and frequently adding bibliographical notes. He had an original way of recording his ownership, which he did by inserting in ink his initial 'P' before the printer's signature 'B', frequently adding two figures to denote the year of his purchase. His library abounded in rarities from English presses of the late sixteenth and the seventeenth century. He collected, not fortuitously, but with fixed aims in view. The leading features of his collection have been well set out as 'Books printed at Oxford; books of Characters; books printed in London in the three years preceding the Great Fire; versions of and commentaries on the Psalms; works of writers connected with Oxford; works of "Royal and Noble Authors"; and works of sixteenth- and seventeenth-century poets'.[1] At the sale of his library at Sotheby's 745 volumes were bought for Bodley at a cost of £427, and are kept as a separate collection under Bliss's name.

4. INCUNABULA, BIBLES, LITURGIES, AND ENGLISH LITERATURE

Book-collecting in the grand manner was a thing of the past. The famous Roxburghe sale of 1812 had marked its culmination and its close. No longer was the library amassing books printed on vellum, *editiones principes* of the classics, and choice Aldines, as it had done under Librarian Price and in the early Bandinel period. Chances of such acquisitions came rarely, but were taken when they came. Of the block-books, which preceded in order of invention if not in actual date of production the book printed from movable type, Bodley possessed Apocalypses in the Douce and Laud collections: it secured a different edition in 1853 for £120.[2] In the same year the library bought for £200 a copy of the *Mozarabic Breviary* printed

[1] *Oxford Bibliographical Society, Proceedings*, vol. iii, pp. 256–8. The note there given on Bliss's library forms a part of S. Gibson and C. J. Hindle's excellent paper on 'Philip Bliss, Editor and Bibliographer'. The miscellaneous antiquarian collections and bibliographical memoranda which Bliss left behind him in the university archives were transferred by its keeper to the Bodleian in 1933.

[2] Auct. M. 3. 14: Macray, *Annals*, p. 464, n.

by command of Cardinel Ximenes at Toledo in 1502; a sum worth paying, since it was the only vellum copy known, and that an immaculate one of what is itself a rare book.[1] There were incunabula to be acquired, notably at the great sale of duplicates from the Royal Library at Munich in 1850, when 320 volumes of early printing were secured for the small sum of £114. Prices varied greatly: £21 was paid in 1849 at a Libri sale for a Sweynheym and Pannartz Pliny's *Historia Naturalis* (Rome, 1473) having a manuscript collation of three early codices by Politian;[2] and £210 to Quaritch in 1874 for a singularly perfect specimen of the *Somme Rurale*, printed at Bruges in 1479 by Caxton's master, Colard Mansion.[3]

Caxtons were still to be had at £20 apiece, that being the sum paid in 1848 for a large-paper but very defective copy of Voragine's *Golden Legend* (1483 edition) which had been sold out of a parish chained library in the Berkshire village of Denchworth,[4] while in 1853 an imperfect copy of the *Chronicles of England* (1480) was bought for £21.[5] Bodley, as was natural, had a nearly complete series of the products of the first press which Theodore Rood of Cologne set up in Oxford in 1479. It was augmented by the purchase of an imperfect copy (formerly William Herbert's), of Mirk's *Liber Festivalis* for £6. 10s. at Utterson's sale in 1852,[6] and of an Oxford school-book (*Vulgaria quaedam abs Terentio in Anglicam linguam traducta*) bought at a sale in 1866 for £36.[7] In this connexion one may make mention of the valuation list which Rood's partner, the Oxford stationer, Thomas Hunt, drew up in 1483 and entered on the fly-leaf of a French Livy, bought for the library in 1860 for £12.[8]

It had been Bandinel's aim to build up a fully representative collection of bibles, and Coxe carried on the tradition, trafficking in English bibles, psalters, and prayer books with the Bristol Quaker and chocolate-maker, Francis Fry, whose own unrivalled collection ultimately went to the British and Foreign Bible Society. From Fry he bought for £100 a perfect copy of Cromwell's first Great Bible of 1539 and a 1541 edition of Cranmer's Bible for £82. 10s. Fry had previously sold to Bandinel in 1858 for £40 a copy of Barker's octavo Bible of 1631, famous for its injunction 'Thou shalt commit adultery',

[1] Auct. I Q. 1. 28: Macray, p. 358.   [2] Auct. Q. 1. 2: Macray, p. 351.
[3] Auct. IV Q. 2. 16: Macray, p. 389.   [4] Auct. V Q. inf. 1. 19: Macray, p. 494.
[5] Auct. QQ. supra 1. 23: Macray, p. 358.
[6] Auct. R. supra 7. Madan, *Oxford Books*, vol. i, p. 261, correcting Macray, *Annals*, p. 159.
[7] Auct. R. supra 2: Macray, pp. 159, 382.
[8] Macray, p. 160. The list is printed in the *Oxf. Hist. Soc. Collectanea*, vol. i, pp. 141–3.

all copies of which were ordered by the Court of High Commission to be thrown into the flames. The first edition of Coverdale's New Testament (printed at Antwerp in 1538) was bought in 1865, and a somewhat imperfect copy of the first Bible to be printed in Scotland (Edinburgh, 1579) in 1867. A Testament and Prayer Book printed by Barker in 1630 and bought for £10 in 1866 is notable for its embroidered binding of silver and gold thread worked on silk, which has been attributed to the Sisters of Little Gidding.[1] By 1870 the Bodleian collection of English bibles prior to 1800 is said to have been wellnigh complete.[2]

Nor were continental editions neglected. The very rare *editio princeps* of the Bohemian Bible (Prague, 1488) was picked up in 1856 for £17. 10s. The still rarer Wittenberg 1529 edition of the Pentateuch and New Testament was bought in the same year for £18. 18s.; and in 1853 a copy of the first complete Lutheran translation of the Bible (Wittenberg, 1534) for £26. 8s. The earliest French version of the New Testament (printed in 1523 by Simon de Colines) was bought in 1848 for no more than £21. And in 1877 the library obtained by gift a second copy of Cardinal Ximenes' famous *Complutensian Polyglott* (Alcala, 1514–17).

The various forms of the Psalter have from time to time attracted book-collectors. Some ninety editions or versions came to Bodley in the Montagu bequest. A collection of early editions of the English prayer book, of the metrical psalter, and of visitation articles was bought for £300 in 1854 from the Rev. Thomas Lathbury, a writer on English church history. Catholic liturgies were equally sought after. In 1877 the Hon. and Rev. Stephen Lawley presented a small collection of breviaries representing the distinct uses of sixteen French and Spanish dioceses. And the library bought two Spanish breviaries of extreme rarity: the Toledo 1502 vellum breviary has been already mentioned; the other, a fine copy of the breviary printed at Lerida in 1479, was bought in 1867 for £36.[3]

The advent of the Malone collection in 1821 had made the library for a time unrivalled in Shakespeariana and Elizabethan drama; and a number of Shakespeare quartos unrepresented in Malone were bought at the Heber sale of 1834 and in the years that followed.[4] Little therefore remained to be added, and it was unnecessary for the Bodleian to interest itself in the Halliwell, Daniel, or Corser sales. An

---

[1] Macray, p. 67. The binding is reproduced as Plate XXII in Salt Brassington's *Historic Bindings in the Bodleian Library* (1891).
[2] Macray, p. 383.   [3] Op. cit., p. 382.
[4] Op. cit., p. 325.

exciting Shakespearian purchase was made, however, at a Sotheby sale in 1865, when the Bodleian had knocked down to it, for £9, an Aldine octavo edition (1502) of Ovid's *Metamorphoses*, having on its title-page what purports to be the poet's abbreviated signature 'Wm She', and on the opposite blank page or 'paste-down' the following note: 'This little Booke of Ovid was given to me by W. Hall who sayd it was once Will Shaksperes. T. N. 1682.' The signature, for long accepted as genuine, has been shown by Sir Edward Maunde Thompson to be a forgery, like the other supposed Shakespeare signature in the British Museum copy of Florio's *Montaigne*.[1] The forger may have intended to substantiate the memorandum: he has merely succeeded in casting doubt on its authenticity. But Maunde Thompson's reasons for rejecting the memorandum also as a nineteenth-century forgery carry less conviction.[2] And if 'W. Hall' were a relative of the poet's son-in-law, Dr. John Hall, some credit may be given to his testimony. The little book still has some claim to have been once owned by Shakespeare.

During the years that followed the Heber sale, the attention that had been given by the Bodleian to early English literature noticeably slackened, most of the rarities acquired being those secured from Bliss's library or bought at a Pickering sale in 1854. The scales were weighted in favour of theology. The printer's copy for the fifth book of Hooker's *Ecclesiastical Polity*, with the author's corrections, was bought in 1878 for £15.[3] Non-juring divines were still in favour at Bodley; 360 of their sermons, preached between 1688 and 1750, being bought in 1849 for 5 guineas;[4] while in 1845 a purchase was made, for £22. 10s., of 300 volumes of tracts, treating chiefly of the non-jurors, and of the Bangorian controversy, so called from the non-jurors' enemy, Benjamin Hoadley, Bishop of Bangor. And in the late sixties Coxe set out to buy editions of Bunyan and early Quaker tracts.[5]

5. FOREIGN LITERATURE AND AMERICANA

German dissertations had a fascination for Bandinel (or perhaps rather for Gaisford), who, as the reader has already been told (p. 22), bought no fewer than 43,400 of them in 1827. By comparison, the

[1] 'Two pretended autographs of Shakespeare'; *The Library*, 3rd ser., vol. viii, pp. 193–217.
[2] They are disputed, with some effect, by F. Madan, in *The Library*, 3rd ser., vol. ix, pp. 97–105. See also Macray's *Annals*, pp. 379–81.
[3] MS. Add. C. 165: Macray, p. 393.
[4] A higher price per sermon was paid next year when 600 English sermons printed between 1600 and 1720 were purchased for £59.
[5] Macray, p. 383.

7,000 bought for £30 in 1846 must seem insignificant. Other purchases of classical dissertations were made at the sales of two Hellenists; Professor Jacobs, editor of the *Anthologia Graeca*, in 1849; and Professor Hermann in 1854.[1] As for earlier German vernacular writings, mention has already been made of two products of Luther's Wittenberg press. The eighty-four volumes of German Reformation tracts bought for the Bodleian in 1818[2] received a very notable addition through the purchase of a collection of 538 works by or relating to Luther and the Reformation in Germany, formed by Dr. J. G. May of Augsburg, which the library secured in 1856 from K. Schneider of Berlin for £300. At the same time the Bodleian bought an analogous collection consisting of books and tracts relating to the history of the Jansenists, who, when forced to leave Port Royal and France, retired to Holland. The collection had been formed by a Jansenist archbishop of Utrecht, and was bought from Mr. Frederick Müller, an Amsterdam dealer, for £151.

In 1838 an American visitor, George Ticknor, had pronounced the Bodleian 'miserably deficient in Spanish literature', a subject on which he was certainly an authority.[3] The complaint was hardly justified, for throughout his librarianship Bandinel was active in buying Spanish books. These were concentrated in the Douce Manuscript Room which hence came to be called the Spanish Room. Mention has already been made (pp. 71, 73) of two works issued under the auspices of Cardinal Ximenes, namely, the *Mozarabic Breviary* and the *Complutensian Polyglott*. The Cardinal's rare treatise on the Christian religion, *Crestia* (Valentia, 1483), was bought in 1863 for £25.

Italian literature had been well represented from the first. It received large additions; first, by a collection of 1,426 volumes on Italian topography, antiquities, and art, formed by Mr. George C. Scott and bought from his brother in 1846 for £234. 6s.; secondly, in 1852 when the Bodleian bought Count Alessandro Mortara's library for £1,000. The Mortara collection[4] is rich in rare sixteenth-century

---

[1] Jacobs's dissertations were bought for £69. 17s. 6d. They are listed in the 1849 *Annual List of Purchases*, pp. 57–68, and are kept as a separate collection. Hermann is perhaps most widely known in this country from the epigram:

> The Germans in Greek
> Are sadly to seek;
> All, save only Hermann;
> And Hermann's a German.

[2] Macray, p. 303.
[3] *Life of George Ticknor*, 1876, vol. ii, p. 169.
[4] Catalogued by the vendor as 'Biblioteca Italica . . . già posseduti dal C. A. M. ed ora passati in proprietà della Biblioteca Bodleiana' (Oxford, 1852).

editions of Italian authors, including early editions of Boccaccio and Ariosto. A considerable number of editions of Petrarch came in 1863 in the Montagu bequest. And occasionally a single rarity would be bought, like the Ferrara 1532 edition of Ariosto's *Orlando Furioso*, bought in 1856 for 100 guineas, or Sir Thomas Bodley's own copy of the *Corbaccio* of Boccaccio (1569) bought at Dr. Wellesley's sale in 1860.

In 1850 the library purchased *en bloc* two collections relating to countries of eastern Europe. One, termed *Libri Hungarici*, illustrated the history and geography of Hungary and other provinces of the old Austrian empire. It contains some 400 volumes and was bought for £78. The other and more important collection is known as *Libri Polonici*. It formed part of the library of the Polish Protestant writer, Jozef Lukaszewicz. It is notable for works printed in Polish in the sixteenth century, particularly books printed at Cracow, as well as valuable translations of the Bible, many of which were scarce in Poland even before the Second World War. The 1,675 volumes forming this collection were acquired for £366.[1]

There were, of course, large gaps in the foreign literature represented in Bodley. 'The Slavonic department', Dr. Neubauer told the Curators in 1878, 'can hardly be said to exist at all.' Much the same complaint had been made to the University Commissioners in 1852 in regard to American books. 'The literature of the United States', said Mr. Strickland, 'is almost wholly unrepresented.'[2] Yet already from 1847, we are told, purchases of works relating to American history began to form a special feature.[3] Stimulus came in the person of Henry Stevens, an active young bibliographer from Vermont. Stevens 'drifted' (he said), or rather blew, in first to the British Museum and then to the Bodleian; 'full of vigour and bother', as Coxe expressed it, adding 'I must be careful in buying, yet his books are good'.[4] Business was conducted by barter, for the Curators gave permission for Bodleian duplicates in American history to be exchanged for American early printed books.[5] Among early Americana bought about this time was Americus Vesputius' *Paesi nouamente retrouati* (Vicenza, 1507), bought in 1856 for £29. 10s., and Dionisio Richel's *Compendio*, printed in Mexico in 1544, bought for

---

[1] A brief account of the Polish books in the Bodleian is given in the *Oxford Magazine*, vol. lxii, p. 127.
[2] *Oxford University Commission Report*, 1852, Evidence, p. 102.
[3] Macray, p. 349.
[4] Diary, 29 Aug. 1864. For Stevens's activities at the British Museum see Esdaile, *The British Museum Library*, pp. 103, 207–8.
[5] Curators' minutes, 29 Nov. 1864.

£26 in 1853. And Coxe interested himself in the collection of works by the New England Puritan, Cotton Mather. Only in 1861 did Bodley obtain, for £75, a set of the Congressional Debates.

6. NEWSPAPERS AND PERIODICALS

Down to 1860, when the Ashmolean united its library to that of Bodley, a newspaper collection could hardly be said to exist. The Bodleian even lacked a complete file of *The Times*, a run of which, for 1839–46, was bought in 1861 for £16. But with Anthony Wood's books there came a series of Mercuries, Intelligencers, and Gazettes from 1657 to 1705. And in 1865 Bodley bought for £200 ninety-six volumes (since split up into three times that number) containing, in chronological order of issue, more or less complete sets of London newspapers from 1672 to 1737. The collection was one that had been formed by the antiquarian printer and publisher, John Nichols. It supplemented a gift made in 1862 by a many-sided collector and university benefactor, the Rev. F. W. Hope. Mr. Hope earned the thanks of the university and a doctor's degree by presenting to Oxford in 1850 his extensive entomological collection which now formed one of the principal contents of the new University Museum. His great collection of engraved portraits, offered in 1859, had come to be lodged in the gallery of the Radcliffe Camera. He had just founded a professorship of Zoology. And his latest gift, the Hope Periodicals, comprised over 1,300 volumes of British newspapers and periodical essays, collected by his father, John Thomas Hope, and covering the whole of the eighteenth century.[1] The Nichols Newspapers and Hope Periodicals combined to set the Bodleian newspaper collection on an entirely new footing; and it was further strengthened by long, albeit imperfect, runs of two journals, namely, the *London Gazette*, 1669–1859, bought in 1865 for £200, and the leading local paper, *Jackson's Oxford Journal*, 1762–1873, presented in 1874 by Mr. Frederick Morrell of Black Hall, Oxford.

Newspapers are one particular form of periodical, and have been defined as periodicals containing current news and published at short intervals. As the nineteenth century advanced, periodical literature grew steadily in importance. The production of a printed catalogue of all periodicals, including the proceedings and transactions of societies to be found in the Bodleian, is due to the initiative of Professor

---

[1] *A Catalogue of a Collection of Early Newspapers and Essayists presented to the Bodleian Library by the late Rev. F. W. Hope* was published in 1865. It is now superseded, except for nineteenth-century publications, by Milford and Sutherland's *Catalogue of English Newspapers and Periodicals in the Bodleian Library* (Oxford Bibliographical Society, 1936).

77

Rolleston, who became a Curator in 1870. On his motion, made in 1875, the Curators resolved to undertake the work, and the sub-librarian, Dr. Neubauer, was entrusted with its preparation. It was probably intended that publication should wait for the completion of the catalogue; but, as the portion dealing with English periodicals was ready in 1878, that section was issued as a first fascicule.[1] The catalogue of foreign periodicals followed as Part III in 1880; but the second part, which was to have contained colonial periodicals, was never compiled.

7. MUSIC

Printed music began to be received from Stationers' Hall under the Copyright Act as early as 1759. It consisted in the main of sheet music and, though considerable in bulk, it lacked the merit of being either exhaustive or selective. Indeed, little attention was paid to it. Down to 1845 the sheets remained uncatalogued and piled up in cupboards. They were then at length routed out and arranged by the Rev. H. E. Havergal, a library assistant and chaplain of New College, and were bound up in three or four hundred volumes.[2] At the same time Mr. Havergal arranged and catalogued in manuscript a more valuable collection which had come to the Bodleian in 1800 by bequest from the Rev. Mr. Osborne Wight, an amateur musician and Fellow of New College. The Wight collection consisted of original folio editions of Handel, Arnold, and Boyce; and works of Purcell, Croft, Greene, and other English composers; also of some 200 volumes of manuscript music,[3] containing many motets, cantatas, and other pieces of eighteenth-century Italian musicians; anthems, some of them autograph, by English composers; and a large number of works —some performed as professorial lectures in the Oxford Music School —by Dr. William Hayes and his son, Dr. Philip Hayes, whose successive tenure of the Chair of Music covered more than half of the eighteenth century.[4]

The reason for the early neglect of the Bodleian musical collection is not far to seek. There was a better and more comprehensive music library in the custody of the Professor of Music, close at hand in the Music School. Consequently it was to the Music School and not to the Bodleian that Dr. Richard Rawlinson in 1752 bequeathed his

[1] As *Catalogue of Periodicals contained in the Bodleian Library*, Part I, English Periodicals.
[2] Macray, *Annals*, p. 257.
[3] Catalogued in the *Summary Catalogue of Western Manuscripts*, vol. iv, pp. 1–36 (nos. 16670–878).
[4] Macray, *Annals*, p. 280.

printed and manuscript music. A hundred years later, under order given in 1850 by the Hebdomadal Board,[1] the Music School Library was catalogued by the Rev. Robert Hake, a chaplain, like Havergal, of New College. And in 1855 the appointment of Sir Frederick Gore Ouseley to the Professorship put new life into musical studies at Oxford which immediately showed itself in a statute (13 March 1856) authorizing, amongst other things, the transfer of printed music from the Bodleian Library and the Ashmolean Museum to the Music School.[2] The statute contemplated the union of the Bodleian and Music School collections under the charge of the Professor of Music. Thirty years later the two collections came to be united under different circumstances (see p. 187), but for the time the enactment remained a dead letter.

In this same year (1856) the Bodleian purchased for £25 some rare sets of English madrigals,[3] but later, in 1877, declined an offer of a collection of manuscript music formed by Dr. William Crotch,[4] who had occupied the Chair of Music for half a century before being succeeded by Gore Ouseley. Only copyright music continued to pour in, and to be stacked uncatalogued in the Logic School. In 1879 the annual intake was estimated as fifty volumes and about 2,500 pieces of sheet music.[5]

8. MAPS

The Bodleian map collection began, in effect, with the opening of the nineteenth century. In 1800, and in one or two years that immediately followed, extensive purchases were made of English and foreign maps, and, at their Visitation in 1813, the Curators ordered a large table to hold their newly acquired maps and books of plates.[6] Then in 1809 the Gough bequest brought into the library the valuable collection known as Gough Maps, consisting of English maps, drawings, and topographical prints, arranged according to counties and bound up in twenty-three large folio volumes.[7] But far the largest bulk of maps were the Ordnance sheets for the United Kingdom which the Ordnance Survey commenced to publish in 1801 and to deposit in the Copyright libraries. The Admiralty followed suit

[1] Hebdomadal Register, 1841–54, p. 199: minute of 11 Nov. 1850.
[2] *Corpus Statutorum*, addenda, p. 545.
[3] Macray, *Annals*, p. 280.
[4] Curators' minutes, 26 May 1877.
[5] Library Records.
[6] Curators' minutes, 8 Nov. 1813.
[7] Listed in manuscript in 1844–6 by a library assistant, F. O. Garlick. Macray, *Annals*, p. 287, n. 1

with its hydrographic charts. By 1882 the library was being inundated with these sheets at the rate of something between three and four thousand a year. In 1877 a committee of the Curators suggested their storage in the Camera gallery; but they remained, for some years to come, in mounting piles in the Douce Room.[1] In default of means for dealing with them and of space for their storage, maps, it is to be feared, were regarded as an encumbrance.

9. A NOTE ON LENDING

The practice of lending had been absolutely forbidden by the Founder. Even Charles I and Oliver Cromwell had been refused permission to borrow, and had bowed to Bodley's behest. Under the Commonwealth the undesirability and the dangers of lending had been the subject of a trenchant paper from the librarian Thomas Barlow.[2] Yet early in the nineteenth century a movement started for the relaxation of the rigour of the early statute. A petition came before the Hebdomadal Board in 1818, and the Board hedged in its reply.[3] In 1833 a pamphlet entitled *A Few Words on the Bodleian Library*, published anonymously by Sir Edmund Head, a Merton graduate, urged the desirability of Oxford following the Cambridge practice of lending. The shortness of the library's hours of opening and the inclemency of its reading-room won converts for his proposal. Its merits and demerits were debated before the University Commission of 1850, when Jowett, E. A. Freeman, and others argued in favour of lending, and other witnesses argued against. In the report which they made in 1852, in which they reprinted Sir Edmund Head's pamphlet, the Commissioners declined to recommend any greater change than that duplicates should be allowed to circulate. Nevertheless, the defences of the old statute had been breached, and, when it was replaced by a new one in 1856, the prohibition of lending was unostentatiously dropped. Few may have noticed its disappearance; no one, at first, took advantage of it.

Thorold Rogers was the first to try his fortune by applying to the Vice-Chancellor for permission to take books out of the Bodleian by grace of Convocation. The Curators declined; whereupon Jowett at once gave notice of a motion that books and manuscripts might be taken out of the library under special conditions with the consent of

[1] *The Bodleian Library in 1882–7*, p. 36.
[2] Macray, *Annals*, pp. 113–18.
[3] 'They do not hereby mean to convey an idea that they are at present prepared to afford encouragement to a plan of which permission to take books out shall form a part.' Hebdomadal Register, 1803–23, p. 502.

the Curators.[1] Nothing followed upon this or upon a motion which Max Müller carried in 1863, allowing professors teaching at the Museum to borrow, for the term, books bearing upon the subjects of their lectures.[2] Notwithstanding, the tide was flowing in the direction of lending. From 1868 the Curators were making frequent grants, on their own authority, of loans both of books and of manuscripts. Nutt, the sub-librarian, was allowed to take manuscripts to his rooms in All Souls; Neubauer, assistant in the Oriental department, was permitted to take a manuscript home for collation.

It was agreed that such practices needed regularization; and early in 1873 the Curators sent up to the Hebdomadal Council a draft statute in which, amongst other provisions, they asked for power to grant loans under certain conditions. Council struck out the proposal and also rejected a suggestion made by Jowett that books might be borrowed for evening use. But when the statute came before Convocation and amendments were moved to it, though the proposal for evening borrowing was rejected by 43 votes to 35, another amendment, moved by the Master of University and seconded by Jowett, legalizing the practice of lending, was carried by 72 to 8. It was a curious piece of drafting. 'Liceat curatoribus', it ran, 'sicut mos fuit, libros impressos et manuscriptos scientiae causa viris doctis sive Academicis sive externis mutuari.'

So lending was made lawful. Free use was now made of the permission. J. L. G. Mowat was allowed to take to his college rooms in Pembroke the MS. archetype of Epictetus, and Mark Pattison to help himself to Anthony Wood's pocket-books. There was no doubt as to the Curators' views. 'We desire also', said their committee on expenses and management, over which Jowett presided, 'to express our unanimous opinion that resident graduates of the University should be allowed to use the books of the Library at their own rooms.'[3] As Coxe told the University Commission in 1877, in the matter of lending 'my Curators are very much more liberal than their librarian'.[4]

Tired, it would seem, of adjudicating upon applications, the Curators delegated their powers under the 1873 statute to the librarian; and it may have been in consequence of that unconstitutional decision, taken in 1878, that what was known as the borrowers' list came

---

[1] Curators' minutes, 29 Oct. and 8 Nov. 1859.
[2] Minutes, 17 Mar. 1863.   [3] Report presented Mar. 1876.
[4] *University Commission*, 1877, minutes of evidence, p. 245. Yet so little was Coxe's attitude understood or remembered that, only ten years later, Robinson Ellis was writing in the *Academy* that he regarded the proposal to reverse the Curators' policy 'with a quite lively resentment as an outrage and desecration to his [Coxe's] memory.' *Academy*, 26 Feb. 1887.

into existence. That list contained the names of persons to whom the privilege of borrowing was accorded by the librarian, and came in the end to include 111 names. Coxe died, and his successor in the librarianship, anxious that rules governing the practice of lending should be framed and codified, got the Curators to appoint a drafting committee. Then was disclosed one of those situations in which a university delights. The 1873 statute had empowered the Curators to borrow, not to lend.[1] A new statute was promoted to repair the flaw, and this gave the opponents of lending their chance. Professor Chandler, a newly appointed Curator, led the opposition; and, when the statute came before Congregation in May 1887, an amendment, prohibiting the lending of any books or manuscripts without the authority of Convocation, was carried by 106 votes to 60. This had the effect of withdrawing from the Curators the power to grant loans without reference to Convocation accorded to them in 1873. And an attempt made a year later to obtain statutory authority for the loan of printed books to heads of university institutions was still more decisively defeated, by 126 votes to 37.[2]

[1] 'Mutuari', not 'commodare'.

[2] The course of events here briefly told is summarized in *The Bodleian Library in 1882–7*, pp. 47–49, and was the subject of two pamphlets by Professor Chandler—*Remarks on the Practice and Policy of lending Bodleian Printed Books and Manuscripts*, 1886, and *Further Remarks*, 1887. The 1888 proposal called forth Falconer Madan's pamphlet, *Bodleian Lending to special persons in University Institutions*, which contains a bibliography of the whole controversy.

Lending systems were already in force for the Radcliffe Science Library and the Indian Institute Library when these were eventually taken over by the Bodleian; and rights of borrowing from the former were safeguarded by the Order in Chancery that authorized the vesting of the Radcliffe Library in the university. Borrowing at the Indian Institute is restricted to books that are the property of the Curators of the Institute. The obligation of obtaining the sanction of Convocation for all loans from the Bodleian was relaxed under the revised library statute of 1938, which made authorization by decree necessary only in cases where the Curators were not unanimous. Under powers given by the same statute the librarian is now authorized to grant loans of books at his discretion to institutions or departments within the university.

Chapter V
Manuscripts and their Catalogues

I. THE PHILLIPPS COLLECTION

In addition to the Ashmole manuscripts and other collections transferred from the Ashmolean Museum, of which some account has
been given in the last chapter (pp. 64–69), the Bodleian came near to
acquiring, about the same time, a far more extensive and valuable
accumulation of manuscripts. The tragi-comedy of the Phillipps
collection is long and complicated. That wealthy, vain, irascible
baronet, Sir Thomas Phillipps, amassed in the course of half a century the largest collection of manuscripts that has ever been brought
together by a private person either in this country or abroad. From
his days as an undergraduate at University College he had retained
some affection for Oxford. As early as 1827 he had approached Bandinel with an offer to sell his manuscripts to Bodley for £20,000. Next
year he made a more formal offer to the Curators that they should
purchase from him his entire collection for the sum of £30,000; it
having already cost him, he said, £50,000. But his terms, as well as the
price he asked, were onerous; for he stipulated, not only that his
collection should be kept distinct, as the Bibliotheca Phillippica, in
a separate room in the Bodleian quadrangle—that could have been
easily arranged—but that he should have the sole management of it
during his lifetime. He was himself ignorant of its full extent. 'I
believe', he wrote to Bandinel, 'there are above 4,000 volumes; but
I would engage to complete them to 5,000.' 'All of his proposals', said
Frederic Madden, 'are so extravagant that the Curators will not
listen to them for a moment.'[1] They declined to consider the conditions which Phillipps attached to his sale, so the offer lapsed, and
nothing more was heard of it for more than twenty years.

At last, in December 1851, after abortive attempts to sell his collection to the British Museum or to the Bibliothèque Nationale, and after
proposals for a separate library-building in Wales had equally fallen
through, Phillipps again approached Bandinel with the request that
he might be allowed to deposit his manuscripts in one of the ground-
floor rooms of Bodley. But this time he was careful to avoid com-
mitting himself as to their ultimate disposal. 'I will *not* say', he wrote
to Bandinel, 'that I *will* give them to the University, because I choose
to remain a free agent.' From then on to 1856 he continued to suggest

[1] Bodley MS. Eng. hist. c. 147, fol. 65.

83

at intervals alternative places of deposit—one end of the Picture Gallery, the Ashmolean Museum, a room in the new Museum in course of erection in the University Parks, or a room in the Taylor Institution. Things began to look more promising in March 1856 when Coxe took over negotiations with the difficult baronet. Phillipps was brought to offer his manuscripts to Oxford upon condition that a room was found for them; that he should be their sole custodian, with power to take manuscripts out for his own use or that of his friends; but, apparently, that there should be no access to the collection except through Phillipps himself during his lifetime. This time the Curators resolved upon acceptance.[1] In October some empty cabinets actually arrived, and the Vice-Chancellor gave leave for them to be temporarily placed in his office, termed the Justice Room, in the Clarendon Building. It was hoped that the manuscripts would follow.

Then came a hitch. The Justice Room was not to be had permanently, and Phillipps was furious at being what he called kicked out of it. His thoughts reverted to the Ashmolean Museum. There seemed a prospect that the whole contents of the Ashmolean would be moved into the new University Museum, not merely the Chemical Laboratory in the basement, and the natural history collections on the upper floors, but the antiquities and ethnographical specimens also; for it was at first proposed that the front ground-floor rooms of the new Museum should be given up to archaeology. A further interview which Coxe had with Phillipps in February 1858 brought negotiations once more to a head. The baronet expressed himself as still prepared to give his manuscripts to Oxford, but only if he was given the Ashmolean for their reception and was allowed to live there himself in the rooms which former Professors of Chemistry had fitted up as lodgings in the basement. He also stipulated that the university should spend £100 a year in printing unique historical manuscripts out of his collection.

It seemed possible that such terms might be arranged. Coxe continued to keep Sir Thomas Phillipps in play, bringing him to Oxford to see Jowett and the Vice-Chancellor, and soothing him down when he became angry over what he regarded as interminable bargaining. Yet when, in May, a formal offer at last arrived, its terms fell far short of what had been hoped. Sir Thomas did indeed state in writing that he was disposed to give the university a hundred boxes containing some 2,000 manuscripts of his own choosing, on condition that these should be kept in the Ashmolean; but the offer can hardly have

[1] Minutes, 14 Apr. 1856.

amounted to one twentieth part of his collection, and he left the ultimate disposal of the remainder an open question, stipulating, however,
that he should be allowed to deposit it in the Ashmolean and have the
use of the rooms below for his life. He was asking, as Coxe pointed
out to him, that the university should surrender to his use a building
badly needed for lecture-rooms or other educational purposes, and
was giving no guarantee that Oxford would ultimately ever receive
more than a small portion of his collection. Council, however, was
unwilling to turn the offer down. It returned a temporizing answer,[1]
and approached the Visitors of the Ashmolean Museum. The Visitors
were prepared to make room for the Phillipps manuscripts provided
they might deposit their own books in the Bodleian. A consequent
request from the Visitors, that the Bodleian Curators should receive
their books, manuscripts, and antiquities, led to the acceptance of
the books and manuscripts, though the offer of antiquities was very
properly declined.[2]

In a report presented to the Curators less than three years before,
the architect Gilbert Scott had advised the fitting up of a room in the
Ashmolean for the use of Bodleian readers in evening hours. The
whole of the rest of the building, he said, might be devoted to some
distinct department of the library, such as the storage of modern
accessions. It so happened that Phillipps's request synchronized with
the arrival of an offer from the Radcliffe Trustees to loan their
library building to the university; and, since this promised to fulfil
just those purposes which Scott had contemplated as being supplied
by the Ashmolean, the Curators no longer felt it necessary to press
for the surrender of the latter building to Bodley. It is true that
Phillipps immediately cast his eye on the Radcliffe Library in the
event of the Ashmolean being unavailable. It afforded more room (he
now estimated his manuscripts at 3,000 foot-run),[3] 'but no bed', as he
rightly observed; and he feared disturbance by the bells of St. Mary's.
He therefore elected for the Ashmolean.

But there were now other claimants for accommodation in the

[1] 'Resolved that this Council return its thanks to Sir Thomas Phillipps for his
munificent intentions, and is disposed to take steps to fulfil his views, as also in case
he should prefer that his MSS. should be deposited in the Radcliffe Library'. Hebdomadal Council minutes (9 June 1858) 1854–66, p. 241; cf. p. 242.

[2] Curators' minutes, 30 Oct. 1858.

[3] This was almost certainly an underestimate. The numeration of Phillipps's manuscripts reaches 36,000; but whole series of manuscripts were frequently entered under
a single number. Their total number will never be known but has been calculated
at about 60,000. The best accounts of the formation of this vast collection are those
given in the *Dictionary of National Biography* and in Seymour de Ricci's *English
Collectors of Books and Manuscripts*, 1930, pp. 120–4.

Ashmolean. Hebdomadal Council received a memorial from the Ashmolean Society (to which they ultimately assented), praying that the old Museum might be retained as a collection of antiquities; and the Oxford Architectural Society offered to present to it its collection of casts and models.[1] The Ashmolean basement had been already evacuated through the removal of the old Chemical Laboratory to the new Museum; and the Curators and a committee of Council, meeting in joint session on 28 May 1859, had agreed that the Arundel and other marbles housed in the Moral Philosophy School should be built into the basement walls.[2]

'Am I to have the *whole* of the Ashmolean?', Phillipps asked. That seemed difficult. Then if not the whole of the Ashmolean, he would require the whole of the Radcliffe. 'How', observed Coxe, 'can the Radcliffe be shut up for fifty years?' Moreover, Hebdomadal Council was in a quandary. It had in the meantime received from Mr. Hope the offer of his collection of engraved portraits (see p. 77), and had suggested to him its deposit in the Radcliffe Library, and Mr. Hope had accepted.[3] So Council called Coxe in to assist in its deliberations, drafted a diplomatic letter for Coxe to convey in person to Sir Thomas, and empowered him to offer the baronet the first floor of the Ashmolean, or if necessary (since this fell considerably short of his earlier demand) 'to offer on the part of the University to do all in their power to meet his views'.[4]

Phillipps received Coxe with unexpected kindliness, but continued to stand out for the Radcliffe Library. It was to be that or nothing; and, since Mr. Hope stood in the way, he would write to Mr. Hope himself. Perhaps it is not surprising that that gentleman declined to stand down. Yet the baronet still persisted. He had a new inspiration, and revealed it in a letter to Coxe on 23 February 1861: 'I do not see any chance of Bodley having my MSS., as Hope is so selfish, unless I were made Head Librarian at Bodley.' Apparently it was immaterial to him that Coxe had himself been elected to that office in the previous November. And the old man (he was close on seventy) was still determined to give no guarantee as to the ultimate destination of his collection. When Coxe pressed him on that point, he broke off correspondence[5] with a letter, dated 30 March, in which he wrote:

---

[1] Hebdomadal Council minutes, 1854–66, p. 267; minute of 21 Mar. 1859.
[2] It was not, however, until 8 Dec. 1862 that a decree was passed assigning the use of the Ashmolean basement to the Arundel Marbles, and only a part of the collection was then moved. The Architectural Society's casts were lodged in the smaller basement; Parker, *Handbook for Visitors to Oxford*, 1875 ed., p. 123.
[3] Hebdomadal Council minutes, 1854–66, p. 307. [4] Ibid., p. 322.
[5] The whole correspondence forms a volume of Library Records. It can be

If you had been really desirous to have my MSS. in Bodley, you would have jumped at the proposition I made, of being principal Librarian of Bodley, you of course becoming second. But it seems your own personal dignity was far more valuable to you than the glory and honour of acquiring for Bodley such a collection as mine. . . . As you require now guarantees, there is an end of the matter altogether.

So Oxford lost whatever chance it may ever have had (and the chance was probably always a slender one) of acquiring the great Phillipps collection by gift from its possessor. Attempts to obtain a considerable portion of it were to be made later (see pp. 195–7), but not until long after Coxe had ceased to be librarian.

2. ACCESSIONS OF WESTERN MANUSCRIPTS

So long as Gaisford was alive, Bodley had a curator who took an active interest in the buying and cataloguing of Greek and Latin manuscripts. Through his means the library had secured in the first quarter of the century the three greatest treasures of its Greek collection—the Clarke Plato, the D'Orville Euclid, and the Saibante Epictetus. The acquisition of Greek manuscripts, though becoming increasingly difficult, did not altogether cease with the purchases which the Dean made at the Meerman sale in 1824. One day in March 1855 Bodley received a visit from Dr. Tischendorf, the discoverer of the Codex Sinaiticus and of so many other treasures of neglected monastic libraries in Egypt and Sinai. He brought with him three early though fragmentary biblical manuscripts. Two (MSS. Auct. T. inf. 1.1 and 2.2) were of the Gospels, one being of the ninth, the other probably of the tenth century. The third (MS. Auct. T. inf. 2.1), which was also ninth-century, was the greater part of Genesis, out of a manuscript of the Septuagint of which other portions went to Petrograd, to the British Museum, and to Cambridge University Library. The three manuscripts were together bought by the Bodleian for £373.

Eighteen months earlier, on 26 September 1853, another would-be vendor of Greek manuscripts had come to Bodley and sent in his name as Constantine Simonides. It was a name familiar to Coxe, for he had received a letter from Sir Frederic Madden, Keeper of the department of manuscripts at the British Museum, warning him against Simonides as a skilful forger.[1] This Greek had imposed on

supplemented, particularly for the earlier period, from the Phillipps correspondence in the possession of W. H. Robinson Ltd. of Pall Mall.

[1] For this we have Madden's own statement made in a letter to the *Athenaeum* for 8 Mar. 1856, reprinted in the *Gentleman's Magazine*, n.s., vol. xlv, p. 375.

Professor Dindorf of Leipzig with his forged palimpsest of 'Uranios', a pretended record of the early history of Egypt, which Professor Dindorf nearly persuaded the Berlin Academy to buy for 5,000 dollars, and of which (through Dean Gaisford) he had induced the Oxford University Press to print a specimen. Madden's warning detracts somewhat from the palaeographical acumen, but not from the courteous wit, both so characteristic of Coxe, attributed to him in the following early account of Simonides's visit.

Simonides had entered the library with no small bundle of rare and curious manuscripts, and one by one they were unrolled before the authorities. 'This is of rather a late date', said Mr. Coxe as he examined one of them. 'What date do you give it?' said Simonides. 'The fifteenth century'. 'Good', rejoined Simonides;—'and this one?' 'The twelfth century'. 'You are correct;—and this one?' and Simonides laid before him, with more than usual care, the discoloured parchment. The librarian's eye sparkled. It was a rare manuscript, and in fine condition. He was not long, however, in giving his opinion. 'This is certainly of the fifth or sixth century.' 'Now Sir', said Simonides, 'I have something here which is still more interesting.' From his breast pocket he proceeded to extract, with the most extreme care, that which was to fill the beholders with astonishment. It was a palimpsest, in torn and tattered condition but still legible. 'What date do you assign to this?' said he. The librarian examined it carefully for a few minutes and then, looking Simonides full in the face— 'The nineteenth century,' he replied. Simonides soon packed up the manuscripts and has not made his appearance at the library since.[1]

The ingenious Greek made a little stir a few years afterwards by claiming to have forged the Codex Sinaiticus.

If Simonides was a prince of forgers, Guglielmo Libri, count Libri-Carucci, takes equally high rank among book-thieves. *L'affaire Libri* was notorious in France, where he had been found guilty in 1850 of stealing books and manuscripts from public libraries; but, fortunately for himself, he had by that time found domicile for his person and safety for his books in this country. The great bulk of his manuscript collections had been bought privately in 1847 by Lord Ashburnham after a vain attempt had been made to secure them for the British Museum, and were eventually sold by the next earl to the Italian Government and to the Paris Bibliothèque Nationale. But there were

---

[1] *Gentleman's Magazine*, N.S., vol. i (Nov. 1856), p. 593. The contributor, who was the Rev. John Macray, father of the Bodleian historian, identifies the forged palimpsest offered to Coxe with that of Uranios. Simonides's very different account of the famous interview is to be found in Charles Stewart's *Biographical Memoir of Constantine Simonides*, 1859, pp. 26–29.

still enough left over to make an important sale in March 1859 when the Bodleian, at the cost of £720, secured seventy Latin and Italian manuscripts.[1] Several of the former were of early date, the most conspicuous being a tenth-century Cyprian from Murbach (MS. Add. C. 15), bought for £84, and a ninth-century Gregorian Sacramentary from Luxeuil Abbey (MS. Add. A. 173), bought for £43.

Few non-Oriental manuscripts of any note were purchased during Coxe's librarianship. Gaisford had died in 1855, and the impulse he gave to classical studies was hardly felt beyond his lifetime. Jowett succeeded to the Regius chair but not to Gaisford's scholarship: his thoughts, so far as Bodley was concerned, were mainly taken up with questions of library administration. The funds at the librarian's disposal were small; purchases made at the Libri sale had exhausted the library's last available reserve; the average amount spent yearly upon manuscripts of all kinds in 1872–81 was little more than £100,[2] of which four-fifths was absorbed by Hebrew purchases. The only sale of manuscripts subsequent to that of Libri at which the Bodleian bought at all largely was that of John Gough Nichols in 1874. John Gough Nichols, son of John Bowyer Nichols and grandson of that John Nichols whose newspaper collection the Bodleian bought in 1865, was third and last in a famous line of antiquarian printers and publishers. His second name attests his grandfather's friendship with the firm's client and Bodley's benefactor, Richard Gough. Among the manuscripts bought for the Bodleian at his sale were a number of notebooks recording tours taken by Gough in 1759–71 and a few volumes of antiquarian correspondence.[3]

Of somewhat greater though not of first-rate importance was the bequest made in 1863 by Captain Montagu Montagu. Mention has already been made (p. 64) of his bequest which included, besides printed books,[4] about sixty manuscripts. The most valuable part of the manuscript collection is a series of twenty-two volumes of autograph letters of which some were bought by Captain Montagu at

[1] Catalogued in *Summary Catalogue of Western Manuscripts*, vol. v, pp. 47–71 as nos. 24709–78.

[2] The average for the years 1872–6 works out at £101, that for 1877–81 at £181, but only by reckoning in £300 given in 1880 for Hebrew manuscripts, of which Mr. Madan observes that 'there seems to be no note to show which they were'. (*Summary Catalogue*, vol. v, p. 583.)

[3] The Gough Nichols manuscripts, though not kept as a collection, are catalogued together in the *Summary Catalogue*, vol. v, pp. 141–50 (nos. 25510–61). Other correspondence from the same source has been acquired in recent years.

[4] For these, and for a sketch of Napoleon which accompanied the collection, see Macray's *Annals*, pp. 377–8. The manuscripts are described in the *Summary Catalogue*, vol. v, pp. 112–34 (nos. 25397–458).

William Upcott's sale in 1846,[1] and others at the sale in the following year of a less well known collector, Walter Wilson of Bath. Upcott was among the first to set the fashion of autograph collecting in this country. Trade in autographs gave new opportunities to the forger, and it must be admitted that the Montagu collection is not wholly free from forgeries. The Montagu autographs are chiefly of the eighteenth and nineteenth centuries, but include two autograph poems by Mary, Queen of Scots: these are no longer kept with the collection but in MS. Add. C. 92. A few years later, in 1872, four volumes of original English state papers of the years 1588–1627, gathered together by a secretary to George Villiers, Duke of Buckingham, were presented to the library by Mr. G. M. Fortescue of Dropmore.[2]

Yet one other manuscript collection received in Coxe's librarianship claims attention. In 1878 the Oxford Archidiaconal Registry moved into new offices, and its Registrar, with the Archdeacon's sanction, transferred his older records to Bodley. They comprised not only the act-books, visitation-books, churchwardens' presentments, and administrative papers of Oxford archdeaconry, but those of Berkshire archdeaconry also, these last having been transferred to Oxford from Salisbury diocese in 1837. The act-books of Oxford archdeaconry commence in 1567, its visitation-books in 1578.[3] The corresponding series for Berkshire commence a little earlier, namely, act-books in 1535 and visitation-books in 1560. Marriage bonds for either archdeaconry were excepted from the transfer: Oxfordshire archdeaconry bonds were deposited eventually in Bodley in 1921;[4] those for Berkshire were retained in the Registry at Reading, only to suffer destruction in a bombing raid in the Second World War. There also came, with the Oxford and Berkshire archidiaconal papers, the records of the various peculiars in the three counties (Oxfordshire, Berkshire, and Buckinghamshire) which make up the diocese of Oxford.[5] Other deposits of ecclesiastical records came to be made subsequently as will be told later (p. 304).

[1] At this sale the British Museum was the principal buyer, securing Add. MSS. 15841–959. Four other volumes of Upcott's collections were bought for the library by the Friends of the Bodleian at a Phillipps sale in 1946.

[2] MSS. Add. D. 109–12. The contents are calendared in the *Historical MSS. Commission's Second Report*, pp. 49–63. Selections have been edited by J. R. Gardiner for the *Camden Society*, 2nd ser. (1871), vol. i.

[3] An index to the Oxfordshire act-books and churchwardens' presentments, compiled by Dr. W. J. Oldfield and arranged under parishes, is kept on the open shelves of Duke Humphrey's Reading-Room. The act-book of the Oxford Archdeacon's Court for 1584 has been edited, with a valuable introduction, by Mr. E. R. Brinkworth, for the *Oxfordshire Record Society*, vols. xxiii, xxiv (1942, 1946).

[4] The *diocesan* series of marriage bonds was transferred to Bodley in 1947.

[5] The papers which came to Bodley in 1878 are catalogued, under subject-headings,

So long as Bandinel remained librarian all miscellaneous accessions of Western manuscripts were added to the long run of Bodley manuscripts. Coxe, on taking office, closed the series, and instituted one called 'Add. Bodl.', which was reformed in 1877 into Additional MSS., classified according to size.[1]

3. COXE'S QUARTO CATALOGUES
(Greek, Canonici, and Laud)

Although Bodley was adding little to the number of its non-Oriental manuscripts, the great stores that it already possessed were gradually being made known to the world in a series of full-scale catalogues. In 1840 Coxe, at Dean Gaisford's instigation, began the cataloguing of Greek manuscripts, a task in which he had already gained some experience when working on the catalogue of the Arundel collection in the British Museum. Gaisford had himself compiled catalogues of two Greek collections in Bodley, namely, those formed by the Dutch scholar, J. P. d'Orville (d. 1751), and by the English traveller, Edward Clarke (d. 1822).[2] And Coxe set out to catalogue the remaining Greek accessions of the early nineteenth century, namely the Greek manuscripts bought from the library of the Venetian Jesuit, M. L. Canonici, in 1817, with those bought at the Meerman sale in 1824 and from the library of the Veronese collector, Giovanni Saibante, in 1820. It seems to have been originally intended that these should be included in a single volume; but, after a start had been made on printing the catalogue of Canonici Greek in 1842, it was decided to continue with the Canonici Latin manuscripts rather than with other Greek collections.

Coxe had started to catalogue the Latin manuscripts of the Canonici collection in 1840, and by October 1843 had finished all but the liturgical section. They fall into three groups. The ninety-three manuscripts referenced as Latin bibles embrace also psalters and

in the *Summary Catalogue*, vol. v, pp. 157–84 (nos. 25579–6120). For further information upon them and upon subsequent additions see notes on 'Ecclesiastical Records in Bodley' by the present writer in the *Bodleian Quarterly Record*, vol. iii, pp. 223–4, and on 'Diocesan Records in the Bodleian Library' by I. G. Philip in the *Genealogists' Magazine*, vol. viii, pp. 7–9.

[1] Viz. B, under 8 in.; A, 8–10 in.; C, 10–14 in.; D, over 14 in.

[2] *Codices manuscripti et impressi cum notis manuscriptis, olim D'Orvilliani, qui in Bibliotheca Bodleiana apud Oxonienses adservantur*, Oxford, 1806. *Catalogus sive notitia manuscriptorum qui a cel. E. D. Clarke comparati in Bibliotheca Bodleiana adservantur*. Pars prior, Oxford, 1812. D'Orville's manuscripts contain texts of post-classical, and a few classical, writers, as well as his own collections on the Greek anthology and collations of Theocritus. Clarke's are chiefly New Testament, patristic, and liturgical.

biblical commentaries. The 232 manuscripts classed as *Latini Patres* or *Scriptores Ecclesiastici* include medieval as well as patristic theology. Of Latin classics there are 311 manuscripts (1–130, poets; 131–311, prose writers). The large miscellaneous section (Canon. Misc.) consists of 576 manuscripts as varied in character as their title suggests. The chief classes of manuscripts in this section are (1) minor theology; (2) medicine, astronomy, astrology, and alchemy; (3) grammar, logic, metaphysic, scholastic philosophy, and Aristotelian commentaries; (4) canon and civil law; (5) literary Latin pieces by Italian writers of the Renaissance.

Although the catalogue of Canonici Greek and Latin manuscripts had been completed except for its index by 1843, it was not published until 1854.[1] It does not include Canonici's 262 liturgical manuscripts. These were incorporated by Coxe into a series of liturgies drawn from various collections to which he gave the name of Misc. Liturg., and had to wait for the appearance of the *Summary Catalogue* before they were catalogued in print. The Canonici Italian manuscripts, 301 in number, are mainly fifteenth-century. They include works of Dante, Petrarch, and other Italian poets; numerous translations of Latin classical and patristic works into the vernacular; legendaries and books of devotion. They were catalogued by a Bodleian reader, Dr. Wellesley's friend, the Count Alessandro Mortara. Mortara's manuscript copy was bought in 1858 for £201 from his executor, the Abate G. Manuzzi. Wellesley, who instigated its purchase, arranged for its publication; it appeared in 1864 with a preface from his own pen but a very inadequate index.[2]

Coxe had no sooner finished cataloguing the Canonici collection than Gaisford decided that he should take in hand a catalogue of all Bodleian Greek manuscripts other than those of Canonici, D'Orville, and Clarke, which had their own catalogues.[3] For this he already had his descriptions of the Meerman and Saibante collections, and he worked away steadily on the remainder until 1852. He had to guide him for most of his task, not merely the old lists in the 1697 catalogue of Bodleian manuscripts, but the fuller descriptions which Dr. Gerard Langbaine had made in the seventeenth century but never published;

---

[1] As *Codices Graeci et Latini Canoniciani* (pars III of the Bodleian quarto series of catalogues). Daremberg refers to it in 1853 as 'depuis longtemps imprimé mais point encore mis en vente', *Notices et extraits des manuscrits medicaux*, p. 7.

[2] *Catalogo dei manoscritti italiani che sotto la denominazione di Codici Canoniciani Italici si conservano nella Biblioteca Bodleiana*. Numbered pars XI in the quarto series. A number of Italian vernacular pieces are to be found in other sections of the Canonici collection.

[3] 'Dean decided that I should now commence the Baroccian (collection)': Coxe's diary, 10 Nov. 1843.

Bandini's full-scale catalogue of the Laurentian Library at Florence served him for a model, and he had the constant assistance and encouragement of the great Dean Gaisford. Coxe's catalogue was published by the University Press in 1853 as the first volume in a quarto series of catalogues of Bodleian manuscripts[1] of which the Canonici catalogue appeared in the following year as *Pars Tertia*. It is comprehensive, for, though it does not include the Greek manuscripts in the D'Orville, Canonici, and Clarke collections, references to them are incorporated in the index. It was the first catalogue of its kind to be undertaken for an English library and may be regarded as Coxe's best work.

The catalogue includes (1) the large collection of 244 massive Greek manuscripts (in which patristic and Byzantine theology and the works of grammarians and scholiasts predominate) formed by Giacomo Barocci of Venice and presented in 1629 by the then Chancellor of the University, William Herbert, Earl of Pembroke; (2) twenty-seven theological and liturgical manuscripts, which bear the name of another and more famous Chancellor, Oliver Cromwell; (3) twenty-nine others, almost all theological, and of which a large proportion are from the library of the monastery of the Trinity at Chalce, given in 1629 by that travelled diplomat, Sir Thomas Roe; (4) the ninety-two manuscripts, again chiefly theological, exegetic or liturgical, given by a third and greater Chancellor, Archbishop Laud, the gem of whose collection was the seventh-century Graeco-Latin Codex E of the Acts of the Apostles; (5) fifty-four manuscripts, some post-classical, some patristic, others liturgical or hagiological, which came in 1659 in the library of the learned John Selden; (6) miscellaneous acquisitions, received at various times, from Sir Henry Savile, Sir Ralph Winwood, and others, of biblical, patristic or liturgical, and classical manuscripts, bearing pressmarks Auct. D, E, or F; (7) thirty-nine manuscripts, chiefly adversaria of classical scholars, which formed part of the multifarious collections of Dr. Richard Rawlinson; (8) the post-classical authors and theological and exegetical writings, in large part from the sixteenth-century library of Bishop Pellicier, bought at the Meerman sale; and (9) the various patristic and liturgical and other manuscripts (among them the archetype of Arrian's Epictetus) from the library of the Veronese collector Giovanni Saibante.

Although one would hardly expect it from its title, Coxe's catalogue also contains descriptions of the classical and theological adversaria of that great scholar, Isaac Casaubon (d. 1614); the notebooks in

[1] *Pars prima recensionem codicum Graecorum continens.*

93

which Dr. Gerard Langbaine, Provost of Queen's College (d. 1658), entered his still valuable lists of contents of Bodleian and Oxford college manuscripts; Dr. Grabe's (d. 1711) excerpts from Greek patristic writers and collations of Septuagint manuscripts; and the manuscripts bequeathed by James St. Amand (d. 1755), which, though in the main Theocritean adversaria, include papers of Sir John Norreys relating to affairs on the Continent in Elizabeth's reign.

Having completed his Greek and Canonici catalogues, Coxe turned in 1854 to the rich collection of manuscripts presented to the university in 1635–40 by Archbishop Laud. For its contents, as for those of other seventeenth-century donations, readers had been hitherto dependent upon a catalogue published in 1698. Laud's manuscripts, other than those in Greek or Oriental languages, are divided into two categories—Latin and miscellaneous. The distinction is deceptive, for the former class of 118 manuscripts only comprises the classical and biblical (and not all the biblical) manuscripts which came from Laud; these and the Greek manuscripts having been separated from their companions, in or about 1790, for shelving in the Auctarium. The majority of the 757 miscellaneous manuscripts are also in Latin. Theology predominates; but liturgies, hagiology, canon law, astronomy, and medieval chronicles are all represented. Most of the English vernacular manuscripts in this section are Middle English poetry, religious prose pieces, and Wycliffite translations of the scriptures. But there are a few Anglo-Saxon manuscripts of importance, above all the Peterborough Version (Chronicle F) of the Anglo-Saxon Chronicle (MS. 636). Among the few historical manuscripts of later date, mention may be made of Sir George Carew's collections for Irish history (MSS. 526, 610–15).

The catalogue of Laud, published in 1858,[1] was the last of Coxe's own catalogues. From that time forward library administration and the preparation of the new general catalogue of printed books engrossed his hours and energy. His catalogues of manuscripts were well up to contemporary standards. Nowadays they would be regarded as deficient in technical description, particularly in their almost entire neglect of illumination and of binding. A modern cataloguer would give the measurements of his manuscripts. He would state the character of the script, note changes of hand, assign provenance, and note the mode and date of acquisition. Later publications of *initia* have since made possible the identification of numerous pieces which Coxe left anonymous. But his *expertise* as a palaeographer was great. He had, however, an unusual tendency to postdate early scripts: a large

---

[1] As *Partis Secundae fasciculus primus* in the quarto series.

proportion of the Laudian manuscripts from Würzburg and other continental religious houses, attributed by him to the tenth century, are now generally accepted as belonging to the ninth.

4. HACKMAN'S AND MACRAY'S CATALOGUES
(Tanner, Rawlinson, and Digby)

Coxe was not alone in his cataloguing. The completion of the three-volume General Catalogue of Printed Books in 1843 set Hackman free to turn to manuscripts. 'Rather dread his intervention', Coxe wrote in his diary. Bandinel put Hackman to catalogue the English historical papers and correspondence of the seventeenth century and other manuscripts bequeathed in 1735 by the antiquarian Bishop Thomas Tanner. The Tanner collection contains a portion of the correspondence of Mr. Speaker Lenthall (d. 1662) and miscellaneous civil war papers which Dr. John Nalson removed from the office of the Clerk of Parliament;[1] the correspondence and ecclesiastical papers of Dr. William Sancroft, Archbishop of Canterbury (d. 1693), and numerous other papers and pamphlets illustrating English history in the late sixteenth and the seventeenth centuries; part of the correspondence of Archbishop Gilbert Sheldon, Dr. Arthur Charlett, Dr. John Moore, Bishop of Norwich, and others, and miscellaneous seventeenth-century correspondence, including that of Tanner himself; letters and papers of Sir Henry Spelman; various manuscripts from Anthony Wood's collections; seventeenth-century correspondence and papers of the Hobarts, a Norfolk family; and a mass of papers, chiefly of the seventeenth century, relating to Norfolk, Suffolk, and Norwich diocese. When all these heterogeneous packets first came in, their contents were thrown together into one chronological series without regard to their origin. Their arrangement, or want of it, dates back to 1741, when Thomas Toynbee of Balliol put in order and summarily catalogued the whole in manuscript. Hackman now started upon the Tanner collection, but was soon drawn away again to edit the supplementary volume of the General Catalogue of Printed Books. When that appeared in 1851, he returned to his work on the Tanner manuscripts; and eventually his full catalogue with its very much fuller index was published in 1860 as *Pars Quarta* of the quarto series.

The vast gatherings of that omnivorous collector of manuscripts, the non-juror bishop, Dr. Richard Rawlinson, swamped the small

---

[1] The other portion of Nalson's collection came into the possession of the Duke of Portland, and while at Welbeck was calendared by the Historical Manuscripts Commission. It has recently been deposited, by His Grace, in the Bodleian Library.

library staff when they arrived in 1755. But by 1771 they had begun to be numbered in what is known as the Old List. Further portions were arranged and listed by Bliss and Bandinel in 1809–12. Bandinel arranged, very methodically, the series called Rawlinson B, while Bliss catalogued, with other sections, a series named Miscellaneous, which subsequently became Rawlinson D 1–407. Reay was subsequently employed to re-reference the manuscripts of the Old List into two new classes, marked A and C. Of these A was formed in 1831; C was not completed till 1850 when Macray was set to work on the collection.[1] As yet only half of Rawlinson's gift was listed, and it was only after Coxe took office that steps were taken to ascertain its yet unknown extent. Of this Macray has left a brief account.

Every corner of the Library was examined, and cupboard after cupboard was found filled with manuscripts and papers huddled together in confusion, while, not least, a dark hole under a staircase, explored by me on hands and knees, afforded a rich 'take', including many writings of Rawlinson's non-juring friends. The whole number of volumes thus brought to light amounted to about 1300.[2]

Macray produced in 1862 the first volume of a Rawlinson catalogue: it embraced classes A and B.[3] This is not the place to enumerate all the varied contents of the Rawlinson collection, which have been so well described by Macray himself in his *Annals*.[4] Let it suffice here to say that the 500 volumes of Class A, of which some sixty are medieval, relate, like the Tanner manuscripts, principally to English seventeenth-century history, and include the State Papers of John Thurloe, Secretary of State under the Commonwealth (MSS. 1–73), as well as correspondence and official papers kept by the diarist, Samuel Pepys, while Secretary to the Admiralty (MSS. 170–95, &c.). Class B (520 manuscripts) is partly heraldic (MSS. 1–146); partly historical (English chronicles and historical collections; MSS. 147–257); partly topographical, arranged in alphabetical order of counties (MSS. 258–474); partly Irish (MSS. 475–514). The Irish manuscripts, some of which are historically important, are chiefly from Sir James Ware's collection. Many of the heraldic and topographical manuscripts came from Sir Peter Le Neve.

In the year after publication of his first volume of the Rawlinson

---

[1] Dr. R. W. Hunt on 'The Cataloguing of the Rawlinson MSS., 1771–1844', in *Bodleian Library Record*, vol. ii, pp. 190–5.

[2] *Annals*, p. 236.

[3] *Codicum R. Rawlinson classes duae priores*, published as pars V, fasc. 1 in the series of quarto catalogues. The catalogue of class A had been completed by Apr. 1858: Curators' minutes.

[4] pp. 231–51.

catalogue, Macray was taken away from the manuscript department to work on the General Catalogue of Printed Books. Yet he kept himself in touch even then with manuscript work, both inside the library by working overtime on a calendar of Clarendon Papers, and outside it by editing the *Evesham Abbey Chronicle* for the Rolls Series and several volumes for the Roxburghe Club, as well as by starting on a calendar of the muniments of his college of Magdalen, which was to occupy him for fourteen years (1864–78). He produced in 1868 the work by which he remains best known, his *Annals of the Bodleian Library*. And he found time to fulfil simultaneously the duties of chaplain at Magdalen and at New College, and of curate in the city church of St. Mary Magdalene.[1]

A change came for him in 1870. Magdalen presented him to the college living of Ducklington, of which he was to remain rector for forty-two years. Residence in a country rectory permitted only half-time work in Bodley. So he limited his attendance to three days a week, and returned to the manuscript department as a special assistant. Working away in the far study on the right of Duke Humphrey, he produced the second volume of his Rawlinson Catalogue in 1878.[2] This covers the 989 manuscripts of Class C, which is of a more miscellaneous character than the two classes he had previously catalogued. Its principal contents are theological, legal (chiefly English common law), and historical. The theological manuscripts comprise medieval Latin works as well as English tracts and commonplace books of the seventeenth and eighteenth centuries, some bearing upon English church history. There are also to be found in this section numerous medical manuscripts, both medieval and modern, and various volumes in Middle English, chiefly religious prose.

At this point Macray was diverted from the Rawlinson manuscripts to recatalogue the collection given to the library in 1634 by Sir Kenelm Digby. Its 236 manuscripts, the great bulk of which had been given to Digby by his Oxford friend, Thomas Allen of Gloucester Hall, are, with few exceptions, medieval, and are mainly of the twelfth to fourteenth centuries and of English provenance. Their cataloguing presented greater difficulty than did the seventeenth-century papers of the Rawlinson collection; but Macray's skill as a cataloguer had increased as he gained experience, and his work was now not inferior to that of Coxe.

---

[1] Materials for Macray's biography are to be found in the account which he has himself given of his career and published works in his *Register of St. Mary Magdalen College*, N.S., vol. vii, pp. 53–59.

[2] *Codicum R. Rawlinson classis tercia cum indice trium classium*, published as pars V, fasc. 2, in the series of quarto catalogues.

The Digby collection is rich in material for the study of medieval science. The subjects most prominently represented in it are astronomy and mathematics, astrology and alchemy; Aristotle and the schoolmen, logic, metaphysics, and natural science; medicine, medieval theology, medieval Latin and Middle English poems, chronicles of English history and hagiologies of English saints. Its most prized treasure is the earliest text of the famed *Chanson de Roland* (MS. 23). Macray's catalogue, begun in 1878, was ready for press by Midsummer, 1881, though it was not published[1] until 1883.

5. CALENDARS (Clarendon, Carte, and Charters)

The Tanner and Rawlinson catalogues had revealed the astonishing richness of the Bodleian in sources for English seventeenth-century history. To the Lenthall and Sancroft papers of the one, and the Thurloe and Pepys papers of the other, there fall to be added two other great collections which go respectively by the names of Clarendon and Carte. The state papers of Edward Hyde, first Earl of Clarendon, came into the Bodleian through various channels, but in the main by bequest from Clarendon's great-grandson, Lord Cornbury, in 1759. Of the 149 volumes which make up the Clarendon collection, the first ninety-three comprise the papers which Clarendon amassed for his *History of the Rebellion*, the correspondence of the Royalist court in exile under the Commonwealth, and state papers for the period of Clarendon's own post-Restoration ministry; all arranged in a chronological series covering the years 1608–89.[2]

An official calendar of the papers in this series was undertaken in 1866. It was at first entrusted to the Rev. Octavius Ogle, Fellow of Lincoln College, and to Macray. Mr. Ogle abandoned his share of the task when he had brought his calendar down to 1645, and it was taken over from him by a Bodleian assistant, W. H. Bliss. Ogle and Bliss's work, covering the years 1523–1649, was published in 1872 as the first volume of a *Calendar of Clarendon State Papers*. Volume II, which was by Macray, had appeared three years before. It calendars the papers for 1649–54. Those for 1655–7 are included in a third volume of the *Calendar*, also by Macray, published in 1876. Further publication was suspended in consequence of the limited extent of the sales,[3] and, though Macray carried on his calendar in manuscript

[1] As pars IX of the quarto series.

[2] The work of arrangement appears to have been carried out in part by Coxe, with possible assistance from Macray, between 1858 and 1863; but in 1842 Frederic Madden saw more than fifty volumes that had been recently bound. Bodl. MS. Eng. hist. c. 155, p. 168.

[3] Macray, *Annals*, p. 227.

as far as 1659, historians had to wait till 1932 before a fourth volume, incorporating Macray's work, appeared under the editorship of Mr. F. J. Routledge.

It was Coxe's intention that the publication of the *Calendar of Clarendon State Papers* should be followed by a calendar of similar documents collected by the historian Thomas Carte (d. 1754). The Carte manuscripts, acquired for Bodley in 1753–7 and 1778, chiefly illustrate Irish and English history for 1560–1720. In large part derived from the Ormonde archives in Kilkenny Castle, they contain the correspondence and official papers of James, first Duke of Ormonde, 1640–89, as well as of two earlier holders of administrative office in Ireland—the Lord Deputy, Sir William Fitzwilliam, 1561–95; and the Attorney General, Sir John Davies, 1603–18. Other component parts of the collection are the papers on English public affairs of the Hastings and Wharton families (16th–17th centuries and 1603–1716 respectively); the correspondence, chiefly on English naval matters, of Edward Montague, first Earl of Sandwich, 1643–71; and papers of Sir David Nairne and others relating to the Stuarts in exile, 1689–1720.

The greater part of this extensive collection remained in boxes until 1862, when Macray arranged it for binding in 288 stout volumes. It was reported upon by Messrs. Hardy and Brewer[1] in 1864, and more fully in 1871 in the 32nd *Report of the Deputy Keeper of Public Records*. At length in 1877 Coxe obtained the Curators' reluctant consent to the engagement of the services of Edward Edwards for the purpose of calendaring the letters and miscellaneous papers which make up 164 volumes of the collection.[2] Edwards had had a chequered career. At one time an assistant in the British Museum of which he subsequently became the historian, he will be always honoured as the pioneer of the Free Library movement. As such he had been chosen, but had not long remained, first librarian of the Manchester Public Library. For the past six years he had been in Oxford, employed on rearranging and recataloguing the Queen's College Library. In his top hat and frock coat, and with his long white whiskers, he presented a very Victorian, if by now a rather dilapidated, figure. From 1877 to 1883 he worked away in Bodley upon the Carte calendar. But redundancy was always Edwards's fatal fault. When he had completed his work, and had received £1,320 in payment, the Curators were glad to dispense with his further services. In 1887 a few pages of the calendar were set up in proof, and Bishop

---

[1] *Report upon the Carte and Carew papers in the Bodleian and Lambeth Libraries.*
[2] Curators' minutes, 28 Apr. 1877.

Stubbs was asked as a Curator to report on its suitability for printing. He found it confused and inaccurate and reported 'that it could not be given to the world without such an amount of labour in the way of correction as would be equivalent to the making of a new abstract'.[1] The bishop's verdict has passed unquestioned, and the slips of Edwards's calendar, chronologically arranged, repose in manuscript, laid down in seventy-five thick folio guardbooks.

The Carte calendar was the last of Edwards's works. The closing scenes in his tragic life have been sketched by the Baptist Minister who gave him shelter at Niton, where he lies buried:[2] 'Late in the summer of the year 1885 Edward Edwards was seen wearily ascending the Shute at Niton in the Isle of Wight. All his belongings he pushed before him on a handcart. So forlorn was his appearance that a passing stranger enquired as to his condition, and drew from him the pathetic story that he had nowhere to go, and no roof to sleep under that night. Edward Edwards and money were never partners.'

Coxe had long hoped that he would have himself found leisure to calendar the large accumulation of charters and rolls which had come to the library by gift from past benefactors.[3] Their number exceeded 20,000. Anthony Wood, Thomas Tanner, and Richard Gough had made the largest contributions to this total. (1) Wood got his deeds from Christ Church. They comprise original deeds of the various religious houses with whose properties that college was endowed. Chief among them were Oseney Abbey; the priories of St. Frideswide and Littlemore; the priories of Wallingford, Daventry, and Tunbridge; certain small priories in Essex, and St. Wolstan's hospital in Worcester.[4] (2) Over 2,000 came in Bishop Tanner's bequest in 1736. They arrived in a saturated state, the barge in which they were brought having sunk in the river on its way to Oxford, but had been arranged and digested by the antiquary, Edward Rowe Mores of Queen's College.[5] They relate chiefly to the counties of Norfolk and Suffolk, and include muniments of the abbeys of St. Benet of Holm and of St. John's, Colchester, as well as the evidences of certain land-owning families—the Hobarts, Jernegans, and Cranes. (3) Gough's deeds also relate in the main to East Anglia. A part derive

[1] Library Records, 'Papers relating to the proposed publication of Edwards' Calendar of the Carte Papers, 1886–8'.
[2] Rev. John Harrison in *Library Association Record*, 4th ser., vol. v (1938), p. 261. A full account of Edwards is to be found in the Life which Thomas Greenwood published in 1902, *Edward Edwards, the chief pioneer of municipal public libraries*.
[3] He notes, for instance, in his diary on 22 Aug. 1863, that he was working on Oseney and Oxford charters most of the day.
[4] Turner, *Calendar of Charters and Rolls*, pp. iii–xiv.
[5] Macray, *Annals*, pp. 211–12.

from the earlier collection formed by Sir Peter Le Neve and these include a few Paston family papers. Le Neve's manuscripts came into the possession of Thomas Martin ('honest Tom Martin') of Palgrave, who added to them a fine series of muniments relating to the town and abbey of Bury St. Edmunds.[1] Eventually a portion of the Le Neve–Martin collection was bought by Gough, who also acquired other deeds formerly in the possession of the Norfolk historian, Francis Blomefield.

Other Bodleian charters are traceable to Rawlinson, Dodsworth, Carte, Furney, and Douce. (4) About 500 deeds came from Dr. Richard Rawlinson, among them a number relating to Yorkshire religious houses which had been gathered together by the Leeds historian, Ralph Thoresby.[2] (5) Yorkshire again predominates among the original deeds bound up in a volume of Roger Dodsworth's collections (MS. Dodsworth 76). (6) There were also deeds of the Hastings family, the earls of Huntingdon, from the Carte collection. (7) A tiny collection of eighteen deeds received in 1755 under a bequest from Richard Furney, Archdeacon of Gloucester, is remarkable for containing no fewer than three royal confirmations of Magna Charta.[3] (8) Francis Douce's are no more than ninety-eight in number and miscellaneous in their nature, but of fine quality.[4]

Being himself unable to undertake the work of calendaring, Coxe sought for and found a helper at hand in William Henry Turner, a retired Oxford chemist. Turner had given up his drug-shop to turn record-agent. Self-taught, he had gained experience in working on the Oxford City archives, and it was through his instrumentality that the records of the Archdeacon's Registry were transferred to Bodley. He was engaged in 1870, in the first place to calendar the Wood charters,[5] and this expanded into the *Calendar of Charters and Rolls preserved in the Bodleian Library*, published in 1878. Useful as this work is, it has many flaws, as may be seen from Macray's profusely corrected copy on the open shelves of the Bodleian reading-room.[6] Unfortunately, it also fails to distinguish *fonds*—the various collections which were thrown together for the purpose of the calendar.

---

[1] For notes on some early twelfth-century grants from the abbots of Bury, see Turner's paper 'on seals attached to Charters in the Bodleian Library' in *Transactions of the Royal Society of Literature*, 2nd ser., vol. x (1874), pp. 505–20.

[2] Macray, *Annals*, pp. 247, 251, n. 1.

[3] Op. cit., p. 252; Turner, *Calendar*, pp. xii–xiv.

[4] They are fully calendared in the Douce Catalogue of MSS., pp. 70–74. Only a few of them are noted in Turner's *Calendar*.   [5] Curators' minutes, 10 Dec. 1870.

[6] Some of the worst mistakes are cited by Nicholson in *Statements of the Needs of the University* (1902), p. 142.

In consequence of what Coxe described as 'the increased interest taken in topographical, genealogical and biographical subjects',[1] Turner was set to card-index in his spare time the topographical collections made by Bishop Tanner's friend, Browne Willis, for the *History of Buckingham*, the *Survey of the Cathedrals*, and Willis's other published works.[2] Then, when the *Calendar of Charters* was finished, his services were retained in order that he might index that vast ocean of fact, the material collected by the great antiquary, Roger Dodsworth (d. 1654), for the *Monasticon Anglicanum*, a projected Baronage, and a projected history of Yorkshire.[3] But after he had indexed the first seven of 161 volumes, and seen his index privately printed, a lingering illness and early death ended his persevering labour.[4]

[1] Minutes, 25 Oct. 1873.
[2] The Willis manuscripts are calendared in the *Summary Catalogue*, vol. iii, pp. 578–602. Turner's slip-index remains in the Bodleian reading-room, and is available for readers.
[3] Curators' minutes, 11 May 1878.
[4] Macray gives an account of him in his *Annals*, p. 392.

Chapter VI
Orientalia, Prints, and Coins

Section I
ORIENTALIA

1. THE ORIENTAL DEPARTMENT

ALTHOUGH no separate Oriental department was as yet officially recognized, throughout the greater part of the nineteenth century one of the two sub-librarians was a Semitic scholar. The youthful but learned Alexander Nicoll, elected sub-librarian in 1814, held that office until his appointment to the Regius Chair of Hebrew in 1822. Reay (1828–60) combined his library post with that of Laudian Professor of Arabic. When Reay fell ill in 1856 the Curators resolved to appoint an under-librarian who should succeed to the regular office upon the next vacancy.[1] Bandinel offered the post to William Wright, a brilliant young Orientalist who had just become Professor of Arabic at Trinity College, Dublin. Unfortunately it became known in Oxford that Wright had delivered a lecture in Dublin in which he declared that the people of Canaan were Semites, and not, as stated in the Book of Genesis, the children of Ham. This was too strong meat for Oxford theologians. Bandinel was badgered into withdrawing his nomination, much to his own subsequent discomfort, for the Curators censured him for so doing,[2] and Max Müller spoke to him with such directness that he and Bandinel were not on speaking terms for a year.[3] Wright joined the staff of the British Museum a few years later, and ended his life as Professor of Arabic at Cambridge.

Payne Smith combined unimpeachable orthodoxy with the patronage of the incoming Vice-Chancellor, the influential Dr. Jeune. His appointment as deputy to Reay naturally led to his succeeding as sub-librarian when the old man retired in 1860. It must be confessed that he was more devoted to Syriac than to librarianship, and Coxe had later to tell him 'that he worked more for himself than for Bodley'.[4] He laboured away at a great Syriac lexicon, and resigned library office in 1865, on being appointed Regius Professor of Divinity. He was to become one day a Dean of Canterbury.

The selection of a successor to Payne Smith caused trouble. Coxe

---

[1] Curators' minutes, 5 Nov. 1856. [2] 31 Oct. 1857.
[3] Max Müller, *My Autobiography*, p. 252.
[4] Diary, 21 June 1862.

consulted Max Müller, then a Curator, as to the qualifications of Edward Cowell, late President of the Sanskrit College at Calcutta, who had recently returned home from India; and Max Müller ended what was probably an embarrassing interview by offering himself as candidate. 'He will never be content to be subordinate,' Coxe wrote in his diary. Nevertheless, on reflection, he began to think that 'Max' would be a good man to have. And Max Müller was content to try it out. 'If you will give me a trial', he wrote to Coxe, 'I shall try whether, even rather late in life, I cannot learn to go in harness. I know you can get on with most horses; but if, after a trial, you find me no go, tell me so, and I shall always cheerfully trot back to my own stables.'[1]

There was a movement on foot, however, to press the claims of Macray, prompted less, perhaps, by an appreciation of the merits of that capable assistant than by dislike of Max Müller's nationality and of his liberalism. He was not merely a liberal and a rationalist, but a German liberal and pushful withal, and for that reason had suffered unmerited defeat in his candidature for the Chair of Sanskrit. A battle was fought out in letters to the press and in broadsheets circulated to Convocation. Max Müller's nomination was challenged on the ground of pluralism: since 1854 he had been Professor of Modern European Languages at a salary of £500. Coxe made answer pointing out that 'the necessities of the Bodleian Library require an under-librarian specially conversant with Oriental literature'. The Curators accepted Coxe's nomination on the understanding that Max Müller should resign his Curatorship; Macray circularized his supporters asking them to withdraw their opposition; and Max Müller was elected. Yet there is no doubt that Macray was bitterly disappointed.

'I do not anticipate comfort to myself', Coxe wrote of the new appointment. Nor did the experiment work. Little more than a year later, one cold morning in January 1867, Max Müller startled his chief by telling him that he had been advised to pass the rest of the winter in the south of France, and the next two or three winters also. He suggested that Cowell, whom he had supplanted, might succeed him. This was not to be, for Cowell was elected instead to the Professorship of Sanskrit at Cambridge. A successor to Max Müller was found in the Rev. J. W. Nutt, a Fellow of All Souls and a student of Samaritan. Rumour was not wanting that the appointment was a job engineered by the Vice-Chancellor, Dr. Knyvett Leighton, who certainly was Warden of Mr. Nutt's college.[2] Nutt held office until his

[1] Library Records, 'Letters to H. O. Coxe, 1855–81'.
[2] There is a clear allusion to this episode in an article on 'The Future of the Bodleian Library' contributed by Mr. Compton Reade to the magazine *Belgravia*,

appointment to the College living of Harrietsham in 1879. Almost from the first he had the assistance of Dr. Adolf Neubauer, a native of Austria-Hungary. Neubauer, whose real first name was Abraham, is reported to have had a humorous turn and to have possessed the shrewdness of his race. In his youth he had fought under Kossuth at the storming of Buda-Pesth. Since then he had made himself a learned Hebrew scholar and an accomplished linguist. He was first engaged in 1868 to catalogue the Hebrew manuscripts in the library which he had come over to inspect two years before; and, when the amiable Hackman resigned through illness in 1873, Neubauer's qualities were recognized by his appointment to the vacant sub-librarianship despite the fact that the senior sub-librarian was also a Hebraist.

2. SEMITIC COLLECTIONS

The *Hebrew* section of the library, begun in Sir Thomas Bodley's lifetime, and strengthened by some fifty manuscripts received from Archbishop Laud and by many printed books from Selden, had been much amplified by the purchase in 1693 of the collections of Pococke and Huntington, the former of which included about 100 and the latter about 225 Hebrew manuscripts. One hundred and ten more came in 1817 with the Canonici collection. But earlier acquisitions were completely eclipsed in 1829 by the purchase of the great Oppenheimer library, containing some 5,000 volumes, of which 780 were manuscript. This at once gave the Bodleian first place among libraries of Hebraica.[1] Down to 1840 the British Museum itself had no more than 200 Hebrew manuscripts.

From 1844 the Bodleian, at Dr. Pusey's instigation, was steadily adding to its Hebrew literature. In that year it bought 483 volumes from the library of the lexicographer Gesenius. Four years later the library of the Jewish bibliophile, H. J. Michael, came up for sale at Hamburg. The British Museum bought Michael's printed books; his manuscripts, numbering 862 volumes, were secured by Bodley for the sum of £1,030. Smaller collections acquired in the next few years were the fifty-nine manuscripts, stated to have been collected in Italy (MSS. Michael adds.) bought in 1850 from the Berlin firm of Bisliches

vol. xxv (1875), p. 180: 'The radical error is that ability and industry in the subordinates are seldom or never rewarded by promotion. The prizes of the institution, namely the posts of Sub-Librarian, when vacant are commonly jobbed away to some fellow who happens to be a friend of the existing Vice-Chancellor, and who brings with him neither antiquarian knowledge nor acquaintance with the routine of the Library.'

[1] Dr. Steinschneider testifies to this in a letter to Bandinel, 28 May 1849. 'Le fond hebreux (*sic*) surpasse maintenant tous les autres bibliothèques, tant en livres imprimés qu'en MS.' Library Papers: 'Steinschneider's catalogue: Letters from the compiler'.

for £100, and the seventy-two volumes of manuscripts, chiefly from Leghorn, bought for £108 in 1853 from the library of the Austro-Italian scholar, Professor Reggio of Goritz. Almost every year the Bodleian was spending considerable sums on systematic purchase of Hebrew printed books and manuscripts, in the main from Asher, the Berlin bookseller;[1] and Dr. Moritz Steinschneider, whom Bandinel invited (through Asher) in 1847 to catalogue the Hebrew printed collection, reports that about 2,100 volumes were added to it between 1844 and 1857.[2]

For references to Hebrew printed books readers had hitherto depended upon the general library catalogue, supplemented by the separate catalogue of the Oppenheimer collection. Steinschneider's learned *catalogus*[3] is in Latin. It is as elaborate as it is hard to use, being part catalogue, part bibliography. It gives no pressmarks and contains a large number of books *not* in Bodley. Steinschneider was at work upon it for eleven years, and it cost the library in editor's salary and in printing the then considerable sum of £2,050.[4] A catalogue of all the library's Hebrew manuscripts, superseding Uri's Latin catalogue, was commenced by Dr. Neubauer in 1868, though not completed till 1886.[5] It incorporates the few biblical codices of the Kennicott collection deposited by the Radcliffe Trustees in 1872, and such Samaritan manuscripts as had been acquired since Uri's publication.

Interest in the *Samaritan* dialect revived in the sixties. Convocation was induced in 1868 by Dr. Pusey to vote a sum of £360 for the purchase of certain supposed Samaritan manuscripts; but they were found on examination by 'a gentleman who could only see with a small part of one eye' to be only Arabic texts written in Samaritan characters. So the purchase was not completed, and the manuscripts were allowed to go to Lord Crawford.[6] A fragment of a Samaritan Targum, bought next year along with two Hebrew manuscripts from Dr. Neubauer for £200, provided occupation for the sub-librarian, Mr. Nutt, who edited it with an introduction on Samaritan history and literature.

[1] Macray, *Annals*, p. 353.
[2] *Catalogus librorum Hebraeorum*, col. 1. They were referenced Oppenheimer Adds.
[3] *Catalogus librorum Hebraeorum in Bibliotheca Bodleiana*, Berlin, 1852–60. Neubauer rightly says that it should rather be called *Bibliotheca Judaica* up to 1732.
[4] Letter from Coxe to the Vice-Chancellor, 5 Mar. 1861.
[5] *Catalogue of the Hebrew manuscripts in the Bodleian Library and in the College libraries of Oxford*, issued as pars XII of the quarto series of catalogues of Bodleian manuscripts.
[6] Macray, *Annals*, p. 384; author's annotated copy.

In 1859 Payne Smith was started by Pusey on a catalogue of the 205 *Syriac* manuscripts which the library then possessed.[1] They included, in addition to those in the older collections, the sixty Syriac manuscripts named MSS. Dawkins after the eighteenth-century traveller James Dawkins, who collected some, but by no means all, of them. Payne Smith's catalogues saw publication in 1864.[2] It is in Latin and arranged by subject, the main heads being biblical, liturgical, theological, and grammatical.

The library's small collection of *Ethiopic* manuscripts, then thirty-three in number, was catalogued in 1848 by Dr. August Dillmann,[3] who had been employed in the preceding year to catalogue those in the British Museum. The Bodleian owes nearly the whole of its Ethiopic manuscripts, including one of the few copies of the Book of Enoch, to that full-blooded but unveracious Scot, James Bruce, explorer of the sources of the Nile. Bruce's collection, which contained also seventy important Arabic manuscripts, had been offered by him to the British Museum nearly seventy years before for £25,000; and, after subsequent abortive attempts had been made to sell it by auction, was bought for Bodley in 1843 for £1,000.

The great Oriental collections accumulated in the seventeenth century had made the Bodleian peculiarly rich in *Arabic* manuscripts. No fewer than 1,400 are briefly described in Uri's catalogue of 1787. The Arabic section of that work was supplemented and corrected in Alexander Nicoll's catalogue in 1835.[4] And now the library's store of Arabic was yet further increased by the Bruce collection, and subsequently, in 1872, by the Radcliffe Trustees' deposit of their Oriental manuscripts. Those that were in Arabic came in the main from the collection of George Sale, translator of the Koran (d. 1736), which had been bought for £157. 10*s*. in 1760 for the Radcliffe Library. Additions were otherwise scanty. Far greater attention was being paid in this period to Hebrew, Persian, and Sanskrit literature.

3. PERSIAN MANUSCRIPTS

Before 1844 the Bodleian's Persian collection was but small in comparison with its wealth of Arabic literature. The number of Persian manuscripts in Uri's catalogue was only 177, though they included

[1] Some of these are manuscripts in the Arabic language but in the Syriac alphabet, or rather in an adaptation of that alphabet called Karshuni.

[2] As *Pars Sexta* of the quarto series of catalogues of Bodleian manuscripts.

[3] Dillmann's catalogue was reissued as *Pars Septima* of the quarto series. Accessions received since 1848 have been recently catalogued by Dr. Ullendorff.

[4] *Catalogi codicum manuscriptorum Orientalium Bibliothecae Bodleianae Pars Secunda, Arabicos complectens.*

some fine illuminated manuscripts from the Pococke, the Greaves, and the Marsh collections. But in 1844 an opportunity arose for increasing them threefold. Sir William Ouseley had recently died, leaving behind him a library of more than 400 choice manuscripts gathered in Persia whither he had accompanied his brother, Sir Gore, on a political mission, and they were bought *en bloc* for the Bodleian for £2,000. One of them, a beautiful text of the Rubaiyat of Omar Khayyam, written at Shiraz in 1460 (MS. Ouseley 140), deserves special mention, for it was from a copy of this manuscript, made by his great friend, Edward Cowell, in the winter of 1855–6, that Edward Fitzgerald made his first acquaintance with the old Persian poet, and so was led on to make his own immortal rendering.[1]

The year after the Ouseley purchase, Sir William Walker presented close on a hundred Persian manuscripts and as many in Sanskrit (with a few in Gujarati and Hindi), collected by his father, General Alexander Walker, while political resident in Baroda. And in 1858–9 the Bodleian authorities acquired, through more than one channel, and so reunited, the yet larger and finer collection formed by Sir Gore Ouseley for which they had previously in vain been in treaty.

Sir Gore, who was one of the founders of the Royal Asiatic Society, had begun forming his library while resident at Lucknow and continued to add to it under yet more favourable circumstances at Teheran, while ambassador extraordinary to the Persian court (1810–14). Thirty-five choice manuscripts from Sir Gore's collection were bought for Bodley in 1858 for £500 from his son, the well-known musical composer, Sir Frederick Gore Ouseley. Sir Frederick, who held the Chair of Music in Oxford and did much to make his subject fashionable there, may have sold other of his father's manuscripts direct to Bodley; but the great bulk of them came thither by gift in 1859 from another collector, Mr. J. B. Elliott of the Bengal Civil Service. That the gift was made to Bodley is due to the action of Mr. Fitz-Edward Hall, afterwards librarian of the India Office. He visited Elliott who was living at Patna, old, infirm, and blind; and, though Elliott had bequeathed his manuscripts to the British Museum by will, persuaded him to alter his disposition of them and present them to Oxford.[2] Thus Sir Gore's collections came together again, though some are referenced MSS. Ouseley adds. and others as MSS. Elliott; and the latter designation also includes the books which Elliott had himself collected over a period of fifty years at Lucknow and

[1] G. Cowell, *Life and letters of E. B. Cowell*, p. 154.
[2] Letter from Fitz-Edward Hall to Bandinel, 6 June 1859, in Library Papers, 'Letters relating to the Elliott Donation of MSS.'

elsewhere in India. Elliott accompanied his manuscripts with a valuable series of Indian and Bactrian coins, some Oriental gems and intaglios, and (possibly less welcome) a consignment of Eastern swords and daggers. The weapons eventually found a more suitable home in the Pitt-Rivers collection at the University Museum, to which they were transferred in 1902.

The Ouseley–Elliott collection (if one may so describe it) consists of just over 600 volumes, containing an abundance of good Persian and Indian illumination. A manuscript of Firdausi's great epic poem, the Shâhnâma (MS. Ouseley adds. 176), furnishes an example of the Timurid early-fifteenth-century school of Persian painting. But the period best represented is the late fifteenth and the sixteenth century, the high-water-mark of Persian art. Though there is no indubitable example of the work of Bihzâd, greatest of Persian painters, a copy of the Khamsah or epic poems of Nawâ'i, written in 1485 in four volumes (MSS. Elliott 287, 408, 317, 339), is adorned with miniatures of his school, one of them signed by his pupil, Kâsim 'Alî. Persian art and literature enjoyed an Indian summer in the court of the Moghul emperors. The finest specimen that Bodley has of Indian book-production is the copy of the poet Jâmî's *Baharistân* or *Spring-garden*, from the library of the Moghul Emperor, Shâh Jahân (MS. Elliott 254). And there are delightful picture-books, produced for the courts of Jahângir and Shâh Jahân, both of the Moghul school (MSS. Ouseley adds. 170, 171, 173) and its successor, the Rajput school (MS. Ouseley adds. 166). Little wonder that Coxe spoke of the Persian manuscripts as 'all the rage'.[1]

Even before the acquisition of the Gore Ouseley collection, proposals had been made for the recataloguing of the Persian manuscripts in Bodley. An article on Persian literature had been contributed by Edward Cowell, then a young graduate from Magdalen Hall, to the volume of *Oxford Essays* for 1855 and had attracted immediate attention. Bandinel was commissioned to engage his services.[2] But Cowell went off to India, and it was only in 1866, after he had returned from Calcutta, that he was able to make a start upon the work. His appointment to the Sanskrit Chair at Cambridge, in the following year, made it necessary to find someone else to take his place. A continental scholar, Dr. Eduard Sachau, was engaged for the purpose;[3] but Dr. Sachau, too, was carried off to be a Professor —of Semitic Languages at Vienna—and the catalogue project made slow progress until a young German from Munich, Dr. Hermann

---

[1] Coxe's diary, 19 Sept. 1859.   [2] Curators' minutes, 3 May 1855.
[3] Minutes, 27 Feb. 1869.

Ethé, was simultaneously engaged by the Curators to take up the task of cataloguing the Persian manuscripts in Bodley,[1] and appointed by the Secretary of State for India to catalogue those in the India Office Library. Although elected three years later to a professorial chair at Aberystwyth, Dr. Ethé continued to devote his spare time to work in the Bodleian, and at length produced his catalogue of Persian manuscripts in 1889, though without an index.[2]

Dr. Ethé's catalogue includes 254 Persian manuscripts from the Fraser collection. James Fraser (d. 1754) amassed his Eastern manuscripts while in the employ of the East India Company early in the eighteenth century. Most of them, it is said, had once belonged to the royal library of Ispahan.[3] They were bought in 1758 from his widow for £500 by the Radcliffe Trustees,[4] who deposited them in Bodley in 1872. The Fraser collection also contains a few Turkish and forty-one Sanskrit manuscripts.

4. INDIA AND THE FAR EAST

It was Colonel Boden's foundation of a *Sanskrit* Chair in 1827 that gave the first impulse to the study of that language in Oxford. Horace Wilson, the first Boden Professor (appointed in 1832), had been in the service of the East India Company and, while in India, had collected a considerable library of Vedic and classical Sanskrit manuscripts. This he sold to the university in 1842 for £500, and the 540 volumes in which it is now bound up form the nucleus of the Bodleian Sanskrit collection. Mention has already been made (p. 108) of the manuscripts, part Persian and part Sanskrit, presented by Sir William Walker in 1845. The Sanskrit and other Indian manuscripts in the Walker collection are a hundred in number. In 1849 the Bodleian purchased for £350 the 160 Sanskrit manuscripts, almost half of them Vedic, which Dr. W. H. Mill, Regius Professor of Hebrew at Cambridge, had collected while he was Principal of Bishop's College, Calcutta. As the result of these three accessions, Max Müller was able to report in 1856[5] that the Bodleian collection of Sanskrit manuscripts, despite its lack of systematic completeness, was the second best in Europe, being surpassed only by that of the East India Company.

It was hoped that the few manuscripts given in 1859 by Mr. Fitz-

---

[1] Minutes, 9 Feb. 1872.

[2] *Catalogue of the Persian, Turkish, Hindustani, and Pushtu manuscripts in the Bodleian Library*, Part I. The Persian manuscripts. Issued as pars XIII of the quarto series of catalogues of Bodleian manuscripts.

[3] Macray, *Annals*, p. 216.

[4] Richard Pococke, *Tours in Scotland* (Scottish History Soc. vol. i), p. 180; Radcliffe Trustees' minutes, 26 Apr. 1758.

[5] Library Papers, 'Report by Max Müller on Aufrecht's catalogue, 1856'.

Edward Hall (to whom Bodley is indebted for the gift of the Elliott collection) would be the precursor of the remainder of his library.[1] That was not to be; but in 1872 the Radcliffe Trustees deposited the forty-one early but fragmentary Sanskrit manuscripts which James Fraser had purchased at Surat and other places in India, and had rightly described as 'the first collection of that kind ever brought to Europe'.

Fraser had formed the intention, from which he was prevented by death, of translating the Veda. It was the Vedic literature that specially attracted the interest of Max Müller and led him to offer to prepare a Sanskrit catalogue. But already by 1855 he found that his engagements would not permit him to complete the task; so he recommended the Curators to engage the services of his compatriot, Dr. Theodor Aufrecht,[2] who had followed him to Oxford to assist in his edition of the Rig-Veda. He still hoped to supply the Vedic section, but the sole result was that, when Aufrecht's catalogue was issued,[3] the Vedic manuscripts were not included.[4] It was a great catalogue, however, for it was pioneer work, as Max Müller explained to the Curators:

Sanskrit literature [he said] has not been studied for much more than half a century; and the number of original texts, edited by European scholars from MSS., is as yet very small. ... The extent of Indian literature is hardly inferior to that of Greece and Rome, and to write a catalogue of one of the largest collections of Sanskrit MSS. involves an amount of reading and research which those are best able to appreciate who have read, for the first time, MSS. in any foreign language, the age, the character, the author and the very title of which had not been previously ascertained. ... In order to catalogue the MS. of a work not yet published, there remains, in many cases, nothing to be done but to read the greater part of the MS. itself.[5]

Aufrecht's catalogue, like the other Bodleian catalogues issued at this time, is in Latin. Manuscripts are arranged in it according to their subjects—the great epics, the Tantra or mystical doctrine, the Kavya or court epics, drama, and so on; and the catalogue concludes with a

[1] He wrote to Bandinel on 24 June 1859: 'It is my intention that these MSS. be followed before any great lapse of time by my entire collection which embraces about 1200 written volumes in the Sanscrit, Hindi, Persian and Urdic languages, which I have procured in India during the last fourteen years.' Letter entered in Curators' minutes.   [2] Curators' minutes, 3 May 1855.
[3] The first part of Aufrecht's catalogue was issued in 1859. The completed work appeared in 1864 as *Pars octava* of the quarto series of catalogues of Bodleian manuscripts.
[4] The defect was not supplied till 1905 when volume ii appeared under the editorship of Winternitz and Keith.
[5] Library Papers, 'Report by Max Müller on Aufrecht's catalogue, 1856'.

synopsis of the collections, in which alone Vedic literature finds a reference. 'It is indeed a *catalogue raisonné*', Max Müller wrote; 'nay, it will be the skeleton of a history of Sanskrit literature.' Mention has already been made (p. 44) of how Aufrecht came near to being appointed a sub-librarian in 1861. In the following year he became Professor of Sanskrit at Edinburgh University, and later returned to Germany to fill a similar chair at Bonn.

Pali is the literary language of Burma, Siam, and Ceylon, and is the sacred language of Buddhism as Sanskrit is of Brahmanism. The two dozen Pali manuscripts then in Bodley were listed by Dr. Oscar Frankfurter in 1880, and his list was published by the Pali Text Society.[1]

Among the languages of India, *Tamil* has the earliest literature after Sanskrit. The Bodleian made the beginning of a collection in this Dravidian tongue by buying a hundred Tamil manuscripts at an auction sale at Hodgson's in 1860 for the small sum of £30.

Chinese books began to come into the library in the lifetime of the Founder, and, though none could read them, were sufficiently prized to be kept within the 'grates' or cupboards at the eastern end of Duke Humphrey. Some more came in the libraries of Laud and Selden, and others by the gift of East India merchants. The first systematic attempt to expand these small beginnings was made in 1856, when 1,100 works were bought for fifty guineas from the family of the Rev. E. Evans, principal of the Anglo-Chinese missionary college at Malacca. Two years later £26 was paid to Mr. James Summers for a collection of treatises on religion, history, and philosophy. The establishment of a Chair of Chinese in Oxford in 1875 directed closer attention to these studies. Next year a catalogue was published of all Chinese works in Bodley,[2] the number of which was further increased through gifts made by Admiral Laurence Shadwell in 1877 and by Dr. Lockhart in 1879.[3]

Section II
PRINTS, PORTRAITS, AND COINS

5. PRINTS AND DRAWINGS

Prints and drawings, portraits, and coins and medals were all alike placed under the charge of Bodley's librarian. The first notable collection of prints to be received by the Bodleian was that known as

---

[1] *Journal*, 1882, pp. 30–31.
[2] A *Catalogue of Chinese works in the Bodleian Library*, by Dr. Joseph Edkins.
[3] The stages in the growth of the Chinese collection have been set out by F. Madan in the *Summary Catalogue of Western Manuscripts*, vol. v, pp. 918–19.

Gough maps, which came in the Gough bequest of 1809. This consisted of topographical engravings and drawings, in addition to maps, all arranged in massive folio volumes under English counties.

Gough's donation was followed in 1834 by that of Francis Douce. The Douce collection of woodcuts, engravings, and drawings[1] carries the impress of its capricious and eccentric collector, who was attracted by the curious more than by the beautiful, and who was in the first place an antiquary and secondly an art connoisseur. His tastes directed Douce specially to the later Middle Ages and to the sixteenth century; to Germany and the Netherlands. He bought so effectively within these limits that his collection of early prints, that is for the period 1450–1550, is one of the most representative to be found outside the National museums of western Europe. His woodcuts are even superior to his engravings on metal. Both are of the highest value for the study of the German Renaissance. The early engravers, Albrecht Dürer, Lucas van Leyden, and the Little Masters, are all well represented. But Douce was far from confining himself to Germany and the Northern Primitives; for the bequest included drawings, engravings, and etchings of various Italian schools; drawings by Holbein and other German–Swiss artists; studies by Watteau and others of the French school; and, among the English drawings, a number of Rowlandsons which Douce acquired direct from the artist.

The third large collection came in 1837 from Mrs. Sutherland. It contained over 19,000 prints, almost invariably in fine condition, of which 15,000 were portraits and the remainder chiefly topographical. They formed extra illustrations to Clarendon's *History of the Rebellion* and Burnet's *History of his own Time*, and swelled those works into sixty-one elephant folios. The portraits are of historical personages of the seventeenth century. All are listed in a printed catalogue which Mrs. Sutherland herself compiled.[2] And she subsequently added to her gift by presenting a grangerized copy of Walpole's *Royal and Noble Authors* expanded to twenty volumes, and yet other extra-illustrated books.

A fourth collection must also be mentioned, though it was not

[1] For the Douce collection see J. G. Mann on 'Francis Douce as a collector' in the *Bodleian Quarterly Record*, vol. vii, pp. 360–5, and K. T. Parker, *Catalogue of the Collection of Drawings in the Ashmolean Museum*, vol. i (1938), p. xi. The best of the drawings are reproduced in Sidney Colvin's *Drawings of the Old Masters in the University Galleries and the Library of Christ Church* (1903–7). The fifteenth-century woodcuts are catalogued, and many of them illustrated, in Campbell Dodgson's *Woodcuts of the Fifteenth Century in the Ashmolean Museum* (1929).

[2] *Catalogue of the Sutherland Collection*, 1837. For the Sutherland collection generally see Macray's *Annals*, pp. 331–5.

under Bodleian management. This was the vast collection of engraved portraits made by Frederick William Hope and accepted from him by the university in 1858. It was lodged in the gallery of the Radcliffe Camera, along with an art library of about 4,000 volumes, and was placed under the charge of a separate keeper. It was described at the time as containing 140,000 portraits, and, in addition, 70,000 topographical prints and twenty to thirty thousand engravings of natural history.[1] The portraits are in the main of the seventeenth and eighteenth centuries, and, though their value is historical rather than artistic, they are singularly representative, and in point of number nearly approach the corresponding series in the British Museum and in the Bibliothèque Nationale.

Dr. Wellesley, himself a considerable print-collector, had pressed for the establishment of a print-room, and, in a memorandum which he addressed to the Curators in 1857, had suggested that the south range of the Picture Gallery might be used for that purpose. He was asked to report on the state of the prints and drawings and to suggest means for rendering them accessible. But nothing followed till five years later when he and Dr. Liddell—Dean of Christ Church and by this time a Curator—were appointed a committee[2] to consider whether the prints could not be arranged in one room, with or near the Hope collection. They reported (not very correctly) that the Bodleian collections had nothing in common with the Hope engravings and ought not to be combined with them, but should be transferred to the print-rooms in the Randolph Galleries. Only prints 'belonging to or closely connected with books as distinct from pure art' should be retained in the Bodleian. Their report[3] was accepted; and the Curators were empowered by statute to place prints and drawings in the Radcliffe Camera or in the Randolph Galleries.[4] Acting on this authority they transferred to the latter building in 1863 the great bulk of the Douce prints. The Randolph or University Galleries were clearly their proper home, for there they supplemented the great collection of Michelangelo and Raphael drawings bought from the Lawrence collection in 1846 by Lord Eldon and other subscribers, and the Rembrandt and Claude etchings and drawings presented to the Galleries in 1855 by Mr. Chambers Hall.

[1] *Gentleman's Magazine*, 1862, pt. 1, p. 787. The portraits and topographical prints now form the Hope collection of engraved portraits in the Ashmolean Museum. The collection of engravings of natural history no longer exists as a separate entity.
[2] Curators' minutes, 12 Dec. 1857; 7 Nov. 1862.
[3] Dated 7 Mar. 1863 and printed as a Council paper.
[4] *Corpus Statutorum*, addenda, p. 677.

Gough maps and the Sutherland collection remained in Bodley, and were now, in 1864, joined by the prints and such extra-illustrated books as Britton's *Beauties of England and Wales* and Nichols's *Literary Anecdotes*, which came as part of Captain Montagu's bequest—a collection, it must be admitted, much inferior in quality to either Gough or Sutherland. Bodleian interest concentrated increasingly upon topographical drawings: hence the acquisition of such grangerized works as the copy of Dukes's *Antiquities of Shropshire*, for which the library paid in 1841 the sum of 40 guineas,[1] and that of Harwood's *History of Lichfield*, bought for £50 in 1878.

6. PORTRAITS

The transfer of pictures mentioned in Chapter I (p. 9) as made from the Bodleian to the Randolph Galleries in 1845, though including a self-portrait of Robert Walker, two fine Reynolds (James Paine and his son, and the Duke of Grafton), and a Battoni portrait of Garrick, had been otherwise in the main confined to landscapes and subject-paintings. In 1861 the sending of a second consignment seems to have been contemplated, and Coxe was asked to confer with the Curators of the galleries over the transfer of pictures having artistic rather than historical value.[2] Radical reformers suggested that *all* the pictures in the Bodleian should be sent to the galleries.[3] Nevertheless, the Bodleian Picture Gallery, though no longer a mixed art collection, was left as a portrait gallery. A few large state portraits hung in the Sheldonian Theatre, and the Music School and Ashmolean Museum had their own series; but the Bodleian Picture Gallery remained the official repository of university portraits. Care was taken over their preservation, and Mr. Hogarth of the Haymarket was called in, in 1862, to carry out much-needed repairs to frames and canvases.

So when, in 1867, Albert Edward, Prince of Wales, presented his portrait after his residence in Oxford as an undergraduate, it was hung at the entrance to the Picture Gallery; and the series of Chancellors was maintained by the addition of Sir F. A. Grant's portrait of the Earl of Derby in 1858. A bust, by Woolner, of Mr. Gladstone, made after he had ceased to be the university's representative in Parliament, was unveiled with some ceremony in 1868. In the late seventies, G. F. Watts was the portrait-painter most in favour: portraits of Coxe, of the Marquis of Lothian (founder of the Lothian Essay Prize), and of Dean Stanley, all come from his studio.

[1] Macray, *Annals*, p. 341. [2] Curators' minutes, 14 June 1861.
[3] Compton Reade in *Belgravia*, vol. xxv (1875), p. 177.

7. COINS

It was no uncommon thing, in the late seventeenth and eighteenth centuries, for a great library to possess a cabinet of coins and medals. The Bodleian coin collection, dating back to a gift made by Archbishop Laud in 1636, is the earliest example of its kind in this country, just as Dr. John Barcham, from whom Laud obtained his coins, is one of the first known English collectors.[1] Laud's collection and the additions made to it in the next hundred years by Sir Thomas Roe, Ralph Freke, Dr. Buck, and others, consisted mainly of Roman and Graeco-Roman with a sprinkling of Greek coins. Thus the fairly large collection, presented in 1704 by William Raye, British Consul at Smyrna, of coins said to have been collected by his cook,[2] was composed chiefly, as might be expected, of Greek autonomous and imperial coins of western Asia Minor. The Ashmolean collection,[3] made by Elias Ashmole himself and increased by subsequent donors, was generally similar to that of the Bodleian, to which it was united in 1860; while that in the Radcliffe Library, formed by its Keeper, Francis Wise (d. 1767), seems to have been limited to Roman republican and imperial coinage. The Radcliffe collection was left behind by the Trustees when the Camera was handed over by them in 1861, and was brought across to the Bodleian coin-room.

We have had occasion already to mention (pp. 11, 35) the name of the Rev. Charles Godwyn, Fellow of Balliol College, as a Bodleian benefactor. In addition to the books and pamphlets and the residue of his property (amounting to £1,050) which he left to the library on his death in 1770, he devised to it a well-catalogued coin collection of picked specimens, having acquired the cabinet of coins formed by Heneage Finch, fourth Earl of Winchilsea (d. 1726).[4] Godwyn may be regarded as the real founder of the Bodleian Greek collection. Yet so soon did memory of his liberality fade, that another donor, Browne

---

[1] As has been pointed out by Dr. Grafton Milne in the *Numismatic Chronicle*, 6th ser., vol. vi, p. 173. See also his note in *Oxoniensia*, vol. i, p. 159.

[2] Macray, *Annals*, p. 173.

[3] The Ashmolean coin-cabinet had been burgled in 1777 by a Frenchman named Le Maître, whom some identify with the notorious French revolutionary, Jean Paul Marat. His trial, of which an account is entered on the fly-leaves of Bodl. Gough Oxf. 70, is the subject of two interesting articles by Mr. J. M. Thompson in the *English Historical Review*, vol. xlvi, pp. 96–117; vol. xlix, pp. 55–73. Most of the coins stolen by Le Maître were recovered. No trace, unfortunately, is to be found in the Ashmolean collection of the 'treasure trove of large gold coins lately found in Sussex' which Charles II, by warrant dated 14 Aug. 1672, ordered John Shelley of Thackham to deliver to Elias Ashmole. Brit. Mus. Add. MS. 32094, fol. 266.

[4] The Winchilsea coins illustrated in Haym's *Tesoro Britannico* (1720) can all be identified with specimens in the Godwyn collection.

Willis, came to be credited with his gift; and it is but recently that
Godwyn has received the recognition due to him.

Francis Douce directed his attention mainly to Roman imperial
bronze,[1] and the series which came to Bodley under his will in 1834
was fine and comprehensive. Douce derived some of his rarer specimens from the French numismatist D'Ennery, whose great collection
was dispersed in 1788. There is no justification for calling Douce's
gift a Douce–Keate collection, for the Keate cabinet to which Douce
himself refers was but a receptacle, like the Calder cabinet which he
bought for 8 guineas.[2] The very large number of bronze coins of the
Emperor Probus to be found in the Bodleian coin-trays suggests an
untraced hoard; and there is direct evidence for a collection of
Roman imperial silver (Hadrian to Quintillus), presented by Dr.
John Reynolds in 1719, being part of a hoard found at Exeter.[3]

The Bodleian series of British, Anglo-Saxon, and English coins
dates from the benefactions of the Buckinghamshire topographer,
Browne Willis, made between the years 1739 and 1760. For although
such coins were once to be found in the Laudian cabinet, the Parlia-
mentarian antiquary, Sir Simonds D'Ewes, had been allowed to
borrow most of them in 1650 upon giving a bond for £500, and the
university neither recovered the coins nor exacted the bond.[4] The
Willis collection[5] was rich in gold and silver, and was further strengthened through a valuable bequest received in 1795 under the will of
Thomas Knight of Godmersham Park. There were English coins
also in the Ashmolean coin-cabinet, and British and Anglo-Saxon
specimens in the small collection left to the Ashmolean in 1850 by
Dr. Ingram, President of Trinity and Keeper of the University
Archives. The Ashmolean likewise possessed a group of Northum-
brian *stycas* from a Hexham hoard; and both the Museum and the
Bodleian received from the Crown, in 1841, parcels of West Saxon
and Carolingian coins from the Cuerdale hoard which became reunited when the Ashmolean was merged in the Bodleian collection.
Irish currency came to be represented when Dr. Caulfield of Cork,
whom his friend Macray describes as an 'enthusiastic and untiring

[1] For Douce as a coin-collector see Dr. Grafton Milne in *Bodleian Quarterly
Record*, vol. vii, pp. 376–9.
[2] Bodl. Lib., MS. Douce e. 66, fol. 18v. Macray's statement (*Annals*, p. 484) that
the Douce collection 'included those of Calder, Moore, Roberts and Keate' consequently requires correction.
[3] Bodl. Lib., MS. Clarendon Press, c. 22, fol. 3. Two other lots, presumably from
the same hoard, are in the Corpus Christi College cabinet deposited in the Heberden
Coin Room in the Ashmolean Museum.
[4] Dr. Grafton Milne in *Bodleian Quarterly Record*, vol. vii, pp. 422–4.
[5] Described by Dr. Grafton Milne, op. cit., vol. viii, pp. 449–52.

Irish antiquary',[1] gave in 1866 a hundred specimens of the coins which the dispossessed King James II so plentifully struck in gun-metal.

One notable element in the Willis cabinet was its tradesmen's tokens. These were struck out of copper, or sometimes out of pewter, by enterprising shopkeepers between 1648 and 1673 to supply their customers with the small change in which the official coinage was defective. Browne Willis was the first numismatist to specialize in them, and he rightly claimed for his collection that it was 'the most numerous of any ever yet made'.[2] Tradesmen's tokens were again struck in England between the years 1760 and 1816. Specimens of this later period were bequeathed to Bodley in 1879 by its former sub-librarian, Archdeacon Henry Cotton.

The medieval and modern coinages of the European continent were but sparsely represented. There were medals, however, both English and continental. Dr. George Clarke of All Souls, dying in 1735, bequeathed his cabinet of medals of Louis XIV and Louis XV. That rather singular university benefactor, the Rev. Robert Finch,[3] gave his collection of Napoleonic medals. The long series of medals struck by the popes of Rome, though not first-rate artistically, have attracted many collectors by the interest of their portraiture. The fine Bodleian series derives from Dr. Richard Rawlinson, who prided himself on the fact that his collection was 'one of the most complete now in Europe'. He left it to the library, by codicil made to his will in 1752, with an annuity of 20s. (which was never paid) for enlarging and continuing the set.[4] It was extended through Godwyn's gift, as well as by a small collection bequeathed to the Ashmolean in 1847 by the Rev. J. W. Mackie of Christ Church. Of other Italian medals there was a fine series for the House of Medici, presented, like the Papal medals, by Dr. Rawlinson. But the gems of the Bodleian medal collection were the beautiful portrait-medals and plaques of the Italian Renaissance, which Douce collected and of which the chief lay hidden and unknown in a secret drawer of his cabinet.[5]

Till the Elliott collection came in 1860, Bodley had practically no Oriental coins. To Mr. J. B. Elliott it owes, not merely so large a portion of its Persian manuscripts, but the coins which he collected during his long residence at Patna. These were in part the historically

---

[1] *Annals*, p. 437, n.
[2] Willis catalogue 2 in the Heberden Coin Room.
[3] Miss Elizabeth Nitchie's *The Rev. Colonel Finch* (1940) is an entertaining biography of this eccentric.
[4] Macray, *Annals*, p. 247.
[5] *Bodleian Quarterly Record*, vol. vii, p. 364.

instructive coinages of Bactrian and Indo-Scythian kings; but there were specimens also of Indian dynasties, both pre-Islamic (the Gupta dynasty) and Islamic (the Pathan and Moghul rulers of Delhi). A small number of Indian coins collected by Sir Bartle Frere in the Punjab was bought in 1872 for £27. And in 1875 and subsequent years Sir Charles Warren presented numerous—but frequently poor —specimens of the coinage of the Mamelukes of Egypt and other rulers of the Near East, found in the course of his survey of Palestine.

Bandinel had been a numismatist; yet the state of the coin-room when Coxe took over was far from satisfactory. Its contents had greatly increased since Francis Wise published his catalogue[1] in 1750. Gifts were not combined in geographical and chronological series but were kept in separate cabinets under the names of their presumed donors. This system, such as it was, increased the difficulty of finding individual specimens, and yet failed to preserve effectively their provenance. For owing, it would seem, to lack of sufficient cabinets, collections became mixed. Browne Willis's collection was one of English coins: the Godwyn collection, which also contained English coins, was consequently placed in the Willis cabinet and its separate origin forgotten. All the bronze Roman imperial coinage received from the Radcliffe Trustees was emptied out of the cabinets which held it, and its identity irretrievably lost.

On Jowett's motion, the Curators set up a committee in 1860 to report upon the coins.[2] Some help in arrangement was given next year by Mr. W. Vaux, Keeper of Coins and Medals at the British Museum, though it was not till 1871, after his connexion with the Museum had ceased, that he was definitely engaged to arrange and catalogue the coins.[3] By 1878 he had produced six volumes of manuscript catalogue, including Greek, Roman, and English coins, as well as the Oriental coins of the Elliott collection. The Curators resolved that as little delay as possible should be made in getting the catalogue into a state in which it could be published.[4] Fortunately, on Vaux's own recommendation, they abandoned a design that would not have justified its cost. Vaux had catalogued over 15,000 pieces: but he had seldom been allowed to enter the jealously guarded coin-room, and much more than half its contents remained unlisted.[5]

[1] *Nummorum antiquorum scriniis Bodleianis reconditorum catalogus.*
[2] Minutes, 30 Oct. 1860.
[3] Minutes, 10 Dec. 1870; 11 Mar. 1871.
[4] Minutes, 27 Oct. 1877. Later, on 16 July 1881, when the idea of printing had been abandoned, Vaux was directed to arrange his manuscript for binding. It is now, with the other Bodleian coin records, in the Heberden Coin Room.
[5] *The Bodleian Library in 1882-7*, pp. 42-43.

Chapter VII

The Library Fabric: Old Schools and Camera

I. THE OLD SCHOOLS

AFTER the Logic School was handed over in 1845, the library ceased for a time to expand, but the need for additional room soon made itself once more felt. Bandinel presented a memorial to his Curators on the subject in 1853. They forwarded it to the Hebdomadal Board,[1] but the Board, engrossed with other matters, took no immediate action. Yet more space for book-storage was badly needed. The question of how it was to be provided was referred in 1855 to Gilbert Scott, the leading architect of his day. 'The increased room required', said Scott in his report,[2] 'is approaching double to that already possessed.' He rejected a suggestion that Bodley should follow the example set by Panizzi in the British Museum and cover its quadrangle with a glass roof. In its stead he advocated an extension programme by which the library should gradually absorb all the adjoining university buildings, not merely the ground-floor Schools, but the Proscholium, Divinity School, Convocation House, and Ashmolean Museum. Even this would not be enough. 'The University would do well', he concluded, 'to obtain full possession of the site of the Clarendon [Building], for, sooner or later, in spite of all you may now do, the Library must push out a second quadrangle in that direction.'

The Curators cannot be blamed if they let these wider projects stand over for another twenty years and concentrated their attention upon the ground-floor rooms of the Schools quadrangle. It will be remembered that of these the room adjoining the Logic School was still in use as the School of Music; that the Schola Metaphysicae and History School were given up to examinations; that the School of Moral Philosophy stored the Arundel Marbles; but that the School of Natural Philosophy on the opposite side of the quadrangle had for a time been virtually out of action.

[1] Hebdomadal Register, 1841–54, p. 289. The terms of the memorial are not recorded.

[2] Scott's report, presented in Dec. 1855, was printed by order of the Curators, 15 Nov. 1856, and reprinted by the Hebdomadal Council in a collection of reports on the Bodleian Library in 1880.

In November 1857 the Curators received a letter from the Vinerian Professor, Dr. Kenyon, suggesting that the Natural Philosophy School should be turned into a Law reading-room. For a hundred years the Vinerian School of Law had occupied the fourteenth-century university library over the Old Convocation House on the north side of the choir of St. Mary's Church. But, though suitable for a lecture-room, it was insufficient to hold a law library. Dr. Kenyon therefore proposed that Bodleian books on law and jurisprudence should be placed in the Natural Philosophy School, and that it should be fitted up as a school for law students. The Curators, doubtless impressed with the paramount need for book-storage, turned down the proposal,[1] but asked Council to sanction the use of the School for library purposes. At the same time one of the Curators, Dr. Wellesley, moved for a consideration of Scott's report with a view to the better adaptation of the Schools building to the uses of the library.

Gilbert Scott was no library specialist, and, as Wellesley remarked in a striking memorandum presented to the Curators in October 1858, his report did not go in search of any new and broad principle. As an architect he was of course alive to the need of strengthening floors to carry increased weights, and he had proposed to buttress the Schools outer walls in order to permit the storage of thirty to thirty-five thousand volumes in dwarf bookcases on the floor of the Picture Gallery—a big architectural change for producing a very small result. But there were better ways open. The genius of Panizzi had already evolved a new element in library planning, the self-supporting stack; and the iron library of the British Museum had revealed a method of library construction which needed only the invention of electric lighting and of air-conditioning to develop into the modern book-stack.[2]

If the British Museum plan were to be applied to the Schools, it would mean, Wellesley pointed out, a decision 'to strike away all the floors, and erect within and clear of the outer walls a pile or system of iron double bookcases from the ground to the roof, with light open iron floorings at distances of 7 feet the whole way up, and iron stair-

[1] Curators' minutes, 14 Nov. 1857. Lawyers had to wait another ten years before getting a reading-room, which was at length provided through All Souls throwing open to university graduates, and to other persons specially recommended, a reading-room in the well-stocked Codrington Library.

[2] Bodley had taken the first step towards stack-construction in 1845 when, on taking over the Logic School, it had not contented itself with wall-cases, which had served for the first-floor rooms, but had erected on the floor six double-sided wooden cross-cases. These cases were 11 feet high. It required only to carry them up a further 5 feet, so as to reach the ceiling, as was done at a later date, to produce a rudimentary stack.

cases clear of the wall-space; the whole entirely lighted from a glass roof: all the present windows to be blocked up, and the present roof removed except over the "H"'.[1] In other words, it would involve the gutting of the existing building, and the building up of iron stack within it, letting the outer walls stand free instead of imposing upon them the heavy strain of supporting wall-cases in addition to that of carrying floors weighted with floor-cases filled with thousands of books.

Had electric light been available at this date it would have avoided the need for top-lighting. As things stood, Wellesley advised against the sacrifice of well-conditioned floors and roofs. (The floors were in fact in far less sound condition than he imagined.) The art of glass-roofing, he rightly observed, was still in its infancy; and a building devoid of intervening solid floors would require complicated, troublesome, and costly appliances for warmth and ventilation. He therefore proposed a modification of the British Museum plan. The suggestion which he laid before the Curators was that at least one, and preferably two, ranges of iron-framed stack should be run down the middle of each ground-floor room and carried up through the flooring into the first-floor rooms; that wall-cases should be similarly continued through the flooring; and that pierced iron platforms should be inserted at mid-height in each room. Whether the Picture Gallery should be similarly treated might be left for future consideration. The scheme put forward had the advantage that one section could be taken in hand at a time, as ground-floor rooms became available.[2]

In presenting his report, Wellesley gave notice of a motion to apply for the use of the Moral Philosophy School. Council had in the meantime replied to the Curators' earlier application for the School of Natural Philosophy by saying that it could not as yet be given up without inconvenience to the university.[3] The establishment of a First Public Examination termed Moderations, in 1849, and the simultaneous creation of two new Final Honours Schools, namely, Natural Science and Law and Modern History, had greatly increased the need for examination-rooms, making it necessary in 1852 to use the Music School for that purpose and to fit up the Natural Philosophy School. But there could be no objection to removing the Arundel Marbles from the Moral Philosophy School, in which they were almost invisible. The Curators discussed the proposal and decided

[1] i.e. over the Old Reading-Room. See above, p. 6.
[2] Wellesley's report was printed as a Curatorial paper in 1858, and has been twice reprinted, namely, for Council in 1880 and for the Curators in 1894.
[3] Hebdomadal Council minutes, 1854–66, p. 218 (15 Feb. 1858).

to raise with Council the whole subject of allocating to Bodley the ground-floor Schools. At their request Council set up a committee which was directed also to consider simultaneously the accommodation required for examination-rooms and professorial lectures.[1] The need for library extension and for increased accommodation for university lectures and examinations were, in fact, inextricably linked. If the library was to take over the whole of the remaining University Schools, the university must find new schools.

The committee of Council and the Bodleian Curators, meeting in joint session on 28 May 1859, agreed that it was desirable that the whole Schools building should be given to the Bodleian at as early a date as possible, and that Council should be recommended to build new Examination Schools. Council accepted the first proposition and, a year later, on Jowett's motion, referred to a committee the subject of a new building for the Examination Schools.[2] In the meantime the problem of book-storage had been temporarily solved in an unlooked-for fashion.

2. ACQUISITION OF THE CAMERA

There was a general demand, voiced by the witnesses who gave evidence before the 1850 University Commission and approved by the Commissioners, for a spacious, well-warmed and properly ventilated reading-room, free from the buzz of conversation, in which books of reference might be placed on open shelves; likewise for evening hours of opening. None of these advantages were to be had in unlit Duke Humphrey; and one of the Commission's witnesses had described the Bodleian as 'practically useless to College Tutors during term-time, owing to its hours'.[3] The Curators did their best by ordering notices to be put up in Duke Humphrey enjoining silence on those who frequented it, as well as by directing that the best bibliographical books should be laid out on a table.[4] They further took power, under their 1856 statute,[5] to provide a room not far from the library ('*Camera* quaedam haud procul a Bibliotheca') in which new publications should be set out, and to which books and manuscripts might be taken for evening reading, the room to remain open from ten in the morning to ten at night. But where was this room, this 'camera', to be found? Bandinel, in giving evidence before the Hebdomadal

[1] 29 Nov. 1858; op. cit., p. 252.
[2] Hebdomadal Council minutes, 1854–66, pp. 275, 277, 303, 308.
[3] *Oxford University Commission Report*, 1852, Evidence, p. 154.
[4] Curators' minutes, 25 Oct. 1856; 13 Mar. 1858.
[5] *Corpus Statutorum*, addenda, pp. 563–4.

Board's committee in 1853, had suggested that a room in the Clarendon Building might be made available for use in the evening.[1] Scott proposed to take over for that purpose a room in the Ashmolean Museum. Gaslight, the sole illuminant then in vogue in public places, could be used with comparative safety in either building. In the daytime the Divinity School, below the Old Library, would serve as an excellent reading-room, 'a use to which, both from its great amount of light and its architectural beauty, it seems pre-eminently fitted'. And if Scott had had his way, he would have introduced decorative glass into its spacious windows and coloured design into its walls and vaulting.

It has ever been the way of our university to obtain additional space in old premises through drafting part of their contents into some new building. So the completion of new quarters for the Clarendon Press in 1831, and the appropriation of the old Printing House for university offices, professorial lectures, and certain scientific departments, had greatly relieved the pressure on the Ashmolean Museum and temporarily freed the Natural Philosophy School. And the erection of the University Galleries and of the adjoining Taylor Institution in 1845 had not merely provided further lecture-space, but, by allowing the transfer of the Pomfret Marbles, had made it possible to appropriate the Logic School to the Bodleian. The claims of art and modern languages had thereby been satisfied, and it was now the turn of science to make its voice unmistakably heard. Already in June 1849 a meeting of graduates had been held to press for the erection of a University Museum; and, before a year had passed,[2] the Hebdomadal Board had resolved that a new Museum should be built 'for a collection in illustration of Physical Science and of Natural History'. A committee of the Board spent two years in discussing alternative sites. At length, on 3 March 1853 Convocation agreed to the purchase of a plot of land in the Parks. The foundation-stone of the new University Museum was laid on 20 June 1855. It was destined to house not merely museums but scientific laboratories, professorial offices, and lecture-rooms.

The art principles of John Ruskin inspired the Rhenish-Gothic design of the new building; and Ruskin's close friend, Dr. Henry Acland, threw himself with enthusiasm into the scheme. Acland had become Keeper of the Radcliffe Library in 1851. That library was

[1] Bandinel's evidence is printed in the Committee's *Report to the Board of Heads of Houses*, pp. 325–8.

[2] 18 Mar. 1850; Hebdomadal Register, 1841–54, p. 185. A full account of the formation of the Museum has been given by H. M. Vernon and K. D. Vernon in their *History of the Oxford Museum*, 1909.

at the outset general in its character, but for forty years its purchases had been confined to medicine and natural history. It was natural, when science was given a home of its own in the new Museum, that books on science should be lodged there also; and a room in it was being set apart as a library. Acland had the wisdom to see that, if the Radcliffe books could be transferred to it to form the nucleus of a science library, it would not merely save much unnecessary duplication, but would set free Gibbs's rotunda in the Radcliffe Square and render that great building available for Bodley. As a witness[1] had already observed to the Hebdomadal Board's committee in 1853, the Radcliffe Library would make a perfect reading-room, like that other round reading-room which Panizzi had just planned for the British Museum.

So the next step followed almost inevitably. The Bodleian Statute, which authorized the Curators to find a new reading-room or 'camera' in proximity to Bodley, had been passed in May 1856; and six months had hardly elapsed when Council received a letter from Dr. Acland suggesting the immediate use of the Radcliffe Library for that purpose. They deferred their answer until Acland had obtained a reply to the proposal he had made simultaneously to the Radcliffe Trustees that the books contained in the Radcliffe Library should be removed to the Museum.[2] On 16 July 1857 Acland's proposal came before the Trustees and was accepted by them; and the Hebdomadal Council immediately appointed a committee to confer with the Trustees on the subject of the proposed transfer.[3] Negotiations had so far advanced that, a year later,[4] Council received letters from Dr. Acland and from Mr. Gladstone on behalf of the Radcliffe Trustees, formally offering the loan of the Radcliffe Library to the university for the purpose of a public library. And at length, on 12 June 1860 the Vice-Chancellor was in a position to announce to the university that the Radcliffe Trustees had signified their readiness to transfer the scientific portion of their library to the University Museum, and also to lend the Radcliffe building for the purpose of a reading-room or for any other purpose of the Bodleian Library; the building to remain

[1] The Rev. R. Hussey, later Professor of Ecclesiastical History; *Report to the Board of Heads of Houses*, p. 236.
[2] Hebdomadal Council minutes, 17 Nov. 1856. Acland's report to the Radcliffe Trustees, in which he recommended transfer of the Radcliffe books to the Museum, and of the building to Bodley, is printed by him as Appendix B to his *Report to the Radcliffe Trustees on the Transfer of the Radcliffe Library to the Oxford University Museum*, 1861.
[3] Hebdomadal Council minutes, 1854–66, p. 194.
[4] 14 June 1858, op. cit., p. 242. The course of subsequent negotiations may be traced from entries on pp. 276, 281–3, 306.

the property of the Trustees and to be maintained by them, no alteration being made in it without their consent.[1]

In the second week of August 1861 the Radcliffe books were transferred to the two first-floor rooms on either side of the central tower
of the newly completed Museum; and on 25 October the Curators
met in the Radcliffe Library to witness Acland hand over the keys of
the building to Coxe as Bodley's Librarian.[2] 'A wonderful day', Coxe
wrote in his diary that evening, after riding 'Punch' over to Wytham
and leaving him there to graze in the paddock for the winter.

There was a *quid pro quo*. It was inevitable that considerable
duplication should have arisen between the Bodleian and the Radcliffe libraries and that there should be gaps in each. The Bodleian
was entitled to receive all British publications under the Copyright
Act, and obtained many more donations, even of scientific books,
from abroad than did the lesser-known Radcliffe. The chief defect of
the Radcliffe Library lay in scientific transactions and periodicals; an
unfortunate cut in the annual grant for purchases from £500 to £200,
made by the Trustees in 1841, having inevitably led to the discon-
tinuance of many subscriptions. Bodley was far richer in this respect.[3]
A scientist, Mr. H. E. Strickland, Deputy Reader in Geology, had
pleaded before the University Commission for co-operation between
the Bodleian and the Radcliffe libraries in the purchase of scientific
literature and for the transfer to the Radcliffe of the books which the
Bodleian already had upon physical science.[4] Steps were immediately
taken to supply the Radcliffe's need for scientific periodicals. By a
statute passed in November 1861 the Curators took power to deposit
books on science in the University Museum.[5] Acland followed this
up by putting before the Curators a request from the science professors for certain periodicals and transactions which they wished to
maintain at the Museum for the prosecution of their scientific work.
The Curators agreed to make the loan asked for, for a term of five

[1] Acland's *Report to the Radcliffe Trustees*, 1861, appendix A.
[2] Acland was by this time himself a Curator, having been appointed in 1857 to the
Regius Chair of Medicine.
[3] Acland, *Report to the Radcliffe Trustees*, pp. 20–21. The inadequacy of the
grant may be judged from Acland's statement to the Vice-Chancellor in 1862 that
£500 a year would barely maintain a scientific library. It was restored to £500 in 1863,
and thereafter was gradually increased till it reached the sum of £1,500.
[4] *Oxford University Commission Report*, 1852, Evidence, p. 101. In a letter written
to the Vice-Chancellor, 22 Oct. 1862, Acland, referring to Mr. Strickland's evidence,
rightly insisted that the Radcliffe Library should be made as complete a scientific
library as possible and that the Bodleian should not waste money in competing with
it in the purchase of costly scientific works. Library Papers, 'Radcliffe Camera
Reports and Letters, 1857–86'.
[5] *Corpus Statutorum*, addenda, p. 652.

years, and approved regulations under which the books lent might be reclaimed on one week's notice.[1]

As befitted a building devoted to science, the Radcliffe Library had been lighted, since 1835, with that novel illuminant, gas. Gas-lamps on well designed bronze pillars stood on the gallery balcony, and others below the gallery. A nine-branched gas standard stood in the centre of the room.[2] For some years before the library was handed over, Acland had experimented in throwing it open to students on one evening a week.[3] The Bodleian Curators, on obtaining possession, resolved that the building should be used as a reading-room, that it should be kept open from ten in the morning until ten at night, and that it should be known henceforth as the Camera Radcliviana or Radcliffe Camera.

For now at length they had obtained the 'camera' or reading-room for which they had been searching, a room equally adapted for day and for evening use; and it was no longer necessary—at least for a time—to press for the surrender of the Divinity School. Further-more, the building could be made to provide the additional storage space that was urgently needed, pending the release of the ground-floor Schools.

3. THE CAMERA IN THE SIXTIES

The Camera was opened as a reading-room on 27 January 1862. '"Twill be a hideous thing', Coxe noted in his diary, 'but will I think work well.' The opening day proved a fiasco, and the expectant lib-rarian, looking in on the new reading-room, found not a soul inside. Despite notices, nobody had come. But knowledge of it grew, and, six or seven weeks later, Coxe was able to record that both Bodley and the Camera were in great request. 'It will be curious', he observed, 'to see if this grows, so as to become a new era in the use of a Library. It may be.'[4]

Let us take a peep into the Camera reading-room as it appeared in the sixties.[5] Above its mahogany folding entrance doors at the

[1] Curators' minutes, 4 Mar., 7 Nov., and 10 Dec. 1862.
[2] It was subsequently removed to the Museum. The bronze pillars of the smaller standards have been reused to form electric standards in the bays below the gallery.
[3] University Notices, 3 June 1856, 8 Oct. 1858.   [4] Diary, 15 Mar. 1862.
[5] The general appearance of the interior of the Camera may be deduced from an inventory of the property left in it by the Radcliffe Trustees (Library Papers, 'Radcliffe Camera Reports and Letters, 1857–86'); the unpublished recollections of W. R. Sims who was appointed to the staff in 1867 (Library Papers); the descriptions in the guide-books, particularly Parker's *Handbook for Visitors to Oxford*, 1858 ed., p. 75; and early prints, of which the best is that engraved from Mackenzie's drawing as heading to the *Oxford Almanack* of 1836 and reproduced in Ingram's *Memorials*, vol. iii.

top of the grand staircase hung Kneller's full-length portrait of Dr. John Radcliffe, whose marble statue by Rysbrack fills a niche over the door inside the reading-room. Strips of coco-nut fibre matting deadened the sound of footsteps on the stone floor. Plaster casts of the Apollo Belvidere, the Discobolus, and other well-known classical statues, given in 1825 by P. B. Duncan, stood at the foot of the great piers that supported the dome, and ringed round, like silent guardians, the central space. In the very middle of the room a round iron and slate table carried a small model of the 'Pancratiastae' or wrestlers. Over it a large metal pendulum was suspended by a cord from the top of the dome; when set in motion by the curious it was found to illustrate the earth's rotation.[1] Facing the door of entrance, and almost blocking the entry to the opposite bay, was an enormous cast of the Laocoon. This was flanked on either side by marble candelabra found in 1769 in Hadrian's Villa, much restored by Piranesi, and presented to the Radcliffe Library by Sir Roger Newdigate.[2] A copy of the Warwick Vase, the original of which had likewise come from Tivoli, perched itself precariously on the gallery balustrade above the Laocoon. Busts stood on pillars in the centre of each bay of the gallery, most notable among them being Roubillac's realistic portrait-bust of crabbed Dr. Frewin, a past benefactor to the Radcliffe Library. Two glazed cases under the gallery contained the Corsi collection of Italian marbles presented by Mr. S. Jarrett to the university in 1827 and subsequently removed to the Geology department in the New Museum. The Radcliffe Trustees had also left behind four coin-cabinets and, for the time being, various collections of non-scientific books and manuscripts.[3] These included Gibbs's architectural books and drawings; Dr. Frewin's classical and historical library; Mr. Viner's law-books; the Hebrew and theological library of their former librarian, Dr. Kennicott; and two collections of Arabic, Persian, and Sanskrit manuscripts, the one made by James Fraser, the other by Sale, the translator of the Koran.

The reading-room gallery, apart from two bays, was not as yet

---

[1] R. T. Gunther, *Early Science in Oxford*, vol. ii, p. 272.

[2] For this pair of candelabra see Michaelis, *Ancient Marbles in Great Britain*, 1882, pp. 593-4. According to a statement made by R. Churton to Convocation, 21 Mar. 1806, preserved in Bodl. G. A. Oxon. b. 19, Sir Roger Newdigate is reported to have paid £1,800 for them. The candelabra are now in the Pomfret Gallery in the Ashmolean Museum.

[3] The Radcliffe Trustees removed the printed books and manuscripts to their new library in 1867 (Library Records: 'Camera Reports and Letters, 1857-86') but redeposited the Oriental manuscripts in Bodley in 1872. In 1893 they presented to Bodley such of their non-scientific printed books as it did not already possess. The Viner collection never left the Camera, and was handed over in 1913.

INTERIOR OF THE CAMERA
from The Oxford Almanack, *1836*

appropriated to the library. It was approached by stone newel stairs at either end, and housed the Hope engravings. The bays under the gallery were handsomely furnished with the eighteenth-century mahogany bookcases, reading-tables, arm-chairs and stools, left behind by the Radcliffe Trustees. Here the readers sat in their quiet recesses. The staff worked at a green baize-covered table behind Laocoon, protected yet further from observation by a pair of crimson curtains. At that table the day keeper, H. J. Sides, took his seat clad in frock coat and tall silk hat: while at the door of the reading-room stood Bayzand, an old stage-coachman and now janitor—idiot Bayzand as Coxe called him when provoked—ready to entertain passing visitors with reminiscences of the coaching days before the new railway reached Didcot.[1]

Readers still entered the building through the iron gates opposite St. Mary's and crossed a large vaulted basement in order to reach the staircase that led them up to the reading-room. As Mr. Strickland had pointed out to the University Commission in 1852,[2] the basement only required the laying down of a damp-proof floor, the insertion of glass windows in the open arcades, and the fitting up of bookshelves to accommodate many years of library accessions. Coxe was of the same opinion; in a letter to the Vice-Chancellor of 10 December 1861, he wrote: 'I think it would be very advisable to go at once to Convocation for a sum of money to enclose and fit up the basement story in such a way as to enable us to provide rooms for books for many years to come, and to carry out the system of classification to which we are bound by statute.'

Having obtained the consent of the Radcliffe Trustees, the Curators commissioned Mr. Sydney Smirke to prepare a plan for the adaptation of the Camera basement to book-storage. The works which he planned and executed included glazed windows behind Gibbs's open-work iron grilles; the construction of the present entrance at the top of a flight of steps on the north side of the Camera; the making of a thoroughly dry floor; a heating apparatus; and bookcases round the walls and main piers. At a cost of £2,771 immediate storage-space was thereby obtained in the basement for 66,000 volumes.[3] The additional accommodation that this gave postponed for a season the need for further expansion; yet it was accepted that, before very long, the library must take over the Old Schools.

[1] His 'Coaching in and out of Oxford' is printed in the Oxford Historical Society's *Collectanea*, vol. iv. [2] *Oxford University Commission Report*, 1852, Evidence, p. 105.
[3] Decrees of 11 June 1863. Smirke's plans are preserved in a volume of plans among Library Records. They show that the shelving round the piers was at first carried up only to the spring of the arches.

Chapter VIII

The Library Fabric: Renovation and Extension

I. NEW SCHOOLS OR A NEW LIBRARY

ALTHOUGH the acquisition of the Camera had postponed the need for further expansion into the Old Schools, Council had agreed to their ultimate absorption by the Bodleian, and this entailed building new Schools. So, on Jowett's motion, a committee of Council was appointed in 1860 to investigate the building of new examination schools. A site for them had still to be found. The committee was in no hurry to report; and when it did so, two and a half years later (4 December 1862), it was to the effect that the most desirable site was 'the land between Kettle Hall and the outer gates of Trinity College', that is to say the area now in large part occupied by the New Bodleian Library; that the next best site was the King's Arms Hotel, if it were big enough; but that inquiry should be made as to the possibility of purchasing the property at the east end of Broad Street, where the Indian Institute now stands.[1]

Another site, almost equally central, came to be considered later. In the eighteenth and early nineteenth century Oxford's chief hotel had been the Angel in the High Street. There Dr. Johnson had stayed, accompanied by Boswell. Nelson had lodged there. And more recently Queen Adelaide, in visiting Oxford, had held in it her little court. But times had changed, and the Angel was for sale. It was eventually purchased for the university in 1865, and a committee, set up by Council to consider the uses to which it should be put, reported in favour of erecting new Schools upon the site.[2] With that end in view, the area was enlarged by the purchase of adjoining properties. At long last, on 6 December 1870, Council sought the assent of Convocation to a decree 'that it is expedient to proceed to the building of new Schools on the site purchased by the University in High Street', submitting to the House at the same time two alternative plans made by T. N. Deane, the architect of the Museum. Convocation jibbed at the probable cost, and threw out the decree by 51 votes to 31.

So the university had saddled itself with an expensive property in

---

[1] Council Committee minute-book, 1857–73, pp. 23–24.
[2] 10 Nov. 1866; ibid., p. 88.

the High, but had declined to take a decision as to its use, and new examination schools were as far off as ever. A step towards determining the issue was taken in February 1872, when delegates were appointed to report on the expediency of building new Schools on the site of the Angel Hotel, or of using the site for some other purpose. And when the delegates reported in favour of proceeding at once to build new Schools upon the site, their report was carried (30 May) in a thin house by 27 votes to 4 against. The next step was to find a design that commended itself to the university. One that was submitted a year later by Mr. John O. Scott showed a modern Gothic building, having a strong likeness to the Natural History Museum in South Kensington. Scott's plan was rejected in Convocation on 23 May 1873, mainly on aesthetic grounds, by 54 votes to 20.

Six months later, on 28 November, a fresh attempt was made. It was proposed that a new delegacy should be set up to proceed with 'the business of building New Schools on the site of the Angel Hotel'. A decree to that effect met on this occasion with strong opposition. It had hitherto been taken for granted that, whatever else happened, the Bodleian Library would remain where it was. But in the debate that ensued, Rolleston, one of the Curators, impressed with the growing congestion of the library buildings, argued that Bodley itself should be moved, and that a new library rather than new Schools should be built in High Street. Other speakers supported him. On a close division the decree was carried, largely through Coxe's intervention, by a bare majority of four votes (55 to 51). 'Shall catch it probably tomorrow', he entered in his evening diary.

The Curators met next day, and the reformers among them secured a committee 'for the purpose of considering the requirements and capabilities of the Library and of the sites adjoining'. Rolleston was on it; also Acland who shared Rolleston's views, Mark Pattison, and the two proctors. They were empowered to seek professional advice, and for that purpose called in an engineer and civil servant, Captain Douglas Galton, Director of Public Works and Buildings. Jowett was not at first on the committee—though he and two of his colleagues were subsequently added—but imparted his views to Captain Galton in the following characteristic letter:

Certain persons, calling themselves a committee of Bodleian Curators, got together lately behind my back and at a time which I choose to consider vacation. They have, I hear, requested you to report as to whether the present buildings and site can be rendered adequate to the demands of the Library. I consider that they are both quite adequate. It is therefore unnecessary for you to report on that point at all. But you will further understand that, whatever you may report, my mind is made up on the subject.[1]

Galton went rapidly to work, and on 25 April 1874, within five months of the appointment of the committee, Acland presented its conclusions to the Curators, with the report it had received from Galton six weeks earlier. The latter set out the structural alterations required in the existing building and the additions that would have to be made to it in order to provide adequate fire-protection and increased accommodation both for books and readers. It gave rough estimates of costs, totalling approximately £40,000; and it compared this sum with the £85,000 *plus* cost of site which, on Galton's calculation, would have to be spent in erecting elsewhere a new fire-proof library building adapted to meet Bodleian needs for half a century.

A choice had to be made between the adaptation of the existing structure and the erection of a new library building on a new site. Acland and Rolleston, the leading spirits on the committee, were in favour of the radical course. As regards convenience, they said in their report, there was 'no doubt a better library than the Bodleian is —better for the storing and arrangement of books and more commodious for students—could be built on a new site. The element of risk arising from non-isolation could also be got rid of. Further, it would be possible to build a Librarian's residence in immediate proximity to the Library, which is a matter of no small importance.' If a new library were built elsewhere, it would no longer be necessary to proceed with the erection of Examination Schools upon the Angel site, since the Old Schools and the evacuated rooms of the Bodleian would serve instead. That site would therefore be available for other uses: a new Bodleian might even yet be erected upon it.

But there were other and more suitable places than the Angel site on which a new library could be built. There was the ground occupied by the Botanic Gardens, if those were removed to the Parks. There was what came in future years to be known as the Broad Street site, 'extending from Trinity Gate to the road to the Park from west to east, and from Trinity Gardens to Broad Street from north to south'. This, the committee reported, 'would be a fine as well as a safe position; but many properties were involved; years would elapse before they could be acquired; and the cost would be very great'. Assuming that site to be practically unattainable, it would be better to look for one in the Parks, in the proximity of the University Museum.

---

[1] Library Records, 'Buildings, etc. 1855–81'.

Coxe, as might be expected, was strongly against removal of the library; and so, as we have seen, was Jowett. The committee, being at variance as to which of the two rival courses should be taken, recommended 'that steps should be taken to obtain the opinion of the University whether it is expedient to proceed with such internal alterations of the Bodleian building as may render it more suitable for a Library, or to undertake, as soon as may be practicable, the construction of a new Library on another site'. Acting on this recommendation, the Curators, at their meeting on 16 May, resolved to request the Vice-Chancellor to lay the report before Council. 'All I could do', Pusey wrote next day to Coxe, 'was to prevent any recommendation, or implicit recommendation, of the plan (for a new Library). It is simply transmitted to Council. The only two spokesmen were Acland and Rolleston, but the V.C. also seemed to lean to it.'[1] Council received the report and ordered it to be circulated to the university.[2]

Coxe took the proposal to move the Bodleian hardly. Goldwin Smith wrote to him: 'It was a real sorrow to me to see you suffering. . . . Don't be unhappy about anything or let anything worry you. It will be a good many years before Bodley is moved.'[3] He was right; and for the moment, perhaps, neither party was ready to press the matter to a division. A final decision was eventually taken, not in Convocation but by the Curators themselves at a meeting held on 27 February 1875. First they agreed unanimously that the Angel site should not be appropriated for the Bodleian. (The committee had itself reported against that particular solution.) Jowett then moved 'that it is not desirable to remove the Bodleian from its present site', to which Acland put an amendment, that 'it may be expedient to surrender the Library for the purposes of the Schools rather than maintain and extend it on its present site'. The amendment was lost, only three Curators voting for it and eight against. And so, with the motion carried, ended what Coxe rightly called a great meeting. Rolleston accepted defeat with the reflection that 'if Sir Henry Savile or Cardinal Wolsey had been living, they would have acted otherwise than we have'.[4]

Now that it had been made clear that the Bodleian would not relin-

---

[1] Library Records, 'Letters to H. O. Coxe, 1855–81'.
[2] As *Report of the Bodleian Construction Committee, together with Captain Galton's Report and a letter from the Bodleian Librarian*. Also printed in the *University Gazette* of 20 Oct. 1874.
[3] Letters to H. O. Coxe, 1855–81.
[4] Letter from Rolleston to Dr. Daniel in F. Madan's collections for Bodleian history.

quish its ancient home, the way was freed for the New Schools delegacy to obtain fresh plans for a Schools building on the Angel site. The plan submitted by Thomas Graham Jackson was the one that commended itself to the delegacy. It had the merit of novelty. He designed a Jacobean mansion, to be built in a stone hitherto unused in Oxford, from the Clipsham quarries on the borders of Lincoln and Rutland. Decrees authorizing the Chest to proceed with the execution of Jackson's plans were passed in June 1876 by large majorities; and so at last the work went forward, and there was prospect that the old ground-floor Schools would be released for Bodley.

2. FIRE PROTECTION

One of the arguments advanced in favour of building a new library was that it could be made fire-proof. For two and a half centuries the Founder's ban on all forms of fire and flame had proved sufficient protection for the library against risk of fire. Artificial lighting was still prohibited, with the result that there was little change in Bodleian hours of opening.[1] But the installation of a steam boiler and heating pipes in 1845 introduced a new element of danger. Sir Francis Palgrave, Deputy Keeper of Public Records, was the first to raise the alarm. Writing in 1855 to his friend Jowett, he enlarged in excited terms on the extreme inflammability of Bodley. 'Fire once caught at midnight, the greater part of the building would collapse in the course of the first half hour and, before Old Tom struck one, the whole would be a mass of ruins.'[2]

The Curators were naturally perturbed and called for expert advice. Mr. Braidwood, superintendent of the London Fire Brigade, advised that the heating pipes should be encased in slate troughs, to prevent their contact with inflammable timber. Gilbert Scott, asked to report on this and on other matters, agreed as to the risk and approved the remedy. The wooden floors of the Schools quadrangle would be burnt through, he said, in ten minutes. It would be far the best course to renew them all in fire-proof construction. If this could not be all done at once, he would still recommend that portions of them should be so secured. And he pointed out that fire-risks could be restricted by carrying party-walls up the whole height of the Schools building, incidentally cutting up the Picture Gallery into a

[1] From 1867 it was opened at nine in the morning in winter as well as summer, and in 1874 the closing hour in the summer months (Apr. till July) was postponed from four to five. Macray, *Annals*, p. 294.
[2] Letter of 1 Dec. 1855 in Library Records, 'Buildings, etc. 1855-81'.

suite of seven rooms, and by the insertion of iron doors in these walls on each story.

Braidwood's proposal for insulating the heating pipes was carried out in January 1857. In compliance with Scott's advice the Curators resolved that the Old Reading-Room should be isolated from the adjoining building by iron doors at either entrance to Arts End. This involved the removal of the old solid entrance door at the top of the main stairs which had probably survived from Sir Thomas Bodley's day, a loss which succeeding generations cannot fail to regret.[1] It was not found possible to adopt Scott's other proposal for dividing up the rest of the building into separate fire-risks, since this depended upon the library obtaining possession of the ground-floor rooms.

When the Curators called in Galton in 1874 they asked him in his turn to advise on the measures that should be taken to protect the library from fire, and in particular to report on the provision of a fire-proof strong-room in which the library's manuscripts and rare books might be kept. There were two stone-vaulted buildings, either of which might be considered suitable for conversion into a fire-proof repository. The one favoured by Coxe and Jowett was the ground-floor of the Camera; the other was the Proscholium below Arts End. Galton was not prepared to recommend the first and suggested, as an alternative to the second, the construction of a new fire-proof building, 100 feet long by 25 feet wide and three stories in height, to be built across the Bodleian quadrangle from north to south. By this he would have bisected the spacious quadrangle, splitting it into two small courts. Galton was an eminent engineer but no architect, and it is perhaps not surprising that his proposal failed to commend itself to the Curators.

So they approached the Radcliffe Trustees over the conversion of the Camera ground-floor into a fire-proof repository; but, as it was thought to be impossible to strengthen the floor over the stone vault without spoiling the appearance of the reading-room, the Trustees withheld their consent. The Curators then fell back upon the idea of the Proscholium, and resolved, on Jowett's motion, that it should be fire-proofed and that valuables should be at once transferred to it. Convocation, though divided in opinion, authorized the Curators to obtain plans and estimates.[2] Sir Gilbert Scott was consequently asked to advise on how the work could be carried out. His report[3] was

[1] Curators' minutes, 2 Dec. 1856. A mason's account among the library bills contains a charge of £2. 2s. 6d. for taking down the old entrance door and preparing for a new iron door, Aug. 1857. The swing-door, put up in 1813 but since renovated, is hung on the inner side of the fire-proof door.
[2] By decree of 4 Mar. 1875.   [3] 14 Apr. 1875.

accepted, and he was asked to prepare specifications and working drawings. These were to include the insertion, in the Proscholium outer wall, of two windows, similar in design to the other windows of the quadrangle; a vandalism that would have ruined the restful dignity of Bodley's panelled façade. At the same time estimates were received for fitting up the Proscholium with fire-proof cases of the type employed at the British Museum. The total cost of the scheme was estimated at £3,000.[1]

At this point the idea of proceeding with the Proscholium was dropped. It had never been popular with the university. As T. G. Jackson subsequently observed, 'It would be a lamentable necessity which deprived Oxford of this stately portico.'[2] And so Jowett appealed once more to the Radcliffe Trustees to allow the Camera ground-floor to be used, as he put it, 'as a strong-box for our manuscripts';[3] this time with greater effect. The Trustees agreed to allow the centre of the reading-room floor, where it touched the stone arches underneath, to be taken up and raised on an iron framework, thus allowing the vaulting of the lower room to be strengthened at its weakest point; and the work was carried out at their expense, and under Alfred Waterhouse's direction, in 1877.

The idea of using the Radcliffe Camera as a repository for manuscripts was almost as old as the Camera itself. Thomas Warton may have originated it, and it won the approbation of Sir William Blackstone.[4] But if manuscripts were to be housed in the Camera, direct communication between that building and the Bodleian was desirable. Pusey had suggested 'a covered way' as far back as 1853.[5] Acland put up to the Hebdomadal Council in 1857 a design by Woodward, the Museum architect, for a gallery, carried on a Venetian Gothic arcade, between the two buildings,[6] and continued to press it upon unconvinced Curators. His colleagues at length, however, resolved upon communication underground, and included, in an extensive programme submitted to Council in 1878, recommendations that the lower story of the Camera should be used as a receptacle for manu-

---

[1] *University Gazette*, 8 June 1875; Report of Committee on University Requirements.

[2] *Selected Reports for the Extension of the Bodleian Library*, p. 20.

[3] Library Records, 'Radcliffe Camera Reports and Letters, 1857–86'; letter to Mr. Arthur Peel, Nov. 1876.   [4] Blackstone, *Great Charter*, 1759, p. xxxv n.

[5] *Report to the Board of Heads of Houses*, 1853, p. 172.

[6] Hebdomadal Council minutes, 1854–66, pp. 188, 194. Acland, *Report on the transfer of the Radcliffe Library to the Oxford University Museum*, p. 14: the Bodleian copy contains a photograph of Woodward's sketch. Acland's plan was for book-trucks to be run on rails along the gallery to the level of the Camera reading-room.

scripts, and that it should be connected with the Bodleian by an underground passage. Thomas Graham Jackson, invited by Council to advise as architect upon the Curators' projects, reported[1] in 1881 that a subway 'would be a very costly contrivance'. One was made in the end, but not until another thirty years had passed.

Jackson thought little of the plan for fire-proofing the ground-floor of the Camera. Although its ceiling had been strengthened, it was still, he held, insufficiently strong to resist the weight of a falling mass of masonry if the dome above caught fire; and he pointed out that nothing had been done to strengthen the vaulting of the side-chambers. He suggested that the large stone-vaulted basement of the Ashmolean Museum would make a fitter strong-room, and that, if more space were needed, it could be got by erecting a one-story fire-proof building on ground between the Bodleian and the Sheldonian Theatre, actually abutting upon both those buildings, his intention being to build northward from the Apodyterium or vestibule of the Convocation House. We shall see, in a later chapter (pp. 231–2), how the Ashmolean basement came to be taken over for purposes of library storage, though not as a strong-room. The library had to wait for more than half a century before it obtained, in the New Bodleian, a book-stack that might be considered fully fire-proof.

It remained to consider what steps could be taken for the better protection of the Old Schools. Galton renewed Scott's proposal for the insertion of party-walls, favoured putting in iron window-shutters, and suggested that one or more sections of the building might be reconstructed in incombustible material. Jackson, however, advised against 'any attempt to form fire-proof rooms in the old building of the Bodleian, which would be a very costly troublesome undertaking'; and consequently nothing was done until, after the Second World War, Scott's plan for renewing floors in fire-proof construction was at length taken in hand.

Galton went into the question of fire-protection very thoroughly, and two of his other proposals deserve a mention. One was for the replacement of the wooden staircases (admittedly a source of danger) by stone; the other was for rising fire-mains in the staircase towers, with cocks on each floor and sufficient length of hose to command the whole building. The latter proposal was adopted sixty years later as part of the general plan for library extension, but the outbreak of the Second World War stayed its execution.

[1] *Report upon the possibility of extending the Library, providing fire-proof book-rooms, and better accommodation for readers*, printed for the Curators in 1894 in *Selected Reports and Plans for the Extension of the Bodleian Library*.

3. RENOVATION OF THE READING-ROOM

One further precaution was taken against the risk of fire. The lead roof over the Picture Gallery had been replaced by copper under Sir Robert Smirke's direction in 1830–1; that over Arts End, Duke Humphrey, and Selden End remained. Galton impressed on the Curators the desirability of replacing lead by copper here also.[1] If the roof caught fire, the lead covering would melt and rain fire into the rooms below. Nor was the roof the only part of the building that needed attention. The whole internal fabric, as the Curators informed Council, required careful examination, and they called for a report on the state both of roofs and floors. The result of an examination by an Oxford firm of builders, Messrs. Symm and Co., was alarming. The inner roof over the Divinity School was reported to be in a very bad state, the ends of the leading timbers having decayed. The south wall had fallen outward about 6 inches, with the result that on that side the outer rafters bore a bare inch and a half upon the outer plate. On receipt of this and of a further report from Galton,[2] estimating cost of repairs to roof and floor at £1,360, the Curators sought and obtained a decree authorizing that expenditure, and started upon the work in the long vacation of 1876.

So the Old Reading-Room fell into the builder's hands. The outer roof was stripped of its lead. To allow of the repair of the roof principals, the seventeenth-century galleries were taken down, never to be replaced, and their contents put into floor cases in the Picture Gallery. Work commenced at the same time upon the floor of Duke Humphrey's Library. This had sunk in the centre till its main timbers rested entirely on the groining of the Divinity School, imposing a dangerous burden upon that noble roof. It was now raised 6 inches, making the corridor level with the alcoves on either side.[3] The old oak floor was replaced by deal, intended originally merely as an under-floor to carry new oak flooring: for, though the oak boards for a new floor were actually prepared, they were never laid down: it was thought in the end to be unnecessary to use the more expensive material since it would be covered by matting.[4]

[1] Curators' minutes, 14 Feb. 1874.
[2] Messrs. Symm's report, dated 4 Nov. 1875, and Captain Galton's letter of 27 Nov., were printed as Curatorial papers.
[3] Galton's report, 24 Feb. 1877, illustrated by diagrams and printed in the *University Gazette*, vol. vii, pp. 287–8.
[4] 'It seems a pity,' T. G. Jackson wrote to Coxe, 'when you are doing so much for the restoration of the building in other respects, that you should leave a deal floor where you found an oak floor.' Library Records, 'Buildings, etc. 1855–81'. The floor of Arts End was not touched at this time. It had to be repaired and strengthened in 1898.

The fine oak bookcases with which Sir Thomas Bodley had furnished Duke Humphrey's Library had to be removed to allow the builders to carry out their repairs to the floor, and, when they went, the Curators appear to have been so pleased with the result that they actually decided not to replace them.[1] Those radical reformers, Rolleston and Acland, presented plans for a drastic rearrangement of Duke Humphrey, and they had the support of Mark Pattison, who found in the Bibliothèque Nationale a model reading-room. But Coxe pleaded hard for the retention of Bodley's presses; and Graham Jackson, called in to advise, reported unfavourably on the plans that Rolleston and Acland had adumbrated. The Curators wavered in their resolution, and gave orders that the presses should be replaced, 'care being taken that they are not fixed as if permanent', and space being left for trying a different arrangement.[2] Reinstatement was none too easy, for, of the eighteen presses, six had been knocked to pieces, their standard ends sawn off; and the fragments lay piled up in Selden End or stacked away with other old wood in the basement of the Sheldonian Theatre.[3] The Curators thought lightly of the matter. Jowett moved that their restoration should not be permanent, but should merely be for one year. Rolleston tabled a motion 'that it is the opinion of the Curators that provision for the accommodation of readers is the chief object to be kept in view in any rearrangement of Duke Humphrey's Library', and both resolutions were carried unanimously.[4] But, for the time at least, Coxe had the satisfaction of seeing 'the dear old cases all up again', and a few days later was able to note 'Dear old Bodley itself again and looking so nice'.[5]

A few months earlier[6] the Curators had set up a committee, presided over by Jowett, 'to report upon the general arrangements of Library rooms'. In dealing with Duke Humphrey it recommended that books should be kept separate from readers, and that readers should be allowed ample space, provided with shelves and drawers, and parted off by a low case from their neighbours—an arrangement which would have involved a clean sweep of the old fittings. The

---

[1] Curators' minutes, 28 Oct. 1876. On this decision Henry Bradshaw, librarian to the sister University of Cambridge, wrote to Coxe, 'I could not have believed such a thing was possible as that Oxford, however "young", would want to destroy such a noble specimen of work, which brings back so vividly the history of the past.' G. W. Prothero, *Memoir of Henry Bradshaw*, p. 415.
[2] Curators' minutes, 10 Feb. 1877.
[3] University archives, W.P. α47 (1), nos. 28, 30, 34, 38.
[4] Minutes, 28 April 1877.   [5] Coxe's diary, 5 and 23 May 1877.
[6] 17 Feb. 1877. The Committee's report was printed as *Report to the Curators of a committee of the Curators of the Bodleian Library, appointed in Lent Term, 1877*, and in part reprinted in *Selected Reports* (1894), pp. 16–18.

report was considered in March 1878 by the Curators, who did not go so far as their committee but agreed that fittings should be restricted to 5 feet in height. Whether they intended to cut down the existing presses or to provide new furniture does not appear from their resolution. Fortunately, Council was wiser than the Curatorial Board and threw out its proposal by a decisive majority (15 votes to 4).[1] So the cases were saved. Graham Jackson, in recommending that the whole of the antique furniture of the Old Reading-Room should be left as it was, wrote very temperately, 'The interior of this part of the Library is one of the most striking and characteristic imaginable, and has in perfection that air of academic study and retirement which befits its history and uses.'[2] Later generations have endorsed his judgement.

4. EXTERNAL REPAIRS

In the report which he made in 1874, Galton informed the Curators that the stone facing of the library was much weather-worn in places, especially in the windows, parapets, pinnacles, and cornices. The whole building, he said, would eventually have to be refaced; and he estimated the cost of such work at £7,500. An unspecified sum was voted by Convocation in May 1876,[3] and repairs were begun under Galton's direction. Galton continued in charge till February 1877, when, at the request of the Curators of the Chest, T. G. Jackson took over the direction of the works. The heads of the windows in Duke Humphrey had by that time been renewed by Galton, and their cusping (which had been cut away) restored. Much else remained to be done. The masonry of Selden End, in particular, was reported by Jackson to be 'in a miserable condition'. Most of the battlementing was in a very dilapidated state, and a great deal actually insecure. A number of the pinnacles were missing and required to be replaced.[4]

The south window of Arts End had already been reported by Messrs. Symm as 'liable to fall at any moment', and the three great windows of Selden End all called for reglazing or renewal of tracery. The introduction of new and not very appropriate tracery, and of grisaille and painted glass in substitution for plain glazing, into the great west window which closes the vista of Duke Humphrey, must have effected a certain change of coloration in that well-known view.

---

[1] Hebdomadal Council minutes, 1866–79, p. 487; minutes of 18 Mar. 1878.
[2] *Selected Reports*, p. 25.   [3] Decree of 23 May 1876.
[4] Jackson's report of 16 Mar. 1877 'on structural repairs and refitting of the buildings containing the Reading-rooms, Divinity School, Proscholium and Convocation House', along with his correspondence with the Chest and its Secretary, Mr. Gamlen, is in University archives, W.P. α47 (1).

The window already contained a number of quarries of sixteenth- and seventeenth-century Flemish or German glass. Unfortunately, when these were taken out for reglazing, nearly every one of them got broken. They were put together again between thin pieces of glass and reinstated, but the cracks remain.

Galton had been using Taynton stone from the Windrush valley. Jackson did his best to persuade the Curators of the Chest to allow him to use Clipsham instead. He had no confidence, he said, in the durability of Taynton stone or in its capacity to withstand the Oxford climate. The price for delivery of both stones was the same, but the hardness of Clipsham added to the cost of labour. On that account the Chest rejected it. Jackson had his way, however, when, the original contract completed, he was invited to examine and report upon the repairs needed to the Old Schools. The report which he made on the masonry of the Schools quadrangle is worth quoting at some length, in view of the interest that has come to be taken in Oxford stone.

This part of the structure was, like the rest, built originally of Headington stone, with Taynton or Milton stone for the pinnacles and copings. The Headington stone has suffered most and is in a lamentable state of decay, especially in the top storey and on those sides of the building that face south, where the case-hardened weather-face to a very great extent is either peeled off or hanging in a ragged state from the walls. The Taynton stone in the upper part has not fared much better than the Headington stone. All the pinnacles but a very few have disappeared entirely; those few that remain have lost most of their crockets and finials, and are in a lamentable condition; and the copings and battlements have already had to be restored with new stone, apparently during the last century. Only a very little of the original Taynton coping remains, and that little is completely decayed. . . . The only stone that has stood well is that of which the cornices and string-courses are cut, which I believe to be the Hard Bed of Headington stone. These are in very fair preservation. The windows have already been renewed on the upper floor towards the south and in some other instances.[1] The material there used is, I believe, Taynton stone, and it is already showing signs of decay. The sills of every other window throughout the building are completely decayed, and, instead of throwing the water off, allow it to soak downwards into the walls, thus adding to the causes of decay. The mullions and jambs of a very great number of the windows are so decayed that they no longer

[1] This was probably done in 1830 when Sir Robert Smirke, engaged in putting a new roof on the Picture Gallery, called the Vice-Chancellor's attention to 'the exceedingly delapidated state of the walls above the windows' (letter of 25 Oct. 1830). Smirke put up new battlements and executed repairs on the eastern range of the Schools.

hold the glass securely or exclude the weather. The Tower is in no better condition than the rest of the building, though it looks better than it really is, having been ingeniously patched with Roman cement, in which a great part of the sculpture has been modelled.[1]

It would be necessary, Jackson said, to renew almost the whole of the parapets and restore missing and ruined pinnacles; to renew the whole of the window-sills and decayed mullions and jambs; to renew some of the strings, labels, and plinths; to reface the whole of the upper story and to patch the worst parts of the first story.

So work was begun by Symm & Co. in 1878, and not till 1884 was it complete. Contract succeeded contract, and for six years the Bodleian precincts reverberated with the screech of stone-saws. The Tower of the Five Orders gave the greatest trouble. Almost the whole of its ornamentation, originally in stone, had been replaced in cement. Bath stone, which had been used for repairs some forty years before, was already beginning to decay. The oriel window over the great gateway facing Hertford College was in so dangerous a state that it 'might with little trouble be pushed out into the street'. Jackson thought at one time that the whole of the tower's two upper stages would have to be pulled down and rebuilt. In the end this was not found necessary, but practically the whole tower was new-faced.[2]

Such repairs were expensive, and cost the university from first to last £26,440.[3] Jackson worked on conservative lines. On the two lower stories of the side facing the Camera he tried the experiment of indurating the Headington stone with a preservative solution. He was satisfied with the result, though he pointed out that it would probably be necessary to repeat the dressing. Elsewhere he refaced with his favourite Clipsham stone, making it his rule, as he said, to touch nothing that might fairly be expected to last for fifty years. This involved patching on the first floor but entirely refacing the tower and the top floor with its battlements and pinnacles. Viewed from neighbouring roofs the result is magnificent and a triumphant vindication of Jackson's faith; for here, as Professor Arkell has put it, one sees 'Oxford reborn in Clipsham stone'.[4] But the usual view-point is from the ground and not so happy; for from this aspect what strikes the eye is the violent contrast between the creamy white of Clipsham ashlar above and the blackened and rougher surface of

[1] *Report from T. G. Jackson to the Curators of the Chest, April 30, 1878.*
[2] *Report to the Curators of the Chest, 10 Dec., 1880.* The dangerous state of the tower had long been known. A report, made in 1825 and now in the University archives, describes its walls as 'rent from top to bottom'.
[3] *The Bodleian Library in 1882–7*, p. 51.
[4] W. J. Arkell, *Oxford Stone* (1947), p. 126 and plate 20.

Headington below, and the unsightly patchwork of the two stones in the middle story. There were doubtless many who regretted the renovation of walls 'clad in the mossy vest of fleeting Time', apostrophized by eighteenth-century Tom Warton.[1] Of such was John Ruskin, who 'was so offended by the restored Bodleian that he would go ever so far round to avoid this eyesore when he had to deliver his lectures'.[2] But Ruskin was already getting a little mad.

5. A PROGRAMME OF LIBRARY EXTENSION

Galton had been asked to explore the capabilities of the existing library building and its capacity for extension. It will be remembered that Scott, to whom the same problem had been propounded nearly twenty years before, had advised taking over the rooms in the quadrangle that were still occupied as examination schools, as well as the substructure of the library, that is to say the Divinity School along with the Proscholium and Convocation House. Scott's report had been pigeon-holed, and Wellesley's bold scheme for converting the whole of the Old Schools into stack on the British Museum model had been held up by failure to obtain control of the ground-floor Schools. Galton approved Wellesley's plan for giving additional support to the floors by running bookcases down the centre of each room, but pointed out that the iron bookcases in the British Museum were of a very expensive construction, and suggested the use of oak instead. He made detailed calculations, and estimated that room could be found in the rearranged Schools for just over half a million more books, and that thereby the library would gain space for accessions for nearly eighty years. And now that the New Schools were actually in course of erection, there was fair prospect of Bodley acquiring the whole quadrangle. The Curators resolved that, as the old rooms became vacant, they should be appropriated to the library, and Council accepted the recommendation, referring this and the Curators' other projects to Graham Jackson for architectural advice.

The Old Schools are splendid Jacobean halls of noble proportions. But Jackson, like his predecessors, was prepared to sacrifice them to the utilitarian requirements of stack. 'These rooms', he wrote, 'will seldom be seen for the future except by the staff of the Library, and it will be unnecessary to consider anything but convenience and the best way of affording the greatest possible space for bookshelves.' He therefore advocated the adoption, with some modification, of Wellesley's plan for subdivision of the new rooms by party-walls with grated iron floors at half the height of each School. By this

[1] Warton, *Triumph of Isis*, 1750, p. 11. [2] Max Müller, *My Autobiography*, p. 216.

143

means he estimated that he would gain space for the accessions of sixty-five years.[1] When Jackson's report on fittings was received in May 1881 the way was clear for the rooms to be taken over. But Coxe was then a dying man, and the task of adapting the Old Schools devolved on his successor.

Readers, as well as books, required additional accommodation. The alcoves of Duke Humphrey may have ceased by this time to be used as private studies, but four at least of them were occupied by staff, leaving only six on either side available for ordinary readers. As no more than three persons could work comfortably at the same time in one alcove, the maximum number of readers who could conveniently be housed at one time was thirty-six. Up to 1878 Selden End afforded no relief, for it was impounded by the cataloguing staff. Still the seating accommodation provided was more than sufficient for those who made use of it, for the daily average of readers in Bodley throughout the year (that is to say of readers present at any one time) was returned to the Curators in 1880 as sixteen. It probably seldom exceeded twenty. Scott had suggested in 1855 that Duke Humphrey should be supplemented by the Divinity School, and that a room should be provided in the Ashmolean for evening reading; but the acquisition of the Camera in 1861 had made this, for the time, unnecessary.

Although the Camera gallery could not be used for reading, since it was occupied by the Hope collection of engraved portraits, still, even without the gallery, the Camera gave seating accommodation for fifty readers. This again proved, at first, more than enough to meet all needs, for it was seldom that more than thirty to forty seats would be occupied simultaneously.[2] The number of those who came to read in the course of the day was of course much higher, and was returned in 1876 as averaging 130;[3] and it is probable that in the next few years it grew rapidly, for in 1880 a Curatorial committee gave the daily average in summer as 200 and in the winter terms as 275.

The cause of the increase was the growing use made of the Camera by undergraduates. Undergraduate-reading was a product of the Honours Schools and a new feature in university life. In the far-sighted evidence which he gave before the University Commission in 1852[4] Mr. Strickland maintained that 'it would be very beneficial

---

[1] *Selected Reports* (1894), pp. 21–24. Galton made his calculations on the basis of a yearly growth of 5,000 volumes, Jackson on one of 8,000 volumes a year.

[2] A census taken one day in Nov. 1875, gives thirty-four readers in the morning and thirty-eight between tea and dinner: almost all were undergraduates.

[3] Report of Bodleian Committee on expenses and management of the library, Mar. 1876.

[4] *Oxford University Commission Report*, 1852, Evidence, p. 101.

to admit undergraduates as well as graduates to the Bodleian Library', and suggested that a special reading-room should be provided for undergraduates. Older and more conservative persons like Pusey thought 'the value of such libraries as the Bodleian to the undergraduate is very much over-rated';[1] but a liberal policy prevailed. The 1856 library statute accorded free admission to all graduates and to other persons on production of a recommendation from an approved person.[2] Henceforward undergraduates were admitted as readers on presenting a written recommendation from their tutors. They were required to wear their gowns.

At the outset they were outnumbered at the Camera by graduates; but already by 1872 complaints were made of the inconvenience caused to graduates through the increased use made of the Camera by undergraduates and unprivileged persons, i.e. readers who were not members of the university, and Coxe had suggested that, if only the Hope collection could be got rid of, the gallery might be turned into a graduates' reading-room.[3] The number of undergraduates admitted to the Camera as readers in the late sixties averaged eighty a year. From 1870 they came in increasing numbers, and in the academical year 1880–1 admittances totalled 193.

Despite the advantages which it indubitably brought, the continued retention of the Camera as a reading-room was by no means generally accepted. Jowett objected to it on the score of expense. Even Acland, through whom it had come into being, lost interest in it when he failed to carry his pet scheme for bridging the space between the Camera and Bodley. There was a movement on foot, much canvassed before the University Commission of 1877, for a new museum of classical archaeology, the Ashmolean having little space for its exhibits.[4] Jowett's committee, set up in 1877, proposed that the Camera reading-room should be transformed into a museum of classical archaeology and art, to which Bodley might transfer its antiquities, coins, works of art, and books of engravings. The

[1] *Report to the Board of Heads of Houses*, 1853, p. 172.
[2] *Corpus Statutorum*, addenda, p. 563. The fee of 11s. formerly charged to all members of the university on qualifying, by graduation, to read in the library, now became merged in degree fees instead of being paid over to the librarian, and that officer was compensated for loss of fees by increase of salary.
[3] Curators' minutes, 26 Oct. 1872.
[4] Following the recommendations of a report (dated 28 Oct. 1862) of the Schools Accommodation Committee set up by Council, the main floor of the Ashmolean building had been made an archaeological museum and its upper floor an examination room. At the same time the great flight of steps leading down from the main floor into Broad Street was swept away and replaced by the existing balcony. Eventually the museum took over the whole building.

Curators, followed by Council, approved the proposal, and Graham Jackson went farther, suggesting that the whole Camera building might fairly be utilized as a museum.[1] But in the end the proposal was dropped, and Oxford had to wait till 1894 before it obtained, in a new Ashmolean Museum, a repository worthy of its archaeological treasures.

It was obvious that, if the Camera was to be given up, as was at this time proposed, other reading-rooms would have to be found to replace it. Jowett suggested that Bodley should aim at providing seats for 150 to 200 readers. Coxe confirmed his estimate, rashly adding 'I do not think that with the libraries, collegiate, scientific, municipal, already existing in Oxford, it is at all likely that the numbers really using the Bodleian will exceed the number stated above'.[2] Galton discussed various ways of obtaining that accommodation, and favoured a new reading-room on the first floor of the building which he proposed to throw across the Bodleian quadrangle. The Curators, disliking that idea but resolved on further accommodation 'with all modern conveniences',[3] proposed, as has been already mentioned, to strip and modernize Duke Humphrey. At the same time they renewed Scott's proposals for taking over one, or even two, of the large rooms in the Ashmolean as an evening reading-room and for making the Divinity School a day reading-room for general readers. It was calculated that the Divinity School would amply accommodate a hundred readers; but, as more might be required in time to come, the Curators suggested that the Proscholium and the Convocation House should also be taken over, and that in each a staircase be inserted leading to the room above. Council threw out the schemes for taking over the Proscholium and Convocation House, and, though it accepted the Curators' proposals for annexing the Ashmolean and the Divinity School, did nothing to implement them.

There was one topic on which Galton had offered no advice, but which came up before Jowett's committee. The library lacked, and continued for another sixty years to do without, any permanent quarters for administrative staff. The Curatorial committee suggested that, since the whole of Selden End was no longer required for cataloguing staff, a portion of it should be screened off to form a librarian's study, the opposite end continuing in use as a cataloguing-room.[4]

---

[1] In 1809 Arthur Young had made the original suggestion that the ground floor or vestibule should be made a museum for agricultural implements. *View of the agriculture of Oxfordshire*, p. 345.
[2] Letter printed as appendix to Captain Galton's report.
[3] Curators' minutes, 24 Apr. 1875.
[4] *Selected Reports* (1894), p. 18.

There was also considerable need of a room for reception, unpacking, and sorting of accessions. At that time and for many years afterwards, down in fact to the Second World War, this work was carried out on the ground floor of the Camera. Coxe had suggested that, if the Convocation House were annexed, its proximity to the cataloguing quarters over it in Selden End made its situation ideal for that purpose. But, as Council refused to part with the Convocation House, Jackson planned an accessions-room in the new building which he projected making between the library and the Ashmolean. From it a stone staircase and a book-lift could give communication to Selden End.[1]

Finally, there was the question of an official residence for the librarian. 'I hold it', Coxe wrote in a letter printed as an appendix to Galton's report, 'to be of the very gravest consequence for the efficiency and safety of such a library as ours, that the Librarian live as directly as possible upon the premises.' The Curators were less concerned, Jowett's committee contenting itself with a recommendation that, 'if this should hereafter be found possible', the librarian should have a house in the immediate vicinity of the library.[2]

This full-dress programme of extension, produced by the committee that had been set up on Jowett's motion in 1877, was sent up to Council; and, after it had been severely pruned by that body, was resubmitted by the Curators in the form of a draft statute in June 1878. But no statute was ever promulgated. The proposal for an archaeological museum in the Camera was referred by Council to the Radcliffe Trustees from whom no answer is on record. When pushed to it by Jowett, Council set up a committee which decided on 15 May 1880 to consult T. G. Jackson as architect upon the scheme.[3] Jackson made his report a year later (20 May 1881), but its discussion was deferred. Coxe paid his last visit to his beloved library on 15 June. Three weeks later he was dead. A year afterwards the Curators made, and promptly withdrew, an application for the use of the Divinity School, contenting themselves with a request for the assignment of the ground-floor rooms in the quadrangle.[4] At the same time, on 6 June 1882, Jackson received formal notice from the Vice-Chancellor that his plan was not adopted.[5] Jowett, succeeding to the

[1] Op. cit., p. 32.
[2] The subject of an official residence for the librarian was revived in Feb. 1902, when, in answer to a letter from the Vice-Chancellor on university needs, the Curators expressed the opinion that 'it would be well that the University should acquire, if opportunity occurs, a suitable house which might in the future be assigned for this purpose'. *Statements of the Needs of the University*, p. 124.
[3] Council Committee minutes, 1873–86, p. 185.
[4] Hebdomadal Council minutes, 1879–96, p. 77; minute of 15 May 1882.
[5] University archives, W. P. α 47 (6), no. 35.

Vice-Chancellorship a few months later, ceased to press for Bodleian extension, finding a wider field for his activities.

And so, for reasons that are not wholly explained, the scheme upon which so much energy had been expended was completely dropped. It is true that a negative conclusion had been reached—not to build a new library; extensive internal and external repairs had been executed or put in train; but the only other outcome of long discussions was the carrying out of an earlier decision to take over the ground-floor Examination Schools as they became vacant, and the production of plans for fitting them up for storage. In the new era that followed on Coxe's death the Curators had much else with which to occupy themselves, and the old projects were laid aside and then forgotten.

6. THE END OF AN ERA

The whole business of library extension told heavily on Coxe's physique, strong though that was. In his younger days he was an unwearied rider, and drew such pleasure from following the hounds that his Victorian conscience became troubled over it. 'Is this fondness for hunting too engrossing?' he questioned himself, adding 'Would willingly give it up if a snare at all, but I don't find it so.' 'Is Bodley's Librarian hunting still?' the Prince of Wales asked when he came up to an Oxford flower-show in 1875. But now age was telling on him. Ever since 1873 new business had been crowding in on his failing energies. He underwent an operation in the autumn of 1874, and in 1878 he sadly commenced his diary for the year with the confession, 'The anxieties and trouble of my profession increase, all tending to increase the force of my malady; the extra exertions of mind and body required in the proposed changes of the Bodleian all tending to make my old age more feeble.'

Across his path there fell with increasing frequency the little shadow of the autocratic Master of Balliol. 'You and I are getting ancient, more's the pity', Jowett had written to him four years before. 'May you live' (he added) 'to see a completed catalogue, a perfectly classified library, a renovated building secured against fire, and then, if you like, depart in peace with a good pension to a living.'[1] Doubtless he would not have been sorry to go. His friend, Sir William Vernon Harcourt, pressed his claim to a deanery,[2] but nothing came of it. There were rows with the Curators. We have told (p. 53) of the crisis over catalogue transcribers' returns in

---

[1] Library Records, 'Letters to H. O. Coxe, 1855–81'.
[2] Coxe's diary, 10 Nov. 1875.

148

1875, and next year came a worse one. It had been decided that library assistants should keep a record of their work, and, when their diaries were presented, the storm broke. It is best described in Coxe's words:

A critical day in my Bodley life. Jowett came up and said the diaries were only half a day's work, and that I ought to have seen it was more. I referred him to the meeting, and, as he did not, I brought it before the meeting, that I am charged with incapacity, and that, if so, I ought to resign. Only Sewell [the Vice-Chancellor] and Rolleston and M. Pattison spoke, the first summing up for Jowett, Rolleston against him and for me, M. P. for me! The matter referred to a committee. What must I do if they decide against me? Resign?[1]

The committee exonerated their librarian but left him with jangled nerves. It was always Jowett; 'Jowett with his measuring rod'; Jowett, 'full of misdirected energy'. Coxe found him 'very civil and sympathetic, but one can never trust him'. And he noted of a Curators' meeting held in May 1878, 'Meeting all quiet and ruling everything as I wished, because Jowett was absent. A most strange change. Now all unanimous. Had he been there, perhaps all *non-placet.*'

He had no one to take the load off his shoulders. In 1879 Nutt gave up his sub-librarianship for a college living, and Coxe repeated the experiment, which had proved unsuccessful in the case of Max Müller, of appointing an eminent scholar to be sub-librarian. Ingram Bywater accepted Coxe's invitation. 'What will he live to see?' Coxe queried in his diary; 'to resign? to be chief?' But Bywater was not the man to submit to the drudgery and hackwork of the class catalogue, or to long hours of enforced seclusion in the library. After only five weeks' trial he told Coxe that he must give up. 'A very great shock', Coxe wrote. Bywater was persuaded to continue for a few months longer, but eventually, in March 1880, sent in his formal resignation, and Coxe appointed in his place Falconer Madan, a young Fellow of Brasenose.

In 1877 his friends had contributed to give Coxe that sure index of declining years, a presentation portrait. G. F. Watts's painting hangs with the other portraits of Bodley's librarians, in the Curators' Room. It shows a worn and weary face. So Mr. Coxe looked, said one of his staff long afterwards, when he came back, tired out from a meeting of Convocation. And Miss Emily Cornish, who knew him well, wrote of Watts's portrait at the time:

Whenever I see Mr. Coxe, my first impression is of the exceeding

[1] Op. cit., 28 Oct. 1876.

brightness of the dark eyes, and contrast with white hair. One's whole impression is of the great vitality and spirit, and entirely of the upper part of the face, of the rather thin fine profile of forehead and nose. . . . Of course I cannot help admiring it as a very fine picture, as every one must: but as Mr. Coxe, no, it is quite an inadequate representation.[1]

On 20 September 1880 Coxe was writing in his diary, 'My sixty-ninth birthday. Can I believe it? My spirit still so young.' Within a fortnight he fell very ill, and, though he rallied sufficiently from his illness to pay short visits to Bodley in the following May and early June, it was but a last flicker of his boyish and indomitable spirit. He died on 8 July 1881, and was buried in the churchyard of his country church of Wytham.

Coxe was an expert Greek palaeographer. Let it be confessed he was not a great librarian. In such matters as classification and cataloguing—the main landmarks of his librarianship—he did not innovate but borrowed from the British Museum. He worked hard himself, but lacked the faculty of making others do so. 'If he had spared himself more', one who worked under him has written,[2] 'by practising devolution in work, and if his trust in others had been less, he would have rendered still greater service. It was sad to see him in his little study, slaving away with such laborious devotion at work which an ordinary clerk could have done just as well.' He was too kindly; too considerate. But there lay his greatness, in the charm and charity of his personal character.

For, as Jowett said in a sermon after Coxe's death,[3] he was 'the friend of all men, overflowing with human kindness, who charmed us all by his courtesy and grace, as well as by his taste and antiquarian knowledge'. He was probably seen at his best when showing, with a running commentary, the treasures of the library to favoured visitors, on whom he confided his impressions to the intimacy of his diary. Such were the dukes of Aumale and Montpensier ('very pleasant and instructive'), Agnes Strickland ('a caution'), Charlotte Yonge ('much amused'), George Eliot and her husband ('very ugly, both of them'), Tennyson ('most pleasant'), Prince Leopold ('very nice, but evidently very feeble, poor boy'), Renan ('thought what an awful responsibility rested on that fat piece of flesh'). He enjoyed good company but bore with bores, and could extract amusement from the fatuous observations of a country clergyman who had detained him for a couple of

[1] 'Letters to H. O. Coxe, 1855–81.'
[2] T. F. Plowman, 'The Bodleian in the Sixties'; manuscript in Library Records.
[3] *Sermons, biographical and miscellaneous*, 1899, p. 134.

H. O. COXE
LIBRARIAN 1860–81
From a portrait by G. F. Watts

hours in the coin-room and who, picking up a Roman copper coin, exclaimed 'This is a real *as*.'

In the pages of Dean Burgon's memoir[1] his drolleries fall flat, but one can still catch in occasional anecdotes the sparkle of his wit. On his introducing Mr. Hicks, the new Fellow of Corpus, to Professor Westwood, the professor heavily inquired whether Hicks was any relation to the man who wrote the *Thesaurus*. 'No,' beamed Coxe, 'Mr. Hicks is a treasure in himself.' And sometimes his replies went deeper. 'Never heard you in better voice,' Lord Abingdon said to him after a sermon at Wytham; 'you were quite eloquent.' Coxe's answer came prompt, 'The Devil told me so before I left the pulpit.'

He did not greatly change Bodley, but, when he died, a light seemed to have gone out of it. This cannot be expressed better than in words that one who knew him well has written of him.[2]

Some there are in every age whose blessed office it seems to be, rather to impart tone and colouring to the circle in which they move, than to influence the historical facts of their time. They are to society what sunshine is to a landscape or expression to the human face. Remove them, in thought, from the scene in which they play their part, and the facts are observed to survive unaltered; but *that* nameless grace which beautifies existence—that secret charm which imparts to the daily intercourse all its sweetness—has fled.

[1] *Lives of Twelve Good Men*, 1888, vol. ii, pp. 122–48.
[2] Op. cit., p. 122, cp. p. 143. It is not difficult to identify 'E. W.' with Miss Elizabeth Wordsworth.

PART III

Nicholson, 1882–1912

Chapter IX

Administration, Finance, and Catalogues

I. THE NEW LIBRARIAN

WHEN Ingram Bywater resigned from the sub-librarianship in April 1880, Coxe noted in his diary that Jowett 'presses Hatch on me as sub, or Nicholson!! Won't have the latter.'

Coxe's death in the following year left the Curators the difficult task of finding a successor to that well-beloved librarian. Mark Pattison, like Coxe, had hoped that it would be Bywater. But Bywater had ruled himself out by resigning the sub-librarianship, that 'necessary but annoying step to the highest post'. 'That you should not be at the head of the Bodleian', Pattison wrote to him after his resignation, 'seems to me a calamity for the Library and for yourself.'[1] He was wrong, for Bywater could not have endured an administrative office; his end was scholarship.

No man was more fitted to preside over a learned library than Henry Bradshaw, librarian to Cambridge University. Bradshaw was approached and was greatly attracted by the proposal. 'Bodley's Librarian,' he said, 'is to my mind beyond any doubt the head of my profession in the country.' But in the end he wisely declined to leave Cambridge.[2] The nomination of Edward Maunde Thompson is also said to have been under contemplation. As eminent a palaeographer as Coxe, he was at this time Keeper of the Department of Manuscripts in the British Museum. He was subsequently to become Director of that great institution, and never, it is said, had it a more impressive figurehead. But he too had fallen out of the field before the Curators proceeded to their final choice.

The more official element among them favoured the senior sub-librarian, the Hebraist Neubauer. Other votes were equally divided between Hatch and Nicholson. Dr. Edwin Hatch represented tradition, in that he was a clergyman, and the Bampton Lectures which he had just delivered on the Organization of Early Christian Churches

[1] W. W. Jackson, *Ingram Bywater*, 1917, p. 89.
[2] G. W. Prothero, *Memoir of Henry Bradshaw*, 1888, pp. 256–7.

had shown him to be also a scholar of liberal views. Jowett at first gave him his support. But there were others who saw in Nicholson a young man, full of energy and of modern methods, supremely fitted to reorganize the Bodleian and adapt it to what they believed to be its new requirements. When Hatch's party transferred their votes to Nicholson, his election was assured, and, though threatened with opposition in Convocation, it was approved by that body without a contest on 16 February 1882.[1]

No greater contrast to Coxe could have been found than that which was provided by his successor. Edward Williams Byron Nicholson began his library career as a boy at school in Tonbridge. He had continued it when, as an undergraduate and scholar of Trinity, he had served as librarian of the Union Society at Oxford. When he was no more than twenty-four he had been appointed to the post, once held by the illustrious Porson, of Librarian of the London Institution. While holding that office and still in his twenties, he successfully launched a scheme for holding in London the first International Conference of Librarians and had acted as secretary to its organizing committee. When that conference gave birth to the Library Association, in which all librarians of the United Kingdom henceforward found their guild and trade union, it was natural that Nicholson should again be one of its two secretaries.

And now he was thirty-three, full of the feverish energy that was to consume him. To those of us who can remember him as he appeared in his later years, he was a somewhat grotesque but still a formidable figure. His magenta tie, his straw hat with Trinity ribbon worn summer and winter; his oblique vision and rather staring and protuberant eyes, in one of them a constantly tumbling monocle, made him a familiar sight in the streets of Oxford. In Bodley he was a tornado, the billowing sleeves of his M.A. gown scattering the papers of library readers as he dashed down Duke Humphrey. He was brusque and lacked the social graces, yet had a fund of unexpected kindness for the young. He was unsparing of himself. His sole aim and the passion of his life was to extend the usefulness of the great library over which he now came to preside.

He had wide and unusual interests, ranging from Keltic (for he always spelt it with a K) to Sanskrit and the obscurer languages of the East; from classical philology to early music. Always acute in his scholarship, he was frequently brilliant, even when, as too often happened, it involved him in controversy.

[1] The account here given of the voting follows one given by Madan in 'Bodleian Notes, 1881–92' (Library papers).

For controversy dogged Nicholson through the whole of his stormy career. Oxford, it is said, while impatient for reform, is always impatient of reformers. It could not avoid contrasting his lack of dignity and manner with the geniality of his urbane and courteous predecessor. Not being academic, his learning and his very real gifts were constantly under-rated. He found himself regarded, he says, as 'well enough suited perhaps to the London Institution, and doubtless fitted to manage the Birmingham Free Library, but not to be mentioned in the same breath with the real heads of his profession'.[1] The criticism was unjust. It was the product of his indiscretions as a passionate reformer.

Bradshaw had warned him on his appointment 'not to despise the traditions of a place where good traditions are of such vital importance if that aroma is to be preserved which gives a charm to the Bodleian and places it at the head of all the libraries in Europe'.[2] He came before long to see the wisdom of that advice, and recanted earlier errors in a memorable report which he made to the Curators seven years after he took office.

If this report [he wrote] ever falls into the hands of a successor of mine coming, as I did, into the Bodleian from elsewhere, and full of enthusiasm for 'practical' librarianship as well as for librarianship of other kinds, I trust that, before beginning stupendous new tasks or any kind of upheaval, he will acquaint himself well with the history of the Library, the stratification (so to speak) of its growth, the conditions attaching to benefactions, the various kinds of current work and the time taken in performing them, and the amount of arrears of work (including cataloguing of old MS. collections); will consider what kinds of new work can profitably be undertaken; will give himself plenty of time to acquire sympathy with all that deserves perpetuation in the system and spirit of the library; and, before deciding on anything new, will try to realize and give full weight to all objections to it—the more especially if what he proposes to do is something which cannot be undone or can be undone only with great difficulty. Had I at the outset applied to myself all the advice I offer to him, I should have saved myself from many ill-considered projects, and, although it is something to have abandoned them, it would have been better never to have entertained them. I can only plead that the questions involved (for the most part at least) were pressed upon my consideration and were not initiated by me.[3]

---

[1] Curators' papers, protest by Nicholson against the recommendations of a Curatorial committee, 30 Nov. 1894.

[2] Prothero, op. cit., p. 257.

[3] Curators' papers, 'Note to a report on the redistribution of the Library', 11 Jan. 1889.

Had he continued to act in the spirit of that frank palinode and to match his ends with the means required to reach them, he would have been a great librarian. Unfortunately for himself—and this was the tragedy of Nicholson's career—he aimed at a perfection that it was impossible to achieve. The merciless logic with which he applied sound principles too frequently led him to absurd conclusions. And so his lode-star proved a will-o'-the-wisp, leading him exhausted into sloughs of extravagance.

Buried in the great mass of records of his librarianship is a little pencil-note, a *cri-de-cœur* of 1890. 'No fresh work can be undertaken without involving time of the Librarian. Deeper and deeper in slough of arrears. Work never so little as seven hours. Worry as well. Appeal to Curators.'[1] The truth is that, even more than Coxe or than their Cambridge colleague Bradshaw, he could not delegate. Everything had to be initiated by him; there was nothing that he would not supervise. In consequence he continuously overworked, and, lacking the grace of proportion, became absorbed in irrelevant minutiae and in unimportant detail. During his first three years of office he took only three weeks holiday in the year, 'working for the rest of it', he says, 'at a ruinous pace'. Life, he found, 'just worth living', and he was buoyed up by the deceptive hope that one day he would have Bodley properly organized and be able to spare himself a little for the future.

But his passion for reform of all kinds brought its nemesis; it provoked opposition which he did nothing to placate. He neither received nor gave quarter. Conscious, and sometimes rightly conscious, of the correctness of his intentions, he was impatient of any interference, and rejected advice even when it was kindly meant. One of his Curators, H. A. Wilson, tried to suggest to him 'that it might be the case that he was prepossessed with the idea that any resolution which came from certain quarters was a hostile resolution, whereas the intention might be very different'. Wilson failed in his well-meaning attempt, finding it 'difficult to get anything out of him beyond clouds of disconnected figures, and defences of himself'.[2]

Easily provoked, Nicholson could forgive but could not conciliate. 'I hate and am weary', he wrote, 'of everlasting conflict'; but his hostile attitude encouraged opposition instead of allaying it, and, in consequence, under the sting of criticism he developed a morbid fear amounting to a persecution mania. At the Visitation of 1894 he passionately broke out to the Vice-Chancellor, 'I live the life of a

[1] Library Records, Librarian's Reports to Curators' Meetings, 1882–90.
[2] Library Records, 'Rev. H. A. Wilson's Memoranda', 30 Oct. and 4 Feb. 1895.

hunted animal, always dreading attack when I'm not being attacked.'[1] Solitary and self-absorbed, his manner was often unfortunate, and conduced little to friendly relations with the Curators whom he might otherwise have quietly guided along the paths of his choice.

Of his quarrels with the Curators we shall have only too frequent occasion to speak. So little sympathy was there between them and their librarian that they often excluded him from their meetings.[2] The last time that Mark Pattison set foot in Bodley, he remarked to Nicholson, 'My experience is that the only way to manage a library is to let the librarian do what he wants.'[3] But that was exactly what other members of the Board were resolved to prevent, and they had some justification. He on his part resented all intrusion: certain Curators, in his view, were determined to 'fetter' him; the word rankled and was constantly on his lips. 'There is no use', he wrote in 1890, 'in my ignoring the fact that, for at least five years past, there have always been a Curator or Curators who have had little or no confidence in the Librarian; who, if he had offered his resignation, would almost certainly have voted for its acceptance.'[4]

Things came to a head in 1898 when, in a printed memorandum on the statutory position of the Librarian and Curators of the Bodleian, he argued that there was nothing in the library statute authorizing the Curators to order the Librarian to do anything or to restrain him from doing anything; that, though they could admonish him, they could not deprive him of office or suspend him from duties; that even the Visitatorial Board could not try him for disobedience to the Curators. 'It has been my full intention,' he exclaimed, 'if further resolutions were passed interfering with the Librarian's statutory rights, to take the highest opinion in the kingdom at once upon their legality.' The Curators on the advice of the then Vice-Chancellor, Sir William Anson, wisely declined the challenge, holding themselves to be responsible for the management of the library, and confident that the Visitatorial Board, as supreme disciplinary body in the

[1] Protest against the recommendations of a Curatorial committee, 30 Nov. 1894.
[2] On 3 May 1890, Nicholson addressed to his governing body a twelve-page pamphlet 'on the increasing exclusion of the Bodleian Librarian from the meetings of the Curators'. A Curatorial resolution passed on 29 Oct. 1887 had required that, after presenting his report, the librarian should withdraw till sent for. This was modified five years later (10 Dec. 1892) when it was agreed that he should be invited to attend all Board and committee meetings on the understanding that he should withdraw upon the request of any Curator present.
[3] Curators' papers, memorandum on 'The statutory positions of the Librarian and the Curators of the Bodleian', 21 July 1898.
[4] Letter 'on the increasing exclusion of the Bodleian Librarian from the meetings of the Curators'.

E. B. NICHOLSON

LIBRARIAN 1882–1912

university, would support them if the Librarian refused to obey their decisions.

Nor was it with the Curators alone that Nicholson came in conflict. For two or three years his relations with his sub-librarian Madan were sufficiently easy, but they were soon to become strained, and eventually communication only passed between them by formal written notes. Madan was not lenient to his chief's failings, nor did he fail to chronicle them with characteristic minuteness. Coxe used to refer to Bandinel affectionately as 'B. B.': to Madan Nicholson was 'D. B.', and the letters stood for *Diabolus Bibliothecae*.[1]

Such then was the librarian, a remarkable man who succeeded at many points in revolutionizing Bodley. It required faults as great as his to obscure the value of his yet greater services.[2]

2. GOVERNMENT AND REVENUE

And what of the Curators? At the close of 1884 the election of Bywater and of the Aristotelian scholar, Professor Chandler, brought on to the Board an element hostile to the Librarian, and thereafter, as Nicholson admitted, there were always one or more Curators who were highly critical of him. He had solid grounds for holding that constant changes in the Board's composition made it difficult to pursue any consistent policy, but the prevailing opinion of the time favoured democratic representation and resented the permanent retention of five seats out of thirteen by Regius Professors. Council, in 1889, submitted to the Curators a scheme, not unlike one that was adopted nearly fifty years later, under which the five Regius Professors should be replaced by representatives of the seven Boards of Faculties. When the scheme came up at a Curators' meeting, Chandler argued that their body was already too large, and put up an alternative plan. Under this the Vice-Chancellor and the Proctors were to remain as *ex officio* members; otherwise the Board was to consist solely of five graduates holding office for five years; of the elected members one was to retire each year, and no retiring member was to be re-eligible until one year after he had ceased to hold office. Chandler's proposal was seconded by Bywater; but, on the motion of Jowett (a reformer but a Regius Professor), the Curators agreed to express no opinion on Council's scheme. So, in default of encouragement, the

---

[1] But he was more popularly known as 'Old Nick'.

[2] The best critiques of Nicholson are to be found in the obituary which appeared in *The Times* for 18 Mar. 1912; in an In Memoriam notice of him which his friend H. R. Tedder contributed to the *Library Association Record*, vol. xvi, pp. 95–108; and in an article in the same journal, vol. li (4th ser., vol. xv), pp. 137–43, by Strickland Gibson, who long served under him.

attempted reform was dropped, and the composition of the Board remained unchanged.[1]

Meetings were more formal than they used to be. Agenda papers had begun to be printed in 1877.[2] Minutes followed suit six years later;[3] and thenceforward sets of printed terminal papers were issued to all members of the Board. From 1889 the Curators drew up, for presentation to Council and publication in the *University Gazette*, annual reports on the working of the library and statements of its accounts.[4] They supplemented their annual Visitation by a 'Perlustration' of the library on the last Saturday in May.[5] Their meetings came to get longer and more congested with business, till at length a change came about that was making itself felt throughout the university—Board government was partially superseded by Committee government.

A Finance Committee set up in 1876 to take charge of accounts and to sign cheques[6] struck no deep root, and, though revived ten years later, was given very limited functions. Meeting on the day before each statutory meeting of the Curators, it contented itself with the formalities of comparing cash-book and pass-book, and of verifying a statement of accounts for presentation to the Curators on the following day.[7] Its replacement in 1892, at Professor Pelham's instigation, by a Standing Committee of five members, meeting weekly in term-time, and charged not only with the signing of all cheques and with the presentation of accounts, but with the supervision of extraordinary expenditure and the rendering, at each Curators' meeting, of a general report on the matters assigned to them, filled Nicholson with alarm, for he found in it a new attempt to 'fetter' him. And he remarked, not without acumen, 'I see that, if such a committee is established, the power of the Board of thirteen Curators will be virtually transformed to a committee of (say) five or seven. If the Standing Committee, either at once or eventually, fulfilled the functions which I have supposed it would, then the active control of the Bodleian would certainly be transferred from the Board to the Committee.' The Standing Committee naturally found its chairman in the

---

[1] Curators' minutes, 9 Mar. 1889.

[2] Under Curators' order of 2 Dec. 1876.

[3] Order of 27 Jan. 1883. The Hebdomadal Council had set an example by ordering the printing of its minutes, 4 Nov. 1878.

[4] A report covering the years 1882–7 was presented to the Curators by Nicholson as the first in a yearly series, and published at the end of 1888 under the title *The Bodleian Library in 1882–7*.

[5] Order of 9 June 1888.

[6] Curators' minutes, 4 Mar. 1876.

[7] Curators' minutes, 19 June 1886 and 18 June 1887.

Board's financial expert, Bartholomew Price, Master of Pembroke. From the outset it met on Fridays in term-time at noon, using the Music School as its committee-room. It has continued to grow in strength, and it may be left to the Curators themselves to judge of the correctness of Nicholson's prediction.

Since 1873 administration of the library estate had been in the hands of another body, the Curators of the University Chest. At the time that Nicholson took office, the Bodleian still owned, undiminished, the property at Cookham with which its founder had endowed it. But Hindhay farm, which formed its larger part, was sold in 1881 for £11,000.[1] Other lands and houses at Cookham and in and about the town of Maidenhead were sold in 1888 at prices aggregating £9,348. 10s.[2] And the water-corn-mill near Boulter's Lock called Ray Mills, with all that was left of the Cookham estate, was sold for £9,330 in 1909.[3] The purchase-money arising from the foregoing sales was invested, and the dividends paid over by the Chest to the library. So the Bodleian ceased to be a landlord.

Library investments in stock, which we have seen (p. 47) amounted in the seventies to £70,600, 3 per cent. Consols, were reduced under a statute passed in 1898,[4] whereby the university resumed £30,000 which it had appropriated to the library in 1845, and made compensation for loss of income by increasing its annual grant. The diminution of the library's own capital resources was only partly made up through bequests made in 1910 by Mr. Reginald Cardwell (£2,000) and by Mr. Patrick Murphy (£5,000).

The Bodleian came, more than before, to rely upon university grants and allowances as the main source of its income. Since 1876 it had a statutory annual grant of £3,350. In addition the library received £800 under decrees, for there was a regular yearly grant of £300 towards the expenses of the Camera; and the £500 a year which had been voted for work on the new author-catalogue continued, after the catalogue was completed, to be given for general purposes. The library therefore received, up to 1898, by statute or decree, a regular annual payment from the university of £4,150. The statute of

[1] Under decree of 30 May 1882.
[2] Under decree of 27 Nov. 1888.
[3] Macray's annotated copy of his *Annals*.
[4] *Corpus Statutorum*, addenda, p. 1022. This statute brought to completion a series of transactions whereby the university, through its want of ready cash, had borrowed, and spent on buildings or on purchases of land, nearly the whole of the £30,000 stock, making up, as it did so, the loss of interest to the library. The £36,000 Consols representing Dr. Robert Mason's bequest had been sold out in 1883 and the proceeds reinvested in a 3¾ per cent. mortgage.

1898, mentioned in the preceding paragraph, increased the statutory grant by £900, without thereby adding to the total library income.

In pursuance of the policy prescribed by the 1877 Commission, various colleges made yearly contributions to the maintenance of the university library. Merton was able to give regularly about £290 a year; but, owing to agricultural depression, All Souls, which had undertaken a yearly payment of £1,000, found it impossible to reach that figure until 1906, and from 1887 to 1898 Bodley would have received nothing at all from the college had not its Warden, Sir William Anson, paid in £100 a year anonymously out of his private purse. Other colleges which came to the help of Bodley included Trinity and Magdalen. Trinity, under the Presidency of Professor Pelham (1898–1906), made a series of annual contributions of £150; and Magdalen from 1905 made an annual grant of £250 for increase of staff.

Grants for special purposes, amounting in all to more than £2,500, were made at various times between 1882 and 1914 by the University Chest. The Common University Fund, into which are paid the sums derived by the university from taxation of the colleges after the fulfilment of their statutory obligations, was another source of occasional special grants. Its delegates paid to Bodley between 1891 and 1914 more than £3,500, of which approximately half went to the binding up of Ordnance Survey maps. The library came to depend more and more upon subventions for meeting exceptional expenditure.

So Bodleian income was made up of the annual revenue derived from library endowment, a fixed university grant, contributions of varying amount made by certain colleges, and occasional grants for special purposes made out of the University Chest and the Common University Fund. During the first ten years of Nicholson's librarianship it averaged just over £7,900. Thereafter, in the main through increased college contributions, it steadily mounted, and the average for his last quinquennium (1907–11) rose to £10,125. Unfortunately expenditure grew with equal rapidity.[1]

3. EXPENDITURE

If one takes the main headings of expenditure, leaving capital outlays out of account, by far the largest item was that of staff. This

---

[1] The library accounts from 1888 onwards were published yearly with the annual report in the *Oxford University Gazette*. From 1924 they will be found in the *Abstracts of Accounts* issued annually as a supplement to the *Gazette*. Mr. Madan has summarized, under its main headings, library income and expenditure for the years 1882–1918 in the *Bodleian Quarterly Record*, vol. ii, pp. 229–34.

amounted in 1882 to £4,293, in 1911 to £6,093. Over 61 per cent. of the library's income continued to go in paying its employees.[1] It could not indeed be said that the Bodleian was overstaffed or that its staff was overpaid. There was not in fact any material change in pay rates. The librarian's salary remained at the £1,000 to which it had been raised in 1873. The statutory maximum for a sub-librarian was still £400, though first Neubauer and then Madan received special rises to £500.[2] Down to 1913 assistants' wages continued to be limited by statute to a maximum of £200. This was not much to support trained members of the staff, some of whom were graduates.

The permanent regular staff hardly increased at all. In 1911 library officers, assistants, and the janitorial and bindery staffs taken together still only numbered 21. What had greatly increased was the number of employees who were not permanent; for 17 'extra staff', 10 catalogue revisers, and 14 boys brought the total number of persons in library employ in 1911 up to 62. Of these the catalogue revisers, of whom we shall speak later (p. 171), were paid out of a special fund. The extra staff consisted of temporary or part-time employees engaged on various forms of cataloguing activity. They formed a kind of librarian's private army, their employment being regulated by the librarian without any reference to the Standing Committee. And then there were the boys.

In a city of the size of Oxford, endowed with good primary and secondary schools, there is bound to be always a considerable supply of boys over school age seeking employment; and, so long as there was no large industry competing for their services, it was not a difficult matter to pick out likely lads for temporary employment in Bodley. The engagement of boys for work in the library is said to have been suggested by Jowett; but it was not entirely a novelty, since Macray was only fourteen when he came on to the staff. Nicholson's aim in recruiting boys was to obtain a cheap form of labour, capable of relieving assistants from mechanical work and of being trained up for eventual promotion to permanent posts. It cannot be said that the fixed rate of 10s. a week was extravagant payment for their services. Only when they had qualified for matriculation in the university were they put up to the higher wage of £60 a year.

They were selected by open competition after an advertisement had been put in the Oxford papers. Every boy was required, on

---

[1] By 1950 the proportion had risen to 67½ per cent.
[2] No effect was given to a resolution taken by the Curators on 13 Nov. 1880 that the senior sub-librarian's salary should rise to £600 and that of the junior sub-librarian to £500, by £15 annual increments.

appointment, to be able to construe fairly well at sight an easy Latin and an easy French author. 'They were expected', Nicholson wrote,[1] 'to spend part of their private time in going through a very varied course of study. They were examined about once a fortnight by the Librarian, usually after Library hours. On days when the Bodleian was closed, they also had lectures on the details of library work.'

The employment of boy-labour did not win the approval of the university as a whole, or even of all Curators. Chandler as usual was outspoken in his comments.[2] 'That the Bodleian is undermanned', he wrote, 'admits of no manner of doubt, yet some, I am sure, agree with me in thinking that, though undermanned, it is considerably over-boyed.' And he disapproved of Bodley's librarian spending his time on tuition. 'At the close of a hard day's work, does this high University officer retire to well-earned literary ease? No; he turns himself for I know not how many hours into a schoolmaster; he gives lessons to little boys; he trains a school of sucking librarians.' And Bywater, if more concise, was no less caustic. 'I cannot approve', he said,[3] 'of the present system by which boys are so largely employed in the Bodleian, and should like this educational experiment to be tried in a less valuable library.'

Nevertheless, the librarian, starting with six boys in 1882, was allowed to increase their number by degrees to eighteen; far too many for permanent absorption. Yet working in Bodley was by no means a dead-end occupation for a promising boy. If, as usually happened, there was no assistantship available for him, he could be put on the extra staff until he had found a job or taken his degree. And to some extent Nicholson achieved his object of making Bodley a training-school for librarians. Boys recruited by him, and trained under his watchful care in all branches of their profession, eventually attained to the post of Keeper of Printed Books in Bodley and to the chief librarianships of the National Central Library, of the London Library, of Chetham's Library at Manchester, of the Shakespeare Memorial Library at Stratford-on-Avon, and of the university libraries of Sheffield and Melbourne.

A library's administrative expenses include, in addition to salaries, the various forms of payment that may be lumped together as establishment charges. Some of these increased greatly during the thirty years of Nicholson's librarianship (1882–1912). The most notable

---

[1] *The Bodleian Library in 1882–7*, p. 23. Nicholson soon found himself too busy to continue giving regular instruction.

[2] In a memorandum dated 10 Nov. 1885.

[3] In a printed paper communicated to Convocation, 27 Feb. 1890.

increase was that in printing and stationery, Nicholson's fondness for notices and forms and for the circulation of printed statements had the effect of swelling expenditure under this head from £58 in Coxe's last year of office to £393 in Nicholson's.

Nicholson was frequently attacked for spending too much on binding. The library had at one time unduly economized in its binding, and in Coxe's last year of office, when the British Museum annual allowance for binding was £6,000, the amount spent at Bodley still fell below £900. Nor did it often exceed that figure until the last five years of Nicholson's librarianship when it came to average £1,235. The charge of excessive expenditure on binding was not wholly justified. It was not so much the amount of binding done as the choice of matter for binding that was at fault. Tradesmen's advertisements —including tailors' trouser-patterns—and Christmas cards and similar products of job-printing could well have been left unbound. Ordnance Survey maps had been better kept loose in file cabinets than mounted on guards in unwieldy volumes of red buckram.[1] And it was objected, with good reason, that expenditure on binding books stood in too high a proportion to the money spent upon purchasing them.

The main defect of Nicholsonian finance was this, that while library revenues increased, all forms of expenditure other than purchases increased likewise, and that the amount remaining available for buying manuscripts and foreign and second-hand books stayed stationary. In 1881 27 per cent. of the library's income was still applied to fulfilling that first duty of all libraries, the increase of its resources by buying in the book market. In the last quinquennium of Nicholson's régime the average yearly amount spent on purchases was £200 less than in the first, and its ratio to total income had fallen from 27 to under 16 per cent.[2] Put in another way, a larger slice of the library's income was being used upon administrative expenses resulting from the acquisition of copyright literature that profited little; and, despite the increase in its revenues, the library was spending less than before on purchases of books of real value.

Low rates of pay, shortage of staff, restriction in purchases, and

---

[1] Between 1891 and 1911 the library received £1,750 in special grants to meet the cost of binding Ordnance Survey maps.

[2] The figure would be raised a little higher if one were to include new books bought for exchange with foreign libraries. Dividing Nicholson's librarianship into quinquennial periods, the average amount spent annually upon all forms of purchase works out as follows: 1882–6, £1,806; 1887–91, £1,800; 1892–6, £1,666; 1897–1901, £1,510; 1902–6, £1,616; 1907–11, £1,585. These figures may be compared with those given in Chapter IV (p. 69) for 1845–79.

entire absence of reserve funds combined to produce that impression of poverty which beset the Bodleian through the whole of Nicholson's time. The annual accounts usually showed a small credit balance on the general fund, but by the close of 1911 this had been replaced by a deficit of £900. The Standing Committee were fully justified in reporting in that year[1] that an increase of from £700 to £800 a year was required in the ordinary income of the library in order to provide for its ordinary expenditure.

Help was already on the way, not only for the Bodleian but for the university as a whole. The need for additional library endowment, together with schemes involving considerable capital expenditure, had been set out by the Curators in 1902 and published in a general statement of the needs of the university. This had caught the attention of an old Balliol man, the Hon. T. A. Brassey. Encouraged by A. L. Smith, tutor and subsequently Master of Balliol, Brassey put forward in 1903 the idea of raising an endowment fund for the university upon which the Bodleian should have a first call. Lord Goschen, who was then Chancellor, thought the time inopportune for an appeal: but in the summer of 1906 Brassey took up once more the cause of university endowment, and by next year, when Lord Curzon succeeded Goschen as Chancellor, had already collected £60,000. Curzon was prompt to turn to account the zeal and energy which Brassey supplied. Immediately after his election he called a meeting to be held in London in May 1907, and there launched a Chancellor's appeal for a quarter of a million pounds. An Oxford University Endowment Fund was thereby brought into being, and its administration entrusted to a Board of Trustees. From 1909 the Trustees made an annual grant of £250 to the library general account. We shall have occasion later (pp. 175, 242, 269) to describe the various forms of library development rendered possible by Brassey's private benefactions as well as by substantial donations from the fund which he had done so much to raise.

4. CLASSIFICATION AND THE SUBJECT-CATALOGUE

From the outset Nicholson was faced with the problem of how to classify accessions. He inherited the subject-classification which Coxe had devised on the British Museum model in 1861, but found its headings too general. Rightly rejecting the temptation to supersede it by the decimal system put out in 1876 by the American librarian, Melvil Dewey, which has since obtained for itself such widespread use and notoriety, he took Coxe's scheme as his basis and greatly

[1] 11 Mar. 1911.

elaborated it. This he did by a process of subdivision. Each of Coxe's classes had a three-figure number. He retained the old notation but added two, or occasionally more, figures to each cypher, and this enabled him to multiply sections a hundredfold. In Nicholson's hands Coxe's seventy-three sections swelled to over 7,000. 'It may be doubted', he wrote in 1888, 'whether in any great library the principle of shelf-classification has been carried out much further than in the Bodleian since 1883.'[1]

The Curators thought that elaboration had been carried too far. Invited by Council in 1896 to consider the possibility of economizing space by alteration of the system of shelf-classification, they agreed that the classification was far too minute and involved much waste of time and space.[2] True it has its blemishes, and one may cite as an extreme example of its minuteness the section 16696091 which Nicholson devised for the physiology of dicotyledons. Nevertheless, a scheme which its author regarded at the outset as provisional has stood the test of time. It works, and is therefore unlikely ever to be materially altered.

There were certain sections, notably those of law and British topography, to which Nicholson's system was not applied. Nor was it ever extended to accessions received before 1883. Jowett remained to the end wedded to his idea of reclassifying the whole of Bodley, and at first brought Nicholson to share his view. 'In my earliest days at Bodleian', Nicholson wrote, 'I entertained the idea of rearranging the entire library according to subjects.' He soon came to see that the great donation collections could not be so treated. And by 1888 his views on reclassification had radically altered, and he acknowledged his earlier errors, saying 'It was simply as a result of longer experience and more careful consideration that I abandoned the idea which I afterwards saw to be thoroughly bad, and, if it had been good, thoroughly impracticable.'[3]

The story has been told, in an earlier chapter (pp. 57–60), of how the Classed Catalogue, that is a subject-catalogue of the contents of the library, had come to be started in 1878 under Coxe as a preliminary to Jowett's plan for re-referencing the older books. It proved a convenient way of side-tracking that project. Otherwise, as we shall

[1] *The Bodleian Library in 1882–7*, p. 33. The fullest account of Nicholson's scheme is that given by G. W. Wheeler in the *Bodleian Quarterly Record*, vol. i, pp. 313–16.
[2] Curators' minutes, 21 Nov. 1896. The larger the number of sections or class-divisions, the greater would be the amount of vacant space on the shelves, since room for additions had to be left after each section.
[3] Library Records, 'Madan's Bodleian Notes, 1882'.

see, the scheme was a failure. 'Who tied the millstone of a classed catalogue round the Librarian's neck, I do not know', wrote one of the
Curators;[1] but the new librarian was content to shoulder the burden
and regarded a subject-catalogue as indispensable. Pushing forward
with the scheme, he estimated in 1887 that the entire mass of materials
would be ready in four years' time for final revision. It could then be
laid down in sheets and bound up in a form similar to the author-
catalogue.[2] But revision, he characteristically insisted, would have to
be done by himself, and he would not commit himself to promising
completion by any date earlier than 1911.

The usefulness of a subject-catalogue and the desirability of proceeding farther with the enterprise had already come to be openly
questioned by Chandler and Bywater. 'A classed catalogue,' said
Chandler, 'is a snare and a delusion, . . . an absurdity and something
worse because all classification is arbitrary; what suits one searcher
for wisdom will not suit another.' And he tartly answered its supporters with the assertion that 'the need which they dumbly feel and
cannot articulately express is for a ready and infallible index to all
literature whatever, or, failing that, to all printed books'. The British
Museum had tried it and abandoned it after spending £7,000 upon the
project. If it was ever completed, it would be but 'a gigantic sham
catalogue which no man fit to use the Bodleian Library would ever
care to look at'.[3] Bywater was equally positive. 'A classed catalogue
for a library like the Bodleian', he advised, 'will be after all only a
very unsatisfactory bibliography.' He persuaded the Curators to set
up a committee to consider whether it should be discontinued; and
although Jowett, as chairman of the committee, secured a favourable
report (with Bywater a dissenting member), its recommendation that
the work should proceed was only carried at a Curators' meeting by
a single vote.[4]

The subject-catalogue had in fact received its death-blow. It will
be remembered that it was to be compiled from the third copies of the
slips that were prepared in triplicate for the author-catalogue. After
1900 their regular sorting and incorporation seems to have come to
an end. For some years they continued to be kept in boxes, waiting
for a sorting that never came. Finally, even the pretence of further
work upon the catalogue was abandoned. Slips were henceforward

---

[1] Professor Chandler, 10 Nov. 1885.
[2] *The Bodleian Library in 1882–7*, p. 32. Later he abandoned the idea of laying
slips down in volumes, and suggested that they should be mounted on cards.
[3] Chandler, *Memorandum on the Subject Catalogue*, 1 Dec. 1885; *Some Observations on the Bodleian Classed Catalogue*, 25 Oct. 1888.
[4] 25 Oct. 1888. The voting was 5 to 4.

made in duplicate instead of triplicate. The vast catalogue no longer grew, and, as it became more and more out of date, the flimsy paper slips of which it was composed ceased to be consulted.

Subject indexes have their uses, provided their range, like that of the *Subject Index to the Accessions of the British Museum*, is strictly limited. But a subject-catalogue of the entire contents of a great library is another matter. Looking back upon the Bodleian project it is easy now to see that it was doomed from the outset. Apart from the question of its necessity (which was bound to be raised as more money was spent upon it without apparent result), its method of construction was at fault. It seemed so easy to compile it out of an unused set of slips of the author-catalogue; and, where the slips represented books that had already been classified, the work was certainly mechanical; but to place under correct headings the catalogue entries of unclassified books was not so easy, since titles do not always give away contents. Author- and subject-catalogues derive their being from very different elements, the first from the title-page, the second from the contents of a book; and so it comes that subject-catalogues, like author-catalogues, can only be constructed from the books they describe.

5. THE AUTHOR-CATALOGUE

Already Nicholson had come to see that the revision of the alphabetical author-catalogue was really more urgent than the completion of the subject-catalogue.[1] The cataloguers of the sixties and the seventies, in transforming the old printed catalogue with its supplement into a written catalogue, had worked from the old catalogue-slips. These had been made according to library tradition; for although Bodleian cataloguers were by that time supposed to observe in the main the famous set of rules which Panizzi had introduced in 1839 for the British Museum, in the absence of any accessible and clearly prescribed code they not unnaturally followed earlier practice. And so, while correcting obvious errors in the old slips, they made no alteration to headings. In consequence, the written catalogue of Coxe's workers reproduced the general arrangement of the printed catalogue of 1843, just as that had retained the headings of the 1738 catalogue, for whose origins one must go back to the printed Bodleian catalogue of 1674.

[1] 'There remains another gigantic task to be superintended, and one which is also really more urgent than the subject-catalogue, namely the revision of the alphabetical catalogue from beginning to end.' Curators' papers, 'Librarian's report on the subject-catalogue', 9 July 1886.

Headings are of the utmost importance in a library catalogue, since it is under the heading that seems most natural to him that the reader first looks to find the book of which he is in quest. Even where this is the name of the author (as is generally the case in what is primarily an author-catalogue), all is not plain sailing in a catalogue, like that of the Bodleian Library then was, which has a preference for Latinized forms, and which treats initial I and J or U and V as one letter. The trouble at Bodley was far greater when the work catalogued was anonymous, and was entered under an arbitrary subject-heading, such as Anglia or Gallia, Carolus or Ludovicus, Army or Parliamentum, or under what is named a 'form-heading', such as Novel or Poesis. In those vast categories it was difficult even for the staff to detect the object of their search; and the Bodleian frequently bought duplicates through inability to trace its own books in its own catalogue. Compared with such difficulties, the Latinization of place-names, of which Argentoratum for Strasbourg is one of the easier instances, was but a minor irritation.

At Cambridge Bradshaw had published a set of cataloguing rules in 1878, and Nicholson was quick to supply the want of them at Oxford. The year 1883 saw the publication of three library cataloguing codes: (1) the American Library Association's rules for an author- and title-catalogue; (2) the cataloguing rules issued by the Library Association of the United Kingdom;[1] (3) the 'Compendious cataloguing rules for the author-catalogue' issued by Nicholson for the Bodleian Library. This last, a set of fifty-six rules, was based on the United Kingdom Library Association code (while departing from it at certain points), just as the latter was modelled upon the American code. The reform was much needed. Henceforward the Bodleian had cataloguing rules that were close enough to those in current use to be generally understood and accepted.

Unfortunately the new rules were perforce limited to new publications: existing catalogue entries were not affected. The old garment remained while continuing to receive new patches; and so a life of Louis XVIII would be entered under the heading 'Louis XVIII, king of France' if it were published in 1883, but, if published two years earlier, would appear under 'Ludovicus XVIII, rex Galliae'.

Nicholson was alive to this defect, though he would not have admitted as defects other faults that might be found in the new cataloguing system. These were that in the first place it tended, like most of Nicholson's work, to be over-elaborate. A conspicuous but

---

[1] These two were subsequently amalgamated in a joint Anglo-American code, first published in 1908.

by no means solitary example of intensive cataloguing is that provided by a collection, bought in 1893, of 419 Icelandic funeral-invitations. In accordance with a strict interpretation of the rules, each separate broad-sheet was entitled to three separate entries, and so a single book made its appearance in the catalogue over a thousand times. But, if Nicholson's fault was elaboration, his chief critic, Chandler, was given to over-emphasis.[1] 'No more should be entered on a catalogue slip', he wrote, 'than will just serve to identify the book; every word beyond that is waste of time, that is waste of money.' Fuller description is often needed for identification of a particular edition than the layman might expect. Bibliographers recognize the fact. All the same there is undeniable truth in Chandler's further assertion that 'Many librarians confound a catalogue of books with a bibliography.'[2]

Further, the system was applied to every printed item in the library, however ephemeral. Coxe, as we have seen (p. 52), got leave from the Curators in 1860 to exclude from the catalogue minor fiction, minor educational works, and other copyright accessions judged to be of no importance. Nicholson, on the other hand, held it to be an elemental principle that everything that came into the library should be catalogued, and, on taking office, gave orders to that effect.[3] And so, said Chandler with his usual crude sense, 'All this rubbish is to be catalogued, at an expense perhaps of one shilling a slip, when the thing catalogued is not worth the tenth part of a farthing.' The Curators did in 1896 resolve to exclude from the complete process of cataloguing the least valuable part of the books claimed under the Copyright Act,[4] but their decision had little apparent effect upon library practice.

Finally, a worse error, because capable of being carried to greater extremes, was that of analytical cataloguing, that is to say, the cataloguing of the contents of collectaneous volumes, of societies' publications, and even of periodicals. Indexes to periodicals and to societies' transactions are in themselves valuable, but should be allowed no footing in a library catalogue. The practice had started under the stimulus of the subject-catalogue; and, though Chandler argued that, if the Bodleian catalogue were to be transformed into an index to all transactions and to all collections, the work of a library might be

[1] 'At the Bodleian', he wrote in 1885, 'we have really nothing to learn from any American librarian.'
[2] Memorandum of 10 Nov. 1885.
[3] *The Bodleian Library in 1882–7*, p. 27.
[4] Curators' minutes, 21 Nov. 1896.

made infinite, requiring infinite sums to pay for it,[1] his colleagues viewed the practice more leniently and, as late as 1909, directed that the separate cataloguing of societies' publications and of articles in learned periodicals, as yet only partially so treated, should be completed.[2] So the subject-catalogue continued to exercise its baleful influence upon the author-catalogue after it had itself, to all intents, been abandoned.

Another disadvantage under which the Bodleian catalogue laboured, like its prototype of the British Museum, was its increasing size,[3] and it was this which first led Nicholson to consider the question of its printing. As early as October 1861, when the Bodleian catalogue was being started, Cambridge University Library had adopted the practice of printing its accession slips. The British Museum followed suit in 1880, and Coxe thereupon raised the question whether Bodley should also take to printing, but in the end he advised against it.[4] Nicholson had not been a year in office before he likewise proposed the substitution of print for manuscript for all additions made to the catalogue from the beginning of 1883. The Curators adjourned discussion and gave no further thought to it.[5] But it remained clear to Nicholson that 'before many years the increase of the already huge bulk of the catalogue will necessitate the introduction of printing instead of transcription, and the gradual reprint of all the old entries'.[6] The way for this was being shown by the British Museum, which commenced printing its General Catalogue in 1881, to complete it in 1905.

It was useless, however, to think of printing the catalogue as it stood. Divergence of cataloguing style was too apparent. Before printing there must come revision, and by 1899 the Curators were coming to regard 'the reduction of the catalogue to a more uniform system' as a matter of urgency.[7] They gave it high priority in their statement to Council in 1902 on the needs of the library, adding that subsequent printing, if it were found possible, would be of great advantage both for space-economy and for readers' convenience.[8] The last service that Professor Pelham rendered to Bodley before his

---

[1] Chandler, loc. cit.

[2] Curators' minutes, 12 June 1909.

[3] The copy of the catalogue kept in the Bodleian reading-room had grown between 1878 and 1897 from 724 to 829 volumes.

[4] Curators' minutes, 28 Feb. and 24 Apr. 1880.

[5] Minutes, 2 Dec. 1882 and 27 Jan. 1883.

[6] Curators' papers, 'Librarian's application for an increase of staff', 5 Nov. 1885.

[7] Curators' papers, 'Report of Auctarium Committee', 17 June 1899.

[8] Needs of the University, pp. 120, 126–7.

death was to get a committee appointed to consider the desirability and feasibility of printing the catalogue and to estimate its cost.[1]

The total cost of the work of revision, for which the engagement of a special staff would be necessary, was estimated by the librarian at £20,000, and the cost of printing and publication at another £30,000. For he now envisaged not merely printing, as at Cambridge, but publication also. Looking upon the catalogue as a work required for external and not merely for internal use, he abandoned his earlier project of printing accessions slips and of transforming the written catalogue into a printed one by a gradual process. Funds supplied by Oxford colleges and by the University Endowment Fund allowed the immediate engagement of staff and the commencement of work in the summer of 1907; and early in 1909 Nicholson was optimistic enough to forecast that the first part of letter A would go to the press in five years' time (that is, in 1914), and that thereafter the revisers' 'copy' would keep pace with the printer.[2]

What blasted early hopes of speedy execution was the amount of unnecessary labour put into the work of revision, in pursuing problems of authorship, and in cataloguing the contents of collectaneous volumes. If the catalogue was to be printed, it required compression. But revision swelled its bulk instead of lessening it, and by 1915 the 829 volumes of 1907 had increased to near 1,200. By that time the First World War was in progress; catalogue revision was brought to a halt, and, as we shall see in a later chapter (p. 270), was finally suspended to be taken up once more under new conditions after fifteen years' interval. In the meantime the library was left with an unrevised copy of its catalogue in the Camera, and a half-revised copy in Bodley; but in this last, since no attempt had been made to bring slips written before 1883 into conformity with the cataloguing rules observed from that date, divergence in the form of catalogue entry still continued. Only in regard to headings—and this was a considerable achievement—had some uniformity been attained.

---

[1] Curators' minutes, 1 Dec. 1906.

[2] Statement by the librarian on revision and printing of the Bodleian Catalogue of Printed Books, for the information of the Trustees of the Oxford University Endowment Fund, 27 Feb. 1909.

Chapter X
Printed Books

I. LIBRARY GROWTH AND THE COPYRIGHT PRIVILEGE

A CALCULATION made in 1885 gave the total number of printed volumes in the Bodleian Library as 406,159, or nearly double the number that had been returned thirty-six years before: one made in 1915 gave it as 1,009,206.[1] The two estimates were made on different bases; the earlier one was of actual volumes, while the later estimate was of books translated into terms of octavo volumes, eight folios being reckoned as equivalent to $14\frac{1}{2}$ octavos. The increase in the thirty years, 1885–1915, may therefore have been rather less than the figures suggest. But the main conclusion is unquestionable: the library was continuing to double its size approximately in the space of a generation.

Estimates of content, and consequently of growth, may be checked by taking the annual rate of increase. The number of items received into the library in 1885 was 45,181; in 1911 it was 73,963. Although these are exact figures, the information which they give is not so precise as might appear. For *items*, in library statistics, are units of very varying size. Each one may represent a bound volume, or a part of a periodical, or a single map or printed sheet. If we have recourse to the imaginary octavo as our standard of measurement, we get a truer idea but less exact data. In an earlier chapter (p. 61) reason was given for thinking that by 1880 the annual intake, excluding periodicals, may have reached, but can hardly have exceeded, 8,000 octavo volumes. But quite early in his career Nicholson was calculating the total intake at 12,000. 'Every eight years we receive an amount of fresh matter equal to about 100,000 copies of the *University Calendar*. To provide for that increase we must provide an amount of shelving about equal to a bookcase $\frac{1}{4}$ of a mile long and as high as a man can easily reach.'[2] The amount grew as years went on; the annual increase in 1898–9 in terms of octavos was returned as 16,249;[3] and in 1916 it was roughly estimated at 20,000.

There were a number of causes contributing to the increase. One was the reception, on a far greater scale than in the past, of academic

---

[1] *The Bodleian Library in 1882–7*, p. 3; Madan, 'Statistical Survey of the Bodleian Library' in *Bodleian Quarterly Record*, vol. i, pp. 254–62.

[2] Curators' papers, Letter to the Vice-Chancellor, 5 June 1884.

[3] Curators' papers, 22 June 1901.

theses from abroad. Nicholson found the library receiving the doc-
tors' dissertations of eleven foreign universities, namely, those of
Prussia and the University of Strasbourg. He persuaded the remaining German universities, the universities of the Scandinavian countries, of Holland and of Switzerland, and the sixteen academies of the
University of France, to follow suit; and thenceforward some 3,000
of these products of profound or immature research poured yearly
into Bodley.[1] But the largest contributor to the library's growth was
the Copyright Act.

From 1885 we are fortunate in having exact returns of what Bodley received under the Act, and can trace the general trend of copyright intake as a fairly steady rise from 31,792 items in 1885 to a peak
of 52,820 in 1913, the last full year before the outbreak of the First
World War, after which came a temporary decline. It is noteworthy
that the sum total of accessions pursued a parallel course throughout
the period, copyright intake accounting for something between sixty
and seventy per cent. of the whole.[2]

In the past the trouble had been to ensure that the library's agent
should collect all the books which he was entitled to claim under the
Act; and in 1881 Jowett, ever insistent on the library's rights in the
matter, persuaded his colleagues to appoint a committee to consider
the collection of copyright books.[3] His efforts proved only too successful. Chandler, for one, saw reason for alarm. 'If we do not take
speedy measures to avert the catastrophe', he wrote, 'we shall, like
Tarpeia, be crushed under the gifts which we solicit.'[4] The comparison was apt, and, ten years after Chandler had made his solitary
protest, a Curatorial committee recommended 'that steps be taken
to diminish the quantity of books received under the Copyright Act'.
Nicholson was not of their opinion; he had always been strict in exer-
cising the library's rights to the full, arguing that 'no printed matter
which the Library receives under the Act is valueless to posterity'.
Despite his protest the Curators entered into communication with
the other privileged libraries with a view to arriving at some limitation of acquisitions, only to find that no agreement was considered at
that time to be possible.[5]

[1] *The Bodleian Library in 1882–7*, p. 9.
[2] The figures for 1885–7 are given op. cit., p. 4; those for the following years are
conveniently tabulated in *Library Provision in Oxford*, 1931, p. 151. No comparison
is possible with returns for earlier years, which are for books and periodicals only,
and do not include maps or music, cards, or single sheets.
[3] Curators' minutes, 5 Mar. 1881.
[4] Memorandum of 10 Nov. 1885.
[5] Report of Committee on Extension of the Bodleian Library, 1 Mar. 1895;

Despite its drawbacks, the free reception of all works published in the United Kingdom was a valuable privilege, calculated to be worth about £2,000 a year.[1] The Bodleian, along with Cambridge and with Trinity College, Dublin, came near to losing it in 1911, when a new Copyright Bill came before Parliament and a series of amendments were moved in both Houses with the aim of withdrawing or restricting the privilege. All attacks upon the position of the university libraries were beaten off by the reasoned arguments of Sir William Anson and of Lord Curzon, and by energetic lobbying on the part of the Cambridge Librarian, Francis Jenkinson.[2] So under the new Act, which became law as 1 & 2 Geo. V, c. 46, the Bodleian was confirmed in its long-established privilege.

2. PURCHASES

When discussing Nicholson's finance we had occasion to speak of the disappointingly small revenue that was left available for book-purchase. Nicholson inherited the financial stringency that had so restricted buying under his predecessor Coxe, and for which he was not himself to blame. The fault of his financial administration was that, while library revenues increased under his rule, the amount left available for purchases tended to diminish. Taking a five-year average of library revenue and of library expenditure on purchases at the end of Bandinel's librarianship and at the end of Nicholson's, one finds that revenue had more than doubled and that book-purchases had fallen by nearly one fifth.[3] Despite Nicholson's attempts to show that expenditure on printed books was as high as could possibly be expected, it is clear that already by 1888 many members of the university were convinced that the library was not buying the books that it needed.

A memorial addressed in that year to the Curators asked that a more systematic attempt should be made to obtain important foreign books as they appeared, and to fill up gaps by second-hand purchases on a larger scale than heretofore; that, to avoid needless duplication, the Bodleian should arrange with the Radcliffe Library at the Museum

memorandum by Nicholson, 'The Hebdomadal Council and the Bodleian', 19 Nov. 1896, p. 11; Reports of Special Committee of the Curators, 13 Mar. and 14 June 1897.

[1] See above, p. 64, for the valuation of £2,108 made in 1879. It is curious to find that the estimate given to Parliament in 1911 was slightly less, namely, £2,067. But the latter figure was arrived at after deducting 25 per cent. from the published price. Partridge, *Legal Deposit of Books*, p. 338.

[2] H. F. Stewart, *Francis Jenkinson*, 1926, pp. 69–75.

[3] The figures are, for 1855–9, average revenue £5,090, average book expenditure £1,946; for 1907–11, average revenue £10,125, average book expenditure £1,585.

and with the Taylorian Library at the Taylor Institution for concerted action in ordering foreign books; and finally that, in order to allow a larger proportion of the library's income to be devoted to book-purchases, the Curators should exercise greater economy in binding, should reduce staff expenses, and, above all, should discontinue the subject-catalogue.

The Curators appointed the inevitable committee to draw up an answer to the memorialists, and, as commonly happened, the committee was presided over by Jowett. Disregarding criticisms of the way in which library money was being spent (for the Curators had given their last blessing to the subject-catalogue a few months before), they returned a disarming answer to the other two points raised in the memorial. More concerted action would be taken between the librarians of the three libraries named. (This proved an empty and a broken promise.) And, expressing a 'hope that a more definite system may be introduced in the purchase of books', they agreed to meet once a week in order to consider lists of books which the librarian proposed to purchase. But these weekly meetings came to an end in the very term in which they were instituted, since it proved impossible ever to obtain a quorum, and the order to hold them was eventually rescinded.[1] With the exception of Bywater and Mowat of Pembroke, none of the Curators were anxious to burden themselves with book-selection; so, despite questions asked in Convocation,[2] no improvement came.

It was left to the Board of Faculty of Modern History some years later, in 1904, to call attention to deficiencies in their field of study, and to the need for more foreign books and periodicals. Their action eventually prompted an offer from Mr. (afterwards Sir John) Fischer Williams, who concealed his identity under the title 'Ex-Prize Fellow', to give £1,000, payable in ten instalments, for filling up deficiencies in works on modern history. The offer was made and accepted in 1909. And increased attention began to be paid to Imperial history when, in 1904, Mr. Alfred Beit and Mr. Wernher between them contributed £500 for the purchase of books on the history of the British Dominions (including that of the American colonies before the Declaration of Independence), and T. A. Brassey gave £100 for books on the history of the British colonies and dependencies. Through these various

[1] Curators' minutes, 1 Dec. 1888; 11 Mar. 1893.
[2] Under the rule allowing ten members of Convocation to address questions to any Board or Delegacy. The questions, put on 4 Nov. 1889, asked what steps had been taken to meet the requests made in the memorial and, in addition, whether the Curators were satisfied with the employment of so large a number of boys on the staff.

means some progress was made in the supply of defects in modern historical literature.

Meanwhile the buying of old and rare books continued upon a modest scale. An annual grant of £150 made by Trinity College between the years 1898 and 1906 was allocated to the purchase of rare books and manuscripts. This relieved the ordinary funds of the library from an expense that they had hitherto borne. But the sum, after all, was extremely small and now went a very little way. For from the middle eighties Robert Hoe of New York and other American collectors were entering on the English second-hand market, and, under the stress of their competition, prices had begun to soar. At the very beginning of the new century the Bodleian Curators informed the Vice-Chancellor that 'the prices which early printed books and desirable MSS. now command are so high that it rarely happens that the sums offered by the Library are sufficient to effect any important purchase at a sale by auction'.[1]

The situation was accentuated by the fact that there were no reserves on which Bodley could draw as in the past. Realizing the want of them, the Curators, in 1902, included in their statement of the library's financial needs, the desirability of such an increase of library income as would allow a balance to be appropriated to special purchases.[2] In default of a reserve fund, or of such addition to its annual income as would make it possible to buy occasionally on a large scale, Bodley was unable either to make any extensive private purchase or to compete seriously in the sale-room, despite the opportunities that presented themselves. There were many such in the eighties, among them the sale of three great ducal libraries—the Duke of Marlborough's Sunderland library which Coxe himself had catalogued; the Hamilton and Beckford libraries of the Duke of Hamilton; and the library of the Duke of Buccleuch.

3. EARLY PRINTED BOOKS

On one occasion when a chance of making a large purchase arose, it was proposed that a special grant for the purpose should be made by the university. This happened in the autumn of 1891, when it became known that Earl Spencer was preparing to sell that most famous of all private libraries which his grandfather, the second earl, had formed at Althorp. The Althorp collection, over which the enthusiastic Dibdin had once presided, included fifty-seven examples of Caxton's press. These were being offered for sale for the sum

---

[1] *Statements of the Needs of the University*, 1902, p. 128.   [2] Op. cit., p. 120.

of £15,510. Of the fifty-seven Caxtons the British Museum wanted fifteen; so its Director, Maunde Thompson, sounded the university libraries of Oxford and Cambridge as to whether they would join in purchasing the lot. Bodley lacked thirty-four of the Caxtons while Cambridge was without twenty-seven. On a report made to them, the Curators agreed to Maunde Thompson's proposal and resolved to apply for a university grant of £2,500. The intention was that the libraries joining in the purchase should share out the Caxtons between themselves, and dispose of duplicates by public auction. But Cambridge proved unenthusiastic; at Oxford the Hebdomadal Council declined to ask for a vote of money; and Lord Spencer objected to public sales which would have put his Caxtons into the hands of private collectors. So the negotiations fell through.[1] A few months later a purchaser was found for the entire Althorp library. It was bought *en bloc* by Mrs. Rylands for nearly a quarter of a million pounds, and now forms the core or kernel of the John Rylands Library which she founded at Manchester in memory of her husband.

Other specimens of English fifteenth-century printing were occasionally forthcoming, as in 1899, when Macray found in the binding of a book in Magdalen College library four sheets, each containing four copies of an unknown proclamation printed in 1496 by Caxton's pupil, Wynkyn de Worde, of which one sheet was presented by the college to the Bodleian. And the library bought from Quaritch in 1892 for £92. 10s. one fifteenth-century book of special Oxford interest. This was a copy, albeit imperfect, of the *Compendium Grammaticae*, composed by Anwykyll, first master of Magdalen College grammar-school; a work printed at Oxford about 1483, of which otherwise only a few stray leaves have survived.[2] The first Oxford printer, Theodoric Rood, eventually returned to his home in Germany, and a volume containing five separate works printed by him at Cologne about 1485 was bought for Bodley in 1899 for the sum of £22. 10s.

It was possible, without incurring any great expense, for the library to keep on adding to the number of its continental *incunabula*, as, for example, in 1899 when £65 was paid for eight rare products of early Spanish presses. Seventy-five fifteenth-century books were bought in one year (1885) and ninety-four in the next. Many *incunabula* had been bought in 1884 on the dispersal of the large library of the Carthusian monastery of Buxheim in Bavaria. And a single year (1884) saw the purchase of as many as thirteen separate editions of

[1] Library Records, 'The negotiations for the purchase of Caxtons'.
[2] Madan, *Oxford Books*, vol. i, p. 257; vol. ii, p. 5.

that most popular of medieval story-books, the *Legenda Sanctorium* of Jacobus de Voragine.[1]

There was as yet no separate catalogue of Bodleian *incunabula*. Bandinel had compiled one in 1827, but it had never advanced beyond the stage of printer's proof. In 1866 the great Henry Bradshaw, on a visit to Oxford from Cambridge, had amused himself by listing the English fifteenth-century books and fragments that he found in Bodley. Prefacing his list with some remarks that reflected on the care that Oxford librarians took of their typographical treasures, he sent it to Coxe with the suggestion that he should print it. Coxe not unnaturally demurred, and returned the manuscript to Bradshaw, with the words 'You must not expect me to thong the whip wherewith we may be lashed.' Bradshaw in a fit of annoyance tore up the list, of which he had no other copy, and threw it into the fire.[2]

Better fortune attended the next attempts that were made to list the early printed books in Bodley. In the later eighties two Oxford undergraduates successively became absorbed in the study of early printing types. They became close friends and established for themselves lasting reputations as authorities on early typography. One was Edward Gordon Duff of Wadham, the other was R. G. C. Proctor of Corpus.[3]

Nicholson engaged Gordon Duff's services in 1886 while he was still an undergraduate and started him on a slip-catalogue of Bodleian *incunabula*. By the time that Duff went down in June 1886 he had gone half-way through the alphabet, bringing his catalogue up to the end of the letter J. Proctor took up Duff's unfinished work early in 1891. When he left Oxford to join the staff of the British Museum he had completed the catalogue, besides listing all the library's fragments of early printing. His catalogue recorded 4,832 *incunabula*, in addition to which the library possessed 605 duplicates and 172 fragments. Nor did his work cease there, but, proceeding to do for the British Museum what he had done for Bodley, he published in 1898 his *Index of Early Printed Books in the British Museum, with notes of those in the Bodleian*. In this work, which at once became rightly famous (for Proctor's sense of type amounted to genius), books printed before 1501 and represented in either of the two libraries are arranged on the principle that Bradshaw had devised, under countries, towns,

---

[1] *The Bodleian Library in 1882–7*, pp. 19, 20.
[2] Prothero, *Memoir of Henry Bradshaw*, pp. 203–5.
[3] A short memoir of Gordon Duff was contributed by Falconer Madan to the *Library*, 4th ser., vol. v, pp. 264–6. A memoir of Proctor by A. W. Pollard appeared first in the *Library*, N.S., vol. v, and was reprinted as preface to Robert Proctor's *Bibliographical Essays*, 1905.

and presses. Those that are in Bodley as well as in the Museum are indicated by an asterisk, and those that are in Bodley but were not then in the Museum are marked by an obelisk. An interleaved copy of 'Proctor', in which Bodleian pressmarks are added, is kept up to date on the shelves of the Old Reading-Room.

There was another cataloguing enterprise inaugurated by Nicholson, in which Proctor similarly carried on what Gordon Duff had begun. The year 1640 marks a dividing line in English bibliography, for it just precedes that Civil War which let loose an unprecedented flood of pamphlets from this country's printing presses. In 1884 the British Museum produced a three-volume catalogue of books in its library printed in England, Scotland, or Ireland, as well as of books in English printed abroad, up to 1640. This was known as the 1640 catalogue, and Gordon Duff was employed by Nicholson to note down all English books which were not to be found in it but which occurred in the Bodleian catalogue. This he did for the letters A–C, but his work then stopped to allow him to make more rapid progress with his catalogue of *incunabula*. It was resumed in 1892–3 by Proctor who made out a rough list for the second part of the alphabet (H–Z), of all English books in Bodley printed between 1500 and 1640. The list was completed, after Proctor left, by other members of the staff. It was a useful piece of work, but has now been superseded by that invaluable book of reference, the *Short-Title Catalogue*, which the Bibliographical Society published in 1927.

4. A SHAKESPEARE FIRST FOLIO AND OTHER PURCHASES

The most famous, though by no means the rarest, of English books of the early seventeenth century is the collected edition of Shakespeare's Plays published in 1623 and universally known as the First Folio. Sir Thomas Bodley had no love of plays and would have excluded them from his library. His successors were better advised. The seventeenth-century catalogues show that the Bodleian had a copy of the First Folio in 1635, though it was no longer in the library in 1674. Presumably it had been included in a packet of 'superfluous Library books' sold in 1664 to an Oxford bookseller for the modest sum of £24, the publication of the Third Folio having made the First (so it was then thought) obsolete. Thereafter the Bodleian had no First Folio until one came to it in the Malone collection.

When, at the beginning of the Hilary Term of 1905, a young B.A. of Magdalen walked into Bodley bearing under his arm an unusually large, but rather dilapidated, copy of the First Folio of Shakespeare, there was no special reason for thinking that anything exciting was going to happen. The book belonged to his father, Mr. W. G. Turbutt of Ogston Hall in Derbyshire, in whose family it had remained for at least five generations. Fortunately, as it turned out, the book was still in a contemporary binding, and Mr. Turbutt sought advice as to its treatment and repair. The volume was shown to Mr. Strickland Gibson, a young assistant in the library but already the author of a standard work on early Oxford bindings. He noticed at once that the book-cover was Oxford work; also that it bore the marks of the clip by which it had once been attached to an iron chain. Obviously it had come from a chained library, and that, presumably, one in Oxford. Could it be the copy that had once belonged to the Bodleian?

In a few minutes the point was established beyond all doubt. Bodley fortunately preserves most of its library records, including the little old memoranda books in which were noted the volumes sent out for binding. An entry in one of them showed that on 17 February 1624 the Bodleian under-librarian gave out 'William Shakespeares comedies, histories etc.', with other books, to be bound by William Wildgoose. It was the habit of Oxford binders at that time to line the inner sides of their book-covers with leaves taken from some printed book. And one of the books bound by Wildgoose on that distant February day was found to contain in its binding consecutive fragments of the same fifteenth-century book as appeared in Mr. Turbutt's Shakespeare Folio.

No doubt was left that the Folio which its owner had sent for inspection was the identical copy that the Stationers' Company had sent in sheets to the library upon publication. On that ground it had an historical interest that no other First Folio possessed. So it was not surprising that, when the existence of the Turbutt copy became known,[1] its owner received from the London booksellers, Sotheran and Co., acting on behalf of an unnamed New York client, an offer to buy the precious volume for £3,000. It was an unprecedented price for an English buyer to pay, even for a First Folio, though the would-be purchaser, who is now known to have been Mr. Henry C. Folger,[2] is reputed to have paid £10,000—at that time the highest price ever

[1] It was exhibited on 21 Feb. 1905 to the Bibliographical Society, and its discovery was announced by Madan in an unsigned article in the *Athenaeum* of 25 Feb. He and Strickland Gibson and young Turbutt collaborated in a monograph published later in the year entitled *The Original Bodleian Copy of the First Folio of Shakespeare*.

[2] An account of the Folger side of the negotiations has been given by Mr. Robert Smith in the *Review of English Studies*, vol. xv (1939), pp. 257-64. See also L. W. Hanson in *Shakespeare Survey*, 1951, pp. 82-84.

given for a printed book—for the Jaggard presentation copy of the First Folio, now reposing, with seventy-eight other copies, in the Folger Library at Washington. Nevertheless there was nothing to be done but to try to raise the sum needed for the restoration of the volume to Bodley. On being informed of Sotheran's offer, Nicholson, acting on his own responsibility, issued to present and past members of the university an appeal for funds for the book's repurchase. The appeal was issued on 11 November: the offer was to remain open until the end of the following March. Mr. Turbutt himself contributed £200, but subscriptions were slow in coming in. On the very last day of March the Regius Professor of Medicine, Sir William Osler, succeeded in obtaining from his fellow-Canadian, Lord Strathcona, a gift of £500, and so, by completing the required sum, secured the Folio for its old home at Oxford.

Other purchases of printed books were insignificant in comparison. The only sale of this period at which Bodley bid on a large scale appears to have been that of the Rev. W. J. Blew in 1895, when many liturgical volumes were bought, chiefly breviaries and missals of continental uses. More attention was paid under Nicholson than formerly to books printed in uncommon languages. A number of books in Finnish or relating to Finland were bought at the Benfey sale in 1883. The year 1887 saw the purchase of four items of considerable rarity— the Gospels and Acts in Slovenish, printed in 1557; the first Polish Bible (1561); the Lindau catechism of 1601, being the first book printed in Romansh; and St. Matthew's Gospel in Dutch and Malay (Enckhuysen, 1692).[1] And some continental literature came by gift. In 1901 the British Museum, having received by bequest from Mr. H. S. Ashbee a library rich in early French and Spanish books, presented more than 400 duplicates from it to the Bodleian. And in 1906 Mr. (afterwards Sir) Oliver Wardrop made the first of a number of gifts to Bodley in the form of a large collection of Russian political papers published at St. Petersburg.

Nicholson was equally on the look-out for first editions of the classics of English literature which had escaped the meshes of the Copyright Act. The purchase-lists for the years 1884–7 include first editions of *The Whole Duty of Man* (1658), of a number of Defoe's works, of Johnson's *Rasselas* (1759), of Wordsworth and Coleridge's *Lyrical Ballads* (1798), and of Bradshaw's *Railway Timetables* (19 October 1839).

---

[1] *The Bodleian Library in 1882–7*, p. 20.

5. RADCLIFFE AND SAVILE LIBRARIES

Except for brief periods in its history, Bodley had depended more upon donations than upon purchases for the increase of its collections. So it was through a body of subscribers that the library recovered the Turbutt First Folio. By the same method it received the Homeric library of Dr. D. B. Monro, Provost of Oriel College, consisting of over 1,000 volumes, which a number of his friends bought and presented on the Provost's death in 1905. In 1893 there had come the Shelley collection, of which we shall have occasion to speak later (pp. 194–5). So far as printed books are concerned, few other gifts of value were made by individual donors while Nicholson was librarian.[1] But Bodley continued to be enriched by other means: two whole libraries and a portion of a third were transferred by their official guardians into its custody.

When Dr. John Radcliffe included among the objects provided for by his will 'the building a library in Oxford', it was without any expressed intention that the library should be specialist in character. Only since 1811 had it limited itself to Medicine and Natural Science. Its eighteenth-century acquisitions included the collections of Oriental manuscripts which the Radcliffe Trustees transferred to Bodley in 1872, as well as much miscellaneous literature. In its new home on the first floor of the University Museum the Radcliffe Library expanded until shelf-room became a problem and the presence of non-scientific books a nuisance. The Radcliffe Trustees therefore decided in 1893 to hand over to Bodley any books on subjects other than science which the Curators might care to take, and to sell the remainder. Under this arrangement the Bodleian secured 766 volumes, including practically the whole of the book-collection which the architect James Gibbs had bequeathed in 1754 to the library which he built. Gibbs's books, all distinguished by his fine bookplate, are mainly works on architecture or volumes of engravings, for the most part Italian.[2] The other books which came to Bodley are chiefly histories and texts of classical authors. Some of them had formed part of the

---

[1] The printed donation-lists which had been issued annually since 1780 were discontinued in 1885. Since then the principal donations have been recorded in the library's annual reports.

[2] Bodl. MS. Eng. misc. c. 28 is a contemporary catalogue of Gibbs's books. Seven volumes of designs and drawings of the Radcliffe Camera and of other buildings of Gibbs's construction, along with a portfolio containing trial designs for the Radcliffe Library made by Nicholas Hawksmoor, are in the Fine Arts Department of the Ashmolean Museum, where they were deposited by the Radcliffe Trustees in 1925. The Hawksmoor drawings are described (by Miss S. Lang) in the *Architectural Review* for Apr. 1949, pp. 183–90, and also in the Bodleian Exhibition catalogue, *Bibliotheca Radcliviana, 1749–1949*, pp. 10–11, 32–34, with plates.

bequest made to the Radcliffe Library by Richard Frewin, doctor of medicine and Camden Professor of Ancient History (d. 1761), whose name is commemorated in Oxford by his residence, Frewin Hall.[1] The volumes not taken for the Bodleian were sold to an Oxford bookseller and so were dispersed.[2]

Unlike the Radcliffe Library, the Bibliotheca Saviliana came to Bodley intact. It has a long and interesting history. The magnificent but scholarly Warden of Merton and Provost of Eton, Sir Henry Savile, was a close friend of Sir Thomas Bodley and an early benefactor to his library, giving to it, in the course of the first twenty years of the seventeenth century, a large number of Greek and Latin manuscripts as well as printed books. But his main benefaction to the university, and that by which his name is still best remembered, was the foundation, in 1619, of two lectureships in mathematical studies, one in geometry, the other in astronomy. The two large schools on the first floor of the east range of the Schools quadrangle—one to the north, the other to the south of the Tower of the Five Orders—were assigned to geometry and to astronomy respectively; and, in between them, the room over the tower archway was given up to the joint use of Savile's professors and known as the Savile Study. Here, in shelved cupboards made for their reception, were placed the books of the professors' common library, the Bibliotheca Saviliana.[3]

Savile was of the opinion that a university chair should have a library attached to it. He pressed this point, though unsuccessfully, upon William Camden, who was at that time establishing in the university the history lectureship destined to become the Camden Chair of Ancient History. 'I for my part,' said he, 'have cleared my study of all the mathematical books which I had gathered in so many years and countreys, Greek and Latin, printed and manuscript, even to the very raw notes that I have ever made in that argument.'[4] Savile's donation comprised a quantity of fine printed books, chiefly of the sixteenth century, some of them enriched with his own annotations, and included about forty Greek and Latin astronomical and mathematical manuscripts.[5] Among the Bodleian records there remains, in

[1] Bodl. MS. Radcliffe Trust c. 35 is a catalogue of about 2,300 volumes, partly medical, partly historical and miscellaneous, left to the Radcliffe Library by Dr. Frewin.
[2] Catalogue of Books from the Radcliffe Library on sale by Blackwell, June 1894.
[3] The terms of the foundation of the Savile lectures are dated 11 Aug. 1619, and are set out in Gibson's *Statuta Antiqua Universitatis Oxoniensis*, pp. 528–37. They were supplemented by orders approved by Convocation on 8 Dec. 1620; op. cit., pp. 537–40.　　　　　[4] Thomas Smith, *Camdeni Epistolae*, 1691, p. 315.
[5] Catalogued, along with Greek manuscripts bequeathed by Dr. Peter Turner and papers by Dr. John Greaves, as nos. 6548–615 in the *Summary Catalogue of Western*

the form of a paper roll, a catalogue, signed by Savile, of the books and manuscripts that he gave to the university for the use of his Readers. They cover the whole field of mathematics, and include the allied subjects of optics, harmonics, mechanics, cosmography, as well as such applied mathematical sciences as surveying, navigation, and fortification. Astronomy is well represented; and although Savile very sensibly put an express embargo upon judicial astrology, that was a subject in which, as we have seen (p. 67), the Ashmolean Library was to become especially strong.

The seventeenth-century Savilian professors all made use of the library; nearly all of them added to it. Dr. Peter Turner, who held the Geometry Chair from 1631 to 1649, was a Greek scholar and bequeathed some half-dozen Greek manuscripts. His colleague, the Astronomy professor, John Greaves (1643–9), added papers of his own. But the first extensive accession to Savile's library was that which came from the most famous of all Savilian professors, Sir Christopher Wren. For, before architecture and the building of St. Paul's absorbed him, Wren held the Chair of Astronomy (1661–73), and, when he retired from it, he left his astronomy and geometry books to the library. Each of them is stamped on its spine with his cypher. Other books in the library bear a monogram which seems to be that of Wren's predecessor, Dr. Seth Ward (1649–61); but, if they are really his, they were not given before 1682, twenty years after the eclipse of the Puritan party at the Restoration had obliged him to vacate the chair.[1]

Wren was succeeded by Dr. Edward Bernard (1673–91). As 'a person admirably well read in all kind of ancient learning'[2] Bernard was thoroughly qualified to be chief editor of the *Catalogi Librorum Manuscriptorum Angliae et Hiberniae*, the first and only attempt to catalogue all public and private manuscript collections in this country; and, though he did not live to see its publication in 1698, he had completed it for the press, inserting in it a catalogue of the printed books, as well as of the manuscripts, in the Savile library.[3] An orientalist as well as a classical scholar, he was himself a great book-collector. His manuscripts, which were chiefly of classical authors and in great part

Manuscripts, vol. ii, pp. 1094–114. A number of important manuscripts of medieval English chroniclers that had belonged to Savile remained in his family until 1860, when they were sold by auction at Sotheby's.

[1] Seth Ward ended his days in 1689 as Bishop of Salisbury, and by his will left half his books to the cathedral library, the other half to a nephew.

[2] Wood, *Athenae Oxonienses*, ed. Bliss, vol. iv, col. 702.

[3] Pars i, pp. 303–13. The catalogue, not a very good one, was compiled by John Caswell, who subsequently became Astronomy professor (1709–12).

bought at Nicholas Heinsius's sale, together with his collated printed texts and his own *adversaria*, were bought for the Bodleian for £200 from his widow, who also sold to Bodley for £140 a selection of his printed books.[1] These, picked over by another great English scholar, Humphrey Wanley, who was at that time working on the staff of the university library, included many rare Aldines and *incunabula*. But nothing came from Bernard to the Bibliotheca Saviliana.

During the whole time that Ward, Wren, and Bernard successively occupied the Chair of Astronomy, and for some years afterwards, the Geometry professorship was held by that Grand Old Man of seventeenth-century Oxford, the Keeper of the University Archives, Dr. John Wallis (Savilian professor 1649–1704). Through him Savile's library received the largest of its accretions. Wallis gave some of his books in his lifetime, but the great bulk of them were presented after his death by his son, and are easily distinguishable by the name 'John Wallis' stamped on a red label, which occurs with monotonous regularity upon the spine of every volume.[2]

As a result of the gifts of Savilian professors, the library of which they had the custody is a very complete collection of mathematical works up to the end of the seventeenth century. Probably, as its official custodians said in 1865, 'no similar collection exists elsewhere in England'. But throughout the eighteenth century the library remained a *caput mortuum*; hardly a book was added to it. Eminent astronomers enjoyed the benefits of Savile's foundation, among them two Astronomers Royal; for Edmund Halley was Professor of Geometry from 1704 to 1742, and James Bradley Professor of Astronomy from 1721 to 1763. But although Bradley's astronomical papers came to Oxford through the medium of Lord North, it was to the Bodleian and not to the Savilian library that they were presented.[3] They were eventually to find an editor in a later Savilian professor, Stephen Rigaud.[4]

Rigaud held the Geometry Chair from 1810 to 1827, exchanging it in the latter year for the professorship of Astronomy. Like his immediate predecessors he combined this last post with that of Radcliffe Observer, and took charge of the Observatory which Dr. John

---

[1] Macray, *Annals*, p. 165. Bernard's manuscripts are catalogued, as nos. 8717–886, in the *Summary Catalogue*, vol. iii, pp. 1–24.

[2] The books given by Wallis junior are roughly listed in MS. Savile 101, fol. 11. Savile A–H and K–M consist almost without exception of Wren, Ward, and Wallis books. Savile's original donation, intermixed with later additions, is to be looked for in Savile N–Z, Aa, and Bb.

[3] The Bradley collection is catalogued, as nos. 16404–54, in the *Summary Catalogue*, vol. iii, pp. 604–13. It includes various lectures delivered by Savilian professors.

[4] Rigaud, *Works and Correspondence of the rev. James Bradley*, 1832.

Radcliffe's Trustees had erected at considerable cost. Besides being a practical astronomer, he was most learned in the history and bibliography of astronomy and of mathematics. A scholar, a man of method and a book-collector, he alone of the later Savilian professors took an active interest in the Savilian library. He catalogued it[1] and added to it in his lifetime. When he died in 1839, and his large library (chiefly of eighteenth-century writers) was sold, his books on astronomy, mathematics, and physics were purchased for £330 by the Radcliffe Trustees for their Observatory. There they remained until 1935, when the Trustees handed over to the Bodleian Library all Rigaud books (about 840 in number) not already represented in it, and sold off the remainder. Rigaud's carefully kept notebooks on astronomy, mathematics, and scientific subjects, including the material for his work on Bradley and for an unwritten biography of Halley, were presented by his sons in 1874 to the Savile library.[2]

Professor Rigaud lived to see the old Savile Study in the Schools tower appropriated, in 1835, by the Bodleian Curators, and the Bibliotheca Saviliana, with its book cupboards, crowded into a dark little room in the south-east corner of the quadrangle. It was an inconvenient place for any library, so it is not surprising that in 1865 the Savilian professors should have suggested its removal thence to the Camera. A committee of Council considered the proposal and advised transfer to the professors' rooms in the University Museum.[3] Nothing was done at that time or until 1884, when the professors agreed to hand over the administration of their library to Bodley's librarian. The books remained where they were until 1940, when they were transferred, with the rest of the contents of ground-floor and first-floor rooms, to a new library book-stack, and their seventeenth-century cupboards went to furnish a Curators' Room.

6. MUSIC

The library of the Music School, which the Bodleian absorbed in 1885,[4] had nearly as long a history as the Savilian library. It too was attached to a professorial chair, for Dr. William Heather, who founded the music lecture in 1626, bequeathed the nucleus of a library,[5] namely a few printed volumes of English madrigals and songs and Italian madrigals, along with a manuscript collection of masses

[1] Rigaud's catalogue is MS. Rigaud 67 in the Bodleian.
[2] They are catalogued as nos. 26203-67 in the *Summary Catalogue*, vol. v, pp. 197-206.
[3] Hebdomadal Council minutes, 1854-66, p. 449; Council Committee minute-book, 1857-73, p. 58.   [4] By statute, 27 Jan. 1885.
[5] Described in *Bodleian Quarterly Record*, vol. v, pp. 23-24.

by early Tudor composers styled, after its first owner, the Forrest collection. From this small beginning the Music School Library grew, as the result of gifts made to it during the seventeenth and eighteenth centuries, until it came to possess about 880 manuscripts,[1] for the most part works by English musicians. Among these were three Edwardian cathedral part-books, perhaps in John Taverner's autograph; and a volume of fantasias, music to masques, &c., in the autograph of William Lawes. There was much English music of the late seventeenth and of the early eighteenth century. The library also possessed a complete set of the court odes which Dr. William Boyce composed for the King's birthday and for the New Year when he was Master of the King's Band of Musicians (1755–79), and the music written for, and performed at, the 'Oxford Act', with which the Encaenia used to be celebrated during the fifty years that followed the Restoration. When the Acts fell into disuse, candidates for musical degrees continued to perform their exercises in the Music School and deposit them in its library. Apart from Italian pieces the School possessed little continental music. Its printed books were comparatively few, and consisted chiefly of Italian instrumental music of the end of the seventeenth century.

Although a statute passed in 1856 empowered the Bodleian Curators to transfer their music to the Music School (see p. 79), no use was made of that permission. The Curators retained custody of their piles of copyright music and of the more valuable Wight bequest. The Music School Library continued to be kept as a separate collection in the Music School even after that room was taken over in 1874 for general examination purposes; and, though it was moved out to the New Examination Schools on their completion, it was brought back in 1885 to the Music School and the Bodleian musical collections were placed there also. So the two libraries were brought together under one control.

The music that came in under the Copyright Act up to 1845 had been arranged and bound, but later accessions had been allowed to accumulate in immense piles, unbound and even unshelved; and, until Nicholson became librarian, no attempt was made to catalogue any of them. Nicholson at once started to bind and to catalogue new accessions and to cope with arrears.[2] 'We shall soon have a separate musical catalogue like that of the British Museum', he wrote in the first burst of enthusiasm.[3] The Bodleian music-catalogue was on slips,

[1] Catalogued as nos. 26342–27119, in *Summary Catalogue*, vol. v, pp. 210–73.
[2] *The Bodleian Library in 1882–7*, pp. 30, 35.
[3] Memorandum dated 25 Oct. 1884.

but towards the end of his librarianship Nicholson was contemplating its transfer on to cards and its eventual printing.

The music section was increased in other ways than by the constant stream of copyright music and by the incorporation of the Music School Library. A grave deficiency was supplied in 1899 when the Oxford University Musical Club presented a complete set of Bach's works and full scores of Haydn and Mozart. The Bodleian also added from time to time by purchase, both to its manuscript and printed collection, buying in 1903 forty-seven volumes of eighteenth-century music and in 1885 five manuscript part-books of Elizabethan motets.

Attention was directed to the amount of early music awaiting investigation in Bodley by Dr. Frere's publication, in 1894 and 1901, of the first but only completed volume of his *Bibliotheca musico-liturgica*. In this he calendared the musical and Latin liturgical manuscripts of the Middle Ages that are to be found in the Bodleian or in Oxford college libraries, and his work therefore serves as a finding-list for their stores of early church music. A little later Sir John Stainer (Professor of Music at Oxford from 1889 to 1899) discovered in a Canonici manuscript, and published, a collection of fifteenth-century Belgian, French, and Italian songs by the Flemish Dufay and contemporary musicians.[1] Two volumes entitled *Early Bodleian Music, Sacred and Secular Songs*, in which Stainer and Nicholson collaborated, followed in 1901, and gave transcripts of a collection of English carols (among them the famous *Song of Agincourt*) contained in a Selden manuscript of about 1450. Nicholson worked intensively during the later years of his life on the earliest Bodleian manuscripts containing musical notation, and the results were published posthumously in his elaborate *Introduction to the Study of the Oldest Latin Musical MSS. in the Bodleian* (1913).

[1] Published in 1898 as *Dufay and his Contemporaries*.

Chapter XI
Western Manuscripts

1. DEPOSITS OF COLLEGE MANUSCRIPTS

FROM the outset of his career Nicholson set himself to persuade the Oxford colleges to deposit their manuscripts in Bodley. The first to come in, in 1882, were those of *University College*. These, 193 in number,[1] were, almost without exception, of English provenance. They include, besides Latin medieval manuscripts, a number of works (chiefly religious prose) in Middle English. Few volumes remain from the college's medieval library, but its manuscript collection was materially increased by the manuscripts which came with the library of printed books formed by Mr. Thomas Browne (d. 1587), and, after the Restoration, by gifts from Dr. Thomas Walker, Master of the College (d. 1665), and from Anthony Wood's Romanist friend, William Rogers of Painswick. Among the latter's gifts was a fine twelfth-century illuminated manuscript of Bede's Life of St. Cuthbert (MS. 165). Other manuscripts can be traced, on internal evidence, as having belonged to Gerard Langbaine, the learned Provost of Queen's College. There are also two chartularies of Fountains Abbey (MSS. 167, 170), and a few statutes and rentals of English ecclesiastical foundations. The college's post-Reformation manuscripts were of minor interest, but among them were at least two stray volumes from Sir George Carew's collections for Irish history (MSS. 90, 103), the bulk of which are divided between Lambeth Library and the Laudian manuscripts in Bodley.[2]

The *Jesus College* manuscripts followed four years later. There were 141 of them,[3] among them an unusually high proportion of twelfth-century copies of works by Bede. The college's principal benefactor was Sir John Price, who took advantage of his position as Commissioner for the Visitation of the Monasteries under Henry VIII to secure a number of manuscripts from Cirencester, from the Benedictine cell of St. Guthlac at Hereford, and from other monasteries in the west midlands. Some of them he bequeathed to Hereford Cathedral; the rest came to Jesus College, though some of these last

---

[1] MSS. 1–188 are catalogued in Coxe's *Catalogus Codicum MSS. Coll. et Aul. Oxon.* pars i, art. 1, and later numbers in *Bodleian Library Record*, vol. iii, pp. 31–34.
[2] See for further details Dr. R. W. Hunt's paper on 'The manuscript collection of University College, Oxford: origins and growth', op. cit., pp. 13–34.
[3] Catalogued by Coxe, op. cit., pars ii, art. 6.

found their way later—one need not ask how—into the Cottonian collection now in the British Museum and into the Laudian collection in Bodley. Special mention may be made of a tenth-century Life of St. Gregory from St. Guthlac's (MS. 37) and, among the Cirencester books, of an early thirteenth-century manuscript of the works of its learned abbot, Alexander Neckham, which contains marginalia in Neckham's autograph (MS. 94). Although, as in most other college libraries, medieval Latin theological writings predominate, Jesus College is notable for its numerous Welsh manuscripts,[1] chief among them being the well-known corpus of Celtic historical and literary pieces styled the Red Book of Hergest (MS. 111), part of which dates from the early fourteenth century. One should not omit to notice a collection, also of the fourteenth century, of English and French poems (MS. 29). Over twenty volumes of later date came from the library of Anthony Wood's friend and patron, Ralph Sheldon,[2] and were intended by him for the College of Arms; but Wood proved faithless to the trust which Sheldon reposed in him, and the manuscripts came to Jesus College instead. They include a few collections of arms and pedigrees, Augustine Baker's collections for a history of the greater English Benedictine abbeys (MSS. 75–78),[3] and the original draft (MSS. 71–73) of the History of Henry VIII compiled by Lord Herbert of Cherbury (to whom the college owes a substantial portion of its early printed books). Two volumes (MSS. 115–16) of Browne Willis's gatherings for his History of Bangor have got separated from the rest of that antiquary's collections in the Bodleian.[4]

The manuscripts of *Hertford College* (deposited in 1890) and of *Brasenose* (1892) were fewer in number and later in date. More interest attaches to the 164 manuscripts which *Lincoln College* deposited in 1892.[5] Richard Flemmyng, Bishop of Lincoln, founded the college in 1427 for theologians, and the manuscripts which he left to his foundation were theological or scholastic. That busy and active theologian, Dr. Thomas Gascoigne,[6] was a benefactor to Lincoln as

---

[1] Described in detail in *Hist. MSS. Com., Welsh MSS.*, vol. ii, pp. 1–90.

[2] As was first pointed out by Mr. I. G. Philip in the *Bodleian Library Record*, vol. i, pp. 119–23.

[3] Baker's collections form the basis of Clement Reyner's *Apostolatus Benedictinorum in Anglia* (Douai, 1626).

[4] Further details are given by Professors Fordyce and Knox in the *Oxford Bibliographical Society, Proceedings and Papers*, vol. v, pp. 56–59. Their account of Jesus College Library is a model for college library histories, of which we possess as yet too few.

[5] Catalogued by Coxe, op. cit., pars i, art. 8.

[6] Miss W. Pronger has given a full account of Gascoigne, of his wide reading and

to other college libraries. As Chancellor of the University he was an influential person in his day. The good relations which he cultivated with the Oxford Franciscans gave him opportunities for raiding the Friars' library, and this perhaps accounts for the presence of a thirteenth-century Grosseteste (MS. lat. 54) among the books which he gave to Lincoln.[1] Gascoigne was a great annotator of books, and his marginalia still have their interest. His two thick notebooks, styled Dictionarium Theologicum (MSS. lat. 117, 118), abound in autobiographical detail.[2]

The founder's nephew, Robert Flemmyng, Dean of Lincoln, was a greater benefactor than either of these, and his books are of a different order. He was one of our early English humanists, had studied at Padua and Ferrara, and had been an emissary to the Roman Curia. His sojourn in Italy gave him opportunities for collecting fifteenth-century copies of classical and neo-classical texts: these he included in the large donation which he made to Lincoln College in 1465. Unlike the books of Humphrey, Duke of Gloucester, Flemmyng's gift has survived almost intact; and it ranks, with the library of books given a few years later to Balliol by Bishop William Grey, as a symbol of the New Learning which was finding by these means a home in Oxford.[3]

Robert Flemmyng studied Greek at Ferrara under Guarino da Verona, and Lincoln still possesses a copy of the Acts and Pauline Epistles in Greek which he presented to it. Much later the college obtained thirty-seven Greek manuscripts, the gift of one who had been a gentleman-commoner. George Wheler[4] made his reputation by travelling in Greece and the Levant in 1675–6, at a time when such travel was rare and difficult. On his return home he received a knighthood, Holy Orders, and a Durham prebend; and he earned an Oxford doctorate in 1683 by adding to the Arundel and Selden Marbles the Greek inscriptions which he had brought back with him

of his benefactions, in the *English Historical Review*, vol. liii (1938), pp. 606–26, and vol. liv (1939), pp. 20–37.

[1] See Anthony Wood, *City of Oxford* (Oxf. Hist. Soc., xvii), vol. ii, p. 381, and A. G. Little, *Grey Friars in Oxford* (Oxf. Hist. Soc., xx), pp. 59, 61. Miss Pronger gives a variety of reasons for taking a more lenient view.

[2] Some, but not all, of the more interesting passages have been edited, in 1881, by Thorold Rogers as *Loci e Libro Veritatum*.

[3] The best account of Robert Flemmyng and his manuscripts is that given by Prof. Weiss in *Humanism in England in the Fifteenth Century*, pp. 97–105. See also the same writer's paper on 'The Earliest Catalogues of the Library of Lincoln College' in the *Bodleian Quarterly Record*, vol. viii, pp. 343–59.

[4] His career has been most fully set out by Dr. Whiting in *Transactions of the Architectural and Archaeological Society of Durham and Northumberland*, vol. x, pp. 83–101.

from his travels. The rest of his spoils he kept during his lifetime. On his death in 1723 he bequeathed to the university a herbarium of dried plants (now in Bodley with the pressmark MSS. Ashmole 1800–3), and left his Greek manuscripts to his old college. Half of them are liturgical, the remainder chiefly theological. Most are late in date, but they include a 'typicon' or monastic rule, of the fourteenth century, illustrated by magnificent portraits of princes and princesses of the Byzantine imperial house of Comnenus (MS. gr. 35).

Some years elapsed before any other college deposited its manuscripts in Bodley, but *New College* eventually followed suit in 1907.[1] The manuscripts with which its founder, William of Wykeham, enriched the college, and those presented to it by early New College men such as William Rede, Bishop of Chichester (who divided his gifts between New College and Merton), and Richard Andrewe, Warden of All Souls and Dean of York, were the Latin texts required in the late fourteenth and early fifteenth centuries by students in the higher faculties of theology, medicine, and canon and civil law.[2] One of the college's first wardens, Thomas Cranley, who subsequently became Archbishop of Dublin, deserves to be remembered for his habit—rare in his time—of entering in each of his manuscripts the date of its purchase and the name of the person from whom he bought it. A later warden, Thomas Chaundler (1454–75), was, like Robert Flemmyng, a promulgator of humanism. He and his patron, Thomas Bekynton, Bishop of Bath and Wells, were both of them benefactors to the college library; and MS. 288 is a presentation copy of Chaundler's literary compositions, with interesting drawings of New College and of Winchester, made for Bishop Bekynton and given by him to New College. Humanistic texts began to come in towards the end of the fifteenth century. New College possesses various manuscripts of the Latin works of Boccaccio and Petrarch, some of them presented to it by John Russell, the learned Bishop of Lincoln; and it has a fair number of Greek manuscripts, particularly of Aristotelian treatises and of the works of Chrysostom, which are in part a gift made in 1557 by Cardinal Pole. Of illuminated manuscripts one alone need be mentioned, but that is a fine one, a psalter illuminated by a known thirteenth-century English artist, William de Brailes (MS. 322).[3] Late accessions to the New College Library include a collection of papers

[1] Its manuscripts number 361. MSS. 1–344 are catalogued by Coxe, op. cit., pars i, art. 7.
[2] Lists of the manuscripts given by the founder, Bishop Rede, and other early donors are printed from the College Register in *Oxf. Hist. Soc. Collectanea*, vol. iii, pp. 213–44.
[3] Sidney Cockerell, *Work of W. de Brailes*, Roxburghe Club, 1930, pp. 7–11.

—chiefly theological and chronological—of Isaac Newton, which had been for some generations in the possession of the Ekins family (MS. 361).[1]

2. CLARENDON PRESS DEPOSIT

Another and a very different deposit was made in 1885 by the Delegates of the University Press. During the closing years of the eighteenth and early years of the nineteenth century a small library had come to be formed in the Delegates' Room at the Clarendon Building, the result of purchase and of bequest. It consisted partly of manuscript, partly of printed books with manuscript annotations. Of one considerable section in it, the books and papers of the Coptic scholar, C. G. Woide, we shall speak later (p. 213). Some volumes of the theological papers of the Church historian and topographer, John Lewis of Margate (d. 1746)—MSS. c. 17–21—were bought, through Gaisford, from a Bristol bookseller in 1820; they supplement papers already received in the Rawlinson collection.[2] Printed Septuagint and Greek patristic texts come from the library of Dr. Robert Holmes (d. 1805), whose numerous volumes of collations made for an Oxford edition of the Septuagint form a separate collection in Bodley.[3] For the rest, the Clarendon Press collection is concerned with Greek classical scholarship, and consists of the notes, collections, and correspondence of scholars who worked for, or whose work was utilized by, the Oxford Press.

Thus Samuel Musgrave's notes on Sophocles (MS. b. 6) were bought by the Press upon his death in 1780.[4] Jonathan Toup, a great scholar though a disagreeable man, dying in 1785, bequeathed to the Press his notes on Polybius (MS. c. 10), and the Delegates acquired in addition many other of his critical papers and collated texts.[5] To these they added transcripts and collations of Plutarch's *Moralia* made by or for the eminent Leyden professor, Dr. Daniel Wyttenbach, whose edition of Plutarch was published by the Press in 1795–1806; collations in the neat hand of the Alsatian, Friedrich Jacob Bast, who died prematurely in 1811; and notes on the Greek dramatists by

[1] Described by Prof. Findlay Shirras in the *Economic Journal*, vol lv (June 1945), pp. 218 et seq.
[2] MSS. Rawlinson C. 155, 409–13.
[3] Catalogued in the *Summary Catalogue of Western Manuscripts*, vol. iii, pp. 614–41, as nos. 16455–617.
[4] *Dictionary of National Biography*, s. v. Musgrave.
[5] His papers were presented by his half-sister; Nichols, *Illustrations of the Literary History of the Eighteenth Century*, vol. viii, pp. 558–61. His books are stated to have been bought at a Sotheby sale in May 1786; *Gentleman's Magazine*, vol. lvi (1786), pt. 1, p. 525.

the Oxford scholar, Peter Elmsley (d. 1825). Taken together, these gatherings represent a period when the Press was making for itself a reputation for Greek scholarship which was to be consolidated in the next generation by the great Dean Gaisford.[1]

3. SHELLEY PAPERS

That the personal and literary remains of that rebel against all constituted authority, the poet Shelley, should come to be among the prized possessions of the library in which he had once aspired to read would have considerably surprised those who sent him down from Oxford. They had remained in the possession of his family, and many were presented in 1893–4 by his son's widow, Lady Shelley. The gift included a copy of the poet's pamphlet *On the Necessity of Atheism*, which had directly led to his expulsion from the university; corrected proof-sheets of one or two other pamphlets; autograph copies and drafts of a number of his poems,[2] of which the chief is the autograph of *Prometheus Unbound*; relics, of sentimental interest, of his short life, from the rattle and coral that he had played with in his cradle to the copy of Sophocles that his drowning hand clutched as he sank below an Italian sea; and, perhaps most important of all, a collection (MS. Shelley e. 1) of letters written by him and by his wife, Mary Shelley. This last was given on the condition that it should not be made available to readers until the centenary of Shelley's death in 1922, and that permission to inspect after that date should be made the subject of special application to the Curators. It would be a mistake, however, to imagine that it had secrets to hide. Nearly all the correspondence had been included in a work entitled *Shelley and Mary* (though of this only a dozen copies are said to have been privately printed), and it had been placed by the family at the disposal of Professor Dowden, who had printed in his *Life of Shelley* all the material that seemed to him to be of any importance.[3]

[1] A manuscript catalogue, by F. Madan, of the Clarendon Press manuscripts is kept in the reading-room. The collection contains, in addition to the works of the scholars mentioned in the text, letters on classical subjects (MS. d. 49) addressed to Thomas Tyrwhitt (d. 1786), who is now perhaps best remembered as the first scholarly editor of our English Chaucer, and the correspondence (MS. d. 23) of the French *emigré*, César de Missy. In 1903 the Delegates of the Press added to their deposit a dozen volumes of transcripts (MSS. c. 30–41) made by the Scandinavian philologist Vigfusson for his publications of Icelandic sagas; and in 1922 they presented the entire collection outright to the Bodleian Library.

[2] A collation of the poems has been given by C. D. Locock, *An Examination of the Shelley MSS. in the Bodleian Library* (Oxford, 1903). The prose has been examined by Dr. A. H. Koszul, *Shelley's Prose in the Bodleian Manuscripts* (London, 1910).

[3] All the letters are listed, and those previously unpublished or only partially

Many years after Lady Shelley's gift, the Shelley collection was greatly strengthened through the donation which Sir John Shelley-Rolls, the poet's great-nephew, made to Bodley in 1946. This included more letters of Shelley and of Mary his wife, a boxful of drafts of Shelley's poems and prose works, and fourteen notebooks in which he had jotted down his verses and prose writings as he composed them. These allow one to trace his verses through every stage of their composition, from a hurried single line, through heavily corrected drafts, down to the fair copy. They supplement six similar green-backed volumes which Lady Shelley had given, and together they form twenty out of the twenty-four known Shelley notebooks, the remaining four being in America.[1]

4. NEGOTIATIONS FOR PHILLIPPS MANUSCRIPTS

When in 1861 Sir Thomas Phillipps brought to an angry close the negotiations for the acquisition of his vast store of manuscripts (see above, pp. 86–87), and so dashed the hopes that Bandinel and Coxe had long entertained, it might well have been thought that all chance of obtaining the Phillipps collection had gone for ever. The old baronet went on accumulating manuscripts and papers until his death in 1872, and devised them as an heirloom to his daughter, Mrs. Fenwick, for her life, with remainder to her third son, Thomas Fitzroy Fenwick. His descendants inherited his collections but not his tastes. The Phillipps library, filling every room of Thirlestaine House, was a white elephant, but marketable; and, in the eighties, rumours began to spread that it might come up for sale. It contained much to tempt foreign buyers. When the library of the Dutch scholar, Gerard Meerman, was sold at The Hague in 1824, Sir Thomas had been the largest purchaser, though Dean Gaisford secured at the sale a number of early classical manuscripts for Bodley. In 1887 it was learned that the Phillipps–Meerman manuscripts had been sold by private treaty to the library of Berlin, and that other manuscripts and documents had been bought by the Belgian Government.

Oxford's interest was aroused, and the Hebdomadal Council inquired of the Curators whether they would care to apply for a grant

published are (with certain exceptions) printed, in R. H. Hill's *Shelley Correspondence in the Bodleian Library*, 1926. The correspondence excluded from that publication consists of letters written by Mary Shelley to persons other than her husband. These have since been printed in the *Bodleian Quarterly Record*, vol. vi, pp. 51, 79, and vol. viii, pp. 297, 360.

[1] From this second Shelley collection Sir John Shelley-Rolls and Mr. Roger Ingpen privately printed in 1934, under the title *Verse and Prose from the manuscripts of Percy Bysshe Shelley*, a selection of fragments in prose and verse, rejected stanzas, drafts, and alternative readings.

of £1,000 for purchase at the sale of the Phillipps manuscripts. The Curators thought that any such application would be premature; but, a year later, things were moving, and by the spring of 1889, after the Delegates of the Common University Fund had voted £1,000 for the purpose, and Hebdomadal Council had informed the Curators that they were prepared to recommend a grant of £4,000 by Convocation, the Curators directed Nicholson to communicate with the British Museum and discover whether the two libraries could agree on joint action.[1] Maunde Thompson, the Director of the Museum, was already in touch with the owners, but he fell in readily with the new proposal, suggesting that Bodley should join the British Museum in spending £10,000 on the purchase of a selected portion of the collection, and that each library should undertake to find half that amount. The Curators concurred, and Convocation voted £5,000.[2] Cambridge now joined in with a contribution of the like amount, and the Treasury was persuaded into making a grant to the Museum of £10,000.

With £20,000 at their disposal, the three libraries opened, in March 1890, their joint negotiations with Mr. Fenwick. It was agreed that the Phillipps collection should be divided into classes and a price fixed for each class. Manuscripts of Latin classics, of which there were 470, were taken by way of trial; but the price their owner set on them (£7,150) was more than double the amount (£2,800) at which they had been valued by the British Museum's experts, and the libraries declined to accept the offer. Mr. Fenwick then came forward with a new proposal, that he should himself select 500 manuscripts and name his price. This too came to nothing, for his selection was unattractive and his price prohibitive.[3]

So in June 1891, following the Museum's lead, the Curators discharged the committee which they had set up to select manuscripts for purchase, and a year later the vote of £5,000 was rescinded.[4] The negotiations for a joint purchase of Phillipps manuscripts had definitely failed, as those for the purchase of the Althorp Caxtons were fated to do a few months later. So the great collection was broken up. In June 1893 there began a series of sales of manuscripts, of which

[1] Curators' minutes, 5 Mar. 1887; 9 June 1888; 9 Mar. 1889.
[2] Decree of 11 Feb. 1890.
[3] Maunde Thompson reported that the selection did not include one first-class manuscript; and that the price worked out at about £18 per manuscript as against the Museum's figure of £6.
[4] Curators' minutes, 6 June 1891; decree of 14 June 1892. The whole story of the negotiations is contained in two volumes of Library papers, 'The Phillipps Collection of MSS.'

eleven had been held before the outbreak of the First World War. The Bodleian bought at nearly all of them, but sparingly, for it had no large funds at its disposal.

5. QUEEN MARGARET'S GOSPELS AND
OTHER PURCHASES

Nicholson was more alive than his predecessor Coxe had been, or than his critics allowed, to the importance of adding by purchase to the library's store of manuscripts. One of his first acts was to get the Curators to appropriate £400 a year to that purpose.[1] For some years the amount was spent in full. But in 1895 the manuscript reserve fund was discontinued; and, though it was laid down that £350 was to be regarded as the normal annual expenditure on the purchase of manuscripts,[2] the sum actually spent steadily dwindled from that date. Had not the yearly grant of £150 that Trinity College began to make in 1898 been applied to the purchase of manuscripts and rare books, the sum available would have decreased more rapidly. As it was, when Trinity withdrew its grant in 1906, there was nothing to take its place. During the last ten years of Nicholson's librarianship the annual expenditure on manuscripts averaged little more than £100. In his last year of office it amounted to a bare £41, a smaller sum than Coxe had ever spent.

Although the money at his disposal was not always wisely expended, Nicholson has to his credit one tremendous bargain. In 1887 a Sotheby sale-catalogue announced that a fourteenth-century Latin manuscript of the Gospels with illuminations was coming up for auction. Nicholson put a ten-pound bid on it at a venture, and, as nobody else was interested in the little volume, it was knocked down to the Bodleian for six pounds. Falconer Madan, then sub-librarian, proceeded at once to catalogue it. He detected at a glance that it had been wrongly described. It was not a complete Gospel-book but a Gospel-lectionary, containing the *capitula* or short lessons read at the Mass; and it was not of fourteenth-century date, but indubitably belonged to the end of the eleventh. Script and illumination marked it as written in this island. And at the end of the volume was a Latin hexameter poem, of a date not far removed from that of the rest, recording a miracle which had happened to this very book.

The miracle happened on this wise. A priest, engaged in taking the little book to an appointed place where an oath was to be taken upon it, dropped it, out of the folds of his robe, into a river which he was

[1] *The Bodleian Library in 1882-7*, p. 15.
[2] Curators' minutes, 11 May 1895.

crossing. The loss was not immediately noticed; but a hue and cry was soon raised, and eventually a soldier who was of the party caught a glimpse of the book lying on the river bed. He dived and brought it up, entirely undamaged—for this was where the miracle lay—but for the two outer leaves which were crinkled from their wetting. And the versifier concludes his tale with the words, 'May the King and pious Queen be saved for ever, whose book was but now saved from the waves.'

It remained to identify the royal lady who had once owned the book. And by one of those coincidences which make the red-letter days of librarians, as Madan sat in his study cataloguing the manuscript, a lady of his acquaintance entered. She was Miss Lucy Hill, daughter of the Johnsonian scholar, Birkbeck Hill. He showed her the manuscript and told her the tale. She recognized it as identical with a story that she had read in a book which Edmund Gosse had given her, a Life of St. Margaret of Scotland. The life was one composed in Latin prose by the queen's spiritual adviser, the priest Turgot. Its author describes the Gospel-book for which St. Margaret had a special affection, and then tells the story of what befell it, a story corresponding in every detail to the hexameter poem in the manuscript.[1]

The little book had strange vicissitudes of ownership. There is at least a probability that it is the 'textus argenteus' presented on Queen Margaret's death to the cathedral church of Durham, of which Turgot became the conventual prior.[2] It reappears in a list of relics kept at Durham in 1383. Stripped, we may imagine at the Reformation, of its silver binding adorned with a crucifix on one side and the Divine Majesty on the other, it fell into the hands of the Elizabethan antiquary, John Stowe; then found its way into the fine library of Lord William Howard ('Belted Will') at Naworth; and in the eighteenth century passed mysteriously to the little parochial library of Brent Ely in Suffolk. From that modest retirement it came into the London sale-room.

Other purchases were less spectacular. One can but mention a few of them. English literature was represented by the autograph corrected copy of Pope's *Essay on Criticism*; by a minstrel's song-book of English and Latin songs transcribed about 1486;[3] and by a

---

[1] The story of the identification has been told by Madan in *Books in Manuscript* (1893), pp. 108–10, and in the *Bodleian Quarterly Record*, vol. ii, p. 199. The manuscript was minutely described in letters to the *Academy* of 6 and 20 Aug. and 3 Sept. 1887, and has been reproduced in facsimile by W. Forbes-Leith as *The Gospel-Book of St. Margaret* (1896). [2] *Bodleian Quarterly Record*, vol. iv, p. 202.
[3] MS. Eng. poet. e. 1. Edited by Thomas Wright for the Percy Society in 1847.

SCS MATTHEUS
EVANGELISTA .

QUEEN MA

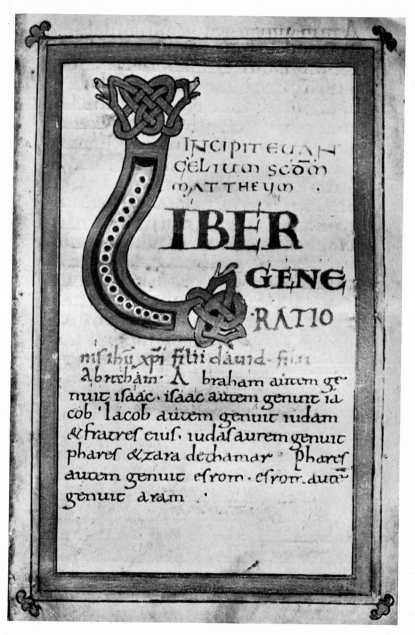

INCIPIT EUAN
GELIUM SCDM
MATTHEUM

LIBER
GENE
RATIO

nis ihu xpi filii dauid. filii
abraham· Abraham autem ge
nuit isaac· isaac autem genuit ia
cob· Iacob autem genuit iudam
& fratres eius· iudas autem genuit
phares & zara de thamar· Phares
autem genuit esrom· esrom autem
genuit aram ·

GOSPELS

rhymed English version, also of the fifteenth century, of Palladius's treatise on husbandry: French literature by a manuscript of Christine de Pisan, bought in 1908 for £45; and medieval Latin literature by the purchase, at a Phillipps sale, of a twelfth-century manuscript of the Polycraticus and Metalogicon of John of Salisbury which had once belonged to Bath Abbey. Eight volumes of Fairfax family papers, bought for £112. 15s. in 1890, came from a large collection at Leeds Castle of which the British Museum has the greater part. A volume of early deeds and manuscript fragments known as the Crawford Charters was bought in 1891. The price paid (£220. 10s.) was comparatively high, but the collection included a valuable set of preconquest documents relating to Crediton, and four royal Anglo-Saxon charters. A purchase of more local interest was that of the muniments of the manor and Augustinian nunnery of Goring on the Thames.[1]

Considerable attention was paid to acquiring liturgical manuscripts. In addition to St. Margaret's gospel-book, already mentioned, the library secured a book of hours containing an office for the martyr-dom of Archbishop Scrope of York;[2] the only copy known of a York gradual (bought in 1901 for £112. 5s.); an eleventh-century Gregorian Sacramentary from Como; a Prague missal, and various continental breviaries. Two biblical commentaries deserve a men-tion: one was an eighth-century commentary on the Pentateuch, for which £47. 10s. was paid in 1891; the other, Capgrave's commentary on Exodus, was of special interest to the Bodleian, for it was a presen-tation copy from the author to Humphrey, Duke of Gloucester, and had been given by the duke to the university library, to which it now returned.

Of the few Latin classical and post-classical manuscripts bought in this period, some were bought at the Wodhull sale in 1886 and had come from Dr. Askew's library; others were Drury manuscripts from a Phillipps sale. Occasionally the Bodleian was able to add to its stock of Greek vellum manuscripts, as in 1882 when it bought for £110 two eleventh-century copies of the Gospels and two twelfth-century Gospel-lectionaries. And a new source of supply of far older Greek writing was by this time beginning to open up—papyrus fragments recovered from the dry sands of Egypt.

---

[1] The earliest in date of the Crawford charters have been published by Prof. Napier and Mr. W. H. Stevenson in *Anecdota Oxoniensia*, medieval and modern series, pt. vii. The Goring charters have been edited for the *Oxfordshire Record Society* (vols. xiii, xiv) by Mr. T. Gambier-Parry.

[2] Published by Madan in a letter to the *Athenaeum*, 4 Aug. 1888.

6. GREEK PAPYRI

The first examples to be discovered of Greek texts written on papyrus were the calcined rolls disinterred in 1752 from the buried Italian city of Herculaneum. Of these Oxford received a small share, for in 1810 the Prince Regent presented four unopened rolls and lead-pencil facsimiles and engraved plates of many others.[1] From 1820 onwards sporadic digging by fellaheen began increasingly to reveal how vast a store of papyrus was awaiting the explorer in the desert areas of Egypt. An immense mass of papyrus fragments belonging to the fifth–seventh centuries A.D. was recovered in 1877 from Arsinoë in the Fayum. The greater portion of the find now forms the Archduke Rainer collection in Vienna, but over a thousand pieces came into the hands of an English collector, Mr. Greville Chester, who passed them on to the Bodleian in 1878 for £20, and presented others in 1887.[2]

Fragments were to be had in plenty, but the Bodleian had no perfect specimens until 1888, when it received ten sheets of a Homeric papyrus, beautifully written in the second century A.D., and containing a portion of the first, and the whole of the second, book of the *Iliad*. The papyrus had been found by Professor Flinders Petrie in a cemetery at Hawara in the Fayum, and was presented by Mr. Jesse Haworth along with the skull of the poor lady who once owned it and had it buried with her. And from 1888 the library began to get papyrus fragments of greater antiquity, dating from the second and third centuries B.C. Some of them had been found by Petrie, used as cartonnage for mummies at Gurob in the Fayum; others derived from Hibeh in the Nile valley.[3] The most important of the Petrie papyri was a long roll containing the revenue laws of Ptolemy Philadelphus (259–8 B.C.).

Petrie had just acquired the Revenue Papyrus (which he passed on to the library in 1894 for £80), when a young Oxford scholar, Bernard

---

[1] The facsimiles were catalogued in Walter Scott's *Fragmenta Herculanensia* (Oxford, 1885). In 1889 the facsimiles of all the Greek rolls which had not by then been either reproduced or edited were photographed for the Oxford Philological Society, by whom sets of photographs, along with an index to the facsimiles compiled by Madan, were presented to the leading European libraries. At Nicholson's suggestion the Delegates of the Clarendon Press published in 1891, under the title *Texts and Alphabets from the Herculanean Fragments*, a limited edition of impressions from the plates, with a prefatory note by the librarian.

[2] The papyrus fragments bought from Mr. Chester were examined and classified in 1886 by Dr. Ulrich Wilcken; *The Bodleian Library in 1882–7*, p. 25.

[3] Published respectively in Mahaffy's *Flinders Petrie Papyri* (Royal Irish Acad., Cunningham Memoirs, viii, ix, xi) and in Grenfell and Hunt's *Hibeh Papyri*.

Grenfell, fresh from the Schools, came out to join him and get a knowledge of excavation. Petrie set his pupil to edit the papyrus,[1] of which Grenfell himself obtained some additional portions when he revisited Egypt in the following winter (1894–5) and did a little digging in the Fayum on his own account. Returning home, Grenfell brought with him a consignment of papyrus and vellum fragments of Roman and Byzantine date which he had found on sites in the Fayum or picked up from dealers. He sold these to the Bodleian. They included a number of classical literary fragments as well as business documents.[2]

Up to now, papyri had been generally bought piecemeal from dealers in antiquities; but in 1895 the Committee of the Egypt Exploration Fund resolved to experiment in systematic exploration. They were fortunate in their second season (1896–7) in securing the site of Behnesa, the ancient Oxyrhynchus, for it proved the most fertile of buried cities. During that winter and again in subsequent seasons Grenfell and his inseparable partner, A. S. Hunt, carried on their diggings for the Exploration Fund, publishing the results in their well-known volumes of *Oxyrhynchus Papyri*. Their very first season produced a sensational find, fitly numbered Oxyrhynchus Papyrus 1. This was the famous *Logia*, a single leaf belonging to the third century of our era, on which are written some otherwise unrecorded sayings of Jesus Christ.[3] The precious fragment was presented by the Exploration Fund in 1900 to Bodley.

The Oxyrhynchus papyri mainly date from the first four centuries A.D. Distributions of them have been made from time to time by the Exploration Fund. The finds that were so presented to Bodley in Nicholson's period include, besides the *Logia*, other old Christian literature such as a portion of the Shepherd of Hermas; a few Biblical scraps, of which the chief is a second-century fragment of the Septuagint version of Genesis; and a fair number of literary texts, among which may be mentioned a part of the fifth book of the Iliad written on the back of a third-century petition from the lady Dionysia, and fragments of a lost play (the *Kolax*) of Menander. With these there came torn business-papers and discarded correspondence, including a delightful letter from the Egyptian schoolboy Theon, begging his

---

[1] As *Revenue Laws of Ptolemy Philadelphus*, 1896. Grenfell's career is admirably sketched by A. S. Hunt in the *Proceedings of the British Academy*, vol. xii, pp. 357–64.
[2] In large part published in Grenfell's *Greek Papyri*, 1st and 2nd series (1896–7). The Bodleian paid £21. 5s. in 1895 and £36 in 1896, and was presented with other fragments from the same source by Dr. F. C. Conybeare.
[3] For the *Logia* see H. G. Evelyn White, *The Sayings of Jesus* (Cambridge, 1920) with its bibliography at pp. xii–xiii.

father to be taken on an outing to Alexandria, and threatening to go on starvation diet if he is not given a lyre.

It was typical of Nicholson's career that he was fully alive to the importance of papyri, and that his treatment of them brought him into serious conflict with his Curators. At a Curatorial meeting in 1891, which Nicholson himself was not called upon to attend, it was resolved that the Librarian be requested to take no further steps in arranging papyrus fragments without consulting the Curators; and, although the request was subsequently withdrawn, an accident through which some passages of the Prophet Ezekiel were rendered permanently invisible led Professor Pelham in 1894 to move for a committee to consider the mounting and arrangement of the papyri then in the library and the propriety of having them catalogued by an expert. Dr. (now Sir Frederic) Kenyon was in consequence invited to investigate and report. Acting on his advice, the Curators authorized the engagement of Grenfell to prepare a short descriptive catalogue of the Greek papyri in the library, and this he carried out with his usual promptitude.[1]

7. REPRODUCTION AND PUBLICATION

It was not over papyri alone that Nicholson met with difficulties. There were squabbles over the exhibition of books and manuscripts, Chandler going so far as to move at a Curators' meeting in 1885 'that no printed book, manuscript, autograph or document belonging to the Library shall be exhibited in the show-cases without the written permission of nine Curators at least'.[2] Nicholson had to face similar opposition to his schemes for making the Bodleian a centre for palaeographical instruction, the Curators declining in 1885 to give the use of a room in the Bodleian to Professor W. M. Lindsay for the purposes of his lectures, though a year later they gave way and accorded to Maunde Thompson permission to give a course of lectures on Latin palaeography within the library precincts.[3]

There were methods other than exhibitions and lectures by which the resources of Bodley might be made known to a wider public. Advantage could be taken of cheap photographic reproduction. There had been a studio for photography in the British Museum since 1875, but it was not until 1887 that the establishment of a photographic department at Bodley was propounded to the Curators.

[1] Curators' minutes, 7 Mar. 1891; 8 Nov. and 1 Dec. 1894; 8 Feb. and 13 June 1896: Kenyon's report, dated 22 May 1896, gives a useful descriptive and historical account of the papyri then in the library. Grenfell's catalogue remains in manuscript on the open shelves of the Old Reading-Room.

[2] Minutes, 2 May 1885.   [3] Minutes, 21 Apr. 1885; 4 Dec. 1886.

Though no immediate action was taken, eighteen months later the Curators appointed three of their number—Professors Price, Chandler, and Bywater—as a committee 'to consider the introduction into the library of facilities for photographing'.[1] Chandler was especially keen on developing this side of library activity, and set out his views in a privately printed pamphlet, trenchant and provocative as was his wont.

But for the lack of adequate knowledge, and the extraordinary apathy, which have been so painfully conspicuous in the management of the Bodleian during nearly thirty years past, the University might before this have been in possession of a new library, capable of containing with ease and safety a million volumes; a building well-arranged, well-lighted, weather-proof and fire-proof. Of such a building a perfectly furnished photographic studio, with all appliances for taking and even for developing plates, would be an almost necessary part.[2]

Chandler's death, self-inflicted, which occurred a fortnight later, held up the presentation of the committee's report; but it was made at last and adopted in November 1890.[3] A binder's room, which had been constructed in 1864 at the west end of the north range of the Picture Gallery, was converted into a photographic room, and the Controller of the University Press was allowed to install his apparatus there and to appoint one of his employees to superintend all photographic work carried on in the library. A circular was issued setting out the Controller's tariff for prints from photographic negatives. Work was at first limited to making silver-prints, bromide prints, and collotypes; but in 1905 the University Press started a cheaper form of reproduction, namely, rotary bromide prints which themselves were negatives, being white on black, and gave to this early form of photostat the name of rotograph. Two years later, when the north wing of the Picture Gallery was made into an upper reading-room, the photographer's enclosure was moved to its eastern end. A new library building completed on the eve of the Second World War contained the 'perfectly furnished photographic studio' for which Chandler had longed, though it was not until the war was over that the Bodleian entered into possession.

The institution of a photographic department led naturally to the production of collotypes for sale to the public. In 1900 Bodleian photographs began to be put on sale at the Press Depository; and,

[1] Curators' minutes, 18 June 1887; 2 Feb. 1889.
[2] Chandler, *Memorandum on Photography at the Bodleian Library*, 12 Apr. 1889.
[3] Curators' minutes, 29 Nov. 1890.

after a few months' trial, Nicholson obtained his Curators' permission to spend £20 on taking photographs of bindings, pictures, and pages of printed books and manuscripts, and to sell them in the library.[1] As yet the enterprise was carried no farther. Production of picture-postcards had still to come.

Besides initiating the sale of cheap reproductions, Nicholson experimented in 1892 in publishing, as a private venture, some of the library's rarest printed pieces in photolithographic facsimile. Only four were issued: namely the unique copy of Caxton's *Ars Moriendi*, Caxton's advertisement of his wares, Columbus's *Epistola de insulis noviter repertis*, and a papal order for a solemn procession in commemoration of the Massacre of St. Bartholomew. Nicholson also planned, but for lack of support was unable to carry through, a palaeographical series of collotypes of Bodleian manuscripts. What he contemplated had already been undertaken on a restricted scale by Professor Robinson Ellis, who received permission to publish a set of facsimile pages from Latin manuscripts in 1885.[2]

That the University Press should undertake the publication of unedited classical texts from manuscripts in the Bodleian Library was a project as old as Archbishop Laud.[3] At Paris the Bibliothèque Nationale set an example to the learned world, and in 1827 Frederic Madden noted in his diary, 'Dr. Bandinel proposes with Bliss to publish a Bodleian Miscellany on the plan of the *Notices et Extraits des Manuscrits*.'[4] Coxe had the same idea. In 1877 he told the University Commissioners that, about twenty-five years before, he had drawn up a specimen printed sheet of a Bodleian periodical to be called *Acta Eruditorum*; and in his advocacy of such a publication he was supported by Robinson Ellis.[5] The sub-librarian, Neubauer, took the same line. 'Surely', he wrote, 'a volume of *Anecdota Bodleiana* for philology and history, published by the Curators, would do honour to our Library.'[6] His colleague Macray was of much the same opinion, and gave it practical expression by engaging on his own account in the publication of certain rare tracts. But the Curators, whose leave

---

[1] Curators' minutes, 9 Mar. 1901.

[2] Of this there are three editions, namely *Twelve Facsimiles* (1885), *Twenty Facsimiles* (1891), and *Specimens of Latin Palaeography* (1903).

[3] Johnson and Gibson, *Print and Privilege at Oxford* (Oxford Bibliographical Society), pp. 10–17.

[4] Bodl. MS. Eng. hist. c. 147, fol. 30ᵛ.

[5] *University Commission, 1877*, minutes of evidence, pp. 130, 247.

[6] Curators' papers, 'Observations by the Librarians on the Report of the Committee of Curators, Feb. 1878'. In selecting his title Neubauer may well have had in mind the *Anecdota Graeca e Codd. MSS. Bibliothecarum Oxoniensium* which Dr. J. A. Cramer published in 1835–7, mainly from Bodleian manuscripts.

had not been sought, looked on Macray's enterprise as piratical, and retorted with a statute 'to prevent the publication of manuscripts without due authorisation'.[1] Ultimately, in 1881, an agreement was come to with the Press, by which its Delegates applied the profits of their Learned Press to a series of *Anecdota Oxoniensia*, devoted to the publication of unedited manuscripts, 'those preserved in the Bodleian and other Oxford libraries to have the first claim to publication'. Through this medium the Press issued a number of oriental and classical texts and, in their medieval series, Napier and Stevenson's *Crawford Charters*, R. L. Poole's edition of Bale's *Index Britanniae Scriptorum*, and M. R. James's edition of Walter Map's *De Nugis Curialium*. For some undisclosed reason the publication of *Anecdota*, apart from one belated issue, was brought to an end in 1914.

8. SUMMARY AND OTHER CATALOGUES

In the earlier part of Nicholson's librarianship the cataloguing of Western manuscripts proceeded on its former lines. Macray, continuing to work away at his catalogue of the Rawlinson collection, produced, for the full-scale quarto series of Bodleian catalogues, the first part of a catalogue of MSS. Rawlinson D in 1893, and followed it up with a second part in 1898 and an index in 1900. Falconer Madan devoted such time as could be spared from the performance of his other duties to the cataloguing of additional manuscripts on a similar scale. But the rate of progress was slow. Although the old catalogue of 1697 included descriptions (some of them imperfect) of all manuscripts then in the Bodleian, a large proportion of the later accessions remained uncatalogued, even in manuscript. A committee of the Curators, reporting this in 1876, stated that they were informed —how optimistically we can now well judge—that about a year and a half would be required to make a general descriptive catalogue of the manuscripts as yet undescribed, and strongly recommended that the work should be begun without delay.[2] A report made next year gave the number awaiting description as 2,600. Three and a half years later, as no action had been taken, Jowett called for a report as to what manuscripts were still uncatalogued.[3] This produced a useful alphabetical list of manuscript collections, drawn up by Madan, recording the state of catalogues and indexes.[4]

[1] 16 Mar. 1880; *Corpus Statutorum*, addenda, p. 869.
[2] Curators' papers, Report of Bodleian Committee on expenses and management of the Library, Mar. 1876.
[3] Curators' minutes, 23 June 1877; 27 Nov. 1880.
[4] Printed in July 1881 as *A Report on the Manuscript Collections in the Bodleian Library*.

There the matter rested until the beginning of 1890, when the Junior Proctor, the Rev. Andrew Clark, gave notice of a motion 'that a summary be prepared, giving the present and intermediate marks of all manuscripts in the catalogue of 1697, and carrying on the series so as to include all subsequent acquisitions, omitting in both cases those separately catalogued'. Clark followed this up with an open letter to members of Congregation.[1] In this he pointed out, at considerable length, the imperfections and inadequacy of existing catalogues, and outlined a scheme for 'a Summary Catalogue of MSS. in the Bodleian Library', very much on the lines that were subsequently adopted. At the same time the Curators received an influentially signed memorial, promoted by one of their own number, T. W. Jackson, expressing 'the benefit to be derived from a summary of those manuscripts which are not included in the existing catalogues of the Quarto Series'. The memorialists suggested that such a summary should include a statement of the date or approximate date of each manuscript, as well as a statement of its former pressmarks, and that manuscripts should be assigned a running number in continuation of those given in the old catalogue of 1697. Bywater, while also in favour of summary treatment, asked for no more than a short list of the manuscripts not yet described in the quarto series of catalogues, the 'Inventaire Sommaire of M. Omont of Paris to be taken as a model'.[2]

The demand for a summary catalogue, voiced from so many quarters, found no support from Nicholson. He was constitutionally averse to the acceptance of proposals that he had not himself originated. Arguing against what he called 'this new and gigantic project', he maintained that the right course to take was 'not to set cataloguers to work on a makeshift summary, but to push on the completion of the Quarto Series of catalogues',[3] which would otherwise be delayed indefinitely. His sub-librarian, Madan, took the opposing view. 'The Summary is a necessity, the Quarto Catalogue a luxury.' If the system of quarto catalogues was to be continued at all, it had better deal in future with subjects rather than with manuscript collections. Madan was alone at the time in holding that opinion; but since his day the idea that the library should aim at the production of class catalogues, that is to say full-scale catalogues of certain categories of manuscripts, has been revived and may one day bear fruit.

After careful inquiry, a committee of the Curators reported in

[1] *The Cataloguing of MSS. in the Bodleian Library: a Letter addressed to members of Congregation by the outgoing Junior Proctor*, 9 Apr. 1890.
[2] Curators' minutes, 8 Mar. 1890.
[3] Curators' papers, 'Observations offered to the Bodleian Curators by the Librarian on the proposal for a Summary Catalogue of MSS.', 7 Mar. 1890.

favour of starting without delay 'a Summary Catalogue of manuscripts hitherto uncatalogued in print on the Quarto system', and of
entrusting the work to Madan. It was agreed that the catalogue
should proceed by collections in the order of their acquisition, beginning with those not included in the 1697 catalogue. Each manuscript
was to receive a running number, and, as those in the old catalogue
were already numbered from 1 to 8716, the numbers to be assigned
to accessions subsequent to 1697 would begin from 8717.

The form taken by the summary catalogue was one that had been
worked out by Andrew Clark and Falconer Madan. Charters, rolls,
and deeds were excluded from its scope. Despite its title of *Summary
Catalogue of Western Manuscripts*, it included oriental manuscripts
in its numeration, and gave references to any printed catalogue in
which they were described. Western manuscripts described in the
quarto catalogues were similarly listed and cross-referenced. In all
other cases the catalogue-entry recorded every item of any size or
importance, and included, in addition to a note of mode of acquisition
and present pressmark, a brief technical description of the manuscript.
This last was a great advance on the more primitive cataloguing style
of the quartos, even if, in respect to medieval manuscripts, it failed to
satisfy at every point the exacter requirements of modern scholarship.

From June 1890, and for so long as he remained sub-librarian,
Madan worked away in his little study upon the summary catalogue
with methodical accuracy and unflagging persistence. He worked
for four or five hours every day, unaided save by a boy employed on
foliation. In 1895 he produced his first volume. It was devoted to the
collections received during the eighteenth century. Of these the
Rawlinson collection, even after subtracting the substantial portions
catalogued by Macray, was far and away the largest. Madan's volume
was numbered III, numbers I and II being reserved for a revision of
the catalogue of 1697. Volume IV followed in 1897. This gave the
collections received during the first half of the nineteenth century,
the principal being that of Douce, together with D'Orville and the
liturgical manuscripts of the Canonici collection. After a longer interval there appeared a fatter volume, numbered V, which was published in 1905. In it were catalogued the collections received during
the second half of the nineteenth century; also the miscellaneous
manuscripts acquired between 1695 and 1890. In the meantime
Madan was not neglectful of current accessions, but catalogued them
year by year, so that the catalogue was thereby kept up to date;
and a fascicule numbered part 1 of volume VI, and containing the

accessions of 1890–1904, appeared in 1906. Thus fifteen years of unremitting toil allowed Madan to prepare, and see through the press, catalogues of all the Western manuscripts in Bodley hitherto undescribed in print. Nor did he pause there, but proceeded without a halt to the accessions (mainly medieval and therefore presenting greater difficulty) of the seventeenth century; and, before he handed over the work to another, he had accomplished half of his new task, the volume of the catalogue numbered volume II, part 1, being almost entirely by him.

There are singularly few errors in Madan's work: omissions are not many. His palaeography was empirical. Its basis was the feeling induced by the handling of thousands of manuscripts. And so his dating was sound: in that he is a surer guide than Coxe. And in one other respect also his summary catalogue was a wonderful achievement. The style that he evolved for himself was admirably adapted for use in a library catalogue: it was perfectly compact and absolutely devoid of ambiguity. It is no criticism of the *Summary Catalogue of Western Manuscripts* to say that in two respects it belied its title. It included oriental manuscripts (to the extent at least of listing them), and, as it proceeded, it ceased to be summary.

The fact is that Nicholson was right in principle: so far as medieval manuscripts are concerned, it is difficult for a cataloguer to be both summary and sufficiently informative. Nicholson usually was right in his principles, only going wrong in their application. And the sin that most easily beset him was that of over-elaboration. This appears —though not so conspicuously as in other instances—in the revision that he planned of Coxe's catalogue of Greek manuscripts. Its entire contents, he held, required 'to be recatalogued on a complete scale, and by comparative and historical methods'. He laid down the lines on which, as a first instalment, the Greek manuscripts of the Laudian collection should be catalogued, working out an improved technical description which should include a note in all cases of the binding, an account of watermarks if the manuscript were on paper, and a statement of the number of gatherings and of lines to a page. In 1902 he engaged the New Testament scholar, Kirsopp Lake, to make the catalogue, but, in consequence of Lake's appointment to a chair at Leyden, work was suspended after only forty manuscripts had been done. In 1906 Nicholson was projecting a new catalogue of Laudian Latin and miscellaneous manuscripts, to be executed by Bodleian assistants under his direction and revision. It was to be prepared and issued in sections, of which the first was to be devoted to the manuscripts from St. Kylian's monastery at Würzburg. The design never advanced beyond a preliminary classification. 'In two months came the proposals for opening a new reading-room, forming an underground bookstore, and revising the catalogue of printed books. These matters', Nicholson wrote shortly before he died, 'have ever since so fully occupied every spare moment of my time, that the new Laudian catalogue has had to be postponed to an indefinite future.'[1]

[1] *Summary Catalogue of Western Manuscripts*, vol. ii, pt. 1, p. 19.

Chapter XII

Oriental and Minor Departments

Section I

ORIENTALIA

1. HEBREW MANUSCRIPTS

In 1886 Adolf Neubauer, senior Bodleian sub-librarian, produced a substantial catalogue of the library's Hebrew manuscripts. This contains descriptions of all the Hebrew manuscripts in Bodley, as well as those in Oxford college libraries, up to the time of publication. Unlike Uri's old catalogue of 1787, it is in English, not in Latin, and the manuscripts described in it are arranged under subjects—biblical, legal, liturgical, theological, and so on. Arabic works written in Hebrew characters are included within its scope. The catalogue was accompanied by an album of well-chosen palaeographical facsimiles.

Ten years previously Neubauer had drawn the university's attention to a source from which Bodley's store of manuscripts might be increased, to 'the treasures which Rabbanitic synagogues might offer from their Genizoth in the East'.[1] A Geniza is a lumber-room, attached to or near to a synagogue, into which all kinds of written and printed material are heaped as into a giant waste-paper basket, and there kept (lest that on which the name of God is written should be profaned by improper use) until such time as they can be carted away for burial in consecrated ground and so perish. One Geniza there was that had been forgotten, so that its contents had escaped interment other than that provided by its own doorless and windowless walls. It was at Old Cairo; and here, under much dust and dirt, lay an unexplored pile, untouched till, about 1870, a Russian Jew named Firkowitch obtained from it some valuable fragments that are now at Leningrad. And it was only about 1890, when the Jews of Old Cairo were rebuilding their synagogue, that they commenced to huckster the contents of its Geniza. In that year the Bodleian obtained, in part by gift from the Egypt Exploration Fund, in part through Mr. Greville Chester, the collector through whose agency the library had obtained so many papyrus scraps from Arsinoë in the Fayum, sufficient manuscript fragments to fill thirty-eight volumes. Successive acquisitions made in subsequent years, partly through Greville

---

[1] *Oxford University Gazette*, 21 Nov. 1876.

Chester, partly through the Assyriologist Professor Sayce, greatly added to the collection; and in 1906 a considerable number of fragments from the same source were bought in Jerusalem. In these diverse ways the Bodleian increased its original holding tenfold, and came to have a collection of Geniza fragments that is surpassed in size only by the more extensive haul of 100,000 pieces acquired in 1898 by the University Library of Cambridge.[1]

Among the Geniza fragments which came to Bodley are some leaves of early printed books which were hitherto very rare, if not entirely unknown.[2] The manuscripts have yielded a richer harvest. Twenty pages of a classified compendium of Jewish Law, one of the principal works of Maimonides, have been recognized as being in the autograph of that great twelfth-century scholar.[3] And one of the fragments which Sayce acquired for the library was seen at once to possess a particular interest. The Book of Ecclesiasticus has come down to us in Greek translations; but here was a portion of the original Hebrew text which had been lost for 1,000 years. The Bodleian manuscript was published separately in 1897, with collotype facsimiles, by Neubauer and his assistant, A. E. Cowley.[4] Other portions have since found their way into other libraries.[5]

The Geniza fragments form the main element in the second volume of the *Catalogue of the Hebrew Manuscripts in the Bodleian Library*, which was published in 1906 over the joint names of Neubauer and Cowley. They were bound up in volumes as they reached the library, so almost every leaf had to be separately described.[6] The task fell upon Cowley, for Neubauer's health had begun to give way in 1894, with the result that in December 1895 Nicholson appointed Cowley, then a master at Magdalen Grammar School, to be assistant sub-librarian. 'Old Nob', as his colleagues called Neubauer, was not really old (he was sixty-three), but he showed increasing signs of brain-failure. He retired upon a pension at the end of 1899, Cowley being appointed to succeed him, and lived on until 1907, a helpless invalid.

---

[1] P. Kahle, *The Cairo Geniza* (Schweich Lectures, 1941), pp. 1–10.
[2] Some account has been given of them by J. L. Teicher in the *Bodleian Library Record*, vol. i, pp. 234–6.
[3] MS. Heb. d. 32. Published in facsimile by Dr. Samuel Atlas as *A Section from the Yad Ḥa-Hazaḳah of Maimonides* (London, 1940).
[4] *The Original Hebrew of a portion of Ecclesiasticus.*
[5] The whole text, so far as it has been recovered, was first published by Israel Lévi as *L'Ecclésiastique ou la sagesse de Jésus fils de Sira* (Paris, 1898, 1901).
[6] A single example will suffice to show how disunited are the fragments. Six leaves of a manuscript of the Targum to the Torah are bound up in three different Bodleian volumes. Two other leaves from the same manuscript are at Cambridge and four at Leningrad. Kahle, op. cit., p. 121.

The second volume of the *Catalogue of Hebrew Manuscripts* is on the same lines as the first, but contains, in addition, a list of dated manuscripts. Manuscripts written in the Samaritan dialect are excluded from its purview for it was hoped at the time that Cowley would one day produce a separate catalogue of all the Samaritan manuscripts in the library.[1] It was Nicholson's intention to follow up the two volumes of the Hebrew catalogue with an appendix giving supplementary palaeographical and historical information, and with a further album of palaeographical facsimiles.

2. OTHER SEMITIC LANGUAGES

Hebrew died out as a spoken language some three centuries before Christ, giving way to *Aramaic*. This necessitated translations of the Scriptures into the vernacular, that is to say into the form of Aramaic spoken in Palestine. Many such translations or 'Targums' are to be found in the Hebrew collection. One manuscript of the Palestinian version of the Scriptures, much older than the rest, came to Bodley from the Cairo Geniza. It consists of only seven leaves, but the writing, which is palimpsest, is of the sixth century.[2]

Far greater antiquity attaches to the Aramaic papyri found at Assuan, by the First Cataract of the Nile. They are relics of a Jewish military and trading settlement on the island of Elephantine in the fifth century before our era. Professor Sayce secured from that source an intact papyrus roll, dating from about 450 B.C., and three Aramaic ostraca, which he presented in 1901 to Bodley. A second roll, obtained in 1904, is of even earlier date, being a contract drawn up in 471 B.C.[3]

A later form of Aramaic developed at Edessa on the Euphrates, and is known *par excellence* as *Syriac*. As has been previously mentioned (p. 107), Payne Smith compiled a catalogue of the Syriac manuscripts in Bodley which was published in 1864. Purchases of Syriac manuscripts continued to be made during Nicholson's period of office. They included a New Testament written about 1000, and a book of the Gospels dated 1219.

Syriac was driven out of current use in Palestine and the Euphrates

---

[1] In 1890 the library bought twenty-four Samaritan manuscripts for £44. Some were biblical, the rest liturgical. For an earlier acquisition see above, p. 106.

[2] Published, with collotype facsimiles, in *Anecdota Oxoniensia*, Semitic series, pts. V and IX.

[3] The papyri have been published by Sayce as *Aramaic Papyri discovered at Assuan* (1906), and in Cowley's *Aramaic Papyri of the 5th cent. B.C.* (1923). The ostraca are described by Cowley in *Proceedings of the Society of Biblical Archaeology*, vol. xxv (1903), pp. 202, 264, 311.

valley by *Arabic*, just as the older Aramaic speech had been replaced in Egypt by Ptolemaic Greek. No important additions were made at this time to Bodley's great store of Arabic manuscripts, though an attempt was made to recatalogue them. Uri's catalogue of 1787 was very unsatisfactory, and both it and Nicoll's catalogue of 1835 were in Latin. David Margoliouth, Laudian Professor of Arabic and a man of great learning, undertook in 1892 a revision of the old catalogues, but made very little headway.

3. EGYPT AND BABYLON

Coptic, the language of native Christian communities in Egypt and itself derived from ancient Egyptian, had long been represented in the Bodleian, for twenty-three Coptic manuscripts came in the Marshall collection in 1685 and twenty-nine in that of Huntington in 1693. One of the earliest of Coptic scholars, the German Paul Ernest Jablonski, visited Oxford in 1718 to work on the manuscripts in the Bodleian.[1] When he died, half a century afterwards, the Radcliffe Trustees agreed to purchase his Coptic manuscripts,[2] and in 1894 they deposited in Bodley the five volumes thus acquired.[3] A later scholar, Charles Godfrey Woide,[4] who settled in London and became an official in the British Museum, is perhaps best known for his edition of the New Testament portion of the Codex Alexandrinus, but he was learned in Coptic, and particularly in the form of it that is called Sahidic. The Clarendon Press gave support and encouragement to his studies by publishing his Egyptian lexicon (1775) and grammar (1778), and on his death in 1790 its Delegates purchased the Coptic portion of his library. This they deposited in 1885 in Bodley. It included Woide's own correspondence, transcripts, and collations, as well as transcripts made by earlier Coptic scholars—Jablonski, La Croze, and Christian Scholz.[5] With these there also came five volumes of early fragments. Among the Woide fragments are some leaves of a Graeco-Sahidic codex of the Gospels of Luke and John, written in uncials of the seventh century. Other portions of the same codex are in the libraries of Vienna, Paris, and London. It is but too common to find that a Coptic manuscript has been parted and dispersed, for Eyptian peasants have unfortunately discovered that they can make a greater profit by breaking up a manuscript than by selling it whole.

---

[1] Jablonski's name is entered in the admission register, 12 Aug. 1718.
[2] Radcliffe Trustees' minutes, 7 Mar. 1768.
[3] They form a little collection referenced MSS. Radcliffe oriental.
[4] Nichols, *Literary Anecdotes of the Eighteenth Century*, vol. ix, pp. 11–14.
[5] MSS. Clarendon Press c. 1–3, d. 4–19, e. 1–30.

The Woide fragments were catalogued in considerable detail by the abbé Hyvernat. He was prevented, however, by absence abroad, from responding to the Curators' invitation that he should make a catalogue of all the Coptic manuscripts in Bodley.[1]

In 1843 there had come intact to Bodley a Coptic papyrus codex which the traveller Bruce had bought about the year 1769 in Upper Egypt. Though its condition has much deteriorated it is yet notable both for its contents and its antiquity. For it is a fifth-century collection of Gnostic writings, and as such has become famous as the Codex Brucianus (MS. Bruce 96).[2] A few miscellaneous papyrus fragments were obtained for the library in 1888–90 by Greville Chester; but in 1908 there arrived a far larger consignment, 'the debris', it has been styled, 'of the monastic library and charter-room' of the Coptic monastery of St. Apollo at Deir-Balyzeh in the Western Desert of Egypt. The site had just been excavated by Professor Flinders Petrie, to whom the Bodleian owes the collection. It is a jumble of fragments of biblical manuscripts, liturgical books, homilies, acts of Egyptian saints, taxation receipts, lists, and monastic accounts, almost entirely written on papyrus but including some vellum leaves. Among them are some Arabic fragments and a few in Greek. The whole lot belong to the sixth, seventh, and eighth centuries.[3]

Specimens of the older forms of the Egyptian language were not to be found in Bodley before Nicholson's day. The first examples to be received of the Ancient Egyptian of the Empire were fifteen ostraca from Luxor, presented in 1907 by Dr. Grafton Milne.[4] They are inscribed in a script (itself derived from Hieroglyphic) known as Hieratic, and date from the period of the Ramesses (12th–13th centuries B.C.). A few of these ostraca are literary, though most are business documents. Hieratic developed, in its more cursive form, into Demotic, a name applicable both to the script, and to the popular form of speech, current in Egypt from the seventh century B.C. to the downfall of paganism; but of this the library had little beyond a

[1] Curators' minutes, 4 Dec. 1886. Hyvernat's catalogue of the Woide fragments remains in manuscript on the shelves of the reading-room.

[2] Its contents were edited in 1905 by C. Schmidt as *Koptisch-gnostische Schriften* for the series of *Die Griechischen christlichen Schriftsteller der ersten drei Jahrhunderte*. And one of the two treatises of which it is made up has been reproduced in facsimile with text and translation by Mrs. Charlotte Baynes as *A Coptic Gnostic treatise contained in the Codex Brucianus* (Cambridge, 1933).

[3] Described by W. E. Crum in Flinders Petrie's *Gizeh and Rifeh* (1907), pp. 39–43. The most striking of the Greek fragments has been published, with facsimiles, by C. H. Roberts and B. Capelle in *Bibliothèque du Muséon*, vol. xxiii (1949), as *An early Euchologion, the Dêr-Balizeh papyrus enlarged and re-edited*.

[4] Published by him in his *Theban Ostraca* (1913).

few papyrus scraps presented to it in 1888 by Greville Chester and by Sayce.

Bodley came equally late into the field in collecting the literature of Egypt's great rivals, the ancient kingdoms of the Tigris and Euphrates valleys. 'Of this', Nicholson wrote in 1902, 'the Bodleian possesses nothing more than a few engraved cylinders; it has not even a single clay tablet.'[1] The defect was remedied when in 1908 the library spent £60 on the purchase of nearly 300 cuneiform tablets.[2] The majority of these, namely 211, were in the early Semitic tongue known as *Assyro-Babylonian*, and nearly all were business documents, the oldest of them dating back to the reign of the law-giver Hammurabi in the eighteenth century B.C.

The remainder of the tablets bought in 1908 were pre-Semitic, the product of a more ancient civilization, that of the *Sumerians*. Fifty additional Sumerian tablets were bought two years later; and in 1911 a gift of 155 tablets from one of the Curators, T. W. Jackson, more than doubled the library's holding. All or nearly all belong to the period of the third dynasty of Ur, which ruled the country before Hammurabi in the second half of the third millennium before Christ. Some are contracts or receipts; others are lists, accounts, and other memoranda made by officers entrusted with administering the vast estates of Babylonian temples.

4. PERSIA AND ARMENIA

Zoroastrianism, the ancient religion of Persia, had for its first European exponent Dr. Thomas Hyde, Keeper of the Bodleian Library from 1665 to 1701. His *Historia Religionis Veterum Persarum* became a classic, but the manuscripts on which his work was based were not included in the collection which passed to Bodley and bears his name, but entered the King's Library and are now among the Royal manuscripts in the British Museum.[3] Zoroastrian literature has come down to us in the primitive form of Persian known as Old Bactrian or *Zend*. Bodley had received, in 1723, from an East India merchant named George Bowcher a Zend manuscript (MS. Bodl. Or. 321) written in the preceding century; but it possessed no very

---

[1] *Statements of the Needs of the University*, p. 150.

[2] The term cuneiform was first applied by a Bodleian librarian, Dr. Thomas Hyde, in 1700, to the wedge-shaped symbols invented by the Sumerians and adopted by the Assyrians, Babylonians, and ancient Persians: Hyde, *Historia Religionis Veterum Persarum*, ed. 1700, p. 526.

[3] MSS. Royal 16 B. Neither Macray's *Annals* nor the *Summary Catalogue* make mention of this secondary Hyde collection, which will be found detailed in Casley's *Catalogue of the MSS. of the King's Library*, 1734, pp. 246–50.

early Zend manuscript until 1889, when Dr. Dastur Jamaspji, High Priest of the Parsees of Bombay, presented a Bactrian text of the Yasna, the principal liturgical work of his sect. It is dated 1323, and is provided with a translation into Pehlavi, the language spoken in Persia under its Sassanian kings. Next year the same donor gave a yet earlier text of the same work (MS. Zend e. 1). This contains a Sanskrit translation. It was written about A.D. 1250, and has been described as undoubtedly the oldest of all Zend-Sanskrit manuscripts.

An account has been given in Chapter VI (pp. 107–10) of the great accessions to its *Persian* manuscripts which the Bodleian received in the collections of the two Ouseley brothers, of Mr. J. B. Elliott, of General Alexander Walker, and of James Fraser, and of the various attempts that were made to have a catalogue prepared of them as well as of the Persian manuscripts in the older collections. Professor Sachau of Berlin did actually catalogue the library's Zoroastrian literature as well as the Ouseley manuscripts. Dr. Hermann Ethé, who took over from him in 1872, completed the task and produced a Persian catalogue, planned on a rather ambitious scale, which was published in 1889. He revised Professor Sachau's descriptions of the Ouseley manuscripts, and arranged his work under the headings of history, poetry, and the sciences and art. The fourth section of the catalogue deals with Zoroastrian literature and is exclusively Sachau's work.

A second volume of Ethé's catalogue contains descriptions of Persian manuscript accessions down to 1894, as well as of the library's Turkish, Hindustani, and Pushtu manuscripts. It was intended to include in it a complete index to the whole work, and an introduction which would have given some account of the various collections of Mohammedan manuscripts in the Bodleian. But Professor Ethé, who died in 1917, did not live to write the introduction that he had planned, or to complete more of the index than a list of book-titles. The volume was eventually published in 1930, but without the projected indexes of authors' names and subjects.[1]

Armenia, a border-land between the civilizations of East and West, fell eventually under Persian influence. Before Nicholson's time the library possessed only some twenty Armenian manuscripts, but from the first year of his librarianship Nicholson set to work to add to their number, and acquired, mainly through purchase, over ninety more in the course of his period of office. The earliest dated manuscript was an antiphonary written in 1296 (MS. Arm. f. 22). Others, which were undated, were older, and included a twelfth-century copy of the

---

[1] An author index has now been prepared and will be issued as part of a third volume.

Gospels (MS. Arm. d. 5) and a translation of Chrysostom's commentary on the Epistle to the Ephesians written in eleventh-century uncials (MS. Arm. d. 11). So the collection became considerable enough to warrant the production of a catalogue. The Rev. Sukras Baronian was entrusted with the task in 1883, and at the time of his death, twenty years later, was still engaged upon it as well as on a catalogue of the Armenian manuscripts in the British Museum which he had begun in 1870. Happily, Oxford had an Armenian scholar of repute in the person of Dr. F. C. Conybeare. In 1912 Conybeare undertook to complete Baronian's unfinished work, which was published over their joint names in 1918.[1] Their catalogue, like other catalogues of oriental manuscripts to be presently mentioned, shows a great advance over earlier cataloguing methods in that it describes the manuscripts and not merely their contents.

Georgia, though neighbour to Armenia, has no affinity with its language. The Georgian collection in Bodley is entirely the creation of Mr. (afterwards Sir) Oliver Wardrop, who commenced in 1910 to transfer to Bodley a library gathered together in the course of his career in the consular service. In addition, he established, in memory of his sister, a Marjory Wardrop Fund for the encouragement of Georgian studies in Oxford. A Menologion or collection of lives of saints of the Iberian church, written about the year 1040 (MS. Georg. b. 1)[2] was presented to the Bodleian by the Fund's Board of Management.

5. SANSKRIT MANUSCRIPTS

An earlier chapter has told (p. 110) how the Bodleian collection of Sanskrit manuscripts came to be formed; a collection so extensive that it was already described in 1856 by Max Müller as surpassed in Europe by one other library only, that of the East India Company. Extensive though it was, the collection was capable of improvement. With one solitary exception all the manuscripts of which it was composed were on paper, and nearly all were of comparatively modern date.[3] Steps were taken to remedy that defect when in 1887 the library spent £200 in buying from Dr. E. Hultzsch, epigraphist of the Archaeological Survey at Madras, 465 Sanskrit and Prakrit manuscripts, some of them being rare manuscripts written on birch-bark.[4]

[1] As pars XIV of the *Catalogus Codicum MSS. Bibliothecae Bodleianae.*
[2] Catalogued in *Analecta Bollandiana*, vol. xxxi (1912), pp. 301–18.
[3] The earliest dated Sanskrit manuscript in Aufrecht's catalogue is A.D. 1370.
[4] Birch-bark continued to be used as material for writing until quite a late period. Bodley bought in 1892 a manuscript (MS. Sansk. b. 33) of the Bhagavata Purana written on birch-bark in 1718 and ornamented with 348 paintings.

A few years later the library succeeded in obtaining some much older examples of Sanskrit writing. In 1898 there was bought for the Bodleian for £50 an extremely ancient birch-bark manuscript (MS. Sansk. c. 17), called from its discoverer the Bower manuscript. It had been disinterred, about 1890, by Lieutenant H. Bower from a buried city in Chinese Turkestan, and consisted of portions of works on medicine and divination, written on fifty long strips of birch-bark in the fifth century of our era.[1] From the same site there came thirty-three fragments written on a primitive woolly paper and probably dating from the fifth to the seventh centuries. These pieces, known as the Weber fragments (MS. Sansk. e. 23), were bought in 1902 for £100 from Dr. Rudolf Hoernle, who presented to the library in the same year, as a tercentenary gift, an arithmetical manuscript, probably of the tenth century and called, from the place of its discovery, Bakshali (MS. Sansk. d. 14).[2] Through Dr. Hoernle's assistance the Bodleian was enabled to purchase in 1900 thirty-four other early Sanskrit manuscripts of the eleventh to the sixteenth centuries, some of them composed of palm-leaves.[3]

Dr. Aufrecht's catalogue of Bodleian Sanskrit manuscripts which appeared in 1859–64, was incomplete even at the time that it was produced. Max Müller was to have undertaken the cataloguing of the Vedic texts, but his section was never written. He must also be held responsible for the omission of a number of non-Vedic manuscripts which were out to him on loan at the time that Aufrecht was making his catalogue. There was therefore a considerable mass of matter, apart from later accessions, that awaited description. In 1896, on Max Müller's recommendation, advantage was taken of the presence in England of Dr. Moriz Winternitz, Professor of Indian Philology at the University of Prague; and a grant of £100 was obtained from the Common University Fund to allow him to start upon a second volume of the Sanskrit catalogue: but next year the Delegates of the Fund declined to renew their grant, and the Professor returned to the Continent. So the work lapsed for three years, to be resumed in 1900–1 by A. B. Keith, a Boden Sanskrit scholar, who was afterwards elected to the Professorial Chair of Sanskrit at Edinburgh which Aufrecht had once occupied, and who was also to make

[1] Edited by Dr. R. Hoernle, for the *Archaeological Survey of India* (new imperial series, vol. xxii), 1893–1912.

[2] Published by the donor, with photozincographic facsimiles, in *Verhandlungen des VII. Internationalen Orientalisten-Congresses*, Arische section, pp. 127 ff.

[3] One of these deserves a special mention. It is an illuminated manuscript of the Buddhist Prajñapāramitā (MS. Sansk. a. 7), written in or about 1099, the paintings in which have been described by Mr. H. J. Stooke in *Oriental Art*, vol. i, pp. 5–8.

a reputation in another field by becoming the leading authority on the constitution of the British Commonwealth. Winternitz and Keith's catalogue was published in 1905. It falls into two sections, namely Vedic (nos. 855–1089) and non-Vedic manuscripts (nos. 1090–621).

As was the case with other catalogues of oriental manuscripts planned by Nicholson, the compilers were working to a scheme formulated by the librarian himself. The scheme provided for a full technical description of each manuscript. The absence of such descriptions from Aufrecht's work led to the production of a supplement to it which was carried out by Keith in 1901–2 and published as an appendix to Aufrecht in 1909. It stands very much to Nicholson's credit that, though no orientalist, he saw very clearly that attention to palaeography is as important in dealing with an Eastern, as it is with a Western, manuscript. 'European palaeography', he wrote in 1905, 'is still only in its youth; Oriental palaeography is only in its infancy.' And so 'another hope I have is to see the production of a separate palaeographical album for each important Oriental language, containing full-size collotype facsimiles, carefully chosen and carefully edited, of dated and early undated Bodleian manuscripts in that language'.[1]

No sooner was the second volume of the catalogue published than fresh accessions of Sanskrit manuscripts began to stream in. The year 1907 brought a number of transcripts made by Dr. W. H. Mill, whose valuable Sanskrit collection had been bought for the library in 1849. When Max Müller died in 1900, his Vedic manuscripts passed to the Japanese University of Tokyo; but, though Oxford did not receive Max Müller's own collection, it benefited in another fashion. A fund was raised by his friends for the encouragement of research into the history, languages, and religion of ancient India. With the help of a grant of £100 made by the administrators of that fund, Professor Macdonell, who then held the Boden Chair, purchased from a Brahmin pundit in Benares about ninety Sanskrit manuscripts and deposited them in Bodley in 1908. They consist of copies of the Vedas—one of these is the earliest known dated copy of the Rigveda—and of the great epic poems styled Mahabharata and the Puranas, and have since been described in a special catalogue compiled by a Bodleian assistant, T. Gambier Parry.[2] At the same time Professor Macdonell drew the attention of the Curators to the desirability of

---

[1] *Catalogue of Sanskrit MSS.*, vol. ii, p. vi.
[2] *A Catalogue of the Sanskrit MSS. purchased for the Administrators of the Max Müller Memorial Fund*, 1922.

acquiring *en bloc* the extensive library from which he had made his selection. On being informed that here was a store that would form a most welcome addition to the Bodleian's treasures, Lord Curzon, at that time Chancellor of the University, prevailed upon the Maharajah Sir Chandra Shum Shere, Prime Minister of Nepal, to buy the collection and present it in 1909 to Oxford.

The Chandra Shum Shere manuscripts, for so they are called in memory of their donor, were reckoned as no fewer than 6,330 in number, and could claim to be the largest collection of Indian manuscripts ever brought to England. Binding, towards which the Common University Fund made a grant of £1,000, has brought them into the compass of 2,152 volumes. Even by that computation their acquisition has more than doubled the size of the Bodleian Sanskrit collection, which in 1905 totalled 1,621 manuscripts. None are of high antiquity, but every branch of Sanskrit literature is represented in them, as may be seen from the still unpublished catalogue compiled by Mr. Gambier Parry.

6. INDIA AND THE FAR EAST

Catalogues were undertaken of manuscripts in other oriental languages. In 1901 the Curators entrusted Keith with the task of cataloguing their *Prakrit* manuscripts. Prakrit, from being a vernacular as opposed to the literary Sanskrit, itself developed into a literary language. A few Prakrit manuscripts had come into the library in the various Sanskrit collections, and some fifty more came with the manuscripts bought from Dr. Hultzsch. Keith's catalogue, though completed in a year, was not published for another ten.[1]

As in their art, so in the literature of their court, the Mohammedan rulers of Delhi were greatly under Persian influence. The *Hindustani* which they spoke is full of Persian borrowings. So it is not inappropriate that the second volume of Ethé's Persian catalogue should contain descriptions of the library's forty-two Hindustani manuscripts, most of which are derived from the Ouseley and Elliott collections. The same volume also enumerates four manuscripts in *Pushtu*, an Iranian tongue spoken in Afghanistan and on the North-West Frontier.

Mention has already been made (p. 112) of the hundred *Tamil* manuscripts bought for the Bodleian in 1860. A catalogue of these, as well as of the library's manuscripts in those other Dravidian languages which have survived in southern India from pre-Aryan

[1] *Catalogue of Prakrit MSS. in the Bodleian Library*, 1911.

times, was made by the Rev. Dr. G. U. Pope and accepted for publication by the University Press,[1] but never reached a state to justify printing.

Bodleian manuscripts in *Malay* were so few, numbering no more than twelve, that Nicholson's choice of them as the subject of a separate printed catalogue may excite surprise; but the fact is that his inquiring mind found a peculiar fascination in the recondite and the minute. The Malay catalogue is the work of Richard Greentree, was executed in 1905, revised by Nicholson himself, and published in 1910.[2]

Although the Bodleian had long possessed early products of the Jesuit missionary press operating in Japan,[3] the *Japanese* language was but sparsely represented before 1881, when the Curators bought a collection of Japanese printed books formed by Mr. A. Wylie. These and a few books and manuscripts presented by Max Müller were catalogued in print in the same year by a Japanese Buddhist priest named Bunyiu Nanjio, who had travelled to Oxford to study Sanskrit under Müller.[4] Bunyiu Nanjio himself added, three years later, forty-one Japanese works and Chinese works published in Japan. Their number was greatly increased by a donation of 328 volumes of Buddhist literature given in 1908 by Sir Ernest Satow, British minister successively at Tokyo and at Pekin.

And lastly, although not the subject of a catalogue, there were the book productions of remote *Tibet*. The Bodleian had secured a few examples of these as far back as 1806, for it bought in that year for £50 certain Tibetan manuscripts which had been obtained in 1785 by Captain Samuel Turner of the East India Company when on a mission to the Grand Lama.[5] A larger consignment, of 102 manuscripts and block-books, collected in Tibet in 1855–8 by the German explorers, Adolf and Robert Schlagintweit, was bought in 1885 from their surviving brother, Dr. Emil Schlagintweit, for £120; and to these the Indian Government added, twenty years later, a more ancient and valuable collection of twenty-one manuscripts and 127 block-books.

[1] *Bodleian Library in 1882–7*, p. 25.
[2] *Catalogue of Malay MSS., and of MSS. relating to the Malay Language, in the Bodleian Library*.
[3] *Bodleian Quarterly Record*, vol. iii, pp. 175–6.
[4] *Catalogue of Japanese and Chinese Books and MSS. lately added to the Bodleian Library*.
[5] Macray, *Annals*, p. 283.

Section II

COIN AND ART COLLECTIONS

7. COINS

On his first coming to the library Nicholson was inclined to think
that the coin collection might be detached from it. When the project
for a new Archaeological Museum should be realized, the coins, he
thought, might be transferred thither.[1] But he soon changed his mind
in that respect, and in 1884 was writing, 'I cannot see where the gain
is to be'. Meanwhile Convocation had set up a delegacy to consider
the housing of the university's works of art. Representatives of the
delegacy attended a Curators' meeting in February 1886 to state their
reasons for desiring the transfer of the coin collection to the old, and
by this time crowded, Ashmolean Museum. The Curators listened
to their arguments but declined to accede to their request.[2] There
matters rested until 1896 when, after a new Ashmolean Museum had
been erected in Beaumont Street, Pelham, by this time a Bodleian
Curator, moved for a committee to consider the desirability and
feasibility of transferring thither the whole or a part of the collection
of coins in the Bodleian. The committee reported that the Ashmolean
was a more natural and proper place for a collection of coins, tartly
observing that 'if Library officials have to be chosen for knowledge
of coins as well as books, the result must often be the selection of one
who is not specially distinguished in either department'. Their report
provoked a violent riposte from Nicholson, and a threat to oppose
any statute that might be put forward. So Pelham, choosing the path
of discretion, moved 'that the Curators do not think the present time
advisable for raising the question', and his advice was accepted. Thus
ended, for the time being, what Nicholson described as 'the Ashmolean attempt to capture the coins'.[3]

Nicholson was no numismatist, but the disordered state of the
coin-room, and the inconvenience of a system under which separate
donations were kept apart instead of being merged in a single series,
acted on him as a challenge. In 1884–7 he was actively carrying out a
campaign of reorganization.[4] In this he had then and later the expert

[1] Curators' papers, 'Librarian's report on the redistribution of the Library', 3 Mar.
1883.
[2] Curators' minutes, 6 Feb. 1886.
[3] Curators' minutes, 13 June 1896 and 6 Feb. 1897; report of committee on trans-
ference of coin collections, 30 Nov. 1896.
[4] Described in *The Bodleian Library in 1882–7*, pp. 42–46, and in reports made to
the Curators 8 Nov. 1884 and 5 Feb. 1886.

assistance of Mr. (afterwards Sir) Charles Oman and Mr. C. L. Stainer. After setting in order the Greek and Roman Republican coins, Oman proceeded to arrange and catalogue the Anglo-Saxon collection, of which it was hoped to print a catalogue.[1] The series of later English currency was enriched by the purchase, in 1886, of fifty specimens from a treasure trove of English gold, ranging from Henry VI to Henry VIII, as well as by a donation of gold, silver, and tokens, given in 1893 by Mr. E. L. Hussey.

There were other donations also. A gift made by Dr. F. Parkes Weber in 1906 included some dozens of Italian bronze medals of the fifteenth and sixteenth centuries. Greville Chester was a frequent donor in his lifetime, and the coins that were received under his will in 1892 were in large part medieval Italian currencies of the Levant. Other accessions chiefly derived from the East. The Egypt Exploration Fund gave some 500 coins from a hoard (Claudius–Marcus Aurelius) found in the Fayum (1896). Ptolemaic, Seleucid, and Jewish coins came in 1888 from Sir Charles Warren; Seleucid and Bactrian coins figured among those that were bought in 1889 from Sir Alexander Cunningham's collection with the help of a grant of £75 from the Common University Fund. That purchase, and a gift of 146 Indo-Scythic and early Indian coins that Lord Curzon made in 1896, expanded the collection that J. B. Elliott had given in 1860. From that collection the Bodleian mainly derived its series of coins of the old Hindu Gupta dynasty, which were first catalogued in 1891 by Mr. E. J. Rapson.[2] The coins of the later Islamic rulers of India, along with all other Mohammedan coins that the Bodleian had received from Elliott, Warren, and other donors, were listed in a printed catalogue made in 1888 by Mr. Stanley Lane-Poole, which was to remain the only Bodleian coin-catalogue issued since the days of Francis Wise (1750). A subsequent gift of 675 Mohammedan coins, collected by Mr. H. C. Kay and presented in 1912 by his son, greatly enriched the Bodleian series of oriental gold coins, for 180 of them were in that metal. Finally, there must not be forgotten a gift of 2,044 Chinese coins made by Mr. G. Uvedale Price in 1903, since this marks the beginning of the university's Chinese coin collection.

8. ART COLLECTIONS

Although Nicholson strenuously and effectively resisted the transfer of coins from the Bodleian to the Ashmolean, he was less averse

[1] Curators' minutes, 27 Jan. 1894.
[2] *Numismatic Chronicle*, 3rd ser., vol. xi, pp. 48–64. See also Vincent A. Smith, 'Coinage of the Gupta Dynasty', *Journal of the Royal Asiatic Society*, vol. xxi (1889), pp. 1–158.

to transferring what might be more properly regarded as museum objects. Many exhibits which had long attracted the eye of curious visitors were dispatched in 1887 to the Ashmolean Museum, then still occupying its old quarters in Broad Street. Among them were Queen Elizabeth's gloves, the platter made out of the Boscobel oak, and the famous Guy Fawkes lantern.[1] And a large number of works of art now found a more suitable home in the University Galleries, to which the great Douce collection of prints had been transferred in 1863. Nicholson's proposal to rid the Picture Gallery of its models of classical buildings by sending these also to the University Galleries for the time being hung fire.[2]

The Bodleian continued to add to its collection of topographical drawings, as, for example, by the purchase in 1885 of seventy-six Oxford drawings made about the year 1804 by J. C. Nattes, and was given in 1890 a fine grangerized set of Ormerod's *History of Cheshire*, enriched with paintings by De Wint, Copley Fielding, and other water-colour artists. The Hope collection of engraved portraits, though not under Bodleian management, was still housed in Bodleian premises, having been removed in 1888 from the gallery of the Camera to the Natural Philosophy School in the south-west corner of the library quadrangle. A proposal to send it packing once more to the top floor of the Old Ashmolean Building was defeated in 1895 in Convocation.

The Picture Gallery remained in use for the exhibition of the university's collection of historical portraits, though few additions were now made to it. When he first became librarian, Nicholson suggested that the whole collection should be transferred to the newly completed Examination Schools, and in 1884 Convocation actually approved a scheme for sending to that capacious building all pictures in the Bodleian and the Ashmolean that were not specially connected with either institution.[3] But the scheme lay dormant. It was only in 1909, after the conversion of half the Picture Gallery into an upper reading-room had made overcrowding intolerable, that the Curators agreed to allow their larger ceremonial portraits, such as those of university chancellors and royal personages, to be transferred to the New Examination Schools.

Yet the Picture Gallery deserved the criticism that Dr. Wellesley had passed upon it in 1858, when he wrote that 'It must be confessed

[1] *Bodleian Library in 1882–7*, p. 47.
[2] Curators' minutes, 11 May 1907.
[3] Librarian's report to the Curators, 4 Mar. 1883. Mrs. Poole's *Catalogue of Oxford Portraits*, vol. i, p. xx. The reference to the Ashmolean is, of course, to the old building in Broad Street and not to the University Galleries.

that a worse-lighted *pinacotheca*, and pictures more chilled blistered and restored, never existed.'[1] A main cause of the poor state of the pictures was without doubt the variations of temperature to which they were subjected. The gallery was unwarmed; its temperature, the Librarian told his Curators, varied from 19 to 82 degrees; its pictures were cracked and blistering. On three separate occasions Nicholson proposed the installation of a heating system: on each occasion his application was turned down or its consideration deferred. Only in 1902 the Curators consented to include the warming of the Picture Gallery in the statement of university needs;[2] and in 1907, at a cost of a little under £1,000, heating was at last installed.

By that time the much-needed work of restoration had been taken in hand and carried through to its completion. The systematic repair of a small number of pictures which most needed it had been begun in 1891. It was taken up on a larger scale in 1903 when, on the initiative of T. W. Jackson, a Bodleian Curator and Keeper of the Hope collection, a fund, amounting approximately to £1,550, was raised for repairing and glazing the Bodleian pictures. The work was entrusted to the London firm of Messrs. Haines and Son, and was brought to a close in 1907. The exhibition of Oxford Historical Portraits, held in 1904–6, had awakened interest in the subject which was further developed by the Oxford Historical Society's publication of Mrs. Poole's scholarly catalogue.[3]

---

[1] Report to the Curators, 1858.   [2] p. 124.
[3] The first of the three volumes of her *Catalogue of Oxford Portraits* was published by the Oxford Historical Society (vol. lvii) in 1912, and contains at pp. 1–130 a complete list of the portraits in the Bodleian Library.

Chapter XIII

Store-rooms and Reading-rooms

I. THE BODLEIAN QUADRANGLE

SOME account has been given, in the first chapter of this work
(pp. 5, 13–18), of how the library spread round the Schools quadrangle, taking over, one after another, the first-floor Schools, and
then in 1845 appropriating one of the Schools on the ground-floor.
Thereafter the university's increasing need of rooms for examinations made further extension in that direction impossible for a time.
Every plan put forward for library extension assumed the eventual
transfer of all the ground-floor rooms to Bodley; but that could not
take place until new Examination Schools had been built. These were
completed and brought into use in the summer of 1882, a few months
after Nicholson took office.

Hesitation and delay over the building of the Schools had produced deplorable results on Bodley. It is true that the acquisition of
the Camera in 1861 had brought relief, but, since that building was
used only for storage of modern accessions (and not for all of them),
in the other parts of the library there was a growing congestion which
made any logical order or methodical arrangement increasingly hard
to achieve. A third part of the Picture Gallery had been closed and
turned into a store-room. In some rooms the books were double-
rowed, that is, one row of books was set behind another; in other
rooms books lacked even that amount of shelf-room and were lying
in large numbers on the floor. Thousands of Ordnance Survey maps
were piled up among the treasures of the Douce Room. Such was the
scene which greeted the Curators on their first formal inspection
under the new librarian and which prompted Dean Liddell to remark,
'Well, Mr. Nicholson, you've got an Augean stable.'[1]

So soon as they were vacated, the Schools were made over to the
Curators.[2] Now would have been the time for the insertion of the
metal stack which Wellesley had suggested in 1858, or for the modification of that plan that had been recently put forward by Graham

---

[1] *The Bodleian Library in 1882–7*, p. 37; Curators' papers, 'Letter from Bodley's
Librarian on the motion of Mr. Mowat', 3 May 1892. Dean Liddell was not the first
to apply the phrase to Bodley. In 1825 Bandinel told Frederic Madden that, when he
succeeded his godfather as librarian, the Bodleian 'was a perfect Augean stable'.
Bodl. MS. Eng. hist. c. 146, p. 272.

[2] Under decree of 23 May 1882.

Jackson. With one exception the fitting up of the Schools was less thorough-going. Instead of Wellesley's free-standing iron stack, carried up through the floors and relieving the outer walls of any weight of books, the Curators adopted the older type of wooden wall-cases, which they supplemented by transverse cases running up to and supporting the ceiling.[1] Instead of inserting pierced iron floors and so dividing each School into an upper and a lower room, as Wellesley and Jackson had both recommended, they carried up their cases a full 15 feet. ('Librarians no more mind going up a ladder,' said Nicholson, 'than sailors mind going up rigging.'[2]) Instead of the fire-proof floors which Scott and then Galton had advocated, they kept the old decayed wooden floors, supporting them by equally combustible wooden cases.[3]

The first School to be taken in hand was the Old Writing School or Schola Metaphysicae, which was fitted up in 1883 at the cost of £1,764[4] and filled with law-books. Next year the two Schools in the south range, namely, the Music School and Schola Naturalis Philosophiae, were partially shelved.[5] But these did not add greatly to the space at the librarian's disposal, since with the Music School there came the old Music School Library, and the major part of the Natural Philosophy School had to be given up in 1888 to house the Hope collection of engraved portraits. It was not until 1887 that the Moral Philosophy School in the north-west corner of the quadrangle was wholly freed from the Arundel Marbles, for, although some of the marbles had been transferred in 1862 to the equally dark cellars of the Ashmolean Museum, others still remained. By a very sensible arrangement the marbles were removed in 1887 from both repositories and reunited in the University Galleries, along with the Pomfret Marbles, under the custody of the Lincoln Professor of Classical Art and Archaeology. The vacated School was promptly fitted up, with the help of a £480 university grant, as a much-needed map-room.[6]

---

[1] The cross-cases which the Curators adopted, following the recommendation of Jowett's committee of 1877 (*Selected Reports for the Extension of the Bodleian Library*, pp. 17–18), had an advantage over Wellesley's longitudinal cases in that they allowed of better lighting. Jackson's scheme for a combination of cross walls and longitudinal partitions would have transformed the Schools into a honeycomb of small cells (op. cit., pp. 22–23).

[2] Curators' papers, 'Observations submitted by the Librarian', 10 Mar. 1899.

[3] In the light of recent examination of the timbers, it seems probable that, without the central support that was given to them in the eighties, the floors would have collapsed.

[4] Under decree of 6 June 1882.

[5] Decree of 17 June 1884.

[6] Under decree of 29 Nov. 1887.

There remained the History School or, as it was called *par excellence*, the Old School. At first roughly shelved for foreign periodicals, it was fitted in 1890 with stack on the lines of the British Museum iron library advocated by Wellesley thirty-two years before.[1] The new fittings cost £2,000. They were designed by J. Osborne Smith, a London architect who had done similar work for the British Museum and the Public Record Office, and comprised an intermediate floor of pierced iron-work and fixed iron-framed cross-cases, 7 feet in height. But advantage was not yet taken of the system of sliding presses which the British Museum had introduced into its iron library three years before. We shall see presently how the sliding press or rolling bookcase came to be brought into use in other parts of our library.

The additional free space which the ground-floor Schools afforded led Nicholson to plan a fundamental change in book-distribution. 'I propose if possible', he wrote in 1883, 'to assign these six rooms to Language, the Greek and Latin classics, Philosophy, Law and Social Science, Mathematics, and Natural Science; and I propose to leave sufficient space in each room to be used, if necessary, as a departmental reading-room.'[2] In his proposal for the establishment of departmental reading-rooms Nicholson showed himself far ahead of his time, anticipating the scheme worked out more than fifty years later by the most recent planners of Bodleian extension. But as he proposed it, the idea was not really practicable: there was not sufficient space in the Old Schools for a combination of reading-room and stack. His great plan began and ended with the conversion of the Schola Metaphysicae into a Law School, into which it was never found practical to admit readers.

Nevertheless he was able to achieve in part a more orderly arrangement of the contents of the Bodleian building. The fitting up of the Old School made it possible to evacuate foreign periodicals from the rooms overhead and leave these free for growing accessions to the sections of British Topography and Oriental Languages.[3] The gifts of Dr. Richard Rawlinson were brought together from the seven corners of the library into which they had been scattered and were placed in a room formerly occupied by Laudian manuscripts. But here, as in so much else, Nicholson did not know when it was wise to stop; and he was checked only by a resolution of his Curators that no shifting of

[1] Decree of 3 June 1890.
[2] Curators' papers, 'Librarian's report to the Curators on the redistribution of the Library', 3 Mar. 1883.
[3] The Gough annexe, as one of the old periodical rooms came to be called, was taken over for topography in 1890, and two years later the Hope Periodical Room was transformed into an Oriental Printed Room.

books on a considerable scale should in future take place without their sanction.[1]

Although nothing further was done to render the Schools building fire-resisting, or indeed to form a fire-proof repository elsewhere, it must not be thought that old warnings or old projects were entirely forgotten. Indeed the risk of fire was ever present to Nicholson's mind. Early in his tenure of office, in 1885, the Curators consulted an architectural expert, Mr. C. J. Phipps, on the methods and cost of fire-proofing a part of the Bodleian. Phipps repeated the advice which Galton had given eleven years earlier; but, of his various proposals, the Curators turned down a recommendation that the main staircase should be reconstructed in stone, and fought shy of his plan for spending £2,739 on the insertion of concrete floors in the southern half of the buildings round the quadrangle. They did decide on putting up to Council proposals for fire-proofing the floor of the Picture Gallery, for inserting iron doors in all party walls, and for protecting windows by iron shutters: but Council agreed to the last alone, and even that modest measure was rejected in Convocation by 63 votes to 13. And so, after much debate, nothing was done.[2] From time to time the proposal for fire-proof shutters was revived, never to be adopted; and the solitary action taken to guard against the danger of conflagration was the expenditure of over £600 in 1907 on the installation of an automatic fire-alarm apparatus, which in due course went out of order and was eventually removed.

The Old Schools were fresh and clean in the Clipsham stone with which T. G. Jackson had in part refaced them, and Nicholson improved their appearance further by opening up the majority of the windows that had been blocked in the course of the past hundred years. Not all his projects were so happy. The Victorians, and in particular the Victorians of Oxford, loved to swathe their buildings with verdure. Thick ivy mantled the walls of Bodley in Exeter garden, and half of the southern face of the Clarendon Building was at this time ivy-clad. Nicholson proposed to plant creepers and climbing plants round the inner and outer walls of the quadrangle, and his proposal was approved by his Curators. But other graduates disliked the idea of turning Bodley into Jack-in-the-Green, and on a petition from forty-one of them the Curators rescinded their order.[3] Nicholson had at the same time proposed the grassing of the quadrangle. This

[1] Curators' minutes, 11 Mar. 1893.
[2] Curators' papers, Report by Mr. C. J. Phipps on fire-proofing, 1 Dec. 1885; Curators' minutes, 4 Dec. 1886; *Bodleian Library in 1882–7*, p. 53.
[3] Order of 31 Oct., rescinded 14 Nov. 1885.

the Curators rejected. Very likely they were right, and a grass lawn would have been out of keeping with its surroundings; yet one could wish that a paved or cobbled surface might one day be substituted for the present expanse of unrolled gravel.

2. CAMERA, SHELDONIAN, AND ASHMOLEAN BASEMENTS

Although the use of the ground-floor Schools gave additional storage-space for the sections of the library kept in the old building, it did nothing to relieve pressure on the ground-floor (or basement as it was generally termed) of the Camera in which the bulk of modern accessions were stored. Further space had to be sought there by carrying up the shelving on its walls and round the central piers until it touched the vault as well as by putting in floor-cases.[1] Nicholson supplemented these last by an ingenious contrivance which was just coming into use in the library world—the rolling bookcase.

The invention of a bookcase running, like a sofa, upon wheels, can be ascribed to a Bradford librarian, Mr. C. C. Virgo. Nicholson had seen a model exhibited in 1877 at the International Conference of Librarians, of which he was secretary; but it was not until his attention had been called to the adoption of an improved type by the British Museum that he introduced it, in 1888, into the Camera. And the Camera fitting was still a primitive affair; a dwarf boxed-in wooden case, drawn forward by handles and running on wheels along grooves cut in the floor.

And now, despite the space gained in the Old Schools and in the Camera, the time had come when the Bodleian could not avoid a further extension of its territory. A Curatorial committee of 1877 had suggested that some 30,000 of the less valuable books in the library might find what they described as 'an appropriate home' in the vaults below the neighbouring Sheldonian Theatre.[2] The use of the Sheldonian basement was offered by the Curators of the Theatre in 1884, and their offer was then accepted, but it was 1887 before the basement was occupied and 1889 before it was formally assigned.[3] Fitted up in 1891 and subsequent years with roughly-made deal shelving, it provided a home for bound volumes of newspapers, and proved the darkest and the most incommodious of all Bodleian store-houses.[4]

The Sheldonian basement was but the first of a series of subterranean retreats to which the Bodleian had recourse in its efforts to

[1] Curators' order for estimates, 3 May 1884.
[2] *Selected Reports for the Extension of the Bodleian Library*, p. 17.
[3] Decree of 26 Feb. 1889. See also *The Bodleian Library in 1882-7*, p. 3.
[4] As may be seen from a photograph in the special number of *Oxford*, Feb. 1937, plate 11.

find storage for accessions. It will be remembered that, as far back as 1855, Gilbert Scott had pointed to the Ashmolean Museum as Bodley's natural *hinterland* into which it might expand, and that T. G. Jackson had subsequently worked out plans for linking up the two buildings (see pp. 120, 147). At the earlier date it had seemed possible that all the contents of the Ashmolean might be transferred to the new University Museum in the Parks. Instead of a complete clearance, the archaeological section of Ashmole's foundation, left behind in the old building, began a new life under the keepership of John Henry Parker, and developed lustily under that of his successor, Arthur Evans, who was appointed Keeper in 1884. It grew and grew, and, despite the room gained in 1886 by transferring ethnological specimens to the Pitt–Rivers collection newly established in the University Museum, it became clear, when Mr. C. D. E. Fortnum started to make gifts from his great collection of renaissance and classical art, that the Ashmolean Museum would have to find a new home. The final decision to move was taken when Mr. Fortnum notified his intention of leaving the remainder of his collection to Oxford, and promised that, if the university would spend £11,000 on building a new museum, he would hand over £10,000 for its maintenance.[1] To this new building, erected on a site adjoining the University Galleries on the north, the name and contents of the Ashmolean Museum were transferred in the summer of 1894.

As soon as it became known that the old building might be vacated, the Curators expressed to Council their desire that it should be appropriated to Bodley.[2] Clearly the basement could be used for storage, but the uses to which the upper floors might be put were not so evident. Scott had suggested that one of them might be made an evening reading-room; but the Camera had come to serve that purpose; and, although Jowett's committee in 1877 had been prepared to surrender the Camera if one or both floors of the Ashmolean took its place as reading-rooms, times had changed and the scheme then contemplated for converting the Camera into a museum of classical archaeology had been given up. Nicholson was clear in his own mind; he wished to see the whole building converted into stack. Thereby, he calculated, 400,000 volumes might be stored, and 'this enormous augmentation would entirely obviate for a generation to come any necessity for considering the erection of new buildings or the occupation of premises in any other part of Oxford'.[3] But the Curators were

---

[1] *Oxford University Gazette*, 31 May 1892.
[2] Curators' minutes, 31 Oct 1891. The request was repeated on 9 June 1894.
[3] Curators' agenda paper, 26 Oct. 1895.

hesitant,[1] and succeeded only in getting the basement. Through their indecision over the upper floors, they lost the chance of securing them. The top floor, to which it was at first intended to transfer the Hope collection of engraved portraits, was appropriated in 1899 to the department of Geography. The main floor for a time stood empty, after a proposal to transfer to it from the University Galleries that white elephant, the Chantrey collection of busts, had been defeated in Convocation (1 December 1896).

On 18 June 1895 Convocation passed a decree assigning the Ashmolean basement to the Bodleian Curators. Thus the library came to possess a stone-vaulted chamber which, as T. G. Jackson had pointed out, was well adapted for the purposes of a strong-room for rare books or manuscripts. But the need for further space for modern accessions was paramount.[2] The books selected for transfer were the bulk of those that had come into the library between 1851 and 1882. They had been previously stored in the Camera and in the Old School. Their removal thence left room for new accessions; and they had the advantage of being 'closed sections' to which nothing further would be added. They had been classified in accordance with Coxe's classification scheme, which has in consequence come to be known in the library as the Ashmolean classification, in contradistinction to the Camera classification inaugurated by Nicholson in 1883.

Before the transfer could be made, the larger of the two rooms of which the basement is composed had to be fitted up. £1,700 was voted for that purpose in 1896–7 by Convocation. An intermediate floor of open iron-work was inserted as had been done in the Old School. Owing to its greater height and the curve of its barrel-vault, the basement lent itself less readily than the Old School did to the purposes of stack; nevertheless greater economy of space was obtained by inserting, between each row of fixed wooden cases, four rows of movable cases. These were in their main features of the same design as those in the Camera; that is to say, they were of deal; they were pulled forward; and they ran on wheels upon rails or in grooves. Storage was found in this way for nearly 100,000 volumes.

[1] On 9 Mar. 1895 they resolved that they were *not* in favour of the proposal to convert the whole of the Ashmolean into a bookstore. And when, on 8 Feb. 1896, they agreed to ask that the whole building *should* be put at their disposal for book-storage, the Hebdomadal Council refused their request. In 1897 and again in 1899 the Regius Professor of Divinity, Dr. Ince, endeavoured unsuccessfully to get his colleagues to take a decision on the appropriation of the upper portion of the Ashmolean: Curators' minutes, 15 May 1897 and 6 May 1899.

[2] 'The long delays,' said Nicholson, 'first in settling the destination of the Ashmolean and secondly in fitting it up, are simply paralysing', Curators' agenda paper, 8 Feb. 1896.

3. NEW SCHOOLS BASEMENT AND UNDERGROUND
BOOKSTORE

And yet before Bodley entered on possession of the Ashmolean basement, it had become evident to some at least of the Curators that the day of small remedies was past, and that the problem of extension must be tackled afresh and on a larger scale. In May 1894 Bywater moved for the appointment of an exploratory committee, charged to search for previous proposals for library extension. Out came once more the old forgotten reports of Gilbert Scott, of Wellesley, of Galton, and of Jackson. These were studied anew, and a year later the Curators resolved that, after the library had exhausted the possibilities of the Ashmolean basement and utilized vacant space that might be found in the basement of the New Examination Schools, 'the University should build on some convenient site a store-house for books; such a store-house to be constructed solely with a view to obtaining the maximum amount of storage room'.[1]

The decision was sound, but there was as yet no agreement as to where the new stack should be erected. Nicholson at first favoured building in the Clarendon quadrangle, that is to say between the Old Clarendon Building and the Bodleian; and this, it may be remembered (see p. 120), was the direction in which Gilbert Scott had said that the library would one day have to expand.[2] But he quickly changed his view, and by 1896 he had decided that the proper course would be to excavate an underground chamber, either in the Bodleian quadrangle, or in the Clarendon quadrangle to the north of it, or under the grass enclosure that encircled the Camera.[3] As to what could be achieved thereby he became, as years passed, extravagantly optimistic. 'Proper use of underground space', he wrote, 'will solve for ever the question of how to provide for accessions of current literature. Radcliffe Square will hold over 3,000,000 volumes; the Clarendon quadrangle 750,000; and almost any amount of additional underground space can ultimately be obtained elsewhere.'[4]

For another three years the scheme lay dormant. Then in 1899 a committee was once again appointed to consider modes of library extension. It took up Nicholson's proposal for an underground chamber, but found at once that it was not practicable to place such

[1] Curators' papers, Report of Committee on Extension of the Bodleian Library, 1 Mar. 1895.
[2] Scott had been in a measure anticipated by Mr. Strickland, who, in giving evidence before the Oxford University Commission of 1852, had suggested that 'ample accommodation for another century's literature' might be obtained by simply doubling the width of the north range of the Schools quadrangle. Evidence, p. 102.
[3] Library papers, 'E. W. B. Nicholson, Draft for Statistics sent to Gladstone'.
[4] *Statements of the Needs of the University*, 1902, p. 129.

a chamber within the Bodleian quadrangle. Excavation showed that, while the foundations on three sides of the quadrangle went down to a depth of 8 or 9 feet, those of the remaining side (the Proscholium) were but $5\frac{1}{2}$ feet deep and would have to be underpinned at great expense. The committee therefore favoured a site contiguous to the Camera, and obtained plans for a subterranean building there from Mr. Edmund Woodthorpe, an architect credited with experience in that type of construction.[1]

The underground bookstore which he designed was to be rectangular in shape and set below the grass sward on the north side of the Camera, with which building it would communicate. Being built in brick, iron, and concrete, it would be fire-proof. It was to be divided by an open iron grating into two stories, each a little over 6 feet high. In the absence of natural lighting, it was necessary that it should be lit by electricity, heated, and artificially ventilated. But the most striking feature of Mr. Woodthorpe's plan was the use made of sliding bookcases. These were of a type much superior to the cumbrous wooden cases in the Camera and Ashmolean basements. They derived from a form of iron book-press invented (independently of Mr. Virgo's Bradford model) by Dr. Tyler for the library which he founded at Bethnal Green. It may be of some interest to trace its history.

In 1887, as the result of a visit to Bethnal Green, Dr. Richard Garnett, Keeper of Printed Books at the British Museum, had introduced sliding presses into the British Museum iron library, after Mr. Henry Jenner, an assistant in his department, had worked out one important modification of the Bethnal Green model. The British Museum cases were suspended from the girders that carried the floor above, instead of running on wheels along grooves cut in the floor below. They were still drawn forward.[2]

The credit for the next stage in the development of the movable bookcase may be attributed to no less a person than Mr. Gladstone. Paying a visit to Bodley on 6 April 1888, he sketched out for Nicholson a design for wheeled bookcases, pulled endways instead of forwards; and he subsequently printed a description of this arrangement

[1] Curators' minutes, 10 June 1899; Reports of Committee on Bodleian Extension, 25 Nov. 1899 and 27 Jan. 1900.

[2] The earlier stages in the development of the rolling bookcase are described by Richard Garnett in an article on 'The Sliding Press at the British Museum', published in *Essays in Librarianship and Bibliography*, 1899, pp. 262–71; by Christian Berghoeffer in an article on 'Bewegliche Repositorien' in the *Centralblatt für Bibliothekswesen*, vol. xiii, pp. 152–7 (Apr. 1896); and by Nicholson in a printed paper, 'The Hebdomadal Council and the Bodleian', dated 19 Nov 1896, among the Curators' papers.

as a footnote to his article on 'Books and the Housing of them' in the *Nineteenth Century*.[1] The change may sound a minor one, but it had radical consequences. If cases were made to slide out endways into a vacant corridor, they could be set up against one another, with practically no intervening space, and thereby two thirds of any building could be packed solid with book-stack.

Mr. Henry Jenner, invited by the Hebdomadal Council in 1896 to visit Oxford and advise on methods of economic storage, made plans to show how the ground-floor Schools might be fitted up with endways-sliding cases on the new model. But though Council recommended that this method should be tried out in one of the ground-floor rooms, the Curators decided at that time to defer the experiment until after they had fitted up the Ashmolean basement.

It was this improved type of case, suspended from girders and rolling sideways along them, that Mr. Woodthorpe proposed for use in his underground chamber. If this type of fitting was adopted, a chamber of the size proposed would give accommodation for 860,000 octavo volumes. It was intended to place in it the bulk of the library's accessions of modern books, the Camera basement, in which they were shelved up to now, being practically full. As the annual increase was calculated at 15,300 octavos a year, the proposed chamber would, it was argued, provide for Bodleian needs for nearly sixty years.[2]

Unfortunately buildings, even if hidden underground, cost money; and the cost of constructing this one, together with the initial expenditure upon rolling cases, could not work out at less than £9,400. And the University Chest lacked money. The calls made upon it were outrunning its resources; and in 1894, after spending £11,000 on the new Ashmolean Museum, the Curators of the Chest had found it necessary to issue a warning that consideration of any measure, such as the erection of new buildings, which would involve further addition to existing expenditure, would have to be postponed.[3] So now, when the proposal to spend near £10,000 on an underground bookstore was put up to them, they declared such expenditure by the university to be impossible. The university had but £12,000 at its disposal; when that was gone, there was no fund remaining out of which

---

[1] Vol. xxvii, p. 396 (Mar. 1890). Nicholson has given an account of Gladstone's visit in his pamphlet *Mr. Gladstone and the Bodleian* (1898), p. 10. Gladstone's invention failed to catch the attention of librarians, and it was left to Mr. J. Lymburn, librarian of Glasgow University, to describe the endways-rolling case in a paper read to the Library Association on 13 June 1892, and printed in *The Library*, vol. iv, pp. 241–2. Mr. Lymburn was unaware that he had been anticipated.

[2] Curators' memorandum, submitted to Council 5 Nov. 1900.

[3] *University Gazette*, vol. xxv, p. 78.

any further capital expenditure could be defrayed. Nor was a loan through the Board of Agriculture possible, since that would involve an additional charge of from £850 to £900 a year, a sum far in excess of the university's means.[1]

So there was nothing that could be done at the moment but make the best of existing buildings and postpone plans for new ones. Some provision had to be made at once, for the Camera basement shelves were already full. It was therefore decided to fit up the smaller of the two rooms in the Ashmolean basement with sliding cases on Mr. Woodthorpe's model, and this was done in 1901. The experience thus gained was applied on a larger scale three years later, when the Curators obtained for library use the large cellar that underlay the entrance-hall of the Examination Schools.[2] During the five years that followed, the new basement was gradually fitted with sliding cases, provided out of special university grants, and filled with the novels which had hitherto kept oddly assorted company with Parliamentary papers in the old Logic School.

Yet neither the Ashmolean nor the New Schools basements could be regarded as substitutes for the large book-stack, specially designed for economic storage, which had been in men's minds ever since Bywater brought up the question of extension in 1894; and when the Vice-Chancellor in 1902 invited the various university departments and institutions to state their needs, the Curators gave first place to the provision of additional space for book-storage.[3] Money was still wanting, but at the end of 1906 a letter came from T. A. Brassey, prime mover in the raising of funds for university endowment. In consequence of this communication the Curators decided to ask Mr. Woodthorpe to revise his plans and estimates for the projected underground chamber, only to find that Mr. Woodthorpe was himself now underground. But Mr. Rutland Saunders, who had succeeded to his business, was at hand to supply the information needed; and in May 1907 the Curators were able to inform Council that sufficient money had been promised to allow the construction to be taken in hand. The Trustees of the Oxford University Endowment Fund had come forward with an offer to hand over £12,000, a sum sufficient to cover the cost of construction of an underground bookstore apart from its fittings.

The Curators had to exert some pressure before they could get

---

[1] Curators' papers, Reply from the Curators of the Chest, 24 Nov. 1900.

[2] Appropriated by decree 7 June 1904. The use of this Schools basement had been first proposed in 1895, but was at that time strongly deprecated by the librarian.

[3] *Statements of the Needs of the University*, pp. 120, 121.

Council to accept the Trustees' offer and approve the plans. Council in the end consented, and Mr. Rutland Saunders was appointed architect. But at the last moment there were fresh difficulties, for the new architect questioned the desirability of having wheeled cases, though these had been regarded hitherto as an essential element in the plan. 'There is a great advantage', he suggested, 'in the fixed book-case scheme.'[1] The Curators were perturbed, but not unnaturally they insisted on the original plan being carried out. They also decided to link the bookstore with the Bodleian by means of a subway starting from the bottom of the library backstairs. As the bookstore was planned to communicate at its other end with the Camera, this provided, though in a very different manner, the passage-way between the two buildings for which Acland had so long pressed.

It was not until late in 1909 that excavation of the ground in Radcliffe Square could be begun; not until 1912 that the building was completed, sixteen years after Nicholson first suggested its construction. Although he was its originator, he did not himself live to see its opening, which was carried out with some ceremony on 27 November 1912. The building was his last enterprise. He had hailed it as one that 'would afford room for some generations to come, and would be a model for economic storage to future generations'.[2]

Hopes had been pitched too high. The underground bookstore failed to win complete success or to achieve all that was expected of it. It was an experiment, for, though the design of the rolling bookcase was not original, it had never been tried out on so great a scale, nor had any library constructed for itself so large a cellarage. Viewed as an experiment, it fully justified itself. And, among all the bookstacks fitted up and shelved at the cost of several thousand pounds during the days when Nicholson was librarian, it alone remains in use at the present day.

4. OLD READING-ROOM AND CAMERA

Under Bandinel, Duke Humphrey's Library was still the jealously guarded preserve of privileged scholars. Only after the Camera was opened under Coxe did undergraduates come in any numbers to read. It fell to Nicholson to make these two reading-rooms more generally useful, and to add a third one before he died.

---

[1] Communication to the Curators, 9 Dec. 1909.
[2] Nicholson, *Crisis of Bodleian History* (1909), p. 3.

During his régime, the number of closed days was cut down;[1] and though there was no material alteration in the hours of opening, that was only because it was not yet considered safe to introduce electric lighting into Bodley. As early as 1880 a number of Oxford scientists memorialized Council in favour of lighting the Sheldonian Theatre and rooms in the neighbourhood, particularly the Camera, with electric light. T. G. Jackson, asked to report on the proposal, advised waiting until electric lighting was further developed: arc lights, he said, were objectionable, since they cast strong shadows, and Swan filament lamps were not yet strong enough to light a large reading-room.[2] But Acland continued to press for the introduction of electric light, and in 1885 an estimate, amounting to £2,660, was obtained for the cost of its installation in the Camera, Sheldonian, and Bodleian Library. The idea was then dropped for a time, probably on the score of expense; and Nicholson, who had begun by thinking of the lighting of the Bodleian as 'involving not the remotest risk whatever', ended by giving it as his opinion that its introduction, as it was then known, into Bodley 'should be permanently vetoed'.[3]

In view of the inflammable nature of the old timber in Duke Humphrey's Library, it was perfectly proper to postpone its lighting until electricians had mastered the art of insulation. The Camera, however, was a lesser risk; so it is not surprising that, when an Oxford Electric Light Company was formed in 1892, and electric arcs began to supersede gas-lamps in the streets of Oxford, the question of lighting the Camera should be raised once more. The cost of installation in the Camera was now very much less than it had been a few years before, amounting to £400. Nevertheless, though Bodleian Curators and Radcliffe Trustees were agreed on having electric light, action was postponed on the familiar ground that other needs were more urgent, and it was not till 1905 that the Camera reading-room at last was lit, at the expense of an Oxford resident, Mr. G. H. Pope of Wadham.

The electric table-lamps at readers' seats in the Camera were not the only new feature in that reading-room. A general cleaning and repainting of the interior was carried out in 1901, perhaps for the first time in the history of the building. Matting laid down on the stone floor now deadened readers' footsteps. Some old acquaintances disappeared. First the Laocoon group and then the Tivoli candelabra

---

[1] By statute of 18 Feb. 1890; *Corpus Statutorum*, addenda, p. 256.
[2] *Selected Reports* (1894), pp. 27–28, 37–38.
[3] Curators' papers, 'Librarian's report on the redistribution of the Library', 3 Mar. 1883; Memorandum on extending hours of opening, 23 Oct. 1909. Nicholson at one time formed the strange idea of lighting Duke Humphrey by rows of small lamps placed *outside* the windows.

were transferred to the University Galleries.[1] The Hope collection of engraved portraits no longer occupied the gallery of the Camera, having been transferred in 1888 to the Natural Philosophy School in the Bodleian quadrangle: its place was taken by more readers' seats, to which iron spiral staircases now gave an easier access than that hitherto provided by the old stone newel stairs.

For readers were steadily increasing in number, and more space had to be found for them. The seating of the gallery brought up the number of seats at the Camera from fifty to eighty-six; yet that was soon not enough, for twenty years later as many as a hundred readers were recorded as present at one time.[2] The increase was largely due to the greater use made of the Camera by women undergraduates. A generation earlier women readers had been hardly known. By 1900 there were said to be often more women reading in the Camera than men.[3]

The men were wearing their gowns; at least a proctorial ordinance issued in 1894 required it. And there were other readers who were neither graduate nor undergraduate. With a view to limiting their numbers, Bywater made the very sensible suggestion, as far back as 1885, that non-academical persons should be admitted only by ticket, and that tickets should require yearly renewal.[4] Well over half a century had to pass before this very modest reform was eventually adopted.

Duke Humphrey was not so overcrowded. Now that the catalogue was completed and Selden End no longer required for cataloguing-staff nor (as had at one time been suggested) for a librarian's study, that western wing could be used to provide reserved seats for a dozen privileged readers. With its two tall floor-cases removed, so that one could now look from one end of the room to the other, it perhaps merited Nicholson's description of it as 'one of the finest Charles I rooms in the kingdom'.[5] Nicholson longed to rid it of its mean furniture (to wit the old cataloguers' tables which still are there), and to throw open the two blocked-up windows in its farther wall. 'If I

---

[1] The Laocoon in 1890, the candelabra in 1894. The Laocoon was broken up in 1927. The candelabra remain to adorn the Pomfret Gallery.

[2] Curators' papers, Report of Underground Bookstore Committee, 27 Nov. 1909. In the seventies the number present at one time had seldom exceeded forty.

[3] *Oxford Magazine*, vol. xviii, p. 393.

[4] Curators' minutes, 2 May 1885. A wider proposal, for the issue of tickets to all readers who were not members of Convocation, was put forward by a Curatorial committee in 1894 but not carried; Report of Depredations Committee, 14 June 1894. Since 1942 tickets of admission have been issued to all readers who are not members of the university.

[5] *Statements of the Needs of the University*, p. 134.

don't succeed before I die', he wrote, 'in getting the University to restore and reopen them, I'll try to "walk" the Selden End until the University does.'[1] But the windows remain blocked, and the poor ghost walks unseen.

The number of readers' seats in the Old Reading-Room may be taken as forty-eight. At first there was sufficiency of room. In 1880 the daily average of readers to be found there at one time had been returned as sixteen. But in 1900 Nicholson had to admit that it was often difficult for a reader to find a place, and by 1909 forty-eight persons were recorded as reading simultaneously.[2] Statistics, so far as material is available, suggest that in the Old Reading-Room, as at the Camera, the number of readers increased in Nicholson's period of office by 150 per cent.

Reading in Bodley had its drawbacks. Heating was better managed than of old, but ventilation was as bad as ever. 'In summer,' said Andrew Clark, himself a Curator, 'you must either catch cold by sitting in a draught to keep you awake, or succumb to the soporific influences of a vitiated atmosphere and the heavy odour of mouldy leather and fermented binder's paste.'[3] And Nicholson spoke roundly of it, saying, 'A worse-ventilated room of its size than the present Bodleian reading-room one would scarcely find.' The library staff were in worse plight than the readers. They sat on benches in front of the two long side-walls of Arts End, the northern half of the floor of that room being then taken up by exhibition cases, as the southern half was by the catalogue stand. Here they worked in a constant draught, and Nicholson informed the Curators that four of his assistants had in consequence gone deaf.[4]

There was another reason, besides crowding and discomfort, for forming a new reading-room; and this was the need, which Nicholson felt from the outset, for a great increase in the number of books on open shelves. A select library for undergraduates, a reference library for researchers, a periodical room, were all objects which had a special appeal for him. In his very first year of office he selected, and

---

[1] *Oxford Magazine*, vol. xiii, p. 81.

[2] *The Bodleian Library in 1882–7*, p. 41; Curators' papers, 'Proposed warming of the Picture-Gallery', 10 May 1900; memorandum by the Underground Bookstore Committee, 27 Nov. 1909. Madan's Bodleian diary, kept in Library Records, contains a daily return of the number of readers in Bodley from 1893 to 1907.

[3] *A Bodleian Guide for Visitors* (1906), p. 50.

[4] Curators' papers, Librarian's memorandum on 'the north wing of the Picture Gallery as an additional Bodleian reading-room', 1 Feb. 1907. The general arrangement of Arts End at this time is well described by Andrew Clark, op. cit., pp. 35–45, as well as by Strickland Gibson in the *Library Association Record*, vol. li, p. 139.

ARTS END IN 1890

arranged in open cases in the Camera, a students' library of about 6,000 volumes, and in the course of the next thirty-six years the number was increased to 15,000.[1] It was a great disappointment to him, as well as to those who had benefited from the select library, when he was forced in 1894, as the result of book losses, to place it under lock and key.

Even before he came, the idea of 'a large reference library in which readers might take down books themselves' had been in the minds of reforming Curators. In 1877 they had the boldness to recommend that Arts End be turned into a reference-room.[2] Nicholson in his younger days went substantially farther. He thought the 'H', that is to say Duke Humphrey and the two ends, might be made to contain a first-rate reference library, 'and the less I felt fettered by the necessity of keeping the older books in their present places, the more complete that library of reference would be'.[3] But now there were Curators who were resolved to 'fetter' him; the extent of whose opposition is revealed by a recommendation that no rearrangement of reference-shelves be made without previous Curatorial sanction.[4] Thus hampered, Nicholson could not go so far as he might have wished; but he did introduce reference-books into dwarf floor-cases at Selden End; he placed all palaeographical works on its western wall; and in Duke Humphrey he added to Sir Thomas Bodley's presses new end-cases for the reception of standard works on bibliography. Useful as these last are as reference-books, it is much to be hoped that the cases in which they are placed may one day be removed, since they spoil the proportions of a noble room by reducing the width of its central gangway.

5. UPPER READING-ROOM

There was still a need for easy access to the learned periodicals which were coming to be of growing importance for scholarship. Ever since Coxe's time current numbers of periodicals had been put out in window-embrasures of the Camera.[5] But that was not enough. Only a new reading-room could give the necessary shelving. At the

---

[1] *The Bodleian Library in 1882–7*, p. 39; *Bodleian Quarterly Record*, vol. ii, p. 169.

[2] 'To the select reading-room should be annexed a large library of reference, in which readers might take down books themselves. For this there is abundant space in the room above the Proscholium.' Report of Committee of Curators on the general arrangement of the rooms of the Library.

[3] Curators' papers, 'Librarian's report on the redistribution of the Library', 25 Oct. 1884.

[4] Curators' papers, Report of 'Committee appointed to consider the accommodation for readers in the Selden End', 15 Nov. 1889.

[5] Under a Curators' order of 2 Dec. 1876.

beginning of his career as Bodley's librarian, Nicholson thought of the Divinity School as a periodical reading-room. But his mind was even then turning towards the use of the Picture Gallery. 'I have come to think', he wrote in 1884, 'that at no distant date the Picture Gallery must almost inevitably become a general reading-room.'[1] Later, in 1892, he elaborated his views. He proposed to re-open all blocked windows, and between the windows to place projecting bookcases, each with its gallery, thus dividing the room into alcoves. 'The room would then be perhaps the lightest and largest reading-room in the world, and would accommodate 70,000 volumes more than it now holds, thus affording space for the fitting up of the finest reference-library in the world.' It would replace Duke Humphrey as the general reading-room of the Bodleian, and leave Duke Humphrey's Library to be used for manuscripts and rare printed books. But it would not be necessary to take the whole in hand at once. Conversion might begin at the north-west end, and advance only as increase in readers made it necessary.[2]

The Curators at that time declined either to agree or to disagree with their Librarian's proposals, resolving only not to carry them out for the present; but in ten years' time, when the novelty had worn off, they agreed to include the provision of a new reading-room in their statement of Bodleian needs.[3] And at length, early in 1907, after receiving estimates of the cost of fitting up the north wing of the Picture Gallery and of supplying it with the necessary heating, Brassey came forward with an offer of the £2,000 required to cover the cost. His offer was promptly accepted, and in October of the same year the northern portion of the Picture Gallery, as far as the Tower room, was opened as an upper reading-room.

Nicholson was enthusiastic over the accomplishment of a measure which he had advocated for over twenty years. 'I doubt', he wrote, 'if so great a gain for so small a sum has ever been proposed before in our history, or will ever be proposed again.'[4] Brassey's gift did not cover the cost of fittings, but this was met out of a donation of £1,000 received from Lord Rosebery. The fittings were not on the lines that Nicholson had originally suggested, for the Curators decided to adopt what is known as the open-desk system. Instead of tables and seats placed in alcoves, readers' tables were set out in the centre of

[1] Report of 25 Oct. 1884.
[2] Curatorial papers, 'Librarian's replies to questions put by a Committee of Curators', 12 July 1892.
[3] *Statements of the Needs of the University*, 1902, pp. 123, 132.
[4] Curatorial papers, Memorandum on 'The north wing of the Picture-Gallery as an additional Bodleian reading-room.'

the room, and shelving was restricted to wall-spaces between the windows. Nicholson was now able to form the collection of learned periodicals which he had so long wanted, and an excellent selection of these and of local archaeological journals was placed on the walls. Heating was introduced at the same time into the gallery at the cost of £945.

6. DEATH OF NICHOLSON

With the lighting of the Camera (1905), the commencement of catalogue revision (1907), the heating of the Picture Gallery and opening of the Upper Reading-Room (1907), and finally the construction of the underground bookstore and the subway leading to it (1912), nearly all the library's requirements enumerated in the 1902 *Statements of University Needs* had been faced. Most were satisfied, but not all. The grant of £250 a year which Magdalen had made in 1905 for staff increase went very little way to providing for that substantial increase in the permanent staff for which the Curators had asked. Despite an annual grant of the like amount made from 1909 out of the University Endowment Fund, the library's regular income was still much below its needs. And there was the great project of printing the catalogue which would have to wait until revision was well forward.

Here were tasks that might well have exhausted a younger man, and Nicholson had turned sixty. He had worked furiously without intermission ever since he was appointed as librarian in 1882. His insistence on doing everything himself allowed him no respite. He was totally incapable of husbanding strength. Consequently in 1902 he had a serious break-down in health from which he never fully recovered. Intensely concerned about his ailments, he sought every remedy save that respite which might have cured them. In 1907 the Vice-Chancellor and Sir William Osler, Regius Professor of Medicine, reported to the Curators that the Librarian's health was far from satisfactory, and the Curators pressed on him the need of devolving more of his work upon others and of taking a long holiday. Already there were signs that he was failing both physically and mentally.

His symptoms grew worse. His neurasthenia intensified. Throughout 1911 he was going steadily down hill and the situation in the library was becoming critical. Library administration was brought to a halt. The librarian who had insisted on supervising everything now supervised nothing.

So in June of that year the Curators began to talk openly of his retirement. Should that become necessary, they told him, before he had completed his thirty years of office which would take place in the following February, they would be prepared to recommend that he should receive his full pension.[1] They met with no response. He would not leave his post. In November a committee set up to inquire into the administration of the library reported 'that in their opinion the Curators would be found wanting in their duty to the University if they did not take such steps as would bring about the resignation of the Librarian'. He was offered a year's leave of absence without loss of pay. He declined to accept it. The offer was repeated, this time couched in the form of an ultimatum. At length he yielded. He gave up the struggle and with it his hold on life. The decree sanctioning his release from duty was passed by Convocation on Tuesday, 13 February 1912. On the following Sunday Nicholson was dead.

Let us attempt to appraise the work of that difficult genius and assess his achievement. The classification scheme which he inherited from Coxe was promptly elaborated by him into something far better; complex in parts and yet generally workable. Of the catalogue projects which he found in Bodley, the subject-catalogue was, fortunately for him but despite his efforts, soon abandoned. He saw the need of revising the author-catalogue and of reducing it one day to printed form, but funds came too late in his career to allow him to do more than make a start upon revision, and by then the reins were slipping from his guiding hand. When he became librarian, the Old Schools that formed the ground-floor of the quadrangle were at length ready to be taken over by the library which had so long coveted them. So he was able to expand. At the same time his omnivorous appetite for every form of publication swelled the proportions of the old problem of storage which he had continually to face. Under his rule the Bodleian was driven underground, and a succession of basements (Sheldonian, Ashmolean, and Examination Schools) were taken over by him and filled to their capacity. By these shifts, and through the adoption of the rolling bookcase, he was able to stave off complete congestion until the new underground bookstore, for which he had long fought, was at length completed. But by that time he was dead.

Fettered by his Curators and clogged by want of funds, he could not always do what he wished. Perhaps that was as well. He was no financier, and was himself in part to blame for the continued and increasing poverty which beset the library despite its growing income.

[1] As the statute then stood, the librarian, on resignation or retirement, was entitled to a yearly pension of £250 if he had completed twenty years' service, and of £500 after thirty years' service.

Yet the marvel is how much he achieved, and that single-handed, for he insisted on doing everything himself. Unacademic and too full of cranks to be a great scholar himself, he nevertheless understood the needs of scholars and saw clearly what the aims of a university library should be. Hence his programme of reform included facilities for palaeographical instruction, reproduction and publication of texts, the provision of full-scale catalogues, the lengthening of the library's hours of opening, the formation of reference shelves, and arrange-ments whereby select books were rendered easily accessible. The Upper Reading-Room stands as his memorial.

He was not the man to attract benefactors and had little money with which to buy books; but he had an eye for the things that were worth acquiring. His purchase of Queen Margaret's Gospel-book for a trifling sum, the recovery of the library's First Folio of Shakespeare, the acquisition of extensive collections of Hebrew fragments from the Cairo Geniza and of Coptic fragments from Deir-Balyzeh, the formation of a collection of Greek papyri that included the famous *Logia*, the beginning of a collection of cuneiform tablets, all stand in varying degrees to his credit and have added to the reputation of the library that formed the passion of his life.

PART IV
Three Librarians 1912–45
Chapter XIV
Administration

1. CURATORS AND LIBRARY OFFICERS

In the foregoing chapters a survey has been taken of two generations in Bodleian history. The first was that during which Coxe was the leading figure; loyal lieutenant to the ageing Bandinel and then his popular successor. The second was the Nicholsonian era of storm and reform. And now there remains to tell of a third period, approximately equal in length to either of the others. This witnessed a new development in library administration, wherein the Bodleian took control of certain external institutions and ran them as dependent libraries; and it led on to the adoption, after a struggle, of an ambitious programme of library extension and to the carrying out of that programme in its main features in a plan of campaign that was eventually halted for a time by war.

For the period about to be described is that covered by two world wars and the years that lay between. It extends over three librarianships, those of Falconer Madan (1912–19), Arthur Ernest Cowley (1919–31), and Herbert Henry Edmund Craster (1931–45), the third of these being the present writer.

At the time of their respective elections each one of them was senior sub-librarian. Madan was sixty-two when he became librarian; Cowley succeeded when he was fifty-seven; Craster was appointed at the age of fifty-two. When the First World War began, Madan had been in office for only two years, and it was natural that he should be granted five years' extension. He only availed himself of four, retiring from office on his first birthday after the Armistice. There were less convincing reasons for extending Cowley, and the prolongation of his tenure coincided with a period of debate and controversy that was little to his taste. Ill health eventually forced him to resign, a year in advance of the time appointed and ten weeks before his death. The present writer reached the normal age for retirement at the conclusion of the Second World War. A change could then be made without causing difficulty, and he informed the Curators that he desired to be released from office.

FALCONER MADAN
LIBRARIAN 1912–19
from a portrait by Percy Bigland

To record events in which one has oneself played an active part might be thought an easy matter. It is not so if one aims at fair historical presentation. The objective standpoint is hard to come by. And, if one cannot pass a final judgement on one's own doings, neither is it easy to pronounce unbiased sentence on those under whom one has served.[1] It will therefore be best to select and summarize, giving only such record as is needed to show how the Bodleian Library that Nicholson knew has developed into the institution that we have today. And, since memories are short, we shall end by explaining the objects which those who carried out library extension had in view, and the steps which were taken to achieve them.

In broad outline the constitution of the library has remained unchanged. It is true that the Latin statute of 1856, under which the library was administered down to the time of Nicholson's death, was superseded in 1913 by an English statute,[2] but this was an adaptation of its Latin model and in large part translated from it. And though it was in turn replaced by a new Bodleian statute in 1938,[3] wherein the same matter was more freely handled, there was no radical change apparent in either—at least on the surface.

The Curators continued to be entrusted with the general control of the affairs of the library. Only their number has been increased. The 1913 statute raised the number of members elected by Congregation from five to seven. And in 1936[4] the Curators, of their own initiative, promoted legislation which gave effect to the proposal made by the Hebdomadal Council in 1889. The five Regius Professors, whom Sir Thomas Bodley had himself designated as Curators, thereby ceased to be *ex officio* members of the Board, and were replaced—much as Council had proposed—by professorial representatives, two professors being thenceforward elected from each of three groups of related faculties. The combined effect of these two changes, and of a further addition made by the 1938 statute, was to raise the number of Curators from thirteen to eighteen. When they were but thirteen, Chandler thought them already too numerous, and proposed that the Board be limited to eight. A large body is not necessarily more powerful than a small one.

A change would probably have come about any way, the change that we have already spoken of as one from board government to

---

[1] The writer has given some appreciation of Madan as a librarian in the *Oxford Magazine*, vol. liii, p. 668. The fullest account of Cowley is that contributed by his friend, T. W. Allen, to the *Proceedings of the British Academy*, vol. xix, pp. 351-9.

[2] 20 May 1913; *Corpus Statutorum*, addenda, pp. 1220-5.

[3] 17 May 1938; op. cit., pp. 1604-8.

[4] 26 May 1936; op. cit., p. 1563.

committee government. During the period of library extension, described in the final chapters of this work, all business relating to new buildings was worked out by a building committee, which soon found it necessary to delegate the preparation of plans to a small planning sub-committee. With this important exception, the practice of appointing *ad hoc* committees gradually fell out of use, and the transaction of the ordinary day-to-day affairs of the library has come more and more into the hands of the Standing Committee over which for eighteen years (1919–37) Dr. Poynton, Bursar and subsequently Master of University College, actively presided.

At its creation in 1892, Nicholson had prophesied that the control of the Bodleian would be transferred from the Curatorial Board to its Standing Committee. Starting as a finance committee, this body has tended more and more to take on the functions of a general purposes committee and to play the part of an inner cabinet of the Curators. Control of finance came to involve control of establishment and pay. And, apart from that, it was found convenient to refer certain non-financial matters that required consideration in detail or prompt settlement, such as disposal of duplicates, applications for loans, and imposition of penalties for breaches of statute, to a body smaller and meeting more frequently than that which assembled round the table at the stated meetings of the Curators.

Though Nicholson was allowed to attend the weekly meetings of the Standing Committee, he was kept off other committees of the Curators. Under his successors a change has taken place. It has come to be recognized that the librarian should attend all committees. Not only so, but he is required to frame their agenda and to draft their reports; and this, coupled with the inevitable tendency to work out measures in committee rather than at Board meetings, has given him far greater opportunities for initiating and directing library policy than he ever possessed before.

A change of seat typifies the change in the librarian's status. No longer does he administer the library from his chair in Arts End, presiding in state over the readers of Duke Humphrey's Reading-Room. Unseen yet omnipresent, he conducts business in the old Curators' Room that opens off the Upper Reading-Room. In 1882 Nicholson had had the room fitted up with bookshelves and had an idea at that time of filling it with incunabula and books on the history of printing.[1] Later he changed his views and suggested in 1907 that it should be brought into use as a private study for the librarian. For Coxe's plan for screening off a portion of Selden End for that purpose

[1] Librarian's report to Curators, 21 Oct. 1882.

had never been carried out; the librarian's upper study at the head of the backstairs was demolished when the Upper Reading-Room was made in 1907; and the only separate apartment which Nicholson had left for his own use was the little closet on the right of the entry to Duke Humphrey. Nor did his successor, Madan, ever have more. Only in 1919, under Cowley, was Nicholson's project realized, and the upstairs room made into a librarian's study.

The assimilation of the librarian's post to that of a director has been assisted by a process of departmentalization. The idea of departments had presented itself as far back as 1857 to the fertile mind of Jowett, who persuaded the Curators that they should resolve to take under their separate charge special departments of the library. And in 1876 a report from the Bodleian committee over which Jowett presided instanced, as suitable departments for Curatorial supervision, the catalogue of printed books, the catalogue of manuscripts, copyright accessions, library desiderata, and the reading-room. But although upon that occasion the Curators reaffirmed their earlier decision, they still took no step towards implementing it.[1] Nor indeed were the Curators as a governing body the proper persons to take individual charge of separate departments. Efficiency could best be attained through assigning departmental duties to senior members of the staff directly responsible to the librarian.

The delegation of duties that this would have entailed was not a course that appealed to the all-embracing activities of Nicholson. Nor yet was it congenial to Madan, who, although in opposition to Nicholson in his lifetime, carried on his policy in this as in other matters after succeeding him in the office of librarian. A close personal attention to every detail of library administration was common to them both. Only in 1927, seventy years after Jowett first moved his resolution, the Curators, having extended Cowley in his office for a further term of five years, conferred upon the present writer the new post of Keeper of Western Manuscripts for so long as he should hold the post of sub-librarian. So the department of Western Manuscripts, which the new Keeper proceeded to form, came into being.

When he became librarian in 1931, there was no difficulty in making that department permanent in the person of another sub-librarian, or in carrying the principle farther and immediately creating an Oriental department. The formation of their necessary complement, a department of Printed Books, had to wait a few years longer. Nevertheless the Curators agreed upon it in principle in 1938,

[1] Curators' minutes, 28 Nov. 1857; Report of Committee on expenses and management, Mar. 1876.

and, after the completion of the New Bodleian had made it possible
to concentrate in a single room the cataloguing staff and the staff that
dealt with library accessions, they appointed their senior sub-librarian,
Strickland Gibson, to be its first Keeper (1 August 1942). Thus, instead of having two sub-librarians, whose activities were for the most
part confined to the production of catalogues, the librarian has come
to have the support of three sub-librarians, each of whom is in charge,
as Keeper, of a particular department.

The number of library officers was further increased through the
creation of a secretariate and the appointment of an official charged
with the supervision of fabric and the control, under the librarian's
supervision, of personnel and service conditions. Nicholson, Madan,
and Cowley each in turn had their private secretary; but secretarial
arrangements were as yet rudimentary. Not until 1919 did the library
possess a typewriter; another twelve years passed before it became the
practice to take copies of outgoing letters; and it was only with the
appointment of R. H. Hill (now Librarian of the National Central
Library) as secretary of the Bodleian in 1933,[1] that a secretariate may
be said to have come into existence. During the years that followed,
the secretary was fully occupied with the multifarious details of
library extension and had no time for non-secretarial duties. Consequently in 1938[2] the surveillance of fabric and of service conditions
was entrusted for a time to a new officer, H. R. Creswick (since
successively Bodley's Librarian and Librarian of the University of
Cambridge), with the title of Deputy Librarian.

To sum up, the Curatorial Board has been enlarged and made more
representative; the powers of their Standing Committee have increased; the authority of the librarian is enlarged, and in its exercise
he has the assistance of four other library officers, namely three sub-
librarians and a secretary, each in charge of a department.

2. DEPENDENT LIBRARIES

The departments or spheres of activity within the library, of which
we have been speaking, must not be confused with what were at first
called departmental, and now are more properly styled dependent
libraries. In the course of this history we have seen how the Bodleian
absorbed other university libraries into its system. Such were the
Ashmolean, the Savilian, and the Music School libraries, whose books
have become so many collections on Bodleian shelves. But to take
over the administration of a living library and fit it into a larger or-
ganism was a different matter. Robarts, with his 'University Library

[1] By decree, 30 May 1933.   [2] Decree, 7 June 1938.

system', had envisaged the possibility of all libraries within the university being brought under a single management;[1] but his address to the 1877 Conference of Librarians had been as a voice crying in the wilderness—remote, unechoed, and forgotten. The idea took new shape when, at another meeting of librarians, Cowley read to the Library Association, in October 1921, a paper on the recent history of the Bodleian Library.

I see the Bodleian of the future [he said] as a great central library, with a number of special libraries as departments of it, housed in buildings adjacent to it but not necessarily all in the same building. Each special library should be under the charge of an expert in the subject, and the whole should be controlled by the central librarian. . . . For the present you would begin with a large library of physical science, another of modern languages and literature, another of archaeology; then you would form a law library, a library of modern history, another of geography including maps, an Indian library, a theological library, and you would add to these as your needs required and funds permitted.[2]

The Curators gave the policy their approval.[3] It may be that Cowley did not always clearly distinguish in his mind between subordinate libraries which were organisms complete in themselves, and special reading-rooms which had no independent existence. And in his later years he may have been led to develop his project further than was warranted, through a desire to relieve pressure on Bodleian book-space by drafting sections of the library to other quarters. (That was an idea abhorrent to Nicholson. 'Don't let them break up the Bodleian' was his last message as he lay dying.) But none the less Cowley's conception has been realized by a development in university library practice which may not yet have run its full course.

An opportunity for taking action came very soon. The 'large library of physical science 'of which Cowley spoke was of course the Radcliffe Library which was at that time still controlled by the Radcliffe Trustees. For long past the wastefulness of two neighbouring libraries duplicating expensive works on natural science had been apparent to many. Mr. Strickland, giving evidence before the University Commissioners in 1852, had advocated co-operation between the two libraries, saying boldly, 'I do not see why they should not be regarded as two departments of one establishment. All the Bodleian books on physical science might then be transferred to the Radcliffe.'[4] After the Radcliffe Trustees had quitted the Camera in 1860 and

[1] See above, p. 50.
[2] *Library Association Record*, vol. xxiii (Oct. 1921), p. 324.
[3] Curators' minutes, 17 June 1922.
[4] *Oxford University Commission Report*, 1852, Evidence, p. 101.

transferred their scientific books to the University Museum in the Parks, statutory power was given to the Bodleian Curators to deposit in it scientific books and periodicals from Bodley.[1] But little use was made of that authorization. Only in 1901, as a return for the permission granted by the Radcliffe Trustees to make a bookstore under their freehold property in the Radcliffe Square, the Bodleian statute was once more amended to allow the Curators to deposit scientific books in the Radcliffe Library and to make loans to it for the use of professors and students.[2]

By that time the Radcliffe Library had outgrown its earlier quarters in the University Museum and entered into possession of a newly erected wing. Dr. Acland had become Sir Henry Acland and had at length resigned after holding office as Radcliffe Librarian for just under half a century. He had been succeeded in 1900 by Dr. Hatchett Jackson, and, when Dr. Jackson died in 1924, Cowley immediately raised with his Curators the question of taking over the administration of the library. Negotiations were opened with the Radcliffe Trustees and an arrangement was eventually come to with them whereby, under a scheme approved by an order made in Chancery on 9 March 1927, they handed over to the university the furniture and equipment of the Radcliffe Library and all manuscripts and printed books comprised in it. So the Radcliffe Science Library came under Bodleian management. The final stage was reached in 1934 when the completion of a building extension to that library made it possible to transfer to it all the modern scientific books, about 170,000 in number, previously kept in the Camera and in the underground bookstore.

Two months before the Radcliffe Science Library was taken over, a second library came under the control of the Bodleian Curators. This was the library of the Indian Institute. The Institute had been founded in 1880 to form a centre for Indian studies in Oxford. Housed in a flamboyant building erected in 1883–96 at the east end of Broad Street, it received two collections of books relating to India that had been given to the university by private donors (Malan and Monier-Williams), and round that nucleus there had been formed a working library of books on Indian history, law, languages, and literature. Inevitably the purchase of English publications, which were obtained free of charge by the Bodleian, was felt to be uneconomic. With that in mind, the Chancellor, Lord Curzon, came down to preside in person at a meeting of the Curators of the Institute in April

[1] 28 Nov. 1861; *Corpus Statutorum*, addenda, p. 652.
[2] 19 Mar. 1901; op. cit., p. 1064.

1909 and persuaded them to approach the Bodleian authorities with the proposal that such Indian literature in Bodley as might be found suitable should be deposited in the Institute, and that the rights which Bodley enjoyed under the Copyright Act should be utilized for the future augmentation of the Indian Institute Library. As a *quid pro quo*, the Curators of the Institute offered to merge their manuscripts in the far greater Oriental collections of the University Library. Their proposal broke on Nicholson's opposition. But the arguments for amalgamation were too strong to be resisted for ever. So it came about that the University Statutory Commissioners, appointed under the Universities of Oxford and Cambridge Act of 1923, framed a statute whereby the Malan and Monier-Williams collections were placed under the charge of the Bodleian Curators, who thereafter took over the administration and control of the whole Indian Institute Library.[1]

A third dependent library differed from the other two in that it was a new creation. Some years after Cecil Rhodes's will had astonished the world and the university that was its beneficiary, the trustees charged with its execution determined to set up in Oxford a monumental building that should be a memorial to him, and should serve as a centre for the advanced study of the political, social, and economic development of the British Empire and of the United States. So plans were made by them for a Rhodes House in South Parks Road. In October 1925 Cowley reported to his Curators that he had been consulted as to the possibility of forming, in the projected building, a specialist library. Its field was less precise than that of the other two dependent libraries. It was originally defined as the history and literature of the English-speaking British Dominions and Colonies, of the United States, and of Africa. The definition has since been made more exact. But historical studies have no clearly marked frontiers, and the consequent physical separation of books dealing with similar subjects was subsequently to lead to suggestions for the incorporation of the Rhodes House Library, as a separate unit, in an enlarged Bodleian.[2] Nevertheless, a free traffic of books between Rhodes House and other parts of the Bodleian Library lessens the drawbacks of separation, and there is a compensating advantage. Rhodes House provides accommodation for the professors and teachers of the subjects represented in its library, and so is able to carry on a closer direction of study than is possible in a large

[1] Statute (*Stat. Tit.* XX. xiii. 2) approved by the King in Council, 22 Apr. 1927; decree of Congregation, 21 June 1927.
[2] *Library Provision in Oxford*, 1931, pp. 100–1.

non-specialist library. On that ground alone the Rhodes House Library, which was first opened to readers in May 1929, has justified its creation.

So between 1927 and 1929 the Curators took over three external libraries. Here the scheme halted. In his address to the Library Association, Cowley had suggested its application to a library of modern languages and literature. This was the library of the Taylor Institution of Modern Languages. The Institution, housed in the classical building (since greatly enlarged) which C. R. Cockerell erected in 1841–4 at the corner of Beaumont Street, is a centre for the Faculty of Modern Languages, and contains what is claimed to be the largest and most important separate library of modern languages in the British Isles.[1] It supplements the Bodleian at other points than European literature and linguistics, for batches of older books on foreign history and topography are equally to be found in it. Apart from this overlap, the separation of the two libraries inevitably produces some drawbacks. It is impossible to isolate form from content; literature from the thoughts it enshrines. That consideration was in some minds when plans for Bodleian extension were being discussed by a Library Commission in 1931, and it was suggested in a minority report that the Taylorian Library should be moved into a wing of a new Bodleian.[2]

Whether the policy which has made the Radcliffe Science Library and the library of the Indian Institute dependent libraries of the Bodleian is ever applied to the Taylorian or to other libraries within the university is a question for the future to settle. If it is, one may be confident that any library brought into the scheme will continue, like the existing dependent libraries, to preserve its own traditions and privileges, and will form with them a group of semi-autonomous units, each operating under the guidance of its own library committee.

3. STAFF AND SALARIES

A library staff is bound to grow with the increasing size of the library which it serves, with the number of buildings in which that library is housed, and with the extent of the facilities provided for study. Under Madan, and in Cowley's earlier years, the number of the Bodleian staff, excluding those employed upon catalogue revision, remained constant at about fifty; but from 1925 it began to increase, and it had reached sixty-two by 1927. That was the year in which the Radcliffe Science Library and the library of the Indian Institute

[1] Op. cit., p. 69.　　　　[2] Op. cit., p. 103.

were taken over. Rhodes House Library followed in 1929. Resumption of catalogue revision in 1935 entailed still further increase; so it is not surprising that by 1938 numbers had mounted to 107.[1] Since the war ended, the library staff has continued to grow, and at the time of writing (1951) it totals 147 persons.

With so large a staff it is natural that service conditions should assume greater significance and occupy to an ever growing extent the attention of the librarian and of his Curators. Up to 1913 there had been no retiring rule for the staff, and no statutory provision for pensions except in the case of library officers. The university had not as yet recognized the need for compulsory retirement, and the Bodleian set an example when by its 1913 statute it provided that the librarian and sub-librarians should retire on the completion of their sixty-fifth year, while allowing for the possibility of four years' extension.[2] Till then the rest of the staff had no pension rights and might at best hope for some *ex gratia* payment of uncertain amount if they did not die in harness. It was not too soon, or by modern standards too generous, when in 1913 the Curators determined that all assistants appointed after that date should be required to come under a contributory pension scheme calculated to produce an annuity of not more than £100 at the age of sixty-five. But herein they were ahead of the rest of the university. Only in 1924–5 Oxford's adoption of the Federated Superannuation Scheme for Universities and of an Employees Pension Scheme set the whole system of university pensions upon a proper footing and removed the need for a Pensions Fund which the Curators had set up.

At the same time, in 1925,[3] there came an improvement in the salaries of the graduate staff to compensate for an increased cost of living. The librarian's salary had been raised from £700 to £1,000 as far back as 1873, and in 1913 it was freed from income tax. It was now fixed at £1,500 and again made subject to tax. Sub-librarians had always been paid low in the past, for it was assumed that those who held the office would be able to supplement their pay by a college fellowship or by some other university post. Under the 1913 statute the maximum salary allowed to a sub-librarian was still only £500. By 1925 successive statutory amendments had brought the minimum

---

[1] A tabular statement setting out staff numbers, 1907–36, is given in the Curators' papers, 'Librarian's report', 24 Oct. 1936.

[2] Pensions were at the same time raised to maxima of £600 for the librarian and of £300 for sub-librarians. By a later statute, in 1924, the date of retirement was brought into conformity with that adopted generally for the university, namely the 31 July following the person's sixty-fifth birthday.

[3] Statute, 9 June 1925; *Corpus Statutorum*, addenda, p. 1444.

salary to £400, the maximum to £800; and at these figures it remained until a general increase in university salaries took place after the Second World War, though £600 came in practice to be accepted as a starting salary.

Below the library officers came the assistants. The term, like that of *ministri*, of which it is a translation, might be, and sometimes was, applied to the whole of the subordinate staff other than manual workers, though Nicholson himself never used it of the boys whom he recruited in such large numbers. Only when a boy had reached the age of seventeen and had matriculated or qualified for matriculation did Nicholson regard him as eligible for nomination to the post of assistant. But in 1912 when, under Madan, boys came to be termed junior assistants, and when some (called minor assistants) were kept on although they were not members of the university, it became necessary to distinguish the higher grade by the appellation of senior assistant, and this term consequently figures in place of *minister* in the 1913 statute. The class was a mixed one, since some of its members were undergraduates, others were university graduates who had perhaps taken an honours degree. This helps to account for the provisions of the 1913 statute, which fixed the annual salary of a senior assistant at not less than £60 or more than £250, exclusive of allowances for overtime or special duties. The initial stipend of a graduate was laid down at that time by library regulation as £100 to £120.

Naturally such low rates could not be maintained after the First World War. In 1921 senior assistants received an improvement in their pay which was confirmed and extended by the statute passed in 1925. Their minimum rate of pay was thereby fixed at £150; their maximum at £400, with a proviso that an assistant might be granted, after twenty-five years' service, a further increase that should not exceed £100. This was the situation in 1931 when a Library Commission, of which we shall have occasion to say much more in a later chapter (pp. 323–5), reported to the university that the proportion of senior assistants employed (then fixed by the 1913 statute at a minimum of ten) might perhaps be reduced, but that their pay was totally inadequate for the class of men required in that grade.[1] Partial effect was given two years later to the Commission's recommendation by a statutory amendment[2] increasing the minimum salary of the grade from £150 to £200, and the maximum from £500 to £600.

Higher standards, alike of technique and of scholarship, had come to be required in every library from an increasing number of its staff.

[1] *Library provision in Oxford*, par. 126.
[2] 16 May 1933; *Corpus Statutorum*, addenda, p. 1523.

In the Bodleian the trend towards specialization that produced library departments and specialist libraries was leading also to a differentiation of grades. For in the past there had been no clear separation of functions. The assistants of Nicholson's day had been required to carry out every form of library activity, from making themselves proficient in Sanskrit or Celtic languages, to counting books upon library shelves. The Library Commission had good reason for recommending that a clearer distinction should be drawn between the responsible duties to be assigned to senior assistants of scholarly attainments and the routine duties which could adequately be carried out by lower grades.

To bring library grades into line with a library's varied requirements was the object of a committee of the Curators, appointed in 1937 to consider the rates of salary and holiday allowances of the staff, and of the two careful and comprehensive reports which they produced in 1939.[1] They made a clean separation of the executive grades employed upon routine work, and the professional or administrative staff to whom the appellation of assistant should thenceforward be restricted. Their scheme abolished the old category of senior assistant, instituting in its place a new but strictly limited class of assistant librarians. This comprised graduates filling posts of special responsibility, such as those held by superintendents of dependent libraries and by superintendents of departments.

Below the assistant librarians there now come two grades of assistants (instituted in 1933) of which grade I is composed of graduates; while grade II is filled by non-graduate members of the staff whose long library experience or technical training justify their promotion.

Routine duties are now reserved for library clerks. Madan had experimented with keeping on the staff one or two young non-graduates to whom he gave the name of minor assistants. The Radcliffe Science Library, when taken over, was partially staffed by non-graduate library clerks. It had long been obvious that the Nicholsonian policy of boy recruitment had its disadvantages and was being overdone; and in 1920 Mr. Wheeler, the wise superintendent of the Camera, protested to the librarian that 'it is in the highest degree desirable that the number of boys employed should be lessened, and that the greater part of the work now done by them should be transferred to a new class consisting of persons of rather more advanced age'. With that object an experiment was made in 1932 in enlisting lay clerks from college choirs for library bookservice. Their musical duties in college chapels were far from giving

---

[1] 25 Apr. and 16 Sept. 1939; Curators' papers, 39: 17 and 35.

them full-time occupation, and from their employment in the library there has incidentally arisen the company of Bodley singers known to listeners to the third programme of the British Broadcasting Corporation. Out of these various elements—the minor assistants of Bodley, the library clerks of dependent libraries, and the book fetchers from college choirs—there has developed the category of library clerks. This includes typists as well as clerks employed on book-service, on invigilation, or upon general clerical work.

The boys, upon whom Nicholson lavished an attention and care that was sometimes well rewarded, disappeared, for a time at least, under the competition set up by heavy industry during the Second World War. Before that war had ended, a Curatorial committee was obliged to report that the recruitment of boys had virtually ceased. The situation has been saved by the employment of female labour.

The first women to enter upon the library service were those whom Nicholson recruited in 1907 for the revision of the catalogue. His nomination of one of them to an assistantship on the permanent staff was opposed by some of his Curators and was only carried on a division. And though during the First World War good use was made of their services by halting catalogue revision and temporarily employing the revisers upon general library duties, when that war ended they were no longer needed and only one remained upon the staff. But even a year before the Second World War broke out, the Curators had resolved in principle upon the employment of girls for book-service and upon minor clerical duties. These juvenile employees, usually taken on the staff upon leaving school, now rank as junior library clerks. The change has affected higher grades also. During the Second World War the temporary appointments that were made were, naturally, almost invariably of women; and, since then, a certain number of women have received permanent appointments, some as library clerks and some (who are graduates) as assistants.

In working out rates of remuneration which should give a fair wage for all these various grades of staff, as well as for the manual workers whom the library was employing in increasing numbers, the Curators' Staff Committee were handicapped by the fact that no common practice was as yet generally recognized in the university. Each university department acted for itself; and, even where scales existed and wages were not determined by individual bargaining, there was a disparity in the rates paid by different departments. There was no generally recognized standard; still less any machinery for periodic adjustment of wages. Standardization has since come about through a committee set up by the University Chest at the end of

1944; and the University and Employees Joint Committee, which has been created since the conclusion of the war, gives effect to a suggestion made to Council in 1939 by the Bodleian Staff Committee that machinery should be instituted for negotiation between university departments and their employees.

Organization, grading, and scales of pay were not the only subjects for settlement by the Staff Committee. As the result of its discussions, and with the object of giving to young persons who left the library service increased opportunities for obtaining employment, the Curators suggested in 1938 to the Hebdomadal Council the establishment of an employment information bureau for the university, and this was eventually brought into being after the war had ended. The Curators recognized their responsibility for assisting out of library funds the younger members of their staff to obtain further educational training, and for granting additional leave to senior members for purposes of study. Holidays with pay were regularized, and additional holidays were granted to persons training in the various forms of National Defence or as members of approved youth organizations. In 1938 a weekly half-holiday—unknown before—was instituted, with a consequent closing of all parts of the library at one o'clock on Saturdays. This was accompanied by an increase in the number of general holidays, and by a curtailment, amounting to a considerable reduction for some grades, in the annual allowance.

This full programme of staff reform had taken two years to prepare; and when the committee's final report was completed in September 1939, war had just broken out. Although the scheme proposed no increase in the maximum rates of pay of the higher ranks of library staff, it did aim at improving the salary scales of young graduates and of the lower grades. For that reason it could not be put into effect without the sanction of the Hebdomadal Council and of the University Chest. Three years later the necessary authorization was at length obtained, and the new wage-scales were brought into effect in January 1943. Like all other university salaries they have been materially improved since the war ended.

4. FINANCE

Augmentation of staff and improvement in pay were only rendered possible by an equivalent increase in library revenue. Bodleian poverty and consequent staff shortage had been a constant subject of complaint under Nicholson, whose genius was little suited to economic administration. The last full year of his librarianship (1911) ended with a deficit of £901. By 1913 the accumulated deficit had grown to £1,831. The Trustees of the University Endowment Fund, who had done much to relieve the necessities of Bodley in the past, could do no more than help to finance the revision of the catalogue and continue till 1916 their annual grant of £250 for general purposes. Prompted by an application from the Curators for an increased grant, the Hebdomadal Council issued in June 1914 an urgent appeal, with a covering letter from the Trustees of the Endowment Fund. The library needed, they said, an additional £2,000 of revenue, and they consequently asked for a capital sum of £50,000.

The appeal was unfortunate in its timing. Two months after it was made, the First World War broke out, stopping further subscription; and of the £50,000 asked for, only £1,400 had been raised. In 1920, after the war was over, the library was fortunate enough to receive, from a single generous benefactor, the sum it had asked for in 1914. Mr. Walter Morrison's gift of £50,000 was the largest money donation ever made to the Bodleian, not excepting that which had come to it in 1841 under the will of Dr. Robert Mason. This and other bequests made in the years 1914–21[1] had the effect of greatly increasing the library's endowment. The amount which the Bodleian received in dividends and interest in 1912 was £2,100; by 1923 that source of revenue was more than trebled and reached £6,932. In the years that followed it continued to rise, but far less rapidly. By 1945 the annual income of the Bodleian estate had increased to £7,545.

Some notable private benefactions were made to the library during the decade 1931–41, though, since in the majority of instances the bequests were made subject to life interests, no immediate benefit was derived from them. Dying in 1931, just after he had ceased to be librarian, Sir Arthur Cowley bequeathed the reversion of his estate to the library over which he had presided. In 1933 the will of that delightful story-teller, Kenneth Grahame, disclosed the fact that he had left to Bodley, subject to life interests, the residue of his estate, including, in addition to investments, the proceeds of copyright and royalties on his writings: the will became operative on his widow's death in 1947, and the income of the fund which thereby passed to Bodley is applied primarily to financing official library publications and to the reproduction of printed books and manuscripts. In 1938 Sir Cyril Cobb, a former member of Merton College, bequeathed a fourth part of his residuary estate, though the first instalment of income was not received until seven years later. Finally, an important

---

[1] Of these the chief were £5,000 by the bequest of Mr. Patrick Murphy received in 1914; £5,000 given by Mr. C. M. Powell, honorary fellow of Corpus Christi College, in 1916; Earl Brassey's bequest of £5,000 in 1920.

benefaction came from across the Atlantic. Samuel Henshaw, director emeritus of the Museum of Comparative Zoology at Harvard, died in July 1941 bequeathing to the Bodleian all his books and the residue of his estate. His books comprised a collection of works by, or relating to, Gilbert White of Selborne; and this the Curators allowed Harvard University to buy on receiving evidence that the testator's final intentions favoured his collection being retained at Harvard. Some years elapsed before the estate was finally settled; but eventually, in 1946, a sum of approximately £20,000 was received by the library, and the major part of it was added to the reserve fund for purchase of rare books and manuscripts.

Besides the revenue which it derives from its own endowment, the library has at its disposal funds assigned to it by the university and by certain colleges. These are in part fixed by statute; in part they are the subject of annual allocations of variable amount. Some colleges have continued to make their yearly contributions, and the failure of others to do so has been more than made up by the action of All Souls, which was not only able from 1906 to fulfil its statutory obligation to pay £1,000 annually, but has been in a position since 1925 to make an additional voluntary payment of a like sum. The statutory payment which the university makes to the library has remained at the £4,250 at which it was fixed in 1898. The university also makes over every year a sum of money voted by decree of Convocation. To the £800 a year which the library has received under decree ever since 1883 there has come to be added a far larger sum for which the library is indebted to State aid administered by the University Grants Committee.

The financial difficulties in which a fall in the value of money placed the university after the First World War were the subject of inquiry by a new Royal Commission set up in 1920. The Commission had in Mr. Asquith a president who was very well disposed to the Bodleian, and its report, made on 1 March 1922, was satisfactory in the extreme. The Commission recommended that the State should make an annual grant to the university of £90,000 for general purposes, and of £10,000 for the Bodleian Library.[1] At first the library had to be content with an emergency grant of £2,000 paid in 1920 and in each of the three following years, and it had long to wait before receiving the full amount designed for it by the Commissioners. The library's share in the Government grant was the subject every year of a decree of Convocation, and was merged, from 1931, with the university's own contribution of £800. Therefore, though

[1] *Royal Commission on Oxford and Cambridge Universities, 1922, p. 250 (par. 159).*

the sum allotted by decree stood at £10,300, the amount which the Bodleian received from public funds was still only £9,500.[1] In 1938 the yearly allocation was increased from £10,300 to £11,000, only to be cut down again to £10,000 and then to £9,000 in the war years that followed.

We shall have occasion in a later chapter (p. 327) to tell of a new university appeal for endowment that was made in 1937 and of the consequent formation of a Higher Studies Fund. An annual sum of £7,000 was appropriated out of that fund to meet the recurrent expenditure entailed by Bodleian Library extension. The first full yearly payment of that amount was made in 1944, but the fund had been drawn upon to a limited extent for some years before.

In addition to what the Bodleian obtains from these and from certain subsidiary sources, there must be taken into account the endowment of the dependent libraries. The Rhodes Trustees meet the whole expenses of the Rhodes House Library. These, during the first ten years of that library's existence (1929–39), averaged £2,920 a year. The Curators of the Indian Institute contribute £275 yearly to the upkeep of their library. The Radcliffe Science Library has for its support £1,500 per annum paid over by the Radcliffe Trustees; a university grant amounting since 1935 to £1,725; an appropriation of £250 voted annually by Brasenose College out of the Hulme Surplus Fund; and £100 interest on Mr. Sanders's benefaction. It also has a small capital endowment derived from successive sales of duplicates. Taking all these sources into account, Bodleian revenue mounted from £11,004 in 1912 to £35,940 in 1939.

So much for library revenue. During Madan's tenure of office a careful economy wiped out the library deficit, allowed funds to be put away to reserve, and left a small credit balance every year. After the First World War the situation changed. Growth of staff, improved salaries, and higher prices combined to increase the cost of running the library to an extent for which the Morrison benefaction and the Government grant failed to compensate. And there were other reasons for the difficulties in which the library proceeded to find itself. Capital expenditure, such as electrical installation, was no longer met, as it had been under Nicholson, by special grants from the Common University Fund or from the Chest; instead of that, and for lack of adequate reserves, it burdened the general account. Over

[1] By a separate decree a further sum out of the Government grant, fixed at first at £500 and subsequently increased, was voted annually for the Radcliffe Science Library; but it was argued with some justification, that when the Commissioners recommended a grant of £10,000, that library had not been taken over, and so was not as yet a charge on the Bodleian.

a period of years the library had to find £500 to £1,000 annually to furnish the underground bookstore with steel stacks. And the new dependent libraries were themselves a liability, for, although the Rhodes Trustees met the whole costs of the Rhodes House Library, there was an annual deficit to be made up on the account of the Radcliffe Science Library where outgoings regularly exceeded the funds appropriated for its upkeep. In 1930, the library, after raiding the whole of its reserve fund, ended the financial year with a deficit of £5,266 upon its general account, and only reached solvency by appropriating £3,000 of a benefaction made anonymously by Mr. Sanders, and by a grant of £2,000 from the Common University Fund. The Curators had reason for informing Council that during the next three or four years the library would require an additional income of £4,000 a year.

That help was not forthcoming, and it was left to the Curators and to a new librarian to devise economies. These were effected through close supervision of every form of outlay; a tightening up of the powers of the Standing Committee which gave them for the first time a real control over staff expenditure; the institution of quarterly financial returns presented by that committee to the Curators; the adoption of such obvious precautions as that no extraordinary payments should be sanctioned by the Curators until they had been referred to the Standing Committee; and the making of cuts in expenditure, some temporary and others permanent, particularly upon binding and in establishment charges. The result showed itself at once. Although revenue remained practically stationary, and every year an additional £200 had to be found to meet increments of salary accruing to a young staff,[1] the library was able, from 1932, to show an annual credit balance.

By 1935 the financial situation had become sufficiently stable to re-establish a general reserve fund out of which the Curators might meet extraordinary items of expenditure. Though it took some trouble to convince the University Chest, the need for reserve funds, to which the Library Commissioners had directed attention four years earlier,[2] was as great as ever. And during the Second World War, when purchase of foreign publications became almost impossible, a way was found, despite a total cut of £8,000 in the university's annual

---

[1] At the time that war broke out, salaries and superannuation contributions absorbed 64 per cent. of the library's total revenue, a proportion slightly in excess of that which had maintained under Nicholson. The amount spent yearly on staff salaries, excluding staff of dependent libraries, had practically doubled between the wars (£16,682 in 1939 as against £8,605 in 1920).

[2] *Library Provision in Oxford*, p. 27, par. 31.

grants to the library, to accumulate £22,000 as a fund to meet the purchase and binding of foreign books and periodicals after the war.

In Bodley as in other institutions financial business has grown greatly in complexity since 1912, when Bodley's Librarian himself made up and distributed the weekly pay-packets of his staff. Accountancy came to occupy at first the spare hours and then the full time of a library assistant. In 1940 a qualified chartered accountant was appointed to carry on the work; for, as in its secretariate, so with its finances, Bodley has developed a business side that would have astonished eighteenth- or even nineteenth-century librarians.

Chapter XV

Accessions and Catalogues

1. COPYRIGHT AND PURCHASE

THE annual growth of the Bodleian Library was estimated in 1915 at 20,000 and in 1930 at 22,000 standard-sized volumes. It derives in the main from the privilege that the library enjoys under the Copyright Act, for about two-thirds of the year's accessions may be reckoned as coming from that source. The number fluctuates, supply varying with the conditions of the publishing trade. During the First World War publishing fell off, and the library's copyright intake showed in consequence a sharp decline, namely from 52,000 items in 1914 to 35,000 in 1918; but, three years after the Armistice, figures rose to a higher level than they had reached before the war.[1]

It had long been questioned whether the Bodleian was justified in availing itself of the copyright privilege as fully as it did. The Nicholsonian policy of demanding everything, however seemingly worthless, met with some sharp criticism.[2] In other quarters the fear was expressed that the library was increasing more rapidly than the university's finances could afford, and it was argued that its rate of growth must be checked. Prompted thereto by Council, the Curators in 1928 set up a committee to consider whether some limitation of copyright accessions was not possible. They reported in favour of reducing the intake of periodicals, and by the beginning of 1930 a list (since greatly extended) of 470 periodicals of trivial or minor importance had been jointly agreed upon by the Oxford and Cambridge university libraries as suitable for rejection, and orders given to their copyright agent that he should cease to make application to publishers for periodicals upon the agreed list. About the same time, in December 1928, Bodley's librarian was authorized to refrain from applying for copies of such subordinate publications as railway companies' time-tables, almanacs, calendars and diaries, fiction magazines, and similar ephemera. The result of these two measures showed itself in a marked reduction in the annual number of copyright items received from 1931 onwards. From 1932 to 1938 this remained fairly constant at 58,000. Thereafter a new world war once again produced a decrease in publishing output.

[1] Statistics of yearly intake from 1888 to 1928 are given in *Library Provision in Oxford*, p. 151. A Curators' paper (40: 12) carries the figures on to 1938.
[2] Exemplified by correspondence in the *Oxford Magazine*, Feb.–Mar. 1915, vol. xxxiii, pp. 218, 238–40, 251.

After copyright publications, the largest factor in library growth is the purchase of foreign books and periodicals. Special attention was drawn to the need for increased spending in the appeal for funds which the Curators made in 1914. 'The greater specialization of studies', they said, 'and the increase in the variety of the subjects of study pursued in the university, make it continually more important that the library should be able, by increased purchases, to make fuller provision of books for use in study and research.'

Instead of increasing, the amount spent on purchases actually fell; perforce during the First World War, when importation of books from abroad was virtually brought to a standstill; but there was small improvement after the war was over. After payment of subscriptions for periodicals and for serial publications, little more than £200 a year was left over for buying other foreign books. In 1928 the Curators informed Council that a further increase of £2,000 was desirable in the yearly purchase of foreign books and periodicals. They had partly in mind the deficiencies arising from insufficient buying in the past. Arrears were to a considerable extent made good by the help of a non-recurrent Treasury grant of £4,500 received in 1930; and, in a communication made to Council in November of that year, the Curators were able to report that the sum spent annually on foreign books and periodicals had reached £2,400 and expressed the opinion that it should be maintained approximately at that figure.

The machinery for book-selection was still defective, despite various efforts that were made to improve it. In 1915 Mr. A. J. Jenkinson, a Fellow of Brasenose, had made the suggestion that the Boards of Faculties should be invited to appoint small advisory committees charged to send in lists of important foreign works periodically to the librarian.[1] An approach on these lines was at length made to the General Board of Faculties at the end of 1931; and by the summer of 1933 the librarian was able to report that advisory committees had been appointed by each of the Faculties and were meeting regularly every term. The system of consultation thus inaugurated has continued to work smoothly and satisfactorily. Lists of recent foreign publications are drawn up by the library staff and circulated to each committee in order that its members may advise as to purchase of books in the subjects on which they are expert. Book-selection committees make for efficient buying and have greatly strengthened the library's stock of modern books without any great increase of outlay.

[1] *Oxford Magazine*, vol. xxxiii, p. 302.

Dependent libraries have their own methods of purchase. The Rhodes Trustees buy, through agents, the books published in the United States and in the Dominions that are required for Rhodes House. At the Radcliffe Science Library an advisory committee selects the scientific works that are needed for that library. These are preponderatingly periodicals, for periodical literature bulks far larger in scientific than in humanistic studies. In the last year before the Second World War, when purchases of all kinds made for the Bodleian and its dependent libraries, including sums spent upon second-hand books and manuscripts, amounted to £5,551, Radcliffe Science Library expenditure on foreign scientific periodicals (though considerably below what it had been six or seven years before) accounted for £1,124. The amount spent by the Bodleian in the same year upon non-scientific periodicals was but £784.

Money had also to be found for the purchase of second-hand copies of older books, English or foreign—books that are required to supply past omissions, or which are valued for their rarity. Unfortunately the resources available to the Bodleian, in a world of rising book-prices, have long been scant. During the First World War and the five years that followed, only about £170 a year was available for buying older books, and, though the library subsequently spent as much as £1,100 or £1,200 in a single year on second-hand purchases, buying was as yet unsystematic and unorganized. Only from 1932, when it was concentrated in the hands of one library officer, and annual purchases of second-hand books were at the same time limited to £600, did the library begin to get full value for its outlay.

The ordinary revenue of the Bodleian gave little scope for that luxury buying which is a necessity for a great library. At the instigation of Dr. Percy Allen, subsequently President of Corpus, a special fund for the purchase of manuscripts and rare books was started in 1916 by a modest allocation of £100. By 1932 this reserve fund had reached the figure of £2,500, and since that time it has been constantly drawn upon to make special purchases, and has been continuously replenished from the general account. Other funds are supplied by well-wishers of the library. Gordon Duff, of whose work upon Bodleian catalogues we have spoken in an earlier chapter, died in 1924, bequeathing his estate in equal shares to the Bodleian and to Cambridge University Library, and directed that it should be applied to the purchase of old or rare manuscripts, printed books, and book bindings. His bequest was made subject to life-interests that are still in force. But, though Bodley has as yet obtained no benefit from this particular fund, it has derived great assistance from a body of subscribers who are grouped together in a society named the Friends of the Bodleian.

Bodies of persons who unite to subscribe funds for gifts to museums and art galleries have been in existence for half a century. The Société des amis du Louvre was formed in 1897; the National Art Collections Fund followed in 1902; and under Sydney Cockerell's impulse the Friends of the Fitzwilliam museum at Cambridge came into being in 1910. It is but a step from museums to libraries. The Société des amis de la Bibliothèque Nationale was started in 1913. A year previously, in June 1912, Mr. H. T. Gerrans, Fellow of Worcester College, in a letter to the *Oxford Magazine* on the subject of Bodleian finance had proposed the formation of a panel of some hundred persons to whom an appeal might be made whenever an opportunity arose of making some attractive purchase for which the ordinary funds of the library were not available.[1] Some years later, Mr. St. John Hornby suggested the creation of a society that should have for its object the provision of a permanent income for the purchase of rare books and manuscripts when library funds were insufficient for the purpose. But it was due in the main to the enthusiastic drive of a Bodleian Curator—Sir Michael Sadler, Master of University—that the Friends of the Bodleian came into being on 16 June 1925.

The society is the earliest instance in this country of an organization of friends of a library. Its formation synchronized with that of similar bodies for the libraries of two leading American universities, namely those of Harvard and Yale. Their example has been widely followed; in England, in 1930, by the Friends of the National Libraries, and in the United States of America, where societies of this nature now abound. Starting with a membership of 281, the Friends of the Bodleian had increased their numbers by 1949 to 387, though at the same time the total of subscriptions had diminished, sinking from £639 in 1926 to £455 in 1949. Despite limited resources, the society has done extremely good service, particularly since 1935, when its advisory committee or council of management commenced to hold regular meetings for discussion of contemplated purchases. In the first twenty years of its existence the society has made purchases amounting to £7,261, besides opening a capital fund account of £1,000 to which the composition fees of life members are now added. Nor does this complete the benefits which the society has rendered to the library; for it constitutes itself a channel for donations from persons outside its body, as well as from its own members, of

[1] *Oxford Magazine*, vol. xxx, p. 384.

whom, in its early days, Dr. J. H. Burn, Honorary Fellow of University College, was the most constant and the chief.

2. THE GENERAL AUTHOR-CATALOGUE

In two earlier chapters (pp. 51–53, 167–71) we have told how the main catalogue, consisting of written slips laid down in many massive volumes, took shape under Coxe and continued to grow under Nicholson. Its defects were apparent, for it was not homogeneous, having been carried out under more than one set of rules. The Bodleian was the first English library to frame a set of cataloguing rules. It is to be found prefixed to the catalogue which Dr. Hyde brought out in 1674. From Hyde's rules derived the tradition that was followed by Bodleian cataloguers down to 1883. The set of rules which Nicholson then introduced was a great advance upon earlier practice, but it created a break in the style of cataloguing. The old entries remained side by side with the new. But it is essential for a good catalogue that it should be uniform in method; and, as soon as the printing of the Bodleian catalogue came to be discussed, it became evident that printing must be preceded by a revision that would achieve uniformity.

So revision was begun in 1907. Unfortunately Nicholson was already a sick man. The careful direction that so complicated a work required was wanting; and, though much useful labour was put into it, from lack of guidance there was little system. Quite rightly the revisers attacked the lengthy subject-headings under which earlier cataloguers had grouped anonyma, and, with a view to their reduction, gave special attention to tracing the authorship of anonymous and pseudonymous works. Money was wasted in the process and progress was slow. By the time that Nicholson died, £3,600 had been spent, yet it was impossible to say how much of the catalogue had been revised.

Madan succeeded as librarian and at once appointed a superintendent of the catalogue revision staff of nine. He instituted a systematic treatment of the catalogue, working through volume after volume. The Trustees of the University Endowment Fund had been contributing £300 yearly towards the cost of revision. T. A. Brassey (by this time Lord Hythe) gave in 1912 a private donation of £3,000 towards the same object, and prospects began to look brighter. Nicholson had estimated that revision would be sufficiently advanced to allow printing to be begun in 1914; and, at the time that he took office, Madan still believed 'that early in 1916 the catalogue will be ready for any scheme of printing that may in the meantime be adopted'. He was soon undeceived. By October 1915 only 300 volumes, or a quarter of the catalogue, had been fully revised, at a cost of £4,100. Rightly or wrongly, it was then decided to restrict the amount of work put into perfectioning the catalogue, and, in place of complete revision, to be content with what was called a survey. In the course of a year a little over 200 volumes were dealt with in more summary fashion. But even this less ambitious work had to be suspended, for the First World War was by this time at its height, and the drain of library staff into the armed forces made it necessary to take women away from catalogue revision to fill the places of the absentees. So revision came to an end, with £8,880 spent, the work half done, and the printing of the whole catalogue as far off as ever.

Yet if for lack of funds that project were to be for the time abandoned, it might still be possible to make a start with printing the catalogue entries of all future accessions. This was what Cambridge University Library had been doing ever since 1861; and Nicholson, on becoming librarian, had suggested that all accessions, from the beginning of 1883, should be catalogued in print. At that time, as on so many later occasions, he failed to carry his Curators with him. But when, from 1902 onwards, they began to envisage the eventual printing of the entire catalogue, the printing of accession slips assumed a new urgency. If the catalogue were to be converted into print, they said in the appeal for funds sent out in the summer of 1914, 'it would at once become necessary to substitute printing for the present mode of transcription in all new catalogue entries.' The war, that broke out immediately after the issue of the appeal, for a time delayed action.

When that war was over, and Cowley had succeeded Madan in office, a decision was at length taken and the change was adopted that Nicholson had advocated nearly forty years before. The cataloguers' entries for all books published in or after 1920 were sent to the printer, and the printed slips went to form a new catalogue, laid down, like the old, in a series of volumes. This method was thought to be better than combining written and printed entries in a single series. So henceforward there were two catalogues—the old 'transcribed' catalogue of all books published up to 1920, and a new printed catalogue of books published from 1920 onwards.

A duplicity of catalogues—the coexistence of two alphabets—is far from ideal; and the formation of the '1920 catalogue', as it came to be called, had a further disadvantage. Nicholson's cataloguing rules, as revised by Madan, continued to be followed in cataloguing accessions of the older (pre-1920) books which still went into the transcribed catalogue, but it was thought that modern books admitted of a simpler treatment. A simplified set of rules was therefore drawn up for use in the new catalogue. Its adoption led to precisely the same result as that which had followed from Nicholson's cataloguing reform of 1883: it produced an undesirable nonconformity. There came to be not only two catalogues but two codes of rules, and their divergence formed a barrier to any eventual merging of the two catalogues into one.

That was a state of affairs that had never been intended to be permanent. A committee appointed to consider the general subject of library extension recommended in December 1926 that the transcribed catalogue should be revised and printed on slips like the printed catalogue. Resumption of catalogue revision could not be undertaken without further endowment. The committee estimated that to complete the revision of the catalogue, to enlarge it by the inclusion of books not in Bodley but in other Oxford libraries, and to print, would cost £100,000. That was the sum earmarked for cataloguing in the report made in 1931 by a library commission of which we shall have much more to tell in a later chapter (pp. 323–5), though the Commissioners then hoped that there would be a balance available for the publication of supplementary catalogues.[1] A closer estimate, made in 1938, gave the cost of staff at £40,000; of printing at £45,337;[2] of paper and binding at £4,877; making a total sum of £90,214. The calculation was made upon certain assumptions, as that salaries and printing costs would remain upon the level at which they then stood, and that the work would be completed by 1951. It would not have been possible to give so low a figure had not decisions been taken meanwhile that had the effect of very materially reducing the bulk of the catalogue.

It was agreed that the catalogue should include the contents of the dependent libraries. On the other hand, the proposal for inserting entries of books in libraries not under Bodleian control was dropped as soon as it was made. Neither did the catalogue have to include oriental books (that is, books in non-European type), music, maps, or doctoral dissertations: each of these classes had their own special registers or card-indexes. It was found that enormous reductions could be effected through the adoption of collective entries for some

---

[1] *Library Provision in Oxford*, pars. 122–5, 134.

[2] In the Bodleian appeal of 1914 the Curators gave the cost of printing alone as not less than £30,000. That had been Nicholson's estimate. A calculation made by Cowley in 1921 that the cost of printing, apart from that of completing revision and seeing the work through the press, would amount to £100,000, went far beyond the mark.

kinds of pamphlets and textbooks.[1] Finally, on the principle that the catalogue should be a catalogue of books and not of the contents of books, the old practice of cataloguing separate articles in periodicals or in collectaneous volumes was abandoned.[2] This limitation of effort had surprisingly extensive results. When an experimental volume was printed in 1938 it showed that the number of entries in the transcribed catalogue had been reduced by one third.

The Library Commissioners reported that 'the revision of the Main Catalogue ought at once to be resumed'. One step had to be taken before any revision was possible. Since revision was suspended in 1916, the '1920' catalogue with its new set of rules had come into existence. It was necessary that these rules and those that were followed for the transcribed catalogue should be revised and reduced to a single code. In amalgamating the two, the rules for the printed catalogue were taken for the model, since these allowed for briefer entries that gave only the essential parts of the full titles of books. The resulting *Rules for the general catalogue of printed books* were drawn up by Mr. G. W. Wheeler, superintendent of the Camera, and were published in February 1933. Six years later they were subjected to further revision in the light of experience gained in the interval, and were published as *Cataloguing Rules*, with an appendix of rules for the cataloguing of music and maps.

Since catalogue entries give pressmarks, it was desirable to know, before printing, whether existing pressmarks were likely to be permanent, and therefore to take an early decision on the old vexed question of reclassification, which Jowett had pressed so hard in Coxe's day. The Library Commissioners of 1931 had pronounced the existing classification to be unsuitable and considered that a good deal of reclassification might prove necessary.[3] We have told in an earlier chapter (p. 57) of how Coxe re-referenced, into the class-arrangement which he started in 1861, the unclassified accessions of 1851–60. An interesting experiment was now (in 1933) carried out in referencing into the current numerical classifications the accessions of 1850. The cost of re-referencing was found to work out at 6*d*. a volume,[4] and it was calculated that the reclassification and redistribution of nineteenth-century accessions which were either wholly unclassified or were classified in less detailed fashion than under the scheme which

[1] So, for instance, 1,312 entries of publications of the International Correspondence School were reduced in the course of revision to sixteen.

[2] To quote a single example, *Shakespeare's England* had about fifty separate entries in the old catalogue.

[3] *Library Provision in Oxford*, pars. 12 and 98.

[4] *Bodleian Quarterly Record*, vol. vii, pp. 515–17.

Nicholson introduced in 1883, would occupy a staff of six persons for four or five years. Though the Commissioners had recommended reclassification, they had omitted to make special financial provision for it, and the Curators resolved to postpone the question until experience had been obtained in the working of readers' direct access to book-stacks.[1]

Catalogue revision was resumed in February 1933, but only preliminary and experimental work could be carried out until quarters were found for a staff of cataloguers. The clearance of the old Schola Metaphysicae in the Bodleian quadrangle, rendered possible by library extension elsewhere, provided a staff-room in which systematic revision was begun in January 1935. Mr. Strickland Gibson was made Director of Cataloguing and laid down the course that the work was to take. The great headings which still encumbered the transcribed catalogue had first to be taken in hand and recast in conformity with modern cataloguing rules. Large non-author headings like Parliament, and the long personal headings derived from the names of sovereigns, had no place in a modern catalogue. Only after these had been cleared away was it possible at length, in 1938, to start from the commencement with the letter A. At the same time an experimental printing of the revised slips of a section of the transcribed catalogue and their production as a specimen volume allowed an accurate estimate to be made, for the first time, of the ultimate cost of the catalogue, and assurance to be given that, at the prices then maintaining, there was sufficiency of funds in hand to carry the work through to its completion.

The aim was clear—the reduction of two catalogues into one, in which the books of the Bodleian and of its dependent libraries should be catalogued in identical form and take their place in a single alphabetical sequence. Publication was not contemplated, but only the printing of sheets which should be cut up, so that their slips, amalgamated with the already printed slips of the '1920' catalogue, might be pasted down into loose-leaf volumes. Printing makes for compression. Four hundred or more volumes would take the place of 1,300. It was hoped at that time that by 1946 the preparation of 'copy' would be sufficiently advanced to allow printing to be begun in that year. (Nicholson had made a similar forecast for 1914.) And, with a view to speeding up the work of revision, six ladies, trained in the London School of Librarianship, were added in 1940 to the cataloguing staff. But by that time war had broken out; the male staff was correspondingly reduced; and, as the war proceeded, it became necessary, as in

[1] Curators' acta, 13 June 1936.

the First World War, to divert cataloguers to general library duties. Care was taken, however, to avoid the mistake then made of halting revision, a mistake which had held up that very necessary work for a generation. Although reduced in numbers to two, the cataloguing staff, now transferred to permanent quarters in the New Library, still carried on. By the end of the war the whole of the letter A and the bulk of B had been revised, the amount spent upon catalogue revision from its resumption up to that date being approximately £10,000.[1]

3. SUPPLEMENTARY CATALOGUES

Other cataloguing activities were being carried on at the same time. A new catalogue of dissertations was begun at the end of 1938 and extended over 200,000 cards. Much, too, was being done at the Radcliffe Science Library. The old slip-catalogue, which it had inherited from the days when it was an independent library, was taken in hand in 1934, and the slips replaced by entries in typed form on standard cards according to the new Bodleian cataloguing rules. The task of revision was completed by 1943. At the same time, in 1934, the scientific sections of the Bodleian were transferred to the Radcliffe Library and were incorporated in the Radcliffe catalogue.

Proposals for a union catalogue which should give references to all books found in college libraries but not in Bodley go far back in Bodleian history.[2] The idea was first bruited in a letter which the learned Dr. Langbaine wrote in 1652 to the equally learned John Selden.[3] Such a catalogue was actually advertised in the second volume of the 1738 Bodleian catalogue as ready for the press. In 1794 the Curators issued notices announcing the preparation of a new library catalogue and their intention of fulfilling the promise made in 1738. They invited the colleges to supply lists of such of their books as were not in Bodley, but only five colleges responded to their request. The project was revived in 1852 by Mr. Strickland in the evidence which he gave before the University Commission.[4] And the idea found final utterance when the committee on Bodleian Extension, which reported in December 1926 in favour of printing the Bodleian catalogue, recommended that the catalogue 'should be supplemented by references to books which, though not in the Bodleian, can be found in other libraries in Oxford'.

[1] A general account of the production of the new catalogue was given in *Oxford*, vol. vi, no. 1 (1939), pp. 62–68.
[2] An account of them has been given by Strickland Gibson in *Oxford Bibliographical Society, Proceedings and Papers*, vol. ii, pp. 201–2.
[3] Letter of 16 Mar. 1651/2, printed in Leland, *Collectanea*, ed. 1715, vol. v, p. 288.
[4] *Oxford University Commission Report*, 1852, Evidence, p. 102.

It is perhaps unlikely that a supplement of this general character will ever be produced. But the compilation of union catalogues has been undertaken in two limited fields, namely in those of periodicals and of early printed books. *A classified list of periodicals and serial works taken in by College libraries etc. in Oxford*, started on the initiative of Professor Haverfield, was privately printed in 1890 and was reissued in revised form in 1913. It has been superseded in regard to foreign periodicals, by a *List of Current Foreign and Colonial Periodicals in the Bodleian and other Oxford Libraries*, which was compiled by the Bodleian staff and published in 1925. This includes periodicals to be found in other university institutes and departments as well as in college libraries, and, so far as Bodley is concerned, supersedes Neubauer's 1880 catalogue of foreign periodicals. It is kept up to date as a card-index in the Bodleian Upper Reading-Room. And a union catalogue of foreign periodicals in the libraries of Oxford scientific departments has been compiled and is kept at the Radcliffe Science Library.

The first attempt to be made in recent years at a union catalogue of early printed books in college libraries proved abortive. Working under the direction of certain college librarians, Dr. Henderson Aitken started in 1911 to compile a descriptive list of fifteenth- and sixteenth-century books that were in college libraries but not in the Bodleian. His death in 1916 brought the enterprise to an end. On the instigation of Mr. G. R. Driver, the project was resuscitated in 1929 by the Oxford Bibliographical Society, and, at a meeting of college librarians called under the auspices of that society, approval was given to a scheme for the preparation of an intercollegiate catalogue of books printed before 1641. The original intention of confining the catalogue to books that were not to be found in Bodley was soon extended to include all early printed books, whether in the Bodleian or not. With the help of a grant towards the cost of editing made by the Committee of Advanced Studies, work was taken in hand by members of the Bodleian staff and progressed slowly until shortly before the war. Since the war ended, work upon the catalogue has been resumed; contributions have been made by the Bodleian and the various colleges to meet the cost of printing; and a volume compiled by Mr. Strickland Gibson will shortly make its appearance. Its scope, like that of the *Short Title Catalogue*, will be limited to English publications, foreign works being reserved for subsequent treatment.

Chapter XVI
Printed Books

THE books or groups of books that have been acquired since 1912, whether by purchase or by gift, have been recorded in the library's annual reports, as well as in the *Bodleian Quarterly Record* and *Library Record* and in the annual reports of the Friends of the Bodleian. It is not possible to give more than a general survey of them here, or to cite more than a few examples of the library's more important acquisitions.

1. ENGLISH LITERATURE

In the field of early English printing, the Bodleian had failed in 1891 to get a share of the Althorp Caxtons, but specimens of Caxton's printing were still to be had. So the library received by gift in 1924 a copy, albeit imperfect, of Caxton's edition of the statutes of the 1st, 3rd, and 4th years of Henry VII, which forms the earliest printed collection of English statutes.[1] Greater interest attaches to a vellum primer, printed in London, about 1484, by Caxton's contemporary, William de Machlinia. It was discovered in 1928 by Mr. George Smith of Great Bedwyn, and was presented by him and Mr. F. B. Benger through the Friends in 1945. The book had been previously known only through some odd leaves found in bindings. Its series of eight woodcuts are the earliest illustrations to appear in any book printed in the city of London.[2]

Falconer Madan established his reputation as a bibliographer by the three volumes of his *Oxford Books* (1895, 1912, and 1931), a full-scale bibliography of books printed in Oxford as well as of works relating to the city and university, which he brought down to 1680.[3] Like Bandinel he was himself a book-collector; and while he was still librarian he presented to the Bodleian a considerable number of books of the Stuart period including 178 Civil War tracts, the remainder of his Oxford collections being subsequently sold to the Stirling Memorial Library of Yale University. As a book-hunter he also

[1] *Bodleian Quarterly Record*, vol. iv, p. 101.
[2] The volume was at one time in Bishop Cosin's library at Durham; *Bodleian Library Record*, vol. ii, p. 112. It has been fully described, and the woodcuts reproduced, by Mr. George Smith in his *William de Machlinia; the primer on vellum printed by him about 1484.*
[3] The notebooks used by Madan for his *Oxford Books*, carrying the record down to 1899, were deposited in the Bodleian on loan by his son, Mr. F. F. Madan, in 1938.

sought out copies of the *Eikon Basilike*, that devotional book which pious Cavaliers foisted upon Charles I, and which won such popularity in Royalist households. Seventy-two editions or issues of this work were given by him to Bodley after his retirement from the librarianship.[1]

Increasing attention has been given by book-collectors of the present century to English literature of the post-Restoration period, and the Friends of the Bodleian have made special efforts to make up the library's deficiencies in that field, particularly in Dryden quartos and Drydeniana. One of the most striking of their acquisitions was a small library of some seventy volumes which they bought in 1931 for £500. This was the Thorn-Drury collection. Mr. George Thorn-Drury, an editor of the poets Randolph and Waller, specialized in the minor poets of the Restoration period. His books, grangerized and profusely annotated, provide a mine of bibliographical information on the poetical writers, not only of the Restoration but on those of an earlier and of a slightly later age.

The eighteenth century has won for itself in recent years a popularity among book-collectors,[2] and the study of its literature has revealed the fact that first editions of some famous English books of that period were not to be found in the Bodleian. Deficiencies[3] have been remedied, largely through the action of the Friends. That society bought and presented a volume containing a set of Swift's *Drapier Letters*, mostly first editions, in uncut, and in some cases even in unopened, state; and at the same time they also acquired, at the Butler sale, a copy of the first edition of Pope's *Essay on Criticism*, of which the autograph manuscript was already in the library. A very fine large-paper copy of the first edition of the *Rape of the Lock*, destined for the library by Sir Charles Firth, was presented by his widow in 1936. Since then, the Friends have bought and given to the library first editions of such famous eighteenth-century novels as Sterne's *Tristram Shandy* and Smollett's *Roderick Random*. The Bodleian collection of eighteenth-century drama has been made more representative through the acquisition of some seventy-five volumes of English plays in the Finch collection, of which we shall have more

[1] F. F. Madan has given bibliographical descriptions of all known editions and issues of the *Eikon* in his *New Bibliography of the Eikon Basilike*, Oxford Bibliographical Society, N.S., vol. iii (1950).

[2] The change of taste has been attributed to the influence of a single bookseller's catalogue, namely one issued by Elkin Mathews in 1925. See John Carter, *Taste and Technique in Book-collecting* (Sandars Lectures, 1947), p. 50.

[3] Attention was first drawn to them in an address given by Dr. R. W. Chapman at the annual meeting of the Friends of the Bodleian in 1929. *Fifth Annual Report*, pp. 7–11.

to say later (p. 283), and by the purchase of 486 Irish editions of plays of the second half of the century.

The Percy collection consists of the residue of the books, pamphlets, and papers of Thomas Percy, Bishop of Dromore; that eighteenth-century divine, *littérateur*, and antiquary who is best known as the editor of the *Reliques of Ancient English Poetry*. The collection was presented in 1933 by the bishop's great-granddaughter, Miss Constance Meade. Percy was a friend of Goldsmith and of Dr. Johnson; and among his books are a set of *The Rambler*, with manuscript notes by Percy, and of *The Idler*, with manuscript notes by Percy and by Johnson, giving information as to the authorship of many of the articles included in those periodicals.[1]

Continuing the tale of first editions down into the early nineteenth century—a period when the acquisition of fiction and poetry was little regarded by librarians—a copy of the very rare first edition of the first of Wordsworth's published works, *Descriptive Sketches* (1793), was bought by the Friends in 1934. The first (1798) edition of the *Lyrical Ballads*—'the black tulip', as Swinburne called it, 'of that sort of literature'—was subsequently presented through the Friends by Mr. J. G. Legge's family, whose gift also included editions of Shelley's *Queen Mab* (1822) and of the Tennysons' *Poems by Two Brothers* (1827). And among the purchases made by the Friends in 1934–6 one may enumerate first editions of Sir Walter Scott's *Waverley* (1814), and of Coleridge's *Christabel* and *Kubla Khan* (1816); the 1820 edition of Keats's *Lamia, Isabella, the Eve of St. Agnes, and other poems*, in which most of the poet's best-known poems make their first appearance in print; and a presentation copy to Southey of Walter Savage Landor's *Simonidea* (Bath, 1806), a fine copy of one of Landor's rarest books.

Mr. John Hodgkin's bequest, received in 1931, brought to the library his almost complete collection of books by or relating to William Beckford, the millionaire author of *Vathek* and builder of Fonthill, and exemplifies a new school of book-collecting, that which confines itself to the works of a single author. Another, and a more curious example of specialization is a very complete collection of about 3,500 volumes relating to the history and use of playing-cards. The collection was formed by Mr. Frederick Jessel and was left by him to the library in 1934.[2]

Finally, typifying the so-called 'cult for moderns', that is to say, for nearly contemporary writers, the Bodleian has received two

[1] *Bodleian Quarterly Record*, vol. vii, pp. 508–9.
[2] *Bodleian Library Record*, vol. i, pp. 116–18.

collections that illustrate the English literature of the eighteen nineties. The Robert Ross memorial collection of over 1,000 volumes is wholly devoted to Oscar Wilde. Formed by Mr. Walter L. Ledger, who bequeathed it to University College, it was handed over by that college to the Bodleian in 1932 upon permanent deposit. The Walpole collection,[1] which the novelist Sir Hugh Walpole formed and which he bequeathed in 1942, is of wider scope, for it consists of over 1,300 picked copies (mainly first editions) of the works of English writers of fiction, poetry, and *belles lettres*, belonging to the last decade of the nineteenth century. Besides printed editions it contains many autograph poems by William Watson, and original manuscripts of the works of that singular writer, variously named Frederick Rolfe and Baron Corvo.

2. BALLADS, BROADSIDES, AND NEWSPAPERS

To collect ballads and broadsides has been a hobby and recreation of more than one Bodleian benefactor; in particular of Anthony Wood, of Thomas Hearne, and of Francis Douce. Hearne's collection of ballads and garlands was long in coming, but it was bought at last in 1912 out of the balance of a Churton Collins memorial fund. A later and quite as considerable a collector of these fugitive products of the printing-press was Sir Charles Firth, who, though a specialist in the political history of England under the Commonwealth, had wide interests which led him into many fields of English social and literary history from the seventeenth down to the early nineteenth century. He found in the ballads that were hawked in the streets of our towns or at our village fairs a specially attractive subject for historical study. Firth was a constant donor to Bodley during his lifetime, and had already given to it in 1906 many street ballads. After his death his widow, Lady Firth, presented to the Bodleian in 1936 the collection which bears his name. It includes twelve large folio volumes of broadside poems and ballads, arranged by subject and mostly of the eighteenth and early nineteenth centuries. The collection is particularly strong in naval and military ballads.[2] With the ballads came also much pamphlet poetry of the later Stuart and Hanoverian times, and a number of rare chap-books, song garlands, and other popular books of the eighteenth and early nineteenth century, as well as eighty-four volumes of political tracts, chronologically arranged and mostly of the later Stuart period.

[1] Op. cit., vol. ii, pp. 40–41.
[2] Firth's manuscript collections of these came to the library along with his printed books, and are referenced MSS. Firth c. 17–18, 20; d. 11–14.

A very early example of a broadside sheet is one that was printed at Leipzig about 1544 and was used for teaching the alphabet. It is entitled *Tabulae ABC Dariae Pueriles*, and the library possesses a copy given to it by the Friends. But the commonest use of broadsides, apart from ballads, was for proclamations. Of these the library has acquired in recent years sets from three sources. In 1928 the Friends purchased for £200, from Major Wentworth of Woolley Park, seventy-six royal proclamations (thirty of which were unique), issued by Charles I at Oxford during the Civil War years (1642–4) when Oxford was the headquarters of the Royalist forces. Three years later the Guildhall Library in London presented 137 proclamations that were duplicated in its own collection, most of which were of the Commonwealth period. And Firth's donation added four volumes of proclamations and other broadsides of the seventeenth and eighteenth centuries.

The Bodleian derives its early English newspapers and periodicals in the main from the collections formed by John Nichols and by F. W. Hope, of which some account has been given in an earlier chapter (p. 77). For the seventeenth century it also has at its disposal the newspapers preserved by Anthony Wood and by Elias Ashmole. Taken together these form a collection that is second in importance only to that of the British Museum. It is especially rich in early newspapers and corantos, Civil War periodicals, London newspapers from 1672 to 1737, and literary periodicals of the eighteenth century. A gift of eleven volumes of the *Mercurius Politicus*, 1650–60, received in the Firth donation, has made the Bodleian set of that leading Commonwealth periodical the most complete known. And since then the newspaper collection has been augmented by gifts from the Friends, in particular through the purchase of a very fine set of the first six volumes of Daniel Defoe's *Review of the Affairs of France (1705–10)*.

It is the exception for any run of an early newspaper to be complete. There are almost sure to be some gaps. For that reason they require a more detailed treatment than can be conveniently given to them in a general library catalogue. This has been provided for Bodley by Milford and Sutherland's *Catalogue of English Newspapers and Periodicals in the Bodleian Library, 1622–1800*, issued by the Oxford Bibliographical Society in 1936. Their work has been rightly described as the most elaborate catalogue of English newspapers and periodicals yet published.

Turning from these ephemeral productions of the printing press to the assured permanence of classical literature, the most interesting single item acquired during the period we are discussing is one that was presented in 1934, through the Friends, by W. W. Vaughan, former headmaster of Rugby. It is John Milton's copy of Euripides (2 vols., Geneva, 1602), and contains a large number of notes and emendations in Milton's hand.[1] And this is but one of many gifts whereby the library has benefited in the past forty years. The Clarendon Press loan collection of classical texts and adversaria, of which some account has been given in an earlier chapter (p. 193), was made over to the library in 1922. In the following year Mr. Henry N. Gladstone presented 256 pamphlets on Homeric subjects collected by his father, W. E. Gladstone, whose Romanes Lecture upon Homer was for long remembered in the university which he had represented in Parliament. In 1931 Mr. John Hodgkin bequeathed his collection of ancient and modern macaronic verse. But more important than any of these is the bequest which Ingram Bywater made, and which came to Bodley upon his death in 1914.

Of Bywater, of his short term as sub-librarian under Coxe, of his curatorship, and of the opposition which he led against Nicholson, we have had on various occasions to speak. His fine scholarship, his strong attachment to books as shrines of learning, revealed themselves in the library which he formed under the inspiration of his friend and teacher, Mark Pattison. Like yet another Bodleian Curator, Sir William Osler, Bywater was a natural bibliophile and loved a fine book. 'The real reason for which to buy a book', he said in his epigrammatic and paradoxical way, 'is the margin. Always look at the margin.'[2] And so the 4,000 volumes which he bequeathed to Bodley are almost all choice specimens and a delight to handle. But Bywater was a student even more than he was a book-collector. He chose his books to illustrate the history of classical learning from Bessarion down to the immediate successors of Scaliger and Casaubon. The catalogue of his library which he printed in his lifetime[3] contains the names of the great, and many of the obscurer, European humanists of the sixteenth and early seventeenth centuries. Aristotle and his commentators are particularly well represented in it. Over fifty of Bywater's books have manuscript marginalia by such famous scholars

---

[1] The annotations were printed in full in 1826 from a transcript by Porson, in *Museum Criticum*, vol. i, pp. 283–91.

[2] W. W. Jackson, *Ingram Bywater*, p. 161.

[3] *Elenchus librorum vetustiorum apud * * hospitantium*, privately issued in 1911.

as Casaubon, Salmasius, Scaliger, and Porson. Near 200 are auto-graphed. There is hardly a book in the collection that is later than 1650. The *incunabula* among them number 152; the number of books printed in the first half of the sixteenth century is 1,159, of which over a third are from the Paris presses specially loved by Bywater. There are no fewer than fifty-three volumes whose binding is stamped with the arms of the great French collector De Thou. And among the gems of the collection it is sufficient to mention a mint copy of the Florentine *editio princeps* of Homer (1488), and a copy of the reformer Melanchthon's *Commentarius de anima* with the autograph of Rabelais.

The Bodleian has added much to its store of Italian literature. That Sir Thomas Bodley himself read Italian in his leisure moments appears from the few books that remain from his private library, one of which, a Boccaccio, has been mentioned in an earlier chapter (p. 76) as bought for the Bodleian in 1860. A second work by Boccaccio, the *Vita di Dante* (1544), with Sir Thomas's autograph on the title-page, was presented by Lord Rothschild through the Friends in 1937.[1] The fine Mortara collection which the Bodleian bought in 1852 was rich in early Boccaccio editions, and the number of these, as well as of the editions of Petrarch which came in the Montagu bequest of 1863, was greatly increased by a gift made to the library in 1912.

This was the first of a series of donations made to the Bodleian by the Dantean scholar, Dr. Paget Toynbee. The numerous Boccaccios which he gave in 1912 are mainly sixteenth-century editions printed at Florence or at Venice. His second donation, made in the following year, was of a more miscellaneous character, but consisted mainly of works in Italian, or printed at Italian presses such as those of Aldus and Giunta, of the sixteenth century.[2] His later gifts were for the most part editions or translations of Dante or commentaries upon the poet. And when he died in 1932, leaving to the library his house at Burnham (of which it pleased him to think that the bricks had come from kilns on Bodley's manor of Cookham), he also bequeathed his entire library, expressing the wish that all his books relating to Dante should be included in the selection made from it. The very compre-hensive collection which Bodley has thereby acquired remains as a memorial to him.

[1] Another personal link with Sir Thomas was given through the same agency by Mr. J. P. R. Lyell in 1945. This was a presentation copy (the only one known) of the first (1605) Bodleian catalogue.

[2] A later Italian printing-press of deservedly great repute was that of Bodoni at Parma. Its magnificent folio edition of Tasso's *La Gerusalemme Liberata* was pre-sented to the Bodleian in 1941 by Mr. Neil Ker of Magdalen College.

That eccentric gentleman the Rev. Colonel Robert Finch, who made a passing entry into Shelley's life and whom we have already mentioned (p. 118) as a donor of Napoleonic medals, left to the university in 1830 a sum of money producing over £100 a year, and a miscellaneous library.[1] This was long kept intact in the Taylor Institution along with an assortment of paintings, drawings, prints, and coins. Eventually, under a scheme sanctioned by the Court of Chancery in December 1918, the collection was distributed between the three institutions of the Taylorian, Ashmolean, and Bodleian. The Bodleian took for its share about 3,500 printed books as well as Finch's correspondence and foreign diaries. The Finch library, thus acquired for Bodley, is especially strong in books on Italian topography, and so forms a useful addition to Mr. George Scott's similar collection which Bandinel bought for the Bodleian in 1846. Along with the books, the Bodleian received one third of the monetary bequest. This, though directed to be applied to maintenance and to the purchase of books suitable to be added to the collection, was merged at first in the library general account, but from 1941 it has been more properly treated as a separate fund devoted to the purchase of books of Italian interest printed before 1800.

Slavonic studies, of which Neubauer had said in 1878 that they were hardly represented in Bodley, have received attention, though not to the extent that they deserved until after the Second World War. Mr. W. J. Birkbeck, a theologian and a liturgical scholar who devoted himself to working for the union of the Anglican and the Orthodox Churches, left to Magdalen College, of which he had been a member, a small collection of Russian books, and these were deposited by Magdalen in 1920. The Birkbeck books, about 300 in number, are mainly theological and historical, and include a copy of the first Slavonic edition of the Bible (Ostrog, 1581). Some early Russian books had come into the library in the Commonwealth period in John Selden's collection, and a *chasovnik* or book of hours, printed at Moscow in 1639, which had once belonged to Selden, was bought by the Friends and presented just 300 years later. To the Friends also the library owes a very rare and fine example of early Slavonic printing—the Four Gospels in Church Slavonic, printed at Belgrade in 1552 in Cyrillic type.

---

[1] A printed *Catalogue of Books in the Finch Collection*, made in 1874, is the work of a Bodleian assistant, George Parker. The Bodleian copy is marked to show which books have been brought into Bodley.

4. HISTORY AND SCIENCE

In the field of European history the Bodleian has received a collection that illustrates the long history of the little island of Malta. This was formed, and presented to the Rhodes House Library in 1937, by the Commendatore Hannibale Scicluna, archivist of the Royal Library at Valetta. It contains some 1,200 volumes dealing with the history, archaeology, and language of the island, as well as with the history of the order of the Knights Hospitallers. Three collections of more limited scope bear upon French Revolutionary and Napoleonic history. Two of them are purchases made by the Friends, who bought twelve volumes containing most of the important periodical literature of the first three years of the Revolution, and a complete set of orders of the day of the army in Egypt which Napoleon commanded from 1798 to 1800. The third is more extensive, and, as befits its donor, is of a more sumptuous character. Lord Curzon's bequest of his Napoleonic collection was received in 1926, and with it came the furniture of the Empire Room in Carlton House Terrace in which it had been kept. Originally brought together by Mr. A. M. Broadley, Curzon bought it *en bloc* at the sale of Mr. Broadley's books in 1916, and made substantial additions to it. It relates in the main to Napoleon's captivity on St. Helena, but also includes extra-illustrated sets of Holland Rose's *Life of Napoleon*, of Lord Rosebery's *Last Phase*, and of Broadley's *Napoleon in Caricature*, the whole grangerized into a magnificent series of thirty-nine folio volumes, copiously illustrated by the addition of thousands of portraits, views, contemporary caricatures, broadsides, autograph letters, and original drawings.

A small library of legal and social history, which started with 300 books from F. W. Maitland's private library, was first opened in January 1908 in a room in the front quadrangle of All Souls, whence it was transferred in 1920 to the Examination Schools. Styled the Maitland Memorial Library of Legal and Social History, it was administered by Maitland's close friend and fellow worker, Professor Vinogradoff; and it received a notable addition when Frederic Seebohm's books on economic history were presented to it by his family. In 1926 Vinogradoff died, bequeathing by will to the Maitland library nearly 2,000 volumes relating to legal and social studies. The library was now taken over by the Bodleian Curators. But with Vinogradoff gone, the vital spirit had departed from it, and it was thought best, in 1933, to terminate its separate existence.[1] Books that were of special interest for historians were put into the library of

---

[1] By decree of Congregation, 23 May 1933.

the Faculty of Modern History, where they are kept together as a Maitland section, and those that were not otherwise disposed of were absorbed by the Bodleian.

The attention that has been given in the present century to the bibliography and early literature of science owes much in Oxford to Sir William Osler, to Dr. Charles Singer, and to Dr. R. T. Gunther, as well as to later workers in the same field. The subject has not always been so highly valued as it is at present. John Selden's copy of the first edition of Descartes's *Discours de la Methode* has by some means found its way into the library of King's College, Cambridge, but it has been replaced by another copy through the good offices of the Friends.[1] When in 1926 All Souls College rid itself of 470 volumes of the medical and mathematical works of the sixteenth and seventeenth centuries, Bodley was the fortunate gainer. And we have already told, in an earlier chapter (p. 186), of how Stephen Rigaud's library of astronomy, mathematics, and physics came in 1935 by gift from the Radcliffe Trustees.

The incorporation of the Radcliffe Library into the Bodleian system brought with it many early scientific works of rarity, including some *incunabula*. With them came a number of the fine large folio editions of works on botany and natural history with coloured plates that were so much admired and so beautifully executed in the late eighteenth and the early nineteenth centuries. Of these the chief are now collected together in the Rare Book Room of the Radcliffe Science Library. Among them may be mentioned Audebert and Vieillot's *Oiseaux dorés* (3 vols. 1802) with its text printed in gold; Le Vaillant's *Oiseaux d' Afrique* (4 vols.) and *Oiseaux divers* (8 vols.); the various botanical works of Jacquin; and Redouté's superb *Liliacées* (8 vols. 1802–16) and *Roses* (3 vols. 1817–24). Some duplicated books already in Bodley. One such case was the *Flora Graeca*, which Dr. John Sibthorp, Sherardian Professor of Botany at Oxford, based on the collection, now in the university's department of Botany, which he had formed during his tours in Greece. The Bodleian, like the Botany department, had a presentation copy; the Radcliffe had a subscription copy. So when, in 1942, Dr. G. Claridge Druce left to the university, along with other bequests, a particularly fine copy of the *Flora Graeca*, this was placed in the Radcliffe Science Library and the Bodleian and Radcliffe copies were sold, the money received for them being added to the Druce Fund.[2]

---

[1] Sir Kenelm Digby's fine copy of the same edition has been recently acquired for the Houghton Library at Harvard. Digby's printed books did not accompany his manuscripts to Bodley. [2] *Bodleian Library Record*, vol. ii, p. 75.

Of non-scientific books with coloured plates one should particularly mention the very fine copy of Blake's *Songs of Innocence*, with twenty-seven out of the thirty-one coloured plates, which Miss A. G. E. Carthew bequeathed in 1940 along with her proof copy of the *Illustrations of the Book of Job*. And other rare illustrated books of the early nineteenth century have been presented by the Friends. Such are Repton's *Observations on the theory and practice of landscape gardening* (1803), Ackermann's *Microcosm of London* (1808–10) in three volumes, and his *Views of County Seats* (1830).

5. BINDINGS

Although the Bodleian did not set out to collect bindings as such, it had an abundance of historically interesting medieval book-covers, and many beautiful specimens came to it in the Douce collection. A publication by Mr. W. Salt Brassington in 1891 of *Historic Bindings in the Bodleian Library*, with twenty-four coloured plates, first drew general attention to the riches of Bodley in this field. It was followed in 1901–4 by Strickland Gibson's thirty-one reproductions of *Some notable Bodleian bindings*; and the same writer's standard work on *Early Oxford bindings*, which the Bibliographical Society published in 1903, contains illustrations of stamped Oxford bindings both in the Bodleian and in college libraries. An addition to Bodley's English embroidered bindings was made in 1911, when the library bought a Gospel Harmony made and bound by Mary Ferrar in the Anglican community of Little Gidding.[1] The Friends of the Bodleian paid special attention in their early days to the acquisition of fine bindings. Their most constant benefactor, Mr. J. H. Burn, presented in 1932–4 three royal bindings—a Matthew Paris (London, 1571) bound in white vellum tooled in gold with the arms of James VI of Scotland; and two from the French court, namely, Ambroise Paré's *La maniere de traicter les playes*, printed on vellum at Paris in 1551 and bound for Henri II, and *L'office de la semaine sainte* (Paris, 1674), bound in red morocco with the arms of Marie Thérèse of Austria, wife of Louis XIV. The Friends have also obtained for the library specimens of the work of contemporary craftsmen, among them Mr. Douglas Cockerell and Miss Katherine Adams (Mrs. Webb).

The Buchanan collection of about 500 printed books, received in 1941, is notable both for its specimens of fine printing and plates and for its specimens of fine binding. Thomas Buchanan showed his

[1] See also above, p. 73.

appreciation of the binder's craft when, as Librarian of the Codrington Library at All Souls (1878–82), he brought out an album of the best bindings in his college library. He soon deserted librarianship for politics, and held minor ministerial office in Liberal governments, but never ceased to be a bibliophile. He bought at the Duke of Marlborough's Sunderland sale of 1881 and at Quaritch's sale of Baron Achille Seillière's books in 1887. Other of his books come from famous collections such as those of Wodhull, Drury, and Heber. His widow carried out his wishes by allowing the Bodleian and All Souls to make their selections from his library. Among the books that came to Bodley are Italian bindings stamped with the papal arms of Urban VIII and Clement XI, a fine French binding executed for Charles de Lorraine and decorated with the heraldry of his house, and many plain morocco bindings bearing the arms of J. A. de Thou and other great French book-collectors. There are a few panel-stamps in the collection, but blind-stamped bindings had generally no great appeal for Buchanan; he preferred more decorative styles. Though English bindings of note are poorly represented, there are here some interesting examples of Scottish workmanship.[1]

6. MUSIC

In treating of music it is convenient to consider printed and manuscript music in combination. To a musical antiquary, Mr. Godfrey Arkwright, who catalogued the manuscript music in Christ Church Library, the Bodleian owes many transcriptions of Tudor church music and of other works of sixteenth- and seventeenth-century English composers, in part made by himself and in part by Professor H. E. Wooldridge. The Bodleian already possessed in the Music School Library a fairly representative collection of early English printed music. Other rare items have since been acquired by the Friends, who bought and presented in 1926 Thomas Morley's *Canzonets* (1597) and Playford's *Choice Ayres* (5 volumes, 1679–85). Purchases have also been made of the publications of John Walsh and his contemporaries. The period in which they lived, that is to say, the first half of the eighteenth century, was one for which the Music School had much manuscript, but little printed, music; and the Bodleian had not then begun to receive the music to which it was entitled under the Copyright Act.

The Bodleian is fortunate in possessing autographs of many English

---

[1] S. Gibson, 'Bookbindings in the Buchanan Collection', *Bodleian Library Record*, vol. ii, pp. 6–12. Two of Buchanan's bindings are reproduced in the Burlington Fine Arts Club's *Exhibition of Book-bindings*, 1891, plates xcix, ci.

composers of the sixteenth, seventeenth, and early eighteenth centuries. Of their successors it had nothing. This defect has been in part made good through the offices of the Friends. Through their medium, Dr. Ralph Vaughan Williams has given the original sketch of his oratorio *Sancta Civitas*, and Dr. Arnold Bax the autograph full score of his Fourth Symphony. The Friends presented autograph manuscripts of Holst's *Savitri* and of his Choral Fantasia before the orchestral score of that composer's more famous work, *The Planets*, was given by Miss Imogen Holst in memory of Sir Hugh Allen. The autograph full score of Elgar's oratorio *The Kingdom* has been deposited for a time in the library.

If less attention has been paid to continental music, it has not been wholly neglected. In 1930 the Friends bought a fine specimen of the exceedingly rare musical part-books printed at Venice by Ottaviano dei Petrucci.[1] Three years earlier they had secured the autograph manuscript of a song (*Tiefes Lied*) by Schubert. More recently, in 1947, they have acquired two Handel holograph manuscripts from Mr. T. W. Bourne, who subsequently devised to the library his Handel collection, including a complete set of the Handel Society's edition of that composer's works.

The music catalogue which Nicholson started in 1883 continued for a time to be carried on in the form of written slips. Nicholson had contemplated replacing slips by cards, and, though he did not live to see this done, a typed card-catalogue was started in 1926 and is still in progress. By 1931, after half a century of work, the very considerable arrears of handlisting and cataloguing Bodleian music had been completely overtaken.

---

[1] *Motetti libro quarto* (Venice, 1505); described in *Bodleian Quarterly Record*, vol. vi, p. 129.

SIR EDMUND CRASTER
LIBRARIAN 1931–45
from a drawing by Augustus John

Chapter XVII

Western Manuscripts

DURING the period 1912–45 there have been no large donations of manuscripts to equal the donations of printed books made by Bywater and Toynbee, by Curzon and Firth. For many years little had been spent out of library funds on the purchase of manuscripts; annual expenditure hardly ever came to as much as £100. But a more liberal policy was adopted in 1927 when a department of Western Manuscripts was created and a sum of £400 was annually set aside for manuscript purchase. Unspent balances are funded in a Reserve Fund for Purchase of Manuscripts and Rare Books, from which, since 1932, sums have been drawn, as need arose, to supplement the annual allocation. From 1925 onwards the Friends of the Bodleian have enabled the library to obtain many choice acquisitions, manuscript as well as printed. And during this period the Bodleian manuscript collection has been enriched by successive deposits of Oxford diocesan archives and by the deposit also of the manuscripts of one Oxford college and of the medieval deeds from the muniment rooms of two others.

1. CORPUS CHRISTI COLLEGE MANUSCRIPTS

In 1935, following the example set by other colleges in Nicholson's day, the President and Fellows of Corpus Christi College deposited their manuscripts in Bodley. They are about 500 in number, and form the most extensive of the college collections so far sent to the Bodleian, for Corpus has been singularly retentive of its older books.[1]

Founded in 1517 by Richard Foxe, Bishop of Durham and then of Winchester, Corpus was a college of the Renaissance, a missionary station of the new learning which was invading Oxford before the Reformation. The books which it received from its founder were the texts that were required for the study of the humanities and prescribed by the founder's statutes as subjects for college lectures. The nucleus of Foxe's collection was a humanistic library of printed books and manuscripts, formed by his predecessor in the see of Durham, Bishop John Shirwood. Out of the sixteen Latin manuscripts which Foxe gave to the library of his new college, six or seven

---

[1] MSS. 1–393 are described by Coxe (who was chaplain and afterwards honorary fellow of Corpus) in his *Catalogus Codicum MSS. in Collegiis Oxon.*, pars ii, art. 3. A continuation by Charles Plummer, privately printed in 1887, lists MSS. 394–438. The later numbers (439–98) are entered in the Bodleian copy of Coxe's catalogue.

had been in Shirwood's possession. It is a pity that Foxe failed to appropriate any of Shirwood's Greek manuscripts: these remained for a time at Bishop Auckland, but all trace of them has long been lost.[1]

Greek manuscripts were not long in arriving. The first person to give public lectures in Greek in the university was William Grocyn, who may be claimed on that score as the leader of the classical revival in Oxford. Eight of his Greek manuscripts were bought for the college after his death from his friend and executor, the famous physician, Thomas Linacre. Most of them were commentaries upon Plato and Aristotle. Eighteen others of more varied character were acquired by Thomas Claymond (d. 1537), whom Foxe had made first president of his college, and were left by him to its library. Most of Grocyn's manuscripts are of the fifteenth century, six of them being transcripts made by Greek refugees who settled in England— Emmanuel of Constantinople and Johannes Serbopoulos.[2]

Claymond was one of the small band of English scholars who were in close touch with Erasmus. His panegyrist says of him that he had read all the authors who had ever written. He certainly read and lectured upon Pliny's *Natural History*, and the four large folio tomes of the voluminous commentary which he made upon that extensive work came to the Corpus Library (MSS. 178–81). He may have also studied Hebrew, for he was the donor of a Hebrew Bible in seven volumes with a thirteenth-century interlinear Latin translation (MSS. 5–11). Erasmus, writing to him in 1519, calls the Corpus Library 'three-tongued', implying that it contained the literature of the three learned languages—Greek, Latin, and Hebrew. Classical learning as yet predominated in it.[3]

With the opening of the seventeenth century the college began to acquire other types of manuscript. The first gift of any size was one that was made between 1618 and 1623 by Henry Parry, eldest son of the bishop of that name who held in succession the sees of Gloucester and Worcester. The bishop died in 1616, bequeathing his manuscripts to his son. Of the thirty manuscripts which the younger Parry gave to Corpus, a dozen can be traced back, with greater or less certainty, to the Gloucester abbey of Lanthony, over a hundred of whose books are now in the Archiepiscopal Library of Lambeth. The others, which probably all came from English cathedral or monastic libraries,

---

[1] P. S. Allen, 'Bishop Shirwood of Durham and his Library', in *English Historical Review* (July 1910), vol. xxv, pp. 445–56.

[2] Allen and Garrod, *Merton Muniments* (Oxf. Hist. Soc., vol. lxxxvi), p. 47.

[3] The history of the library in the sixteenth century has been well sketched by J. R. Liddell in *The Library*, 4th series, vol. xviii (1938), pp. 385–416.

include the earliest surviving manuscript of Florence of Worcester (MS. 157), itself a Worcester book, and an important manuscript (MS. 78) of the French version of the Brut chronicle.

The college owes a much larger debt to one of its Fellows, Brian Twyne. A very great Oxford antiquary, to whom Anthony Wood did scant justice, Twyne was the chief compiler of the Laudian code and was the first to hold the office of Keeper of the University Archives. He published only one book, but he was always collecting, and Wood's debt to him was far greater than Wood acknowledged. A taste which he had for science and magic, or a desire to recover books that his grandfather had once owned, attracted him to the extensive library of manuscripts formed by Dr. John Dee, that singular combination of scholar and dupe or charlatan. Dee died in poverty, and his books were for a time the subject of litigation. When they were put up for sale in 1625, Twyne secured a large number of the manuscripts for the very modest sum of £15 and offered them to Corpus. His offer was declined, but Twyne had the good sense to leave them, with the rest of his library, to the college by will, and so they came to it in 1644. Thus it happens that Corpus possesses far the largest portion, that is to be found in any one place, of a library which, in its leading features, resembles the Thomas Allen books incorporated in the Digby collection and the library formed a century later by Elias Ashmole.

For Dee's interests lay chiefly in the direction of medieval science, medicine, and mathematics. He specially sought out the works of the Oxford Franciscan Roger Bacon. Yet the sixty-three Corpus manuscripts which can be identified as certainly or probably coming from Dr. Dee's study are not wholly confined to these subjects. They include a Richard Rolle bought by Dee from John Leland (MS. 236), and, among other philosophical writings, a Latin translation of Plato's *Phaedo* and *Meno* made in 1423 for Humphrey, Duke of Gloucester (MS. 243). Seven of the Dee manuscripts which passed to Corpus once belonged to St. Augustine's Abbey at Canterbury, and there is some reason for thinking that Dee may have acquired them from Brian Twyne's grandfather, John Twyne, master of the grammar school in that city.[1]

An eleventh-century manuscript of Bede's *Historia Ecclesiastica* in Anglo-Saxon (MS. 279) and a twelfth-century Life of St. Oswin (MS. 134), which came to Corpus from Brian Twyne, may or may

---

[1] Dee's manuscripts have been enumerated, and as far as possible traced, by Dr. M. R. James in his 'List of MSS. formerly owned by Dr. John Dee', published in supplement No. 1 (1921) of the *Bibliographical Society's Transactions*.

not have belonged to Dee. The fourteenth-century chartulary of St. Frideswide's Priory (MS. 160) certainly reached him from another source, for it was given to him by Thomas Allen. Of Twyne's own notebooks, a dozen volumes of very miscellaneous content are in the Corpus collection (MSS. 254–65). His ample and more ordered collectanea on Oxford University history, consisting of some thirty volumes, were left by him to the university and preserved in its archives, but since 1921 they have been deposited in the Bodleian. Most important among them are the full transcripts which he made from the city's medieval archives which have since perished.[1]

Two notebooks (MSS. 266–7) of an earlier Oxford antiquary who was also a Corpus man are of minor importance. Their compiler, Miles Windsor, left them to his college on his death at an advanced age in 1624. William Fulman, who belonged to the next generation, was a more considerable person. A Fellow of his college, an editor of English chronicles, and a friend of Anthony Wood,[2] when still young he was expelled from Corpus by the Parliamentarians, and returned there to a Fellowship at the Restoration. He is described as 'a severe student in various sorts of learning', and, when he died in 1688, he left to the college twenty-two volumes of collectanea and a good many scattered notes, together with a few medieval manuscripts of which the chief are a late-tenth-century copy of the Rule of St. Benedict in Latin and Old English which belonged originally to the abbey of Bury St. Edmunds (MS. 197), and one of the oldest manuscripts of Chaucer's Canterbury Tales (MS. 198). The twenty volumes of his collectanea or notebooks (MSS. 296–315)[3] include three, retained by the college, that form material for the history of Corpus; two volumes of short lives headed 'Memorials and remains of famous and learned men', and a third similar volume for poets, this last widely known for its biographical notice of Shakespeare, and many others that contain transcripts from monastic chronicles and copies of papers bearing upon university affairs and upon English seventeenth-century history.

Of other Corpus manuscripts one need mention but a few. An Irish missal (MS. 282), one of the only four that are known, still

[1] The fullest account of Brian Twyne is that given by Strickland Gibson in *Oxoniensia*, vol. v (1940), pp. 94–114. His collections are described, and Wood's debt to him considered, in Andrew Clark's *Wood's Life and Times*, vol. iv (Oxf. Hist. Soc., vol. xxx), pp. 202–26. The contents of the Corpus volumes have been enumerated by Coxe in his catalogue, pp. 105–14.

[2] Wood's letters to Fulman are in MS. 310. Fulman's side of the correspondence is to be found in MS. Wood F. 41.

[3] To these should be added a part at least of MSS. 317–19 which are given in Coxe's catalogue as Collectanea of Richard Davis of Sandford.

retains its leathern satchel and dates from about 1200.[1] To about the same date belongs a life of the Norwegian St. Olaf (MS. 209), which was once in the library of Fountains Abbey and was given to Corpus by John Rosewell, headmaster of Eton. An interesting day-book kept by a Dutch bookseller, John Dorne, who set up shop in Oxford, records the daily sales which he made in 1520 (MS. 131).[2] There is also a volume of the correspondence which the astronomer, John Flamsteed, had with Sir Isaac Newton and Dr. John Wallis (MS. 361). Fifty-six manuscripts out of the Corpus collection have been retained by the college and form no part of the deposit. These include all those with illuminations, the most notable being two volumes of a French Bible-history illuminated for King Francis I (MSS. 385–6) which General Oglethorpe, founder of the colony of Georgia, gave in 1772 to the college of which he was a gentleman-commoner; and eleven volumes of landscape sketches (MS. 443) made at the end of the eighteenth century by the Oxford musician and drawing-master, J. B. Malchair.[3]

2. CLASSICAL AND MEDIEVAL MANUSCRIPTS

The Bodleian collection of classical papyri was started, as we have seen (p. 200), by Nicholson. An important part of them, including the famous *Logia*, came from Oxyrhynchus and were presented by the Egypt Exploration Fund. That body continued to make distributions of its finds down to 1923: since then it has been found convenient to keep back the great mass until the whole has been sorted. Among the Oxyrhynchus papyri presented since 1914 are fragments of the Greek lyric poets, Alcaeus, Sappho, and Callimachus; recovered portions of lost plays—the Hypsipyle of Euripides and the Kolax of Menander; and a fourth-century fragment of Achilles Tatius's romance named Clitophon and Leucippe.[4] Although not a papyrus, one should also here mention a single leaf of a little codex of the sixth book of Esdras in Greek. It was written in the fourth century, and is the earliest specimen of a vellum book that the Bodleian possesses.

[1] Edited with facsimiles, by F. E. Warren, *The MS. Irish missal belonging to* . . . *C. C. C., Oxford* (1879).
[2] Edited by F. Madan for the Oxford Historical Society, *Collectanea*, vol. i, pp. 73–177; vol. ii, pp. 453–78.
[3] All the drawings in this collection that relate to Oxford and its neighbourhood have been listed by Mr. H. Minn in *Oxoniensia*, vols. viii–ix, pp. 159–68.
[4] The papyri here named have been published in *Oxyrhynchus Papyri*, vols. vi, x, xi. Miss Wegener has edited, as 'Some Oxford Papyri', for *Papyrologica Lugduno-Batava*, vol. iii A (1942) the more important of some non-literary papyri which came to the Bodleian on Dr. A. S. Hunt's death in 1934.

Latin literary papyri are much rarer than Greek, but Oxyrhynchus has yielded a page of a fifth-century papyrus of Sallust's Catiline. Two waxed tablets have come from a different source. One, a folding tablet on which is entered, in a good cursive hand of A.D. 147, a Roman birth-certificate[1] was bought through Bernard Grenfell. The other was acquired by Professor Sayce in Cairo and was presented by him in 1919. It is a Latin-Greek diptych, recording the appointment of a guardian made in A.D. 198, and is in a remarkably good state of preservation.[2]

Apart from papyri, there is little to tell in the way of acquisition of Greek or Latin classical texts. The few which were received in 1914 out of Professor Bywater's library are chiefly humanistic pieces and Latin translations from Greek authors made in the fifteenth century in Italy. The bequest was followed by a gift of Bywater's collations and classical notes, and of his correspondence, including that which he had with the German student of Scaliger and friend of Mark Pattison, J. Bernays. The papers of classical scholars of an earlier generation, which the Delegates of the Clarendon Press had deposited in the library in 1885,[3] were presented by them outright in 1922.

Among many manuscripts of medieval literature six may be mentioned as of particular interest. In 1932 the library bought a twelfth-century manuscript (MS. Lat. th. d. 17) of an otherwise unknown dialogue which a Yorkshire monk, Robert of Bridlington, composed on the Augustinian rule. A 'Compendium Physicae' bought in 1940 (MS. Lat. misc. e. 91) is a fifteenth-century transcript of a twelfth-century compilation from Hugh of St. Victor and William of Conches. A manuscript once in William Morris's possession, bought for the library in 1942 (MS. Lat. th. b. 4), contains the Decretals which Pope Gregory IX promulgated in 1234. It is a very early copy, being written at Modena in 1241, and is interesting not only for its miniatures but as containing the earliest known redaction of the Glossa Ordinaria composed by Bernard of Parma.[4] In 1943 the Curators purchased a fourteenth-century Apocalypse with an Anglo-Norman metrical commentary (MS. French e. 22) since edited in *Anglo-Norman Texts*, vol. vi. A Latin dictionary, termed Campus Florum, which was compiled by an English Cistercian monk, Thomas

---

[1] Reproduced in *Proceedings of the Society of Biblical Archaeology*, vol. xxvi, p. 195, plate iv.
[2] It has been described by Grenfell in the *Bodleian Quarterly Record*, vol. ii, pp. 258–62, and reproduced in facsimile with a description in the *New Palaeographical Society*, 2nd series, pl. 100.   [3] See p. 193.
[4] The manuscript forms the subject of a joint article by Dr. Kuttner and Miss B. Smalley in the *English Historical Review*, vol. lx (1945), pp. 97–105.

of Merevale, has survived only in part, and that in one manuscript. This unique fourteenth-century manuscript was bought in 1942 and is now referenced MS. Lat. misc. f. 37. Finally, the library owes to a gift made through the Friends by Dr. H. Watney a late-fourteenth-century collection of Wycliffe's sermons (MS. Don. c. 13), containing several religious lyrics.[1] These half-dozen manuscripts may serve as examples of the acquisitions that were made when money came to be available.

Other medieval manuscripts illustrate the history of the religious orders, notably a fourteenth-century chartulary of St. Laurence's hospital at Canterbury (MS. Top. Kent d. 3), bought at the Clumber library sale in 1938; a late-fifteenth-century manuscript containing short notices of the founders and patrons of Tewkesbury Abbey and its cells, with their arms and portraits (MS. Top. Glouc. d. 2), which was at one time kept in the abbey treasury and was bequeathed in 1938 by its owner, the Rev. C. H. B. Hudson;[2] and an interesting collection of Franciscan manuscripts. This last was presented in 1940 by Dr. A. G. Little, who devoted his life to the study of the order. Perhaps the most important of the manuscripts in this little collection are a late-thirteenth-century register of general and provincial constitutions and decrees made in the general chapters of the Franciscans (MS. Lat. th. d. 22, formerly Phillipps MS. 207), and a collection of pieces dealing with the life of St. Francis (MS. Lat. th. d. 23, formerly Phillipps MS. 12290).[3]

During the second decade of this century a trio of liturgiologists might have been found daily reading and conversing in Selden End. Two of them, Dr. Wickham Legg and the Rev. F. E. Brightman, bequeathed, when they died, printed liturgical works out of their private libraries. The third, Dr. H. M. Bannister, a student of early music and a great palaeographer as well as liturgiologist, left to Bodley upon his death in 1919 his invaluable notes on liturgical manuscripts in English and foreign libraries and on English and foreign liturgical calendars.

The number of English medieval service-books has been increased by the gift, made by Mrs. Martin in 1918, of a late-fourteenth-century

[1] Two which were otherwise unknown have been printed in the *Bodleian Quarterly Record*, vol. vii, pp. 1–7, where one is ascribed, with considerable probability, to Richard Rolle.

[2] Described in *Transactions of the Bristol and Gloucestershire Archaeological Society*, vol. xxxiii (1910), pp. 60–66, and in the *Bodleian Library Record*, vol. i, pp. 14–15.

[3] The latter has been fully described in Little's *Collectanea Franciscana*, vol. i, pp. 9–113 (British Society of Franciscan Studies, V).

psalter that was written for Norwich Priory (MS. Lat. liturg. f. 19) and by the acquisition of several Sarum books that belonged to pre-Reformation country churches. A manual of the fourteenth century (MS. Lat. liturg. f. 25), apparently the earliest one extant, had been immured in the chancel wall of West Lavington church in Wiltshire, from which it was recovered early in the nineteenth century, and was eventually bequeathed in 1941, along with an illuminated Sarum book of hours, by Mr. Eustace F. Bosanquet.[1] A late-fourteenth-century noted breviary that had once belonged to the Berkshire church of Denchworth (MS. Lat. liturg. b. 14) came in 1934 under a bequest made by Prebendary H. B. Hyde. And in 1933–4 Sir John Noble gave through the Friends two fine missals of the early fifteenth century in memory of their late owner, John Meade-Falkner. One of them (MS. Don. b. 5) had belonged to another Berkshire church, that of Buckland; the other (MS. Don. b. 6) had been perhaps written and illuminated for the Benedictine abbey of Abbotsbury and had passed to the Dorset parish church of Closworth.

The Bodleian has a good store of illuminated books of hours, some of the finest being those that form a part of the Douce collection. Of the fifteen Continental *horae* of various uses which Thomas Buchanan collected and his widow presented in 1939, ten are from France, two being of the school of the celebrated French miniaturist, Fouquet (MSS. Buchanan e. 3, 4). And although it is a far cry from Jean Fouquet to William Morris, one may conveniently make mention here of two specimens of Morris's decorative writing which have come by gift from his daughter, Miss May Morris. Both are on vellum. One (MS. Don. f. 3) is of the Rubaiyat of Omar Khayyam;[2] the other (MS. Lat. class. e. 38), of which the illumination is unfinished, is of the Odes of Horace.

3. HISTORICAL AND ANTIQUARIAN MANUSCRIPTS

From various manuscripts that bear upon the medieval history of England one may pick out for special mention one of the three known originals of the Great Charter of King Stephen with the great seal attached. It came to the library in 1916 from St. John's College in a volume of original documents relating to Hereford (MS. Rawlinson Q. b. 8) which had once belonged to Thomas Hearne. An early copy

[1] Described by him in the *Wiltshire Archaeological and Natural History Magazine*, vol. xl (1918), pp. 142–7.

[2] Another calligraphic transcript of Fitzgerald's Omar, made by Graily Hewitt and illuminated by Florence Kingsford, was bequeathed in 1931 by a former Bodleian assistant, Mr. C. M. Firth (MS. Eng. poet. e. 35).

of Magna Carta, dating probably from the first quarter of the thirteenth century,[1] was given in 1926 in memory of Mr. John Eliot Hodgkin. A survey made of the honour of Denbigh in 1334 came to Bodley with a few other manuscripts from the Maitland Library.[2] Two rolls of household accounts deserve special mention: one is that of Richard de Swinfield, Bishop of Hereford, for 1289-90,[3] the other (MS. Eng. hist. c. 267 R) is for Lord Dacre's household in 1542.

The Tudor period is represented by a narrative of the Reformation written by a Yorkshire parson, Robert Parkyn, in the reign of Queen Mary;[4] and by William Wodwall's contemporary metrical chronicle of the reign of Elizabeth, illustrated with pen drawings.[5] For English seventeenth-century history there is a diary kept during the Civil War by the Oxfordshire Rector of Ducklington, presented by Mr. Neil Ker, who bought it at the Campsall Hall sale in 1942, and a large collection of newsletters (MSS. Don. c. 37-40) given by the Friends in 1933. These last were written from Sir Joseph Williamson's office between 1669 and 1701 for Sir Daniel Fleming, head of a Westmorland family, many of whose papers have been edited for the Oxfordshire Historical Society.[6]

To a gift made by the Pilgrim Trust in 1932 the Bodleian owes a large and important collection of historical papers of the seventeenth, eighteenth, and early nineteenth centuries. They came from Wroxton Abbey, the seat of the North family. There is much family correspondence among them including a series of letters to Sir Dudley North (1636-70), papers of Lord Keeper North, eighteenth-century correspondence of the first Earl of Guilford, and General Sir Charles Doyle's papers relating to the Peninsular War. And besides private letters and household books, there are numerous government papers —official data collected by George III's prime ministers, Lord Bute and Lord North; Customs House ledgers for 1762-80, and accounts of Secret Service and Civil List expenditure for 1707-41 and

---

[1] *Bodleian Quarterly Record*, vol. v, p. 29.
[2] Edited as vol. i of the British Academy's *Records of Social and Economic History*, 1914.
[3] Printed in 1853-4 by the Camden Society, 1st series, vols. lix, lxii.
[4] MS. Lat. th. d. 15; printed by A. G. Dickens in the *English Historical Review*, vol. lxii (1947), pp. 58-83.
[5] MS. Eng. hist. e. 198. This very odd poem, if one can call it poem, is described in *Notes and Queries*, 4th series, vol. iii (1869), pp. 305-7.
[6] The whole collection, formerly at Rydal Hall, is reported upon in the Historical Manuscripts Commission's 12th report, appendix, part vii, where many of the newsletters will be found calendared. Dr. Magrath's edition, *The Flemings in Oxford* (Oxf. Hist. Soc., vols. xliv, lxii, lxxix), prints all letters and other documents relating to Oxford, 1650-1700.

1762–70. The whole collection has been arranged, and bound up at the expense of the Pilgrim Trust, in 331 volumes.[1]

Another collection of a semi-public nature, bought in 1916 (MSS. Eng. hist. c. 66–118) comprises the fifty-three volumes of letter-books of George, Lord Macartney, governor of Madras from 1780 to 1786, which supplement a series in the British Museum. And in 1943 a purchase was made of the correspondence that passed in 1759–1808 between Laurence Sulivan, chairman of the East India Company, and the Company's officers, chief of whom were Sir Robert Palk, Robert Vansittart, and Warren Hastings. Finally, two sets of papers that have been received by donation illustrate different chapters of nineteenth-century history. The first consists of the political correspondence (1847–58) of Baron Ward, the shrewd Yorkshire jockey who became chief minister to the reigning Duke of Parma: this was given by his family in 1936.[2] The other is a gift made in 1939 to the Rhodes House Library by the family of the Rev. Horace Waller, an intimate friend of David Livingstone. It includes the diaries of the first university's mission to East Africa, proofs of Livingstone's journal containing passages that have not been published, and many letters from Livingstone and from General Gordon.[3]

The acquisition of the Ashmole Library had made the Bodleian rich in heraldry. It is impossible in this brief survey to do more than draw passing attention to the collection of armorial manuscripts bequeathed in 1932 by Dr. F. P. Barnard, or to the 268 visitations, volumes of pedigrees, ordinaries of arms, and other heraldic manuscripts which Mr. W. Harry Rylands, a mainstay of the Harleian Society, left by will in 1922, and which his widow supplemented in 1941 by a gift of fifty-nine volumes of genealogical, heraldic, and ecclesiastical notes, relating largely to the northern counties.

Bodley's possession of the manuscripts of the great seventeenth-century antiquary, Roger Dodsworth, which so largely relate to Yorkshire, made it fitting that opportunity should be taken for securing two similar collections. One of these was bought in 1938. It consists of the Yorkshire monastic collections of John Burton (1710–71), compiler of *Monasticon Eboracense*. Burton was fortunate in having access to the original charters rescued by Dodsworth from St. Mary's Tower in York, which have since disappeared. The other collection comprises manuscripts formerly in the possession of Mr.

[1] A general account of the North Papers has been given in *The Times* for 9 Nov. 1932, and in the *Bodleian Quarterly Record*, vol. vii, p. 142.
[2] The correspondence, now referenced MSS. Ital. c. 28–66, has served as material for J. Myers's *Baron Ward and the Dukes of Parma*, 1938.
[3] *Bodleian Library Record*, vol. i, pp. 145–6.

Bacon-Frank of Campsall Hall. The Bacon-Frank manuscripts were dispersed by sale in 1942, when some were bought for Bodley out of library funds and others were presented by Mr. Neil Ker. These contain valuable material for Yorkshire history and, like Burton's papers, are closely connected with Dodsworth's gatherings. Two of the volumes are the work of Dodsworth himself; the rest are mainly collections made in the late seventeenth century by another Yorkshire antiquary, Nathaniel Johnston, which have been added to in the next century by Richard Frank. One of the volumes contains sixty-seven letters addressed to Johnston by Sir William Dugdale.[1]

The correspondence of Sir Symon Archer,[2] extending over the years 1627–46 (MS. Eng. letters b. 1), which was bought for the library in 1931, is also chiefly with Dugdale, for it was from Archer that Dugdale received his initiation into Warwickshire history. Another very important volume of letters was one that was acquired in 1942 for £400 from Mr. James Fairhurst of Oldham (MS. Selden supra 108). It contains the correspondence which one of the Bodleian's chief benefactors, the learned John Selden, conducted with English and foreign scholars, orientalists and antiquaries, and includes sixty-four letters addressed to Selden by Dr. Gerard Langbaine, Provost of Queen's College.[3] Other Selden manuscripts have been bought more recently from Mr. Fairhurst for the Bodleian, which also secured in 1921 the manuscript of Selden's autobiography (S. Seld. c. 23), and purchased more of his collections at the Clumber Library sale in 1938.

Lastly in this section we come to that spinner of fantastic theory who was yet a great field-archaeologist, Dr. William Stukeley. A number of valuable Stukeley manuscripts, chiefly consisting of plans and drawings, had come to Bodley in Richard Gough's collection. The rest stayed with his descendants until they were dispersed by sale in 1924. The Bodleian then acquired the whole of his archaeological diaries, the bulk of his correspondence, and the more important of his sketch-books, and in consequence it now possesses the major portion of Stukeley's papers.[4]

---

[1] A fairly full account of the Bacon-Frank collection is given in the sixth report of the Historical Manuscripts Commission, pp. 448–65, to which the library annual report for 1942–3 supplies references.

[2] Mr. Philip Styles has described and utilized this correspondence in a paper on 'Sir Simon Archer, 1581–1662'—*Dugdale Society Occasional Papers*, no. 6 (1946).

[3] *Bodleian Library Record*, vol. ii, pp. 73–74.

[4] *Bodleian Quarterly Record*, vol. iv, pp. 149–50. For Stukeley see Stuart Piggott's amusing biography, *William Stukeley*, 1950. The Stukeley manuscripts in the Bodleian are there listed at pp. 189–93. Mr. Piggott gives at pp. 206–24 a topographical index to the drawings and plans in Stukeley's manuscripts, most of which are in the Bodleian collection.

4. ENGLISH LITERATURE

The increased attention mentioned in the last chapter (p. 277) as paid to English literature of the seventeenth and subsequent centuries shows itself as much in the department of Manuscripts as in that of Printed Books. The Friends of the Bodleian have specially devoted themselves to acquiring contemporary seventeenth-century texts of English poets. The library is also indebted to them for two documents that bear upon the history of publishing in the first half of the eighteenth century. One, which has been called the basis of the most remarkable literary transaction of that century, is the original agreement made between Alexander Pope and his publisher, Bernard Lintot, for the publication of Pope's translation of the Iliad (MS. Don. a. 6). The other (MS. Don. b. 4) is the ledger in which William Bowyer, chief English printer of his day, kept account of his paper stock and entered the number of sheets printed of the books of such well-known authors as Swift, Pope, Defoe, Richardson, and Fielding, with the dates upon which copies were delivered. And among the Johnsoniana which the Friends have given is his diary (MS. Don. f. 6) for the last months of 1782. The diploma by which the university conferred upon Johnson the degree of D.C.L. in 1786 has been recovered from the Malahide collection and presented to the library in 1938 by Colonel Ralph Isham (MS. Lat. misc. c. 61).

For manuscripts of English authors of the nineteenth century the Bodleian had nothing except the Shelley collection. Here, too, the Friends have been active. Their gifts include a packet of letters from George Crabbe to his friends and booksellers (MSS. Don. d. 16–17); upwards of 200 letters written by Robert Southey to his brother Henry (MSS. Don. d. 3–5); literary pieces by the rustic poet, poor mad John Clare (MS. Don. c. 64); and nine small notebooks (MS. Don. e. 1) in which Christina Rossetti transcribed her poems. And if one turns from poets to prose writers, it is to the Friends again that the library owes a little book called *Volume the First* (MS. Don. e. 7) in which Jane Austen wrote her girlish compositions;[1] the letters that the authoress of *Our Village*, Mary Russell Mitford, sent to Sir Thomas Talfourd (MS. Don. d. 38); papers and family letters relating to the life and works of Thomas Love Peacock; a series of publishers' agreements, correspondence, and working-tables kept over nearly forty years by one who made novel-writing a business and yet was a great novelist—Anthony Trollope (MSS. Don. c. 9–10); and the last

---

[1] Edited from this manuscript by Dr. R. W. Chapman in 1933.

unfinished essay (MS. Don. d. 84) which a more laborious and studied writer, Walter Pater, wrote upon Pascal.

Other memorials of writers of the Victorian Age have come by direct gift to the library. Such are the correspondence, letter-books, and diaries of that eminent Victorian, Sir Henry Taylor; the original manuscript of one of Tennyson's Idylls—*Gareth and Lynette*—which his son Hallam gave in 1922 (MS. Eng. poet. b. 3); two volumes (MSS. Eng. poet. d. 43, 44) in which Dante Gabriel Rossetti wrote out his sonnets for 'Janie' Morris; and a holograph of Swinburne's *Ode to Proserpine* (MS. Eng. poet. c. 24) once owned by Ruskin. Of Ruskin himself the library has purchased many letters. Transcripts of his diaries and correspondence over a period of fifty years (MSS. Eng. misc. c. 209–33, Eng. letters c. 32–52) were presented in 1936 by Mr. A. H. M. Wedderburn, joint editor of the supreme edition of Ruskin's works.[1]

Nor have the autograph writings of more nearly contemporary authors been neglected. Colonel T. E. Lawrence presented in 1923 the manuscript of his *Seven Pillars of Wisdom* (MS. Res. d. 33), a work possessing a history as out of the common as its author. John Galsworthy gave through the Friends in 1928 the autograph of *Strife* (MS. Don. d. 6) as 'the first draft of (perhaps) my best play'; and in 1933 the Friends bought and presented the corrected typescript of James Elroy Flecker's *Hassan* (MS. Don. d. 30). Finally, the Bodleian has acquired by gift the original manuscripts of two immortal children's tales—*Puck of Pook's Hill* (MS. Res. c. 5) which Rudyard Kipling gave in 1926, and *The Wind in the Willows*, which the author's widow, Mrs. Kenneth Grahame, presented in 1943, along with the letters to their boy in which the work originated (MSS. Eng. misc. e. 247, 248; d. 281).

5. LETTERS

A mass of private correspondence and journals has been acquired or made available for readers since 1912. The institution, in 1928, of a new class of MSS. English Letters is a sign of the growing element that correspondence had come by then to form in the library's manuscript accessions. Twelve volumes of correspondence received by the botanist and antiquary, Dr. Richard Richardson (1663–1721), were bought out of Miss Currer's library at Eshton Hall in 1916 by the Radcliffe Trustees and were deposited by them as MSS. Radcliffe Trust c. 1–12. They are interesting as containing many letters

---

[1] The original diaries, in about thirty volumes, and some thousands of Ruskin's letters, are in the possession of Mr. J. Howard Whitehouse.

from William Sherard, Ralph Thoresby, and Thomas Hearne.[1] The twenty volumes of the correspondence of the learned non-juring bishop, Thomas Brett (1685–1744), was bought, largely through private subscription, in 1916 (MSS. Eng. th. c. 24–43), and increase the stock of non-jurors' papers which came to the Bodleian in the Rawlinson collection.[2] Dr. Paget Toynbee gave in 1920 practically the whole of Madame du Deffand's surviving letters to Horace Walpole. Madame du Deffand was one of the most gifted of French letter-writers, and her correspondence, filling fourteen volumes (MSS. Toynbee 1–14), covers the years 1766–80.[3]

The Bodleian has also come to be possessed of the private papers of two Keepers of the British Museum department of Manuscripts— Francis Douce and Sir Frederic Madden. Douce was one of the greatest of Bodleian benefactors. His notebooks and correspondence remained unopened in the British Museum until its Trustees deposited them in Bodley in 1931, and furnish abundant information regarding the formation of his collection.[4] Madden, dying in 1873, left his private journals and other papers by will to the Bodleian, with the stipulation that they should remain unopened until 1920. His ample journal (MSS. Eng. hist. c. 140–82) extends from 1819 to 1872. The quarrels and bickerings to which his difficult nature made him prone belong to a forgotten past, and his diary forms a narrative that is brim-full of information regarding manuscript collections. Madden had a good eye for manuscripts, was watchful of opportunities, and was most energetic in making acquisitions for the museum in whose department he served first as assistant and then as Keeper from 1828 to 1866.

Another locked chest came to the library in 1884. It contained the papers of a former Curator and a leading Oxford figure of his day, Mark Pattison, Rector of Lincoln. The outspoken Memoirs which Pattison dictated in his last illness narrated the events of his life down to the year 1860, and it was popularly believed that the chest would

---

[1] Many of the letters are printed in Nichols's *Illustrations of the Literary History of the Eighteenth Century* and in Dawson Turner's *Extracts from the Literary and Scientific Correspondence of Richard Richardson, M.D.*, privately issued in 1835.

[2] The wanderings of this collection have been well worked out by Canon Ollard in *Theology*, vol. ii (June 1921), pp. 283–90. The Brett papers form the basis of Mr. Henry Broxap's *Later Non-Jurors* (1924).

[3] The most recent editions of the letters are those by Mrs. Paget Toynbee (*Letters of Horace Walpole, chronologically arranged*, 1903–5) and by Mr. W. S. Lewis in the *Yale Edition of Horace Walpole's Correspondence*, vols. iii–vii (1939).

[4] Articles by Sir James Mann and Dr. Grafton Milne in the *Bodleian Quarterly Record*, vol. vii, pp. 362–4, 376–9, make use of the diary in which Douce recorded the antiquarian purchases made during the last thirty years of his life (1803–34). For the Douce correspondence see op. cit., pp. 380–2.

be found to contain a continuation of the story. When the box was opened in 1912, the belief was found to be mistaken. The Mark Pattison collection[1] contains the material from which the Memoirs were written; Pattison's earlier diaries and commonplace books, and a very extensive correspondence, complete, however, only to 1862. Various additions have since been made to it, including further correspondence; Pattison's notes for lives of Saumaise, the Scaligers, and Casaubon (MSS. 79–105); and diaries for the years 1843–84 and notes for his autobiography (MSS. 128–38), given by his niece, Mrs. Newton Robinson; while the part played in the rector's life by the engaging 'Mrs. Mark', subsequently Lady Dilke, is illustrated by a collection of her letters (MS. 118) presented in 1925 by Lady Thursfield.

The vaster and more varied correspondence of one who was an equally well-known figure in late Victorian Oxford, Sir Henry Acland, was given in 1926 by his son, Mr. H. D. Acland, with limited right of access. Acland was for very many years Librarian of the Radcliffe Library, and has been mentioned on various occasions in these pages. In addition he held the Regius Chair of Medicine from 1858 to 1894. As a Regius Professor he also was a Curator of the Bodleian Library. His extensive correspondence, kept together as the Acland collection, has in it a long series of intimate letters which John Ruskin wrote to him over a space of nearly fifty years, many letters from Dean Liddell of Christ Church, over a hundred from Mr. Gladstone, many from Florence Nightingale on the subject of nursing services, and one delightful little note (familiar from picture postcards) from a child, Prince George of Wales, who subsequently became His Majesty King George V.

One large collection of correspondence is as yet unavailable for readers. T. E. Lawrence was one of the best of English letter-writers. A collection of his letters, written mostly to his mother between the years 1905 and 1934, was presented to the library by his family in 1940 upon condition that it should be reserved for at least another ten years.[2] And it has been supplemented by a gift made by his brother, Dr. A. W. Lawrence, of copies of many more of Lawrence's letters. These typescripts fill seventeen volumes, but will not become accessible until 1970, or be available for publication until the year 2000.

6. MUNIMENTS

Some account has been given, in an earlier chapter (p. 90), of a collection of ecclesiastical records that was deposited in Bodley in

---

[1] MSS. Pattison 1–78, catalogued in *Summary Catalogue of Western Manuscripts*, vol. vi, pp. 372–9.   [2] *Bodleian Library Record*, vol. i, p. 147.

1878. It consisted of the act-books, visitation-books, churchwardens' presentments and other administrative papers, of Oxfordshire and Berkshire archdeaconries, which had till then been stored in the Oxford Archidiaconal Registry. A third archdeaconry, annexed to the diocese of Oxford in 1845, is that of Buckinghamshire. The archives kept in its registry at Aylesbury were transferred to the Bodleian in 1914. They were wider in their scope than the Oxfordshire and Berkshire records already in Bodley, for, in addition to acts of court from 1521, they included terriers of glebe lands, marriage bonds, and the copies of parochial registers that were annually sent in to the diocesan office by incumbents and are known as bishops' transcripts. These last have their genealogical value in so far as they supply the place of missing registers.[1]

Berkshire archdeaconry formed till 1837 part of the diocese of Salisbury: hence it comes that its terriers and bishops' transcripts are still preserved in the diocesan registry of that cathedral city, and that its marriage bonds were 'blitzed' in the Archdeacon's Registry at Reading. The parish register transcripts and terriers for Oxfordshire came to the Bodleian along with a mass of episcopal and archidiaconal papers from the Oxford Diocesan Registry in 1915, and they were followed in 1921 by the marriage bonds for Oxford archdeaconry. Since then, in 1947, some 300 boxes of papers have been transferred from the same office. In addition to the registers of the see from its foundation in 1544, and a vast store of other official records, they include the diocesan marriage bonds and allegations, which have thus joined company with the series of archdeacons' marriage bonds for Oxfordshire and Buckinghamshire. So, as the result of successive transfers, the Bodleian has become the chief repository of the ecclesiastical records of three counties.[2]

Bodley has long been recognized as a suitable place for the custody of college manuscripts. The library has extended its policy by encouraging colleges to deposit in it their earlier archives. Christ Church took the lead by sending in 1927 the medieval deeds and rolls that were in its Treasury. The great bulk of the Christ Church archives consist of the muniments of those monastic houses that were

---

[1] A list of the Buckinghamshire transcripts is given in the *Bodleian Quarterly Record*, vol. iv, pp. 115–18. Those for the years 1604–14 have since been deposited by the Lincoln Diocesan Record Office.

[2] For a more detailed account see I. G. Philip in the *Genealogists' Magazine*, vol. viii (Mar. 1938), pp. 7–9. It is worth recording that in Apr. 1841, the Hebdomadal Board received and declined a request from the Diocesan Registrar, Mr. Robert Morrell, for the use of the Law School on the north side of St. Mary's Church as a depository for his official papers. Hebdomadal Register, 1833–41, p. 240.

suppressed to endow Wolsey's Cardinal College. Chief of these are
the great Oxford Benedictine abbey of Oseney and the Augustinian
priory of St. Frideswide. The Oseney deeds form the originals of
a great number, though by no means all, of the documents entered
in the abbey's chartulary.[1] Those of St. Frideswide are almost wholly
confined to Oxford City properties, for the priory's lands outside
Oxford were not included in the endowment of King Henry VIII's
new foundation.[2] The other main contributors to the series of monastic muniments are the Berkshire priory of Wallingford (a cell of St.
Albans), and the Cluniac priory of Daventry in Northamptonshire,
a house for which many original charters will be found in the Harleian collection at the British Museum. A considerable number of the
deeds of these and other religious houses that were once in Christ
Church Treasury were already in the Bodleian and included in Coxe
and Turner's *Calendar of Charters and Rolls*,[3] for Anthony Wood
had been allowed to carry them off, and so they had passed from the
Ashmolean to Bodley in the Wood collection. As the result of the
deposit made by Christ Church, after the lapse of two and a half centuries they have become reunited with their fellows.

In 1930 Queen's College followed the example that Christ Church
had set in depositing its medieval archives. In addition to the pre-
Reformation title-deeds of College properties lying principally in
Oxfordshire, Berkshire, and Warwickshire, the series includes the
numerous charters of Monk Sherborne priory in Hampshire as well
as those of the Domus Dei or Hospital of St. Julian in Southampton
from whose estate the college derives its main revenue.[4]

Colleges are not the only Oxford bodies that have deposited their
records in Bodley, for the library received in 1934 on deposit those
of one of the churches in the city—St. Peter in the East—with its
very early churchwardens' accounts, commencing in 1444.[5]And the

[1] They have been printed in Salter's edition of the *Cartulary of Oseney Abbey*,
Oxf. Hist. Soc., vols. lxxxix–xci, xcvii, xcviii, ci (1929–36). Denholm Young's *Cartulary
of the Medieval Archives of Christ Church*, Oxf. Hist. Soc., vol. xcii (1931), lists the
original deeds printed in Salter's first two volumes but not those in vols. iii–vi.
[2] Calendared in Denholm Young, op. cit., pp. 21–48, with references to S. R. Wig-
ram's edition of the *Cartulary of St. Frideswide*, Oxf. Hist. Soc., vols. xxviii, xxxi.
[3] In his calendar of Daventry and Wallingford charters Denholm Young has
included (op. cit., pp. 49–156) all those deeds in the Wood collection that were insufficiently calendared in Coxe and Turner.
[4] A typed calendar, in two volumes, of the deeds that form the Queen's College
deposit was made by Mr. Denholm Young and is kept on the open shelves of Duke
Humphrey's Reading-Room. Transcripts of some of the earlier Sherborne and
Southampton deeds are printed in the Historical Manuscripts Commission's Fourth
Report, appendix, pp. 451–5.
[5] *Proc. Soc. Antiquaries*, 2nd ser., vol. x, pp. 25–28.

records of various Oxford trading guilds are now lodged in the library. Those of the dissolved Oxford Barber Surgeons (a corporation within the university) were bought in 1890 from the family of its last master.[1] In 1925 the heirs of Mrs. Frederick Morrell of Black Hall presented the records of the Oxford Company of Cordwainers, the sixteenth-century accounts and other books of the Tailors' Company, and the later annual accounts of the Mercers and Woollen Drapers.[2] The earlier accounts of the last-mentioned company were deposited by its officers in 1942.

Opportunities have been taken, as they arose, of buying up court rolls of neighbouring manors. So between 1932 and 1936 the library obtained the court rolls of Headington (13th–17th centuries), Cumnor (1419–1817), and Beckley (1580–1662). In 1927 Sir George Dashwood had deposited on loan a good series of court rolls for Kirtlington from 1500,[3] together with a large number of deeds and documents relating to that estate. The court rolls of Dinton, Bucks., beginning in 1383, were bought for the library in 1926.

Many deeds have come in of other Buckinghamshire properties. The principal estate held by the Radcliffe Trustees is that of Wolverton. Its title-deeds were placed in 1755 in a little closet opening off the main staircase of the Radcliffe Camera, which served as an evidence room, and here they suffered much from damp and want of ventilation, though, as the Trustees' solicitor observed, 'it fortunately happens that they are all of very ancient dates'.[4] When the building was handed over to the university, the deeds were moved to the Radcliffe Observatory; and they were eventually, in 1928, deposited by the Trustees in the Bodleian Library. They go back to the twelfth century and include the papers of the Longueville family. Other Buckinghamshire charters, mainly of the thirteenth century, were bought in 1941 from Hartwell Hall; and next year the library purchased from Earl Manvers's collection at Thoresby Park about 400 deeds of the thirteenth and following centuries relating to Beaconsfield and other properties in the county.[5]

There was also bought from Earl Manvers a field-map with terrier made in 1635 of the Nottinghamshire village of Laxton. The map has attained some celebrity, for it is not merely unique in its amount of

---

[1] They are listed as nos. 31110–27, in the *Summary Catalogue of Western Manuscripts*, vol. vi, pp. 19–21.

[2] *Bodleian Quarterly Record*, vol. iv, pp. 222–4.

[3] Specimen extracts are printed op. cit., vol. v, pp. 179–88.

[4] Radcliffe Trustees' minutes, 22 Jan. 1755; 6 June 1817.

[5] A typescript calendar is in the Old Reading-Room. The remainder of Lord Manvers's deeds were bought for the British Museum.

detail, but Laxton is the only village in England that has retained its old open-field system to the present day.[1] Another historically interesting map of about the same date is that made by the Dutch military engineer, Sir Bernard de Gomme, in 1644, showing the line of fortifications thrown up during the Civil War round Royalist Oxford.[2]

[1] See Orwin's *Open Fields*, 1938, pp. 112–19, &c., with its accompanying diagrams.
[2] Reproduced and described in *Oxoniensia*, vol. i, pp. 161–72.

Chapter XVIII
Orientalia, Art Collections, Manuscript Catalogues

Section I
ORIENTALIA

1. NEAR AND MIDDLE EAST

I⊤ has been mentioned in an earlier chapter (p. 214) that *Demotic*, the popular form of speech current in Egypt for 1,000 years from the seventh century B.C., was as yet unrepresented in the Bodleian save by a few scraps of papyrus. The defect was in part made good in 1918, when 1,000 fragments of burnt papyri, found by Flinders Petrie in 1884 at Tanis, were given by the Egypt Exploration Fund. They were chiefly hieroglyphic, Demotic, and Greek, and among them was a long hieroglyphic roll which proved to be a kind of religious gazetteer, giving town-names and lists of feasts and sanctuaries. It has come on this account to be known as 'the geographical papyrus'.[1] A Demotic papyrus given by Professor Griffith in 1922 (MS. Egypt a. 40) deserves mention because of its early date: it is a contract of marriage made in 527–526 B.C. Demotic and Greek are both alike represented in a gift made by Dr. Grafton Milne in 1919 of thirty-seven mummy labels from Panopolis and seven inscribed wooden tablets dating from 157 to 100 B.C.[2]

Papyrus was not the only common writing-material in use in Ancient Egypt. A cheaper substitute existed in the pottery-sherds that are termed *ostraca*, and these were found useful for casual notes that were not intended for permanent record. The first specimens to enter the library came in 1889. Some years later, in 1906, the Bodleian received, through Dr. Grafton Milne, some thirty Greek ostraca from Oxyrhynchus; and in 1907 and at subsequent dates many more, both in Greek and Demotic, from the more prolific site of Luxor or the Egyptian Thebes. These were in the main receipts and accounts of the Ptolemaic and Roman periods.[3] The same donor gave subse-

---

[1] Published with lithograph facsimile by Flinders Petrie for the Egypt Exploration Fund in *Two Hieroglyphic Papyri from Tanis*, 1889.

[2] The tablets have been published in the *Bodleian Quarterly Record*, vol. ii, pp. 314–18.

[3] The Greek, and a selection of the Demotic, ostraca are published in Grafton Milne's *Theban Ostraca* (Oxford, 1913).

quently, in 1921, eighty-four Demotic ostraca from another site, that of Dendereh; and sixty-four Coptic ostraca came in 1939 by gift from Dr. W. E. Crum.

A far larger donation, made in 1914 by Professor Sayce, made the Bodleian collection of ostraca the largest in the world. The ostraca which he then presented had been garnered by him while wintering at Karnak in 1884–6. They were upwards of 4,000 in number, and were chiefly tax-collectors' receipts. Most were in Greek, a considerable number were in Demotic, a few in Coptic, and there was a sprinkling of Arabic. In 1916 the total Bodleian collection of ostraca was reckoned to include 1,328 Egyptian, 2,802 Greek, 203 Coptic, and 16 Arabic specimens,[1] and to this it received further additions. A start was made in publishing a corpus of *Greek Ostraca in the Bodleian Library* in 1930, when Mr. J. G. Tait published his first volume for the Egypt Exploration Fund, including in it all of the Ptolemaic period except those already described in Milne's *Theban Ostraca* and in Wilcken's *Urkunden der Ptolemäerzeit*, Bodleian ostraca of the Roman and Byzantine ages being reserved for a second volume.

Ostraca, however, require museum treatment and, though important for palaeography, they are better fitted to be regarded as museum objects than to be shelved in a library with manuscripts and rolls. On that ground it was decided, shortly before the War, that the whole library collection of ostraca and inscribed tablets should be transferred to the Ashmolean Museum.[2]

The Ashmolean has also become the main repository of a similar type of document, the *cuneiform* inscriptions on baked clay tablets that came from the Euphrates valley. Yet the Bodleian has continued to add to the collection begun by Nicholson, notably through gifts made by Dr. Stephen Langdon and Mr. H. Weld Blundell. From the former the library received a bilingual tablet, dated 80 B.C., on which an epic poem is inscribed in Sumerian and Semitic. Mr. Blundell presented a fine barrel-shaped cylinder recording King Nabonidus's restoration of the temple of the Moon-God at Ur of the Chaldees in 547 B.C. The Neo-Babylonian tablets in Bodley have been catalogued by the late Dr. Campbell Thompson.[3]

An almost equally remote antiquity attaches to the contents of the post-bag of Arsham, Persian Governor of Egypt under King Darius, which the library contracted to buy in 1944. They consist of fifteen letters, written on leather in *Aramaic* in 411 B.C. or a year or two

---

[1] *Bodleian Quarterly Record*, vol. i, pp. 81, 352.   [2] Decree of 13 June 1939.
[3] *A Catalogue of the Late Babylonian Tablets in the Bodleian Library*, 1927.

later, relating to the management of domain lands in Egypt. At the time of purchase, war conditions made delivery uncertain; but the documents, with their post-bag, reached Oxford safely as soon as the war was over. So the Bodleian acquired the only known original official documents of the Achaemenid Empire.[1]

Additions have continued to be made to the Bodleian collection of *Hebrew* printed books,[2] the riches of which may be gauged by the fact that, out of about one hundred known dated Hebrew incunabula, Bodley possessed by 1915 sixty-seven, a proportion exceeded only by the British Museum.[3] Steinschneider's learned though cumbrous catalogue served as their guide, but its defects were very apparent, and it was resolved in 1916 that the work should be undertaken afresh. Cowley's *Concise Catalogue of the Hebrew Printed Books in the Bodleian Library*, begun in that year, was completed and published in 1929.

Although there has been as yet no further publication of catalogues of Oriental manuscript collections, Dr. P. E. Kahle has prepared one of the Bruce collection and all other *Arabic* manuscripts previously undescribed. These last include two Korans written in Kufic characters of the late tenth or eleventh century, the one presented by the Friends of the Bodleian, the other by Major Robert Anderson and his brother. An Arabic translation of part of the Materia Medica of Dioscorides, dated A.D. 1239 and illustrated by numerous coloured drawings of plants, was left to the library by Sir William Osler under the terms of his will.

Thanks to the donations made by Sir Oliver Wardrop, the Bodleian now possesses the most important collection of *Georgian* manuscripts to be found in Europe.[4] The Wardrop donation is rich in material for the ecclesiastical, and still more for the secular, history of Georgia. Most of the Wardrop manuscripts are of the eighteenth century, but the Bodleian Georgian collection contains some that are much older. In addition to the early volume of lives of saints mentioned in a previous chapter (p. 217), it possesses a palimpsest leaf, from the Cairo Geniza, of a codex of the Prophet Jeremiah that dates from the seventh or eighth century.[5]

[1] Professor Driver in *Bodleian Library Record*, vol. ii, pp. 123–4.
[2] e.g. by the purchase of a unique Hebrew Pentateuch (Venice, 1527); of Tissardus's Hebrew grammar (Paris, 1508), the first Hebrew book printed in France; and of Brythner's *Manipulus messis magnae* (London, 1638), one of the earliest specimens of Hebrew printing in England, and of which only one other copy is recorded.
[3] *Bodleian Quarterly Record*, vol. i, p. 204.
[4] It has been described by the Archimandrite Gregory Peradze in an article on Georgian manuscripts in England; *Georgica*, vol. i (1935), pp. 84–87.
[5] Robert Blake in the *Harvard Theological Review*, vol. xxv (1932), pp. 225 et seq.

The number of *Persian* and *Turkish* manuscripts has been increased through a co-operative purchase of manuscripts from Tiflis made in 1920 in conjunction with the British Museum and the School of Oriental Studies, and through the transfer of a collection of eighty-four manuscripts bequeathed in 1922 to the Indian Institute by Mr. E. H. Whinfield, a Persian scholar and translator of the immortal Omar.

2. INDIA AND THE FAR EAST

The various manuscript collections that were the property of the Indian Institute have now been taken over by the Oriental department of the Bodleian. The chief of them is that which was given in 1883 to the Institute by its founder and first Keeper, Sir Monier Monier-Williams. This includes Persian, Turkish, and Arabic manuscripts, but the bulk are *Sanskrit* or in other Indian languages. They were collected by their donor upon several journeys which he made to India for the purpose of obtaining material for his new foundation. His interests were not, like those of Max Müller, in the Vedas, but lay in classical Sanskrit. The manuscripts which he collected comprise a considerable number of the sacred poems called Tantras, and a valuable series of Jaina books in Prākrit which Sir Monier procured in 1877–8 through Professor Georg Bühler. His gift also contains what is probably the most complete collection in existence of Indian paintings of the Kālighāt school which flourished in the nineteenth century in Bengal.[1]

In addition to manuscripts, Monier-Williams endowed the Institute with Oriental printed books to the number of about 3,000. A library given in 1885 by the Rev. S. C. Malan[2] was larger in size but more varied in character, and the non-Oriental books that were in it were disposed of when the Institute was taken over by the Bodleian in 1928. A printed catalogue of the Institute's Sanskrit and Prākrit manuscripts was published in 1903:[3] it includes those in the Monier-Williams and Malan collections and a few derived from other sources.

Yet one more collection of Sanskrit manuscripts, 370 in number, was deposited in the Institute on loan in 1911 by Sir Aurel Stein and was bequeathed by him when he died in 1943. The manuscripts came from Kashmir, having been collected by Stein chiefly at Srinagar

---

[1] H. J. Stooke, 'Kālighāt Paintings in Oxford', *Indian Art and Letters*, N.S., vol. xx (1946), pp. 71–73.

[2] Correspondence relating to the Malan gift is printed in A. N. Malan's *Life of Solomon Caesar Malan, D.D.*, 1897, pp. 341 seq.

[3] A. B. Keith, *Catalogue of the Sanskrit and Prākrit MSS. in the Indian Institute Library*.

between 1885 and 1905.[1] And upon his death there came also to the library a mass of diaries and notebooks which Sir Aurel kept with meticulous accuracy on his travels of exploration in Central Asia.

The finds of early *Chinese* literature which Stein made in the course of those journeys have gone to the British Museum, but the Bodleian Chinese collection has been enriched from other sources. Starting from small beginnings, it was increased, both in size and value, by a purchase of over 600 works which were bought in 1882 from Mr. Alexander Wylie for £110. No further addition of note was made until 1913, when Mr. (afterwards Sir Edmund) Backhouse, a gentleman long resident in Pekin, made the first of a number of considerable donations. The Curators showed their appreciation of the value of his gifts by contributing £1,840 towards the cost of purchase and transit, and by reflooring and refurnishing the old School of Natural Philosophy in 1925 as a Chinese Room, after it had been vacated by the Hope engraved portraits.

Backhouse was a scholar of repute, a collector of Ming editions of which the Bodleian now possesses over 200. Of editions printed under the earlier Sung dynasty the library has as yet got no undoubted example. One of the most notable works acquired in the Backhouse collection is a copy of a large-paper Palace edition of the vast encyclopaedia named *T'u Shu Chi Ch'êng*, published in lithograph at Pekin in 1726 in 5,000 volumes, of which the Bodleian copy is the only complete set still in existence.

Taken as a whole, the Chinese collection in Bodley[2] is well representative of the works contained in the Confucian canon, and it has been decided to continue to specialize in religion and philosophy. With that end in view, the library purchased in 1938, with the help of a contribution made by Mr. and Mrs. H. N. Spalding, the Tokyo edition of the Chinese version of the Buddhist Tripitaka. The literature of the neighbouring state of Korea has come to be represented through a gift made in 1927 by the bishop of that country, the Right Rev. Mark Napier Trollope. The books he gave include a dynastic history of Korea in twenty-five volumes and a fifty-volume encyclopaedia.

[1] They have been catalogued by G. L. M. Clauson in the *Journal of the Royal Asiatic Society*, 1912, pp. 587–627.

[2] A report on the Bodleian Chinese collection, made by a member of the staff of the National Library at Peiping, is printed in the *Bodleian Quarterly Record*, vol. viii, pp. 228–31. See also the account given of the first Backhouse donation in *The Times* for 2 Dec. 1913.

Section II
ART COLLECTIONS

The Bodleian has come to be very rich in topographical prints and drawings of Oxford and the neighbourhood. It already possessed a basis for its collection in Richard Gough's donation. In more recent times the foundations for the study of Oxford topography were systematically laid by Herbert Hurst, whose topographical collections,[1] including his drawings of old buildings in and near Oxford, were presented by his family in 1913. Mr. Percy Manning, whose early death in 1917 was a marked loss to local history and archaeology, left to Bodley eighty-seven portfolios of local engravings and drawings as well as many books and manuscript gatherings relating to the antiquities and social history of Oxford and Oxfordshire. His collection includes (MS. Top. Oxon. b. 93) thirty drawings by Malchair (d. 1800) and twenty-three made by Nattes in 1804. Three large volumes (MSS. Top. Oxon. b. 89–91) of topographical drawings by the nineteenth-century artist Joseph Fisher and others, were bought in 1919. Five other large folios (MSS. Top. Oxon. a. 35–39) of pencil drawings, chiefly by Fisher and Pugin, but also containing architectural drawings and plans of Blenheim by Vanbrugh, were bought in the Rev. B. W. Bradford's sale at Sotheby's in 1928, and constitute a collection of which the nucleus had been formed by William Upcott. The library bought largely in 1925 at the sale of Mrs. Frederick Morrell of Black Hall, and secured, in addition to much manuscript material relating chiefly to the city of Oxford, the original drawing for one of the two engravings which Loggan made of the interior of the Bodleian in 1675, and drawings of old houses in High Street by William Turner (MS. Top. Oxon. a. 31), as well as an extra-illustrated copy of Anthony Wood's *City of Oxford* formed by the Oxford antiquary, Alderman William Fletcher.[2] Those excellent artists of the first half of the nineteenth century, F. Mackenzie and the Bucklers, are also well represented by acquisitions made at various dates, notably through purchases made by the Friends in 1929 of 141 sepia drawings (MSS. Don. a. 2, 3) made of houses in Oxford in the eighteen-twenties by J. C. Buckler (many of whose pencil-sketches are in the British Museum), and of a large-paper copy of Joseph Skelton's *Antiquities of Oxfordshire* (1823) with a set of proof engravings and 111 of the original drawings by Skelton and Mackenzie (Don. b. 2, 3).

[1] Catalogued in *Summary Catalogue of Western Manuscripts*, vol. vi, pp. 396–403 (nos. 36022–55).

[2] MSS. Top. Oxon. c. 299–300. Fletcher had himself presented the library in 1818 with his extra-illustrated copy of Wood's *University and Colleges* (MSS. Top. Oxon. c. 14–20).

A great number of portraits and caricatures, illustrative of English history from 1603 to about 1830, came to the library in 1936 as part of the Firth collection. They fill twenty-four large folio volumes, and consist of engraved portraits and historical prints of the Stuart period, and a fine series of satirical prints, chiefly political, of the eighteenth and early nineteenth centuries. These last supplement the caricatures of the Napoleonic period which came in the Curzon collection.

It is natural, however, for prints and drawings that are primarily of artistic value to be housed in the Fine Arts department of the Ashmolean Museum. The Hope collection of engraved portraits, which had long occupied coveted space on Bodleian premises, was at length transferred to the Ashmolean in 1924 and its library incorporated in that of the department of Fine Arts. The bulk of Francis Douce's prints had gone there long before, and a further exchange of Douce prints was made between the Bodleian and the Ashmolean in 1915. Twelve volumes of drawings and prints which James Gibbs collected and left to the Radcliffe Library were deposited in the Ashmolean in 1925 upon revocable loan. An original design by Albrecht Dürer, discovered in another of Gibbs's volumes, was transferred by the Bodleian Curators to the Ashmolean in 1938. And in 1943 the decision was taken to transfer to the new print-room of the Museum the whole of the magnificent Sutherland collection of engravings.

Similar reasons have prompted the transfer to the Ashmolean of various busts which formerly adorned the Picture Gallery—Edward Pierce's bust of Sir Christopher Wren, Rysbrack's bust of the first Duke of Marlborough, and Woolner's bust of Mr. Gladstone, while others have gone to the Examination Schools. The plaster casts of classical statuary that were once in the Camera reading-room have joined the university collection of casts in the Ashmolean or have been given to Stowe School, and the architectural models from the Picture Gallery have been sent to the School of Architecture in London University.

On the other hand, the Bodleian has kept its portrait collection, adding to it by the gift, from subscribers, of the Holton Park portrait of Oliver Cromwell; the presentation, by the artist, of Laszlo's portrait of Pope Pius XI (who was a librarian before he was a pope); the bequest of another portrait by Laszlo, that of the botanist, G. C. Druce; the deposit, by the Radcliffe Trustees, of Kneller's full-length portrait of Dr. John Radcliffe; and the gift, through subscribers, of a portrait of the present writer by Augustus John. This last hangs in the Curators' Room, along with the portraits of earlier librarians.

Transfers have also been made from time to time to the Ashmolean department of Antiquities, notably in 1927, when Dr. Richard Rawlinson's collection of seal matrices was transferred thither upon revocable loan. The great majority of the matrices are of Italian seals, having been acquired by Rawlinson from a collection made by G. A. Lorenzani in the seventeenth century.[1] Other objects from the Rawlinson donation, including his clock and an ancient bronze vessel with Hebrew inscription, were sent to the Ashmolean in 1932, along with a painted set of Elizabethan fruit trenchers and many miscellaneous antiquities. At the same time a collection of moss agates from the Elliott collection and a fossil egg of the struthiolithus, a prehistoric bird that once inhabited northern China, found a more suitable home in the University Museum.

The long-drawn dispute over the Bodleian coin collection has at length been ended. Within a year of Nicholson's death the Curators agreed to send their coins to the Ashmolean. Money to endow a properly qualified keeper was not then forthcoming. But a little later, under the impulse of Dr. Heberden, and through the benefaction of his college of Brasenose, means were found to establish and endow the Heberden coin-room in the Ashmolean, to which the Bodleian coins were in 1920 transferred.

Section III
MANUSCRIPT CATALOGUES AND REPRODUCTIONS

When Madan became Librarian in 1912, he had perforce to lay aside the work upon the *Summary Catalogue of Western Manuscripts* upon which he had so successfully laboured for more than thirty years. All Western manuscripts acquired since the appearance of Bernard's great *Catalogus* of 1697 were now described in print, and the task of recataloguing seventeenth-century accessions had not merely been taken in hand but was almost half done. It was proposed that, when that work was accomplished, it should be issued as volume II of the *Summary Catalogue*, volume I being reserved for a general introduction and conspectus of pressmarks. The scale of cataloguing was much fuller than that which had been adopted by Bernard; so volume II had eventually to be divided into two parts, of which the first was seen through the press by the present writer in 1922. The second part, which is of composite authorship,[2] followed in 1937.

[1] A full report upon the collection, made by Dr. F. P. Barnard, is printed in the *Bodleian Quarterly Record*, vol. vi, pp. 132–8.
[2] In this volume the catalogue of the *E. Mus.* collection is almost wholly the work

The cataloguing of accessions was continued by the present writer. A fascicule containing those for 1890–1904 had appeared in 1906, and an entire volume, numbered VI, covering the years 1890–1915, was eventually issued in 1924. It still remained to carry on the cataloguing of current accessions, to prepare comparative tables of press-marks, and to print the index. Until publication is undertaken, it is necessary for readers to consult the material available for them at the entry to Duke Humphrey's Library.

When the battle was being fought out between the advocates of a summary catalogue and those who favoured a continuance of the more detailed quarto catalogues, Madan, as we have seen (p. 206), expressed the view that any future quarto catalogues should deal with subjects rather than with manuscript collections. Rules for class-catalogues were approved by the Curators in 1937, and a catalogue, on those lines, of Bodleian canon and civil law manuscripts was begun by Professor Hermann Kantorowicz but suspended by his death. Another unfinished cataloguing venture was the *Calendar of Clarendon State Papers*, of which three volumes had been published in 1869–76. Macray had brought it down to the end of the year 1656. With the help of a donation made for that purpose in 1913 by Mr. Vernon Watney, a fourth volume, in which Mr. F. J. Routledge revised Macray's written slips, was published in 1932. It continues the calendar to the eve of the Restoration. Papers of later date are fewer in number and are reserved for a final volume.

Various card indexes have been taken in hand and are available to library readers. They include an index to the extensive literary correspondence of the early eighteenth century contained in the Rawlinson and Ballard collections; a classified index to all Oxford topographical prints and drawings that are in the library; and an index to the first lines of English verse in Bodleian manuscripts. This last has been carried out by post-graduate students and members of the library staff under the direction of Mr. Percy Simpson.

The issue of reproductions of Bodleian manuscripts was a project which Nicholson had much at heart. Facsimiles of some important manuscripts were published by outside agencies during his librarianship.[1] Others of equal or greater renown have since followed, the Roxburghe Club having issued reproductions of the Douce Apoca-

of Madan; the Casaubon and Hatton collections and MSS. Dodsworth 1–61 are by Craster; the remainder is the work of Mr. N. Denholm Young.

[1] They include the 'Miracles de Notre Dame' for the Roxburghe Club in 1885, Charles II's Council Notes for the same society in 1896, Queen Margaret's Gospels in 1896, the Clarke Plato in 1898, Eusebius's Chronicle in 1905, and the Bible moralisée in 1911. See *Bodleian Quarterly Record*, vol. vii, pp. 340, 428.

lypse, the Herbal of Apuleius, the famous manuscript of the Chanson de Roland, and selected plates from the Ormesby Psalter and the Bromholm Psalter in the Ashmolean collection. A sumptuous facsimile edition of the Caedmon manuscript was published at the expense of the British Academy in 1927. Other manuscripts that have been reproduced in their entirety are the Irish Annals of Innisfallen and the Mexican Mendoza Codex.

The library has also had its official publications. In 1929, upon the occasion of the fourteenth centenary of the abbey of Monte Cassino, the Curators published, with a detailed description by Dr. Lowe, four plates from the Hatton manuscript of the Regula Benedicti, the most ancient book in Bodley that can definitely be said to have been produced in this island. And four years later, with the help of a donation of £1,000 from an anonymous Friend of the Bodleian, they published at the Clarendon Press a facsimile of the library's best-known illuminated manuscript, the Romance of Alexander. The edition is furnished with a description of the manuscript and its illuminations by Dr. M. R. James, and with four coloured plates, the gift of private donors.

The issue of a library journal which should be devoted in part at least to the publication of Bodleian manuscripts had been canvassed for the best part of a hundred years before the first number of the *Bodleian Quarterly Record* appeared in April 1914. The new magazine had for its primary objects the printing of lists of the library's chief accessions, the publication of notes on current events and discoveries made within the library, and the printing of documents and other essays. The *B.Q.R.*, to give it its familiar title, owes its origin, next to Mr. Madan, to Sir William Osler, for it was Osler's financial help that carried it through its earlier stages. It had its predecessors in other libraries, notably in the *John Rylands Library Bulletin*. It has had its imitators, as in the *Harvard Library Notes* (1920), precursor of the *Harvard Library Bulletin*; in the *British Museum Quarterly* (1926), and the *Huntington Library Bulletin* (1931). And although it no longer exists in its original form (for even before the Second World War its production was found to involve the library in an annual loss), it has been replaced, since 1938, by the *Bodleian Library Record*, which appears at less frequent intervals, but fully keeps up the standard of its articles.[1]

---

[1] Other library publications include a series of handbooks for the use of staff and readers, particulars of which will be found in the *Bodleian Library Record*, vol. i, pp. 78–80.

Chapter XIX

Library Extension (Part I)

1. ALTERNATIVE COURSES

In 1900 the Bodleian Curators had informed Council that the underground bookstore, which they were planning to make in the Radcliffe Square and which was eventually completed in 1912, would provide for library needs for nearly sixty years. Nicholson was even more hopeful and hailed the scheme of underground storage as one that would solve for ever the problem of housing modern accessions. When, at some future date, the underground bookstore was full, another chamber could be made on the farther side of the Camera. The possibilities of excavation were limitless.

The new bookstore was designed to receive rolling bookcases on both its floors. Yet the system of solid packing, though economic of space, was not found really satisfactory. Capacity was gained at the cost of accessibility. And so it came that only the upper deck was ever filled with rolling stack. When the lower deck was fitted up in 1923 to receive the foreign periodicals which had been previously kept in a congested room of the Bodleian quadrangle, it was furnished in the ordinary way, with ranges of fixed stack separated by gangways.

The abandonment of rolling stack greatly reduced the bookstore's expectation of life. Cowley calculated at the time that the lower floor would accommodate all periodicals for about twenty years, and that the floor above, with the Camera basement, could cope with accessions until about 1940. In 1925 he revised the statement that he had made two years earlier. The Old Library building was practically full already, and the underground chamber would only suffice for the normal accessions of another ten years. The Curators hastened to forward their librarian's memorandum to Council, informing that body that the time was rapidly approaching when extension on a very great scale would be necessary.

From the discussions that followed during the next few months there emerged five alternative proposals for providing more bookspace. These were clearly set out in a pamphlet drawn up by one of the Curators, Sir Michael Sadler, and circulated to members of Congregation in the summer term of 1926.

First, there were those who thought that the sole function of a university library is to serve what are called the higher studies, and that the Bodleian had the remedy in its own hands—that it could contract its future intake and discard its past accessions and be none the worse for it. The Curators set up a committee to go into the question and received a report that favoured both methods of relieving congestion —the limitation of intake and the steady discarding of publications which could under no circumstances advance knowledge.[1] Yet it was apparent even from the first that the relief that could be gained in this way was extremely small, and that it afforded no solution to the library problem.

Then there was what may be called the orthodox solution, propounded in the past by Nicholson and still at that time advocated by Madan.[2] This was to continue the system of underground chambers. But, apart from other natural drawbacks, there was the risk that excavation would imperil the foundations of surrounding buildings. Architectural advice was taken on the question whether an underground bookstore could be constructed with safety between the Camera and St. Mary's, and the answer given was unfavourable.

The third course, favoured initially by a committee of Council, was to put up a building outside Oxford, designed to accommodate about half a million volumes and capable of indefinite expansion. The Bodleian might follow the example set by the British Museum in 1905 and send to such a building its files of newspapers. Thither might also go all runs of old directories and sets of periodicals that were not frequently wanted. This idea was no novelty. As far back as 1881 the Rev. E. S. Foulkes, Vicar of the University Church of St. Mary's, had urged on the Curators that 'some spot in the suburbs where land is still cheap should be selected as the site of a repository for the mass of ephemeral publications'.[3] Bywater in 1894 had suggested to his colleagues on the Curatorial Board the building of a bookstore 'for books which have merely to be kept and are not likely to be used'.[4] And the erection of a book-stack within 3 miles of Oxford had been advocated by members of Congregation in 1909 as an alternative to the construction of the underground bookstore.

Here at least was a plan that merited consideration. No site for a building capable of indefinite expansion could be found in the immediate vicinity of the Bodleian. On the other hand, the university had undeveloped land in the suburbs at Wolvercote. The principle of

[1] Statutory power was eventually taken in 1938 to eliminate from the library material of no literary or artistic value or of an ephemeral nature, and is used with circumspection.
[2] In a pamphlet entitled *The Ideal Bodleian*, 1928.
[3] Letter of 13 July 1881 filed with Curators' minutes.
[4] Curators' minutes, 1 Dec. 1894, as noted by Rev. H. A. Wilson.

providing a site for a repository of little-wanted books was approved by Congregation,[1] and eventually five acres on University Press property was definitely assigned for the purposes of a future Bodleian repository.[2] It was left to the future to decide on what kind of books are so little wanted that they could be safely sent to a distance.

From the outset, however, it was clear that even if a suburban store-house were erected, there must still be some very considerable extension of the central premises. Otherwise, as Mr. Scholfield, the Librarian of the Cambridge University Library, pithily expressed it in a letter which he wrote to Cowley: 'Soon you would find that you are driven to putting in your annexe books that *are* wanted. In another half-century your annexe will be as big as Bodley itself. But, long before that, you will have virtually two libraries. Make two libraries, and you will halve the usefulness of Bodley while doubling its cost.'

One seemed therefore to be thrown back upon some enlargement of the Bodleian building. Two methods were reconsidered that had been proposed in the eighteen-fifties. One was the plan that Wellesley had originated and Galton and Jackson worked out for filling the Old Schools with modern stack. Its adoption would have provided book-space but have made it impossible to find additional reading-rooms. The other was a scheme for following the Panizzi model and roofing over the quadrangle. Gilbert Scott had rejected this in 1855, and it found little support.

More weight attached to proposals for a new book-stack on ground lying north of the Bodleian, the direction in which Scott had told the Curators that the library must inevitably expand. With library extension in view, he had advised the university to obtain full possession of the Clarendon Building. It was occupied then, as it still is today, by university offices for which the building was not really suitable. If new offices could be erected on the opposite side of Broad Street, then, Cowley now suggested, the Clarendon Building might be gutted and a modern book-stack, capable of holding a million octavo volumes, could be built up within its walls; and at some future date this could be linked up with the Bodleian by a wing fronting Catte Street.

Already, however, a growing number of the younger Oxford tutors were becoming impressed with the advantages that were to be had in America, where, in libraries built on modern lines and lit

---

[1] By decree of 12 Mar. 1929 and resolution of 26 May 1931.
[2] The lines on which a repository might be constructed, with an estimate of cost, form the subject of a report made to the Curators on 21 Jan. 1932.

throughout with electric light, readers had access to the shelves and could work in or near the stack. These advantages, it was thought, were essential for the proper prosecution of modern studies, and could only be had in a new library; and the place best fitted for a new Bodleian was the west side of the University Parks. The old proposal, which had been turned down in 1875 and since then completely forgotten, was up before the university once more. Its execution was likely to cost half a million pounds.

2. SCHEME A AND SCHEME B

A month after the issue of the pamphlet in which these alternative schemes were adumbrated, Sadler received a message from an American citizen that he was prepared to consider offering a gift of half a million for the purpose of a new library building. Armed with this message, Sadler pressed the Curators to appoint a committee to consider and recommend a site. The committee, of which he was chairman, got to work very rapidly and produced a report which was approved by the Curators four weeks later (4 December 1926). It recommended that the old Bodleian building should be retained as an administrative centre, but that it should be modernized by the installation of electric light, the provision of a large work-room for library staff, and the redistribution of so much of its contents as would permit the creation of additional reading-rooms equipped as special libraries, with open shelves accessible to readers. It rejected Cowley's proposal for converting the Clarendon Building into book-stack, and proposed instead that a new Bodleian building should be constructed on the north side of Broad Street, with an east front facing Parks Road. Details of the scheme, which also included the provision of a site for an annexe or repository outside of Oxford, and the revision and printing of the library catalogue, were communicated to the potential donor. It soon became generally known that he was Mr. J. D. Rockefeller.

It is curious to find that, so far back as 1777, an old Rector of Lincoln College, Edward Tatham, had picked upon what now came to be known as the Broad Street site as eminently suitable for a library building. He regretted, in fact, that the Radcliffe Camera had not been built upon it.[1] In 1862 a committee of Council had selected it as the most desirable position for new Examination Schools; and a little later, in 1874, after another site had been secured for the Schools, the advocates of a new library proposed that it should be constructed on the area between Trinity gate and Trinity gardens. That solution

[1] Tatham, *Oxonia explicata et ornata*, 1777 ed., p. 22.

had been rejected at the time, partly because the properties suggested were not as yet in the university's hands; but certain of them had since been bought with money supplied in 1909 by the Trustees of the University Endowment Fund.

The scheme of library extension adopted by the Curators at the end of 1926 was very similar, in general outline, to the one that was finally approved by the university five years later. Time was pressing, for Cowley had warned his Curators that, after 1935, 'chaos will reign in the Library'. Yet there was hesitation and delay. A scheme had been proposed, but opinions still differed as to its merits. The university remained uncommitted. Cowley still clung to his plan for a new wing to the Bodleian and the absorption of the Clarendon Building, while admitting that a large book-stack might ultimately be built in Broad Street. He was averse to any larger scheme. The problem, in his view, was one of book-storage. He was due for retirement at the end of July 1927, but, at the same meeting at which the Curators approved the proposals of Sadler's committee, they resolved that he should retain office for another five years. Meanwhile the movement in favour of a much larger and bolder plan was gathering strength. The growing demand that the library should be made more generally useful by an extension of shelf-access seemed to many to be incapable of satisfaction except by building a new library, and this was the course to which Sadler himself inclined.

It was high time that the university should be invited to make its choice between rival plans. So eventually, after much discussion by the Curators and the Hebdomadal Council, two alternative resolutions were framed for submission to Congregation. One, which was styled Scheme A, proposed the building of a new university library, which should include rooms for advanced study and research as well as for the administrative work of the library. The other, named Scheme B, was for a bookstore which should be designed to provide some access for approved readers, and which should be built on what had now come to be called the Broad Street site.

Scheme B was supported by the majority of the Curators and of Hebdomadal Council. The Broad Street site had in its favour the centrality of its position. Those who took the other view and preferred Scheme A argued that, although the designated area in Broad Street was central, it was an island site incapable of expansion. They expressed doubts as to whether it was large enough to allow shelf-access or give space for special rooms for study, and they contended that theirs was the only scheme that provided the concentration that was essential for efficient and economic management. So the Bodleian controversy, as it was called, raged with some fury for a number of months, until at length, on 8 May 1928, both schemes were put before Congregation and both were rejected—Scheme A by a large, and Scheme B by a small, majority.

3. A LIBRARY COMMISSION

The rejection of the two rival schemes led to the appointment of a joint committee of the Curators and of Council, and to the eventual production of a majority report which advocated the building of a repository outside Oxford, the exclusion of ephemeral publications, and the erection of a building in Broad Street. A minority protested that these measures gave even less than had been proposed in Scheme B. Even so, they said, the scheme would admittedly require a large benefaction, but it would be unlikely (as subsequent events proved) to attract a benefactor if it became known that the university had not taken steps to collect and examine information about the solution of library problems elsewhere. They therefore pressed for an inquiry into the conditions maintaining in other libraries, with special reference to the needs of universities.

On 12 March 1929 Congregation accepted, without a division, a decree empowering the University Chest to receive donations towards the cost of carrying out library extension on the lines proposed in the majority report. But it was widely known, outside Oxford as well as in it, that the official project had only been adopted after a larger plan had been rejected, and that it had been accepted with reluctance by those who felt it fell short of an ideal solution. Negotiations that were carried on during the summer between Lord Grey of Fallodon as Chancellor of the University and representatives of the Rockefeller Foundation did in fact disclose the improbability of financial aid being forthcoming for a scheme arrived at without official inquiries into the methods of equipment of recently constructed university libraries. A difficult situation was overcome by an offer, made on behalf of the Rockefeller Foundation, to meet the expense of any commission that might be appointed to visit modern university libraries. Representatives of the university and of Bodley were informed of the offer at a memorable conference over which the Chancellor presided on 13 October.

So it came about that on 4 March of the following year (1930) a decree was passed accepting the Rockefeller Foundation's offer and appointing a Commission 'to visit modern University Libraries in Europe and America; to report to the University upon the organization, planning, equipment and methods of administration of such

Libraries; and generally to advise the University, upon the basis of their investigations, as to the best method of securing such library provision at Oxford as shall be abreast of modern requirements'. The Commission, of which Sir Henry Miers was appointed chairman, set to work at once, and, after visiting libraries on the Continent and in the United States, produced a lengthy report which was printed under the title *Library Provision in Oxford* and circulated to members of Congregation in March 1931.

After reviewing the whole situation *de novo*, the Commission decided against the construction of a complete new library. It would entail the abandonment of the Bodleian as a home for research, and to abandon that historic building 'would indeed be "a pillage of man's ancient heart"'. They recommended the erection of a supplementary building on more modern lines in Broad Street, and to that extent their plan bore a general similarity to Scheme B and to the project of March 1929. But the Commissioners' report went much farther than those earlier schemes. Hitherto the building in Broad Street had been looked on as an additional book-stack; larger certainly than any of the stacks the library had already, but in no way superseding them. The Commissioners advised the better plan of general concentration of storage. The new building should be made to house all the library's books except such as were required for reference shelves. This meant the evacuation of the inconvenient basements in which so large a proportion of the library's books were kept, and, in addition, the emptying of the rooms on the ground floor and on the first floor of the Bodleian quadrangle.

This led to the second new feature of the Commission's scheme. The setting free of the Old Schools, which had been impounded for book-storage, would allow the library to find on the ground floor of the quadrangle the rooms that it so much needed for administrative purposes; while the whole of the two upper floors, into which the Upper Reading Room had already intruded, could be transformed into reading-rooms, housing (with the Old Library) at least 100,000 volumes. Thus the university would be provided with an open reference library about five times greater than that in the main reading-room of the British Museum. The consequent great development of open shelves, on which could be gathered together all the apparatus of research, was rightly regarded by the Commissioners as the very core of their scheme.

The measures advocated in the Commission's report were summarized in thirteen recommendations.[1] These were embodied in a

[1] See appendix.

decree which was submitted to Congregation on 26 May 1931 and approved without a division. So at last the university arrived at a well-thought-out scheme of extension that met with very general agreement. It had not as yet got the money for carrying it out; and the capital expenditure involved, together with the provision of a maintenance fund, was calculated by the Commission to fall very little short of a million pounds.

The acceptance of the Commission's report was the last outstanding event in Cowley's librarianship. He was already mortally ill, and found it necessary to resign his office as from 31 July 1931. A knighthood came to him as a reward for public services, but he did not live to enjoy his honour, and he died on 12 October. A fortnight later, on 24 October, the present writer was elected as his successor.

4. THE FINDING OF STORAGE-SPACE

It was necessary to act, and that speedily; nor could one wait until the funds for the full extension scheme had been secured. The new librarian reported the position to his Curators three months after taking office.

The Bodleian building is practically full. Parts of it are badly congested. There is little room left in it for accessions of older books, and no space for more maps. The New Schools Basement is full. Parliamentary papers overflowed some time ago from the Sheldonian Basement into even less satisfactory quarters in the Bodleian subway. The Camera Basement and the Underground Bookstore cannot possibly provide accommodation for more than four years' normal accessions to the classes of books already stored there; and during that limited period the task of finding the necessary shelf space will grow steadily more laborious, since the amount of book-shifting involved will increase as the space available diminishes. It is consequently certain that all parts of the existing buildings will be full up with books before any section of the proposed new building in Broad Street is ready.

The prime need was to find additional space for book-storage as rapidly as possible. Unless that was done, the library might be expected to reach saturation-point in the course of 1934. How to find it was the first problem that had to be settled. The immediate erection of a repository outside the city was considered and rejected in favour of a better course.

One of the minor measures recommended in the Commission's report, to which the university had now given its approval, was the extension of the Radcliffe Science Library. The building in the southwest corner of the Museum area, which it had occupied since 1902,

was the work of Sir Thomas Graham Jackson and had been given to
the university by the Drapers' Company. It was already overcrowded
with readers, and its storage-space would be used up in another ten
years. The Commissioners therefore advised the erection of a wing
at the west end of the existing building, having reading-rooms on its
upper floors and bookstores below. This the Curators resolved to put
in hand at once. The additional storage which it provided would not
be required immediately for scientific books, and could be used, in
part at least, as a temporary store for books from the Bodleian. By
this method the difficulty of finding book-room pending the completion of the Broad Street stack could be overcome.

In June 1932, within three months of taking their decision to proceed with the Radcliffe Science Library, the Curators found an
architect in the person of Mr. (now Sir Hubert) Worthington; and
in March of the following year (1933) a contract for a new building
was signed and operations were begun. Work was completed in the
summer of 1934, and the new wing was formally opened by the Prin-
cess Royal on 3 November. It cost little more than £40,000, a sum
well within the Commission's estimate. The extension nearly doubled
the building in size. Its two large reading-rooms were calculated to
provide seats eventually for 120 additional readers; but the larger part
of one of them was (and still is) temporarily given up to the use of a
mathematical institute. And below them three decks of book-stack
had shelving for a quarter of a million volumes.

Into the Radcliffe book-stacks there were moved, in the Long
Vacation of 1934, 170,000 books. These were mainly science sections from the Camera and the underground bookstore, and thus all
modern scientific works were brought together for the first time in
one building. The books transferred also included the contents of one
of the ground-floor rooms of the Bodleian quadrangle, the old Schola
Metaphysicae; for an empty room was needed for the staff that was
being formed to revise the library catalogue. So the Radcliffe Science
Library was enlarged; a start was rendered possible on the greater
project of catalogue revision; and sufficient storage-space was found
to satisfy all immediate needs. These results were reached in 1934, the
year in which it had been predicted that the Bodleian would find
itself filled to capacity.

5. WAYS AND MEANS

In the meantime the university had secured the funds that were
considered necessary to carry out the complete programme of

extension. On 24 May 1932 Congregation accepted by a unanimous vote an offer from the Rockefeller Trustees to contribute up to three fifths of the total cost, conditionally upon the university finding the remaining two fifths within a stated period. The university's share worked out at £337,720. Times were unfavourable for raising so large a sum of money, for the world was still in the trough of a financial depression. A general appeal to the public seemed to be out of the question; but nothing prevented a private and limited appeal being made to Oxford colleges and to certain other institutions. The university had in hand, as a substantial contribution towards the sum required, the value of the building sites which it had acquired in Broad Street, and these were assessed at £79,000. College contributions totalled, in all, £65,050. The Trustees of the Oxford University Endowment Fund, which had been raised on the appeal that Lord Curzon launched in 1907, made over the whole of their assets, amounting to £48,000. In one way or another almost a quarter of a million pounds (actually £245,405) was raised in cash or promises to pay; and the balance required to make up the university's contribution was obtained through the University Chest guaranteeing annual payment of £7,000 a year, pending the provision of equivalent funds from other sources.

The university had been given four and a half years in which to find the money. It was found in less than one, and so the conditions set out in the Rockefeller Foundation's magnificent offer were fulfilled. The Rockefeller Trustees thereupon expressed their willingness to make payments, as needed, of their share of building costs up to the end of 1941.

By the beginning of 1937 it was considered that the time was favourable for issuing the public appeal that had been postponed five years before. The Chancellor's appeal for funds, which was issued on 9 February 1937, was not limited to the purposes of library extension. It asked for half a million pounds for the better endowment of humane studies and of natural science in the university. Only the first of its objects was to raise a sum that would relieve the university of liability for the payment of £7,000 a year which it had undertaken to make for Bodleian extension, and to provide in addition a surplus of £20,000 to meet increased cost of library maintenance. The appeal was inaugurated by a contribution of £100,000 from Lord Nuffield and met with complete success. The sums raised were funded in what is known as the Higher Studies Fund. The first full annual payment of £7,000 was made out of that fund in 1944, and from then onwards became part of the library's permanent income.

The money was secured, and it remained to devise the administrative machinery needed for putting the library extension scheme into execution. Ultimate responsibility lay with the Curators; but the drawing up of building plans had perforce to be entrusted to a smaller body, capable of meeting at more frequent intervals. A Building Committee, composed of Curators and co-opted members, was set up in May 1932; and, when plans were being worked out for the new library building in Broad Street, the whole of that business fell, in the first instance, on a small planning sub-committee of three, to whom the Librarian and the library secretary submitted all points on which decisions had to be taken. The sub-committee, over which Professor (now Sir Maurice) Powicke presided as chairman, reported to the Building Committee, whose findings were approved by the Curators and, when necessary, were forwarded to Council and to the University Chest, for confirmation. Informal weekly meetings of the Librarian, the University Registrar, and the Secretary of the Chest, held throughout the whole course of the extension period, made for easy intercourse and mutual understanding between the university bodies primarily concerned.

To replace an old library by an entirely new one is a comparatively simple matter; but to retain and transform the old and add to it a great new library building is much more complex. Work must be carried out by stages; the various parts of the plan must be so fitted and dovetailed that they avoid mutual interference; and the stages must be defined at the outset. A time-table was subsequently drawn up by the librarian in November 1932,[1] allowing for a ten-year programme of library extension, and was the basis on which the Rockefeller Trustees limited their commitment to the period closing with the end of the year 1941. There was every prospect of building operations having been brought to completion by that time. In the event, it was found possible to adhere strictly to the time-table until, in the autumn of 1939, the outbreak of a Second World War first slowed down building-work, and finally brought it to a standstill.

---

[1] Revised in May 1933 and again in June 1934.

Chapter XX
Library Extension (Part II)

1. PLANS FOR THE NEW LIBRARY

AFTER the completion of the Radcliffe Science Library wing in the summer of 1934 there came a pause in major building operations. The next and far the largest item in the programme of library extension was the construction of the building in Broad Street which is today popularly known as the New Bodleian. That building, it must be remembered, was intended primarily for storage; but it had been agreed, on the Library Commission's recommendation, that it should also contain rooms for the reception, handling, and cataloguing of books, and that a considerable amount of free space should be left in it and placed at the librarian's disposal. Furthermore, Congregation had also agreed to the making of 'experiments in library administration, including the use of carrels and research-rooms adjoining appropriate sections of the stacks'.[1] The library authorities were consequently left with considerable freedom in deciding on what should be included in those portions of the new building that were not devoted to storage. It was impossible, however, to arrive at any final conclusion on the point before finding out the extent of the demand for special reading-rooms and research-rooms, and whether it could be supplied by rooms in the old Bodleian building. The requirements of the new library could only be assessed after determining the capacity of the old library to meet the new needs: their respective functions had first to be clearly defined.

A trial scheme for the future allocation of the rooms that surround the Bodleian quadrangle was approved in May 1934, making it possible to proceed with the new library building. The Bodleian Building Committee turned to the selection of an architect. The sister University of Cambridge was in the act of completing its new library which had been built to the designs of Sir Giles Gilbert Scott. It was decided that the same architect should be employed by Oxford, and his appointment was formally ratified by decree of Congregation (12 June 1934). A month later, Sir Giles Scott and the Librarian set out to visit some of the great libraries on the Continent; and their journey was followed by a more extended tour of inspection of American libraries, made by the Librarian and the Secretary in September and early October.

[1] Resolution of 26 May 1931.

The next step was to frame instructions to the architect. The problem that had been set was not an easy one to solve. The area chosen was an island site measuring a single acre. Upon that ground the university had committed itself to erect a building capable of holding about five million books. The height to which the building might be raised was limited by aesthetic considerations and by city by-laws, and the depth to which it could be carried was determined by the water-level. More had to be got on to the site than the Library Commission originally contemplated; for they had merely envisaged a stack screened by outer rooms on one side only, namely, that of Broad Street, whereas the university's supplementary resolution of 26 May 1931 implied a disposition of rooms round the stack.

It had been assumed at the outset that the building would receive natural lighting from light-wells, but the Librarian's visit to America led him to a different conclusion. While in the States he had the opportunity of seeing the just-completed new library of Columbia University in New York, and of examining the plans made for the annexe to the library of Congress at Washington; and he became convinced that a building on similar lines provided the sole possible solution to the problem. He accordingly proposed the construction of a solid building, only partially dependent on daylight, in which outer ranges of rooms should surround a square central stack, artificially lit and ventilated.

The idea was elaborated at meetings of the Planning Sub-Committee, held weekly during the succeeding months, and led to a detailed specification of plans for the new library building. Embodied in a ten-page pamphlet entitled 'Instructions to the architect', the specification was adopted by the Curators on 1 June 1935 and remitted to the architect a fortnight later, after approval by Council and the University Chest. Preliminary plans were submitted by Sir Giles Scott in October. Before the year ended, they had been approved by the university authorities, and the architect was directed to proceed with the lengthy task of preparing working drawings. When these were in readiness, firms were invited to tender; and eventually, in December 1936, a contract was sealed with the Oxford building firm of Benfield and Loxley.

2. PROGRESS OF THE WORK

The work of clearing the site began on 1 December 1936. A row of houses in Broad Street and Parks Road had first to be demolished. Some of the Broad Street houses concealed, behind their Victorian exteriors, architectural features of the early seventeenth century, and of these and of their domestic fittings careful records were taken.[1] Nor was this all. During the months of 1937 when a mechanical excavator was removing vast masses of gravel to make way for basements, a careful watch was kept for objects of archaeological interest.[2] A mass of medieval pottery recovered from the pits and wells that studded the site has helped to establish the sequence of pottery forms current in Oxford during the thirteenth century; while three mammoth's teeth now in the University Geology department date from a far more ancient past.

The gravel in which these finds were made formed a bed 20 feet in thickness. Subterranean water, pouring over the last foot or so of gravel at the rate of two to three thousand gallons an hour, necessitated iron sheet-piling round the edges of the excavations, so that the whole building is set, as it were, in a water-resisting tank. Below the gravel lies solid blue Oxford clay, giving firm bedding for the foundations of the heavy building imposed upon it.[3] Excavation was still in progress when, on 25 June 1937, Her Majesty Queen Mary formally laid the foundation-stone of the new building.

During the period of construction the Building Committee was still kept busy revising the distribution of rooms and taking decisions as to internal fittings and furniture. The Librarian and the Secretary were having weekly conferences with the architect's representative, settling every kind of detail. The structural steel-work—a three-dimensional network of stanchions and girders flared with the names of Brown and Redpath—reared itself up to the height of 80 feet above the street. By the end of the summer of 1938 it was all in position, and a beginning—it was a mere beginning—had been made in laying floors and in building up the outer walls. Then came the Munich crisis with its threat of war in Europe. But that danger passed and the work proceeded.

A year later all work on the exterior had been practically completed. Floors had been laid down; staircases and internal partitions were in position; walls and ceilings had been plastered. The fitting up of the stack lagged behind; but the heating system was already in operation, drying out the building. Arrangements had been made for a royal opening on 14 June 1940.

[1] W. A. Pantin, 'The Recently Demolished Houses in Broad Street', *Oxoniensia*, vol. ii, pp. 171–200.

[2] E. T. Leeds, 'Glass vessels of the XVI century and later from the site of the Bodleian Extension' (op. cit., vol. iii, pp. 153–61); R. L. S. Bruce-Mitford, 'The Archaeology of the site of the Bodleian Extension' (op. cit., vol. iv, pp. 89–146).

[3] The geology of the site has been described by Professor Arkell, op. cit., vol. iii, pp. 1–6.

On that day the German armies were marching into Paris. The scene had changed. From September 1939 England was at war. The outbreak of the Second World War had little immediate effect, however, upon the building operations. Acting on the architect's advice, the Curators decided that work should be continued, and, although the pace became slower, by the summer of 1940 the building was practically complete.[1]

It was fortunate that it was so, for the completion of the stack allowed the contents of the library, other than reference books, to be gradually transferred to a building that was comparatively secure from blast and conflagration; while the outer rooms were each in their turn taken over, as soon as the workmen were out of them, for use by university departments or by non-university bodies. We shall speak more of these war-activities later (p. 343), and confine ourselves for the present to a description of the building and of the purposes which it is designed to fill.

3. THE NEW BOOK-STACK

The New Bodleian is a rectangular building, 172 feet square, with frontages 41 feet in height and a central block which rises 78 feet above street-level. It is a steel structure, with floors of reinforced concrete, and is consequently fire resistant. Only its external walls are stone-cased. The style chosen by the architect is neo-classical, with a minimum of ornament, neither competing with, nor conflicting with, the university buildings that confront it on the opposite side of Broad Street. It has had its critics as well as its admirers, for Oxford is a home of criticism, though its initial judgements are not always final. 'I remember', Max Müller wrote,[2] 'the outcry against the Taylor Institution, the only Palladian building at Oxford; and yet everybody is now grown reconciled to it, and even Ruskin lectured in it.'

The stack, which forms at once the core and the substructure of the building, consists of eleven decks. The three lowest are below ground-level and cover the whole building-site, for they extend below the surrounding private roadway. Taken together, the basement decks provide as much storage-space as is to be found in the whole building above-ground. The two topmost decks rise above the outer ranges of rooms and consequently possess natural lighting; but they are set so far back from the street as to be hardly visible from it.

---

[1] The steel sub-contract was not fully completed until Nov. 1940. Work on the electrician's sub-contract was carried on spasmodically until Apr. 1943.
[2] *My Autobiography*, p. 216.

THE NEW BODLEIAN

The intermediate six decks are encased by three stories of outer rooms: each story corresponds with two decks of the stack, and is itself capable of conversion into stack. It will be understood from this brief description, that the building has a far larger capacity than its outward appearance suggests. It fulfils the Library Commission's requirement that it should be capable of holding about five million books.

Each deck of the stack is a little over 7 feet in height, and all except the two lowest are already fitted throughout with ranges of steel stack and shelving of a special design supplied by Messrs. Roneo. Lifts[1] and internal staircases, all of steel construction, provide communication between the decks. Being almost wholly dependent upon artificial lighting, the stack is electrically lit. Electric power works the lifts, and heating is provided by a thermal storage plant which circulates water from cylinders heated by electric power. In so changeable a climate as ours, air has to be conditioned in order to maintain the amount of moisture that is needed to prevent books from getting too damp or too dry. The washed and warmed air that is circulated through the book-stack keeps the place at a suitable temperature and provides the correct humidity.[2]

In order to allow rapid transmission of books from the stack to the reading-rooms in the Old Bodleian, a tunnel has been driven underneath Broad Street and links the two buildings. A belt-conveyor has been installed in it and continues at either end as a vertical elevator. Books are conveyed by this mechanism to and from the reading-rooms and are automatically discharged at the required floor.

Books are distributed over the stack according to a scheme drawn up by the Librarian and approved by the Curators. Classified sections fill the seven top decks, periodicals and non-periodical literature occupying different parts of each deck.[3] Manuscripts are on the ground-floor; newspapers, unclassified collections and early printed books are on the deck immediately below. They look well upon their shelves, despite the forecast made by one writer[4] in 1875 that 'the old

[1] Although the Curators agreed on 6 May 1882 that the librarian should report on the construction of a lift or lifts, the Bodleian had not so much as a book-lift till 1913 or a single passenger-lift until 1928.

[2] The system aims at maintaining a relative humidity range of 50 to 60 per cent., and a temperature range of 55° to 62° F. in the stack, these being the best conditions for the preservation of books and for the comfort and efficiency of persons working in the stack. Temperature is maintained at 62–67° F. in the outer rooms.

[3] In a memorandum dated 25 Oct. 1884 Nicholson pointed out that the earlier Bodleian practice of keeping *all* periodicals together had resulted in a series of breakdowns. All the periodicals which deal with special subjects, he rightly held, should be placed with those subjects.   [4] Compton Reade in *Belgravia*, vol. xxv, p. 179.

volumes of the date of Caxton will look strangely out of place in some spic and span, brand new, semi-maniacal specimen of the architecture of the future'. The vast expanses of the two lowest decks have been left unshelved, for it was calculated that the floors above them would allow for storage of accessions up to 1964, though it would be necessary to begin making further provision of stack in 1948.

The idea that readers might be permitted to enter library stacks and consult books upon the shelves was first propounded (though not in Oxford) in 1892.[1] Shelf access gradually won its way to favour in the library world, and was one of the privileges for which the reforming party pressed in the days of the Bodleian controversy. The Library Commission approved of restricted access to the stack; and the Curators agreed in principle in 1938 that it should be allowed to members of the university Faculties (that is, to all persons actively engaged in teaching in the university), to persons recommended by the Boards of Faculties and approved by the librarian, and to other persons at the librarian's discretion.

With the same object in view, Congregation resolved in 1931 on experimenting with carrels in the stack—little private studies such as Dr. Scott, of Greek Lexicon fame, had unexpectedly pleaded for before the University Commission of 1850.[2] Consequently a couple of dozen have been provided on the upper decks of the stack, and there is room for a hundred more. They are intended to be allotted to readers who desire to work for long periods in close proximity to certain classes of books. Over fifty movable desks and chairs in different parts of the stack are available for readers who are not provided with carrels.

4. EXTERNAL ROOMS

Besides sanctioning carrels, Congregation authorized the experimental making of research-rooms adjoining appropriate sections of the stack. A number of the external rooms have consequently been assigned for this purpose and placed at the disposal of those Faculties that required them. The whole of the first floor on the north side of the building is occupied by a large special reading-room for modern studies, with seats for eighty readers. Round its walls are more than 6,000 volumes, forming a select library of philosophy, political science, and economics. The adjoining gallery, which is intended

[1] By James Duff Brown in an anonymous article entitled 'A plea for liberty to readers to help themselves', published in the *Library* for Dec. 1892 (vol. iv, p. 302).
[2] *Oxford University Commission Report*, 1852, Evidence, p. 114.

eventually to house a copy of the library catalogue, has helped in post-war years to relieve the pressure on the reading-room.

A spacious room on the first floor of the eastern range has been fitted up for the consultation of maps; and, with the specially constructed filing-cabinets on the corresponding floor of the stack, has provided, for the first time, proper accommodation for the Bodleian map-collection. Its present quarters are very different from those of the old map-room in the north-west corner of the Bodleian quadrangle, where Ordnance Survey maps were stacked in huge piles of three or four hundredweight. The collection has greatly increased in size as the result of large donations made during the Second World War by the Geographical section of the War Office. It is now not merely better housed but is in process of being properly catalogued under a set of Bodleian rules devised in 1939.

Next to the map-room is a room designed for the study of local records,[1] though it has not as yet been brought into use for that purpose. A room on the floor below is set apart for the study of practical bibliography, a subject which Sir William Osler did much to encourage when he was a Bodleian Curator.[2] Bibliography is a study that is ancillary to librarianship; and it was therefore right and proper that an Oxford Bibliographical Society, on the model of the older bibliographical societies of London and Edinburgh, should have been founded in 1922 under Bodleian auspices.

In the Bibliography Room there is kept the Albion hand-press which Dr. C. H. O. Daniel, sometime Provost of Worcester, acquired in 1882. On it he set up, in Fell type of the late seventeenth century, the minor works which he took pleasure in printing for his immediate circle of friends.[3] The Bodleian collection of Daniel Press books and fly-sheets is now practically complete, thanks to a purchase made from Mr. F. F. Madan in 1940 by the Friends of the Bodleian.

Prior to Nicholson's death, exhibition cases were confined to Arts

---

[1] One of the many interesting suggestions made by Mr. Strickland to the Oxford University Commission of 1850 (Evidence, p. 102) was that a room in the library should be set apart for Oxford local literature.

[2] In an unpublished and unfinished paper written in 1907, Osler proposed the foundation, in Oxford, of what he called 'The College of the Book', in which everything could be learned in regard to the production and treatment of books, and of which a school of bibliography should form a part. 'To carry out a scheme of this extent', he wrote, 'would require a rearrangement of existing conditions at the Bodleian and the Press; a separate fire-proof building in underground communication with the present ones, and which should be devoted to administration, reading-rooms, department-rooms and teaching-rooms.' Harvey Cushing, *Life of Sir William Osler*, 1940, pp. 767–8.

[3] Falconer Madan's bibliography, *The Daniel Press*, was printed upon this press in 1921.

End, but from 1912 the Picture Gallery was also brought into use for exhibition purposes. The idea of having special or temporary exhibitions of books and manuscripts was first started by Madan, whose Shakespeare Tercentenary Exhibition of 1916 met with considerable success. From 1931 temporary exhibitions became a regular institution. So, when the new library was built, two exhibition rooms were included in the south range, the one devoted to special exhibitions, the other to permanent exhibits. These two rooms form the only portion of the building to which visitors are normally admitted, and here are on sale the picture postcards which the library started to print in 1922.

The whole of the western range is given up to staff quarters. Prior to 1935, when a room in the Bodleian quadrangle was cleared for the reception of a newly formed body of cataloguers, the staff had no separate working-quarters but were left to carry out their duties as best they could in the reading-rooms and store-rooms of the library.[1] A new and larger cataloguing-room in the New Bodleian was taken into use before the war ended. There are also rooms for the reception and handling of accessions. Binding-repair used at one time to be carried on in a study built at one end of the present Upper Reading-Room, and then, after the coin collection had been sent to the Ashmolean, in the cramped quarters of the old coin-room. A much larger staff of binders is now spaciously housed on the ground floor of the western range. In place of an enclosure in the Upper Reading-Room the photographic staff has a set of studios occupying the whole of the top floor of the north side of the new building: these include a room for the reading of microfilms and a closet for reading and photographing by the light of an ultra-violet-ray lamp.

There is a common-room for the staff and a staff canteen. A janitor's lodge is built over an archway adjoining the library. Workshops and the complicated apparatus of a vast heating chamber fill a part of the basement. And perhaps one should not omit to mention a fumigating chamber that deals destruction to bookworms. Whereas the Bodleian got along comfortably without an internal telephone until 1913 and without a Post Office telephone until 1919, an extensive telephone system is now installed. These mechanical appliances, together with loud speakers and with pneumatic tubes for the delivery of messages and book orders, help to make the New Bodleian a building that is typical of its age, and give it a very different character from the Old.

---

[1] The staff seats which filled the northern half of Arts End will soon be forgotten. They are shown in plate 12 of the special number of *Oxford* (Feb. 1937).

The Library Commission had estimated the cost of construction of what they called 'the Broad Street Building' at £400,000, to which £6,000 had to be added for the tunnel. The adoption of a compact type of building allowed a saving to be made on construction to the amount of £35,000, and this was capitalized to meet the increased expenditure required upon lighting and ventilation.[1] Thus a sum of £371,000 was left available for the building, a sum that in the long run was only slightly exceeded, the total expenditure on construction and furnishing working out at £379,300.

5. THE CAMERA

With the construction of the new library the main part of the building programme was completed. The problem of housing books had been solved for the space, it was hoped, of one or even of two centuries. But it was not for books alone that accommodation had to be found, but for the users of the library. There was need of additional reading-rooms. For a long time past the number of readers had continued to show a steady increase. In the appeal for funds issued in 1914 the Curators calculated that it had more than doubled since 1892. Attendance in Bodley and the Camera was said to average 260 a day throughout the year, the Camera accounting for two thirds of that number; and naturally readers were far more numerous in term than in vacation. In 1920 the average number of readers using the Camera in the course of a day in term-time was estimated as being between five and six hundred. On almost any morning in term the place was more than full, and in the following years the numbers still grew.

The dependent libraries drew a considerable number of students away from the Bodleian. They were libraries, to a great extent, of open access, and reading could be carried out in them under easier conditions than were formerly to be found in Bodley. Hence came a demand for specialized reading-rooms with a wide and well-chosen range of textbooks on open shelves. In 1923, at the request of the Law Board, such a room was fitted up in the Examination Schools and made a reading-room for English Law. The Curators agreed in principle in 1926 to the creation of more reading-rooms for special studies, in which readers should have access to open shelves. And in pursuance of that policy a portion of the Picture Gallery next to the Upper Reading-Room was taken over in 1929 as a reading-room for

[1] The running costs of electric lighting and power and heating were calculated at £3,800 a year. To run boilers on gas or oil or solid fuel would have increased the cost of heating.

English literature, and was furnished with forty-eight seats. As its readers were mainly undergraduates, its opening did something to relieve congestion in the Camera.

Additional seating in the gallery of the Camera brought the number of seats in its reading-room up to 116. That, however, was far from exhausting the capacity of the building. The central space below the Dome was as yet entirely occupied by floor-cases and catalogue-stands, arranged on no particular plan. The Library Commission pointed out that many more seats could be got in if the bulky library catalogue were removed. Before that was done, and as a preliminary to it, the lighting of the room was transformed. The installation carried out in 1905 consisted entirely of table-lamps; there was no general lighting. At night a canopy of darkness surrounded readers as they sat at their lamp-lit desks. The need for rewiring in 1932 gave opportunity for a complete remodelling of the reading-room lighting. All desk-lights were eliminated and over-head lighting substituted, with indirect lighting of the alcoves under the gallery. A few years earlier, in 1925, the room had been cleaned and redecorated, and the distempered interior of the dome had been tinted to bring out its plaster decoration.[1] But now for the first time, with the new system of lighting, the architectural features of the building stood fully revealed.

This was the first step. The second was to remove the general catalogue. It was sent at the end of 1934 to the Upper Reading-Room, where it still is. There it replaced the partially corrected copy of the catalogue which was required by the revisers for their new cataloguing room. The place of the full catalogue was supplied in the Camera by a book-catalogue of all works kept in the reading-room, and by a card-catalogue of selected entries from the general catalogue giving references to the books most likely to be required for undergraduate reading.

It was now possible to rearrange the centre of the reading-room, which had up to now been full of furniture and empty of readers. Far back in 1883 Dr. Acland had expressed the view that tables should be set in it radially, and that the surrounding statues should be removed.[2] The course that he proposed was at last adopted. In 1935, under Mr. Worthington's direction, a staff enclosure was formed in the centre of the room, and tables radiating out from it provided seats for fifty-two additional readers, raising the total number of seats in the reading-room from 122 to 174. In the following

[1] There had been an earlier cleaning and repainting in 1902.
[2] Library papers, 'Radcliffe Camera correspondence, 1883–7'.

year the casts of classical statuary found a new home in the Palladian school-buildings of Stowe.

There still remained the ground floor to be dealt with; that stone-vaulted basement which formed a crowded store-room for modern accessions. In 1928 the Curators had resolved that, so soon as its contents could be housed elsewhere, the room should be converted into a special reading-room, perhaps for history and economics. Nothing could be done until the stack in the new library was in readiness; when that was finished, the contents of the Camera ground floor were the first books to be placed in it. And so in 1940, although war was gradually closing down all building-work that was not military or governmental, it was found possible to dismantle the room, to clean down its walls and the ceiling that had been blackened by the dim light of a single gas-jet, to install electric lighting and heating, and to supply tables and chairs for forty-four readers. The select library of the English Reading-Room was transferred thither from the Bodleian building, and so was that of the Law Reading-Room which had been evicted from the Examination Schools on the outbreak of the war. In May 1941 the Camera ground floor was brought into use as a reading-room, and it now provides for treble its original number of readers.

Thus in the course of ten years the internal arrangements of the Camera were transformed and its seating accommodation doubled. In 1936 its outer appearance was equally altered by the levelling of the surrounding lawn and the removal of its iron railing, with the help of a benefaction given for that purpose by Lord Justice Greene. Since 1927 the Camera has been university property, the freehold having been handed over in that year to the university by Dr. John Radcliffe's trustees.

6. THE OLD LIBRARY

Under the time-table that had been adopted for carrying out the programme of library extension, the years 1940 and 1941 were set apart for the final phase, that is to say, for work upon the Old Bodleian building. We have told already (p. 329) of how it was found necessary to work out in some detail the uses to which the different parts of that building might be put as a preliminary to the formulation of plans for the new library. The scheme adopted followed the general lines of the Library Commission's report, in assigning the ground-floor rooms of the Bodleian quadrangle for use as administrative offices and (in part) for co-operative research, and the two upper floors for conversion into reading-rooms in special subjects—namely, law, theology, oriental studies, languages, and history—while Duke

Humphrey's Library remained a general reading-room and Selden End was destined to be a room for the study of manuscripts. The Library Commissioners estimated that these rooms should be capable of housing, upon open shelves, at least 100,000 volumes, and still have room for expansion. The Boards of Faculties were invited to co-operate in selecting books for the proposed special reading-rooms, and their task was almost completed before the outbreak of the war.

No work could be carried out upon the rooms round the quad-rangle until the books with which they were packed had been moved into the new stack in Broad Street; and that, as we have seen, was not in readiness until after the war had actually begun. When the rooms were eventually cleared, an examination of their floors revealed the extent to which the timbers had decayed. The discovery was not un-anticipated. Quite early in the library's history, in February 1703, the floor beams of the Schools had been reported to Sir Christopher Wren as being quite broken and cracked at the jointings, and Wren had replied that 'he is absolutely for taking away the floors that now are, and putting new ones in their place'.[1] A century and a half later, Sir Gilbert Scott had advised that all the floors should be renewed in fire-proof construction with the object of reducing fire-risks. And now examination revealed their rottenness. Where the main joists entered the walls, timber had been reduced to powder, and the floors were found to have largely depended for their support upon the lofty bookcases that reached up to the ceiling. There was nothing to be done but to substitute steel girders and concrete for wooden joists and floors, an operation that had the double advantage of tieing the outer walls together and of freeing the buildings from the danger of fire.

A beginning was made in 1940, and new floors were put into the section of the eastern range that lies south of the tower. Then the war brought work to a standstill, not to be renewed until after peace had returned. But it had been found possible, before work ceased, to bring one of the Old Schools into new use. Under Mr. Worthington's direction, the Schola Logicae, which a hundred years before had held the Pomfret Marbles, and since then had been filled with close-packed bookcases, was stripped of its ungainly fittings, lined with Jacobean panelling taken from behind bookcases in various parts of the library, hung with the portraits of past librarians, and brought into use in 1941 as a handsome meeting-room for the Curators.

Nothing further was possible at that time, save some work in the north-west corner of the quadrangle and an enlargement of the Bod-

[1] Correspondence cited in *Oxoniensia*, vol. xiii, pp. 45–46.

THE CURATORS' ROOM, BODLEIAN LIBRARY

leian boiler-house which should make it eventually possible to heat all parts of the building. So extension for the time ended. The New Bodleian had been built, the Camera had been transformed; but work upon the Old Library had barely begun. The attention of the librarian, and of a staff that steadily diminished as its members joined the fighting services, was transferred to one object, the security of the library.

7. THE BODLEIAN IN WAR-TIME

Six months before the war, arrangements had been made for the library to be partially closed in the event of hostilities. As things turned out, it was found possible to keep all parts of the library open, and the Bodleian may therefore claim to be the only great library in the country which continued to give in war-time almost as complete a service as in peace. Hours of opening of the Radcliffe Science Library, where a good deal of research was being undertaken for the Government, were actually extended. The staff was soon reduced to less than half its former strength, sixty of its members being absent on war-service, and all able-bodied personnel who remained were engaged on part-time civil defence. Yet, despite reduction in numbers, it was found possible not merely to carry on normal service, but to remove the entire contents of the library into greater security.

Requisitioning of the Examination Schools on the outbreak of war necessitated an immediate and hurried evacuation of the 200,000 volumes (chiefly fiction) that were kept in its cellars, and dumping them in the basement of the unfinished new library. That done, in the second month of the war a bricked enclosure was built in the basement, and some 60,000 of the library's most valuable books and manuscripts were removed into it. Here at least they might be considered out of the reach of fire and blast. It was then possible to proceed with a systematic transfer of the contents of the Camera basement, underground bookstore, Ashmolean basement, and the rooms round the Bodleian quadrangle to the shelves that awaited them in the new library. Thither also went, for the duration of the war, all the old books that formerly filled the highly inflammable bookcases of the Old Reading-Room. So Duke Humphrey's Library was stripped bare, and the Old Schools stood desolate; but the books were safe, and, almost unnoticed, the whole contents of the Bodleian, amounting to a million and a half of volumes, had been ranged in order in the new stack. Despite the staff's diminishing numbers, the work was complete by the summer of 1942.

Only one thing was needed to bring to a successful conclusion the programme of concentration of storage laid down by the Library Commission. This was to reduce to order and remove to the underground bookstore (the heating and ventilation of which had been remodelled in the interval) the fiction that had been so unceremoniously bundled out of the Examination Schools, together with dissertations and other less-used categories of books. That also was done by the summer of 1944.

It was not for itself alone that the Bodleian provided shelter in the new book-stack. At the time of the Munich crisis the Curators had circularized Oxford colleges, offering to make the new library basement available for the deposit of their treasures. So, when war came, thither went the pictures of Christ Church, the stained glass of New College, the Grinling Gibbons carvings of Trinity, the manuscripts of Merton and Balliol, the University Archives, the libraries of the English School and of the Modern History faculty, and books from other university departments, such as the Botanical department and the Hope department of Entomology. Nor did the Bodleian shut its doors to libraries outside Oxford, but gave hospitality to books from the British Museum Natural History departments, the King's Library from the British Museum, the Goldsmiths' Library from London University, the Dyce collection from the Victoria and Albert Museum, books and specimens from the herbarium of Kew Gardens, the records of the Court of Arches, and the books of such learned societies as the Linnaean and the Royal Society. All these and many more were war-time companions in the cellars of the New Bodleian, and were returned, when peace came, in safety to their owners.

Librarianship in time of war is an affair of stirrup-pumps and sand-bags, of static water-tanks and trailer-pumps, and of the many activities that go by the name of A.R.P. From the first the Bodleian had its volunteer fire-brigade, formed from the library staff. From the first also it had its nightly guard of fire-watchers, strengthened, after the first eighteen months, by enlisting the services of undergraduates. In the summer of 1942 the dangers arising from indiscriminate bombing, and the threat of the so-called Baedeker raids, made it necessary to take more stringent precautions; and, before the end, Bodley had a night-guard of thirty persons, sleeping on library premises, and all trained to some degree in fire-fighting. As an additional measure of security, 2,000 of the library's greatest treasures were removed by road in June 1942 and deposited in the underground galleries of a stone-quarry near Bath, put at the Curators' disposal by the authorities of the British Museum.

The City of Oxford had also to provide for the safety of its inhabitants in the event of air-attack, and the lowest basement of the New Bodleian was placed at the disposal of the city authorities for conversion into a public air-raid shelter. The shelter, completed by July 1942, had accommodation for 1,100 people, but no occasion ever arose for its being brought into use. The floor immediately above it had in its centre the library's brick treasure-chamber, round which were ranged the war-time deposits of other libraries. Bodleian books filled the upper portions of the stack. The surrounding rooms were given up to a variety of uses, for the library retained for its own purposes one room only—the catalogue room. The destruction of the general catalogue would have been so great a loss that it was essential that the revised copy should be placed in a fire-resisting building.

The other rooms were occupied, partly by other university departments such as the Institute of Statistics (which had had the misfortune of being evicted from one set of offices after another), and by the Slade School of Art; partly by non-academic bodies engaged on various forms of war-work. Among these last were the British Red Cross Society, the regional offices of the Blood Transfusion Service and of the Royal Observer Corps, the Royal National War Libraries, the Educational Books Section of the Prisoners of War Department (well known to prisoners of war in Germany) and, most important of all, naval intelligence departments of the Admiralty. Readers in the reading-room of the New Bodleian may be interested to know that the room played some part in the working out of plans for the Normandy landing on D Day.

The expulsion of the German armies from France in the autumn of 1944 brought relief, and dispensed a hard-worked staff from further fire-watching. When Germany made its unconditional surrender on 9 May 1945, the old familiar books were already in course of being reinstated in Duke Humphrey and in Arts End. Before June was out, the library's great treasures had been brought back from the stone-quarry in which they had reposed for the past three years. When on 31 July 1945, the present writer retired from office under the age-limit that the statute prescribed, the war was very near indeed to its end. A week later the first atomic bomb brought it to a sudden and dramatic close. Another week elapsed and Japan surrendered. The Bodleian had passed unscathed through a war of unparalleled destruction.

8. EPILOGUE

How different was the Bodleian then from the library over which Bandinel had presided a hundred years before! That had been confined to a single building of which it was not even the sole occupier. Round the Bodleian quadrangle all the ground-floor rooms but one were still used as University Schools. Since that date the library had absorbed the remaining Schools. It had acquired the Radcliffe Library, renamed the Camera. It had made for itself an underground bookstore between the Camera and the Old Bodleian. It had taken over three outlying libraries, namely, the Radcliffe Science Library and the libraries of Rhodes House and of the Indian Institute. And now it had built for itself, and was about to take full possession of, the great new library on the farther side of Broad Street.

Where there had been a single reading-room there now were eight. Electric light had been introduced, and whereas the library had formerly closed its doors at four in the afternoon, or even at three in winter, the Bodleian now remained open until seven throughout the year, and the Camera and the Radcliffe Science Library until ten at night. Extension of hours, additional reading-rooms, and the innovation of placing thousands of select books upon open shelves, had combined to produce a vast increase in the number of those who made use of the library. A hundred years ago there were no undergraduates and no women readers. It is doubtful even whether, in 1845, there were often more than ten people reading in the library at the same time. A count, made on a morning in February 1947 of all those who were reading in one or other of the library's reading-rooms or in a dependent library, showed that at half past ten there were 620 readers hard at work. In the middle of the afternoon of the same day their number had risen to 714.[1]

With the great increase in the use made of the library, staff has expanded to meet the services required by additional readers and enlarged premises. In 1845 the entire staff was no more than nine, of whom four were graduates and all four were in orders. At the outbreak of the Second World War the staff numbered 107. Since its conclusion, the opening of the new library has necessitated rapid expansion, so that now (in 1951) the number of library employees stands at 147. Sixty of these (or 41 per cent.) are women and girls, and all, it may be added, are laity.

The small annual revenue of £4,650 which the library received in 1845 soon became insufficient to meet its financial burdens. Constant appeals for increased endowment succeeded in augmenting the library's resources. But it was not until 1920, when the university began to receive a State grant and to pay over a portion of it to Bodley, that the position was materially eased. By 1939 library revenue

[1] *Bodleian Library Record*, vol. ii, p. 159.

amounted to £36,000, having more than trebled itself in the course of twenty-seven years. Recent increases have fully compensated for the fall in the value of money. In 1949–50 Bodley received from university sources (including Government grant) over £56,000, twelve times the whole income that sufficed it in 1845; the Bodleian Extension Fund produced a further £15,470; and total receipts approached £90,600.[1]

In 1845 the Bodleian contained fewer than a quarter of a million printed books. In 1915, the latest year for which figures are available, it had over a million. We have given reasons for thinking that it has been doubling its size with each successive generation; and, by the same token, it should now be approaching, if it has not already reached, the two million mark. Thus in the course of a century has the Bodleian Library developed, and the pace of its growth become ever more rapid, fulfilling still its founder's prayer—

QUOD FELICITER VORTAT

[1] Outlay on the library in the last year before the war formed 6·76 per cent. of the total university expenditure. In 1950–1 the percentage had risen slightly, namely, to 7·13.

APPENDIX

Three Extension Programmes

I. The first of the schemes here set out takes the form of resolutions of the Bodleian Curators as amended by the Hebdomadal Council on 18 March 1878 (Hebdomadal Council minutes 1866–79, p. 487). A statute to give effect to the resolutions was drafted but was never brought before Congregation. See p. 147 above.

1. That the rooms on the ground floor of the Schools quadrangle be annexed to the library.

2. That, after due provision shall have been made for the Divinity Professors and Divinity exercises, the Divinity School be used as a reading-room by day.

3. That the upper Ashmolean room and, as soon as provision shall have been made for the Ashmolean collection, the lower room, be fitted up as a reading-room for the Bodleian. The Ashmolean to be connected with the library by a covered communication.

4. That the basement story of the Radcliffe be used as a receptacle for manuscripts and more valuable books.

5. That it be connected with the Bodleian by an underground passage.

6. That the upper story be employed as a Museum of Classical Archaeology and Art.

II. In the *Statements of the Needs of the University* issued in 1902 the needs of the Bodleian Library were summarized (at p. 120) as follows:

1. Further provision for the storage of books.

2. A substantial increase in the permanent staff of the library.

3. Reducing the Catalogue of Printed Books to a uniform system.

4. Such an increase in the regular income of the library as may make it possible, without unduly restricting expenditure on the ordinary work and purchases, to appropriate sufficient sums to work on arrears and to special purchases of books.

5. Providing for a careful inspection of the pictures and for the treatment of such of them as may be found to require immediate attention.

6. The printing of the Catalogue of Printed Books, so soon as the progress of revision makes it possible.

7. The electric lighting of the Camera.

8. The provision of a covered passage to the Radcliffe Camera, if not included in the scheme for storage.

9. The provision of a new reading-room.

III. The following recommendations were made in 1931 by the Library Commission (*Library Provision in Oxford*, pp. 83–84), and were adopted in the form of a decree by Congregation on 26 May 1931:

(*a*) The continuance of the historic Bodleian, mainly as an enlarged range of reading-rooms with direct and easy access to about 100,000 of the books most in demand.

(*b*) The use of the ground floor of the quadrangle for administrative offices, cloakrooms, and other purposes, including advanced teaching and research, at the librarian's discretion.

(*c*) The continuance of the upper floor of the Camera as a reading-room for undergraduates, with additional seating accommodation.

(*d*) The use of the ground floor of the Camera as an exhibition room.

(*e*) The concentration of storage in a special building on the Broad Street site, capable of holding about 5,000,000 books.

(*f*) The preservation of the amenities of Broad Street by a front section screening the stack and containing (1) rooms for the reception, handling, and cataloguing of books, and for the housing of special collections, and (2) a considerable amount of further free space at the librarian's disposal.

(*g*) The maintenance of a rapid service of books by mechanical means through a tunnel between the Bodleian and Broad Street.

(*h*) Some extension, at the discretion of the librarian, of the privilege of direct access to the store-house shelves.

(*i*) The enlargement of the Radcliffe Science Library by the addition of a new wing.

(*k*) The enlargement of the Taylorian Modern Languages Library on a site in St. Giles's adjoining the Institute.

(*l*) The development of the existing system of subsidiary special libraries under the control of the Faculties by the provision of accommodation in a new building adjacent to the Examination Schools.

(*m*) The preparation of a new working catalogue for the Bodleian.

(*n*) An improvement in the salaries of the Bodleian staff.

Index

INDEX

Bruce, James, his MSS., 21, 107, 214, 310.
Bruges, 72.
Brut Chronicle, 291.
Buchanan, Thomas, bequest, 286–7.
Buchanan, Mrs., donor, 296.
Buck, Dr. William, gift of coins, 116.
Buckingham, George Villiers, 1st Duke of, 90.
Buckinghamshire, archidiaconal records, 304; deeds, 306.
Buckland, Berks., 296.
Buckland, William, geological collections, 2.
Buckler, John Chessell, drawings of Oxford houses, 313.
Bühler, Prof. Georg, 311.
Bunyan, John, 74.
Burgon, John William, Dean of Chichester, 31; *Lives of Twelve Good Men*, 151.
Burleigh, William Cecil, Lord, portrait of, 9.
Burn, Dr. John Henry, benefactor, 269, 286.
Burnet, Gilbert, Bishop, his *History of his own Time*, 21, 113.
Burton, John, MS. collections, 298.
Bury St. Edmunds, muniments, 101; MS. from, 292.
Buss, R. W., aquatints, 5 n., 6 n.
Bute, John Stuart, 3rd Earl of, official papers, 297.
Butler, H. T., sale, 277.
Butler, Samuel, Bishop of Lichfield, sale, 21.
Buxheim, Bavaria, 177.
Bywater, Prof. Ingram, appointed sub-librarian, 149; resignation, 149, 152; elected as Curator, 157; critical of employment of boys, 162; opposes the subject-catalogue, 166; on book selection, 175; on photography, 203; on a summary catalogue of MSS., 206; moves in the matter of library extension, 233, 319; proposes readers' tickets, 239; bequest, 281–2, 294; collations and correspondence, 294.

Caedmon, 317.
Cairo, MSS. from the Geniza, 210–11, 310.
Callimachus, 293.
Cambridge University Library, 52, 54, 87; cataloguing rules, 168; printed accessions slips, 170, 270; joint action with Oxford over copyright, 62, 63,

174, 265; negotiations for joint purchase of Caxtons, 177; the like for Phillipps MSS., 196; Geniza fragments, 211; new library, 329.
Camden, William, 183.
Campsall Hall sale, 297, 299.
Canonici, Mathew Luigi, his MS. collection, 13, 20, 105; catalogues, 25, 91–92, 207.
Canterbury, MSS. from St. Augustine's, 291; St. Lawrence's hospital chartulary, 295.
Capgrave, John, *comm. on Exodus*, 199.
Cardwell, Reginald, bequest, 159.
Carew, Sir George, MSS., 94, 189.
Caricatures, 284, 314.
Carte, Thomas, his MSS., 99, 101.
Carthew, Miss A. G. E., bequest, 286.
Casaubon, Isaac, 93, 282, 303.
Caswell, John, Savilian Professor, 184 n.
Caulfield, Dr. Richard, gift of coins, 117.
Caxton, William, *Chronicle*, 72; *Golden Legend*, 72; *Ars Moriendi*, 204; advertisement, 16, 204; *Statuta*, 276; publications in Althorp library, 176–7.
Chalce, MSS. from, 93.
Chandler, Prof. Henry William, opposition to lending, 82; elected as Curator, 157; proposes the reform of the Curatorial board, 157; criticizes employment of boys, 162; opposes the subject-catalogue, 166; his views on cataloguing, 169–70; on copyright accessions, 173; urges development of photography, 203.
Chandra Shum Shere, Sir, gift of Sanskrit MSS., 220.
Chanson de Roland, 98, 317.
Chantrey, Sir Francis, busts, 9, 232.
Chap-books, 16, 68, 279.
Charles I, bust, 7; application to borrow, 80; proclamations, 280; *Eikon Basilike*, 277.
Charles of Lorraine, 287.
Charlett, Dr. Arthur, correspondence, 95.
Charters and deeds, 69, 100–1, 199, 304–6.
Chaucer, Geoffrey, *Canterbury Tales*, 292.
Chaundler, Thomas, Warden of New College, 192.
Chester, Rev. Greville John, donor, 200, 210, 214, 215, 223.
Chettle, Henry, 48.
China: Chinese books, 112, 221, 312; coins, 223.

5439 · 355 · A a 2

Headington, stone, 141; court rolls, 306.
Hearne, Thomas, 7; ballads and garlands, 279; MSS., 296; letters, 302.
Heather, Dr. William, 186.
Heber, Richard, his sale, 22, 73, 287.
Heberden, Dr. Charles Buller, President of B.N.C., 315.
Hebrew printed books and MSS., 17, 21, 105–6, 210–12, 290, 310; inscription, 315.
Heinsius, Nicholas, sale, 185.
Henry II of France, 286.
Henshaw, Samuel, bequest, 261.
Herbaria, 192.
Herbert of Cherbury, Edward, Lord, 190.
Herculaneum, rolls from, 200.
Hereford, MSS. from, 189–90, 296.
Hergest, Red book of, 190.
Hermann, Gottfried, sale, 75.
Hermas, shepherd of, 201.
Hewitt, Graily, calligrapher, 296n.
Hexham, Northumberland, coin hoard, 117.
Hibeh, 200.
Hicks, Edward Lee, Bishop of Lincoln, 151.
Hieratic writing, 214.
Hieroglyphic papyri, 308.
Hill, Birkbeck, 198.
Hill, Lucy, 198.
Hill, Reginald Harrison, secretary of the Bodleian, 250; work on library extension, 328, 331.
Hindhay farm, Berks., 35, 47, 159.
Hindi MSS., 108.
Hindustani MSS., 216, 220.
Hoadley, Benjamin, Bishop of Bangor, 74.
Hobart family, correspondence, 95; evidences, 100.
Hodgkin, John, bequest, 278, 281.
Hodgkin, John Eliot, 297.
Hodgson, Messrs., sale, 112.
Hoe, Robert, book-collector, 176.
Hoernle, Dr. Rudolf, donor, 218.
Hogarth, —, picture restorer, 115.
Holbein, Hans, drawings by, 7, 113.
Holm, co. Norfolk, Abbey of St. Benet, 100.
Holmes, Dr. Robert, collations of Septuagint, 193.
Holst, Gustav, autograph, 288.
Holst, Imogen, donor, 288.
Homer, papyrus fragments, 200, 201; Towneley MS., 21; edito princeps, 282; Monro collection, 182; Gladstone collection, 281.
Hooker, Richard, Eccl. Polity, 74.

Hope collection of engraved portraits, in Camera gallery, 77, 114, 129, 144, 145; removed to School of Nat. Phil., 224, 239; proposal to transfer to Old Ashmolean, 224, 232; transferred to Ashmolean Museum, Beaumont Street, 314.
Hope, Frederick William, gift of British periodicals, 64, 77; gift of engraved portraits, 77, 86, 114.
Hope, John Thomas, 77.
Hopyl, Wolfgang, printer, 68.
Horace, 296.
Horae, 16, 199, 296.
Hornby, C. H. St. John, 268.
Howard, Lord Henry, gift of Arundel Marbles, 5.
Howard, Lord William, of Naworth, 198.
Hudson, Rev. C. H. Bickerton, bequest, 295.
Hugh of St. Victor, 294.
Hultzsch, Dr. Eugen, sale of MSS., 217, 220.
Humphrey, Duke of Gloucester, 191; MSS. belonging to him, 199, 291.
Hungarian books, 76.
Hunt, Dr. Arthur Surridge, 201, 293n.
Hunt, Thomas, Oxford printer, 72.
Huntington, Bishop Robert, his MSS., 105, 213.
Hurst, Herbert, Oxford topographical collections, 313.
Hussey, Edward Law, donor, 223.
Hussey, Prof. Robert, 125n.
Huth, Henry, book collector, 71.
Hyde, Prebendary Henry Barry, bequest, 296.
Hyde, Dr. Thomas, Bodley's Librarian, 215, 269.
Hyvernat, Abbé Henri, 214.

Icelandic MSS., 23, 194n.
Ince, Dr. William, Regius Professor, 232n.
Incunabula, 15, 72, 177, 185, 282; catalogue of, 178.
India, MSS. collected in, 108–9, 219–20; Indian painting, 109, 311; coins, 109, 119, 223; books relating to, 252–3; Government of, 221.
India Office Library, 108, 110.
Ingram, James, President of Trinity, bequest of coins, 117.
Ireland, John, Dean of Westminster, bust, 9.

Nabonidus, King of Babylon, 309.
Nairne, Sir David, his papers, 99.
Nalson, John, Civil War papers, 95 and n.
Nanjio, Bunyiu, *Catalogue of Japanese and Chinese Books*, 221.
Napier, Dr. Richard, 66.
Napoleon I, portrait, 89 n.; medals, 118; orders for the army in Egypt, 284; Curzon collection, 284.
Nattes, John Claude, drawings, 224, 313.
Nawâ'i, 109.
Neckham, Alexander, autograph, 190.
Neubauer, Adolf, sub-librarian, 59, 70, 76, 81, 105; *Catalogue of periodicals*, 78; *Catalogue of Hebrew MSS.*, 105, 106, 210, 211; sale of MSS., 106; candidate for librarianship, 152; proposes a library publication, 204; retirement, 211.
New York, Columbia University, 330.
Newdigate, Sir Roger, 128.
Newspapers, 67, 68 n., 77, 280; storage, 230.
Newton, Sir Isaac, MS. papers, 193; correspondence, 293.
Nichols, John, collection of newspapers, 77, 89; *Literary Anecdotes*, 115.
Nichols, John Gough, sale, 89.
Nicholson, Edward Williams Byron, elected librarian, 152–3; his character and quarrels, 153–7, 202; introduces boy-labour, 161–2; employment of women, 258; financial policy, 163, 174; elaborates subject-classification, 164–5; views on reclassification, 165; cataloguing rules and practice, 168–70, 269; proposes printing the catalogue, 170–1; catalogue revision, 167, 171, 269; increases library intake, 172–3; catalogues of incunabula and early printing, 178–9; raises funds for purchase of Turbutt First Folio, 181; attention given to first editions, 181; starts a music catalogue, 187–8, 288; publication of early music, 188; encourages deposit of College MSS., 189; purchase of Queen Margaret's gospels, 197–8; work on papyri, 202; schemes for palaeographical instruction, 202; production of facsimiles, 204; opposes the idea of a summary catalogue, 206; plans revision of Coxe's catalogues of MSS., 208–9; plans for catalogues of Oriental MSS., 212, 219, 221; acquisitions of Oriental MSS., 212, 215, 216; reformation of coin collection, 222; presses for heating of picture gal-

lery, 225; redistribution of contents of Bodleian rooms, 226–9, 333 n.; acquisition of storage in Old Ashmolean, 231–2; plans and carries out underground bookstore, 233, 237; formation of select and reference libraries, 240–1; creation of upper reading-room, 241–3; illness and death, 243–4, 251; his achievement, 244–5.
Nicoll, Alexander, sub-librarian, 103; catalogue of Arabic MSS., 107, 213.
Nightingale, Florence, letters, 303.
Noble, Sir John, donor, 296.
Non-jurors, 74, 302.
Norfolk, 95, 100.
Norreys, Sir John, 94.
Norris, John, janitor, 33.
North family papers, 297.
North, Sir Dudley, letters to him, 297.
North, Francis, Lord Keeper, papers, 297.
North, Frederick, Lord, donor, 185; official papers, 297; bust, 9.
Norwich, 95, 296.
Nuffield, William Morris, Lord, 327.
Nutt, John William, sub-librarian, 81, 104, 106, 149.

Ogle, Octavius, 98.
Oglethorpe, General James, gift to C.C.C., 293.
Olaf, St., life of, 293.
Oman, Sir Charles, 223.
Omar Khayyam, 108, 296 and n.
Oppenheimer, David, Hebrew library, 17, 20, 105; catalogue, 23.
Ordnance Survey, 79, 163, 226, 335.
Ormerod, George, *History of Cheshire*, 224.
Ormonde, James Butler, 1st Duke of, his papers, 99.
Oseney Abbey, *see* Oxford City.
Osler, Sir William, Regius Professor, 243; assistance in obtaining First Folio, 181; interest in bibliography, 285, 335 and n.; helps to start *B.Q.R.*, 317; bequest, 310.
Ostraca, 214, 308–9.
Oswin, St., life of, 291.
Ouseley, Sir Frederick Gore, Professor of Music, 79; MSS. bought from him, 108.
Ouseley, Sir Gore, his MSS., 108, 216.
Ouseley, Sir William, his MSS., 21, 108, 216, 220.
Ovid, 74.
Owen, Humphrey, Bodley's Librarian, 7.

INDEX

INDEX

PRINTED IN GREAT BRITAIN
AT THE UNIVERSITY PRESS, OXFORD
BY CHARLES BATEY, PRINTER TO THE UNIVERSITY